AF777826

SECOND EDITION

STRUCTURED BASIC

IBM® PC / TRS-80® VERSION

JAMES F. CLARK
Fulton County Schools
Atlanta, Georgia

WILLIAM O. DRUM
DRA Software Training Center
Tucson, Arizona

J84

Published by

SOUTH-WESTERN PUBLISHING CO.

CINCINNATI   WEST CHICAGO, IL   CARROLLTON, TX   LIVERMORE, CA

Copyright © 1989
by SOUTH-WESTERN PUBLISHING CO.
Cincinnati, Ohio

ALL RIGHTS RESERVED

The text of this publication, or any part thereof, may not be reproduced or transmitted in any form or by any means, electronic or mechanical, including photocopying, recording, storage in an information retrieval system, or otherwise, without the prior written permission of the publisher.

ISBN: 0-538-10840-1

Library of Congress Catalog Card Number: 88-60368

2 3 4 5 6 7 8 9 0 Ki 7 6 5 4 3 2 1 0 9

Printed in the United States of America

IBM is a registered trademark of International Business Machines Corporation.

TRS-80 is a registered trademark of the Radio Shack Division of Tandy Corporation.

CONTENTS

PREFACE

Computers have become indispensable tools for businesses, professional people, and governments. The ability to program computers has thus become vastly more important, both as a career opportunity and for personal use. The advent of microcomputers has resulted in a literal explosion of computers using the BASIC language.

This text teaches the BASIC language, with an emphasis on programming business, mathematical, and general applications. The emphasis is on business because the great majority of career opportunities are in business programming. In preparing this second edition of the text, the authors drew on the experiences of many teachers who used the first edition. The changes suggested by these teachers have resulted in a book that develops in the student a proper appreciation of programming in a structured and easy-to-understand fashion.

The idea of designing a program before coding it is presented beginning in Chapter 1. The design and coding of programs in modular form are introduced in Chapter 3. This early introduction enables students to use good planning and coding techniques which produce structured programs. Proper program documentation is emphasized throughout the text, and the use of structured programming is developed without burdening the student with technical jargon. Hierarchy charts, program documentation sheets, and module documentation sheets are used instead of flow charts. These forms of documentation are much easier to understand and are much less frustrating to students.

All programming principles are presented in the context of practical applications. Each chapter is divided into two topics. Topic 1 presents general principles—principles that apply regardless of the computer language being used; Topic 2 explains how to apply those principles using the BASIC language. As each BASIC keyword is presented, its general form and an example are given.

Each chapter contains example programs using newly presented keywords. This helps integrate the new keywords with previously learned materials. Each topic includes review questions, and at the end of each chapter are lists of vocabulary words and BASIC keywords that were presented (both vocabuary words and keywords appear in bold on first reference in text).

The text is written specifically for BASIC as used on the IBM® PC[1] and compatibles and the TRS-80®[2] Models III and 4. Therefore, it is not necessary to wade through material related to some other computer's very different version of the language in order to find material for the computer you are using.

Throughout the text, long variable names are used. Since variable names relate directly to their function, it is much easier to understand the programs than if cryptic one-character or two-character variable names were used.

Each chapter contains ten programming assignments that progress in level of difficulty. This enables the teacher to more readily accommodate the needs of various students. In most chapters, there are business, mathematics, and general programs at each level of difficulty. At the end of each part is a programming project designed to help the student integrate the learning from the preceding chapter.

Five end-of-the-book items are handy references once particular programming ideas have been learned. A glossary contains new vocabulary words presented in the text, making review much easier. A quick reference guide to all BASIC keywords (see Appendix A) is a handy reference for refresher purposes once the keyword has been learned. Each entry in the reference guide refers the student to the page in the text that will give full information. Appendix B gives suggestions for debugging programs, and Appendix C provides an ASCII code table for use when writing programs that do character manipulation. Appendix D introduces flowcharting and is for use in courses of which flowcharting is a part.

---

[1] IBM is a registered trademark of International Business Machines Corporation. Any reference to the IBM Personal Computer or the IBM PCjr refers to this footnote.

[2] TRS-80 is a registered trademark of the Radio Shack Division of Tandy Corporation. Any reference to the TRS-80 or to the Radio Shack Microcomputer refers to this footnote.

PART ONE
A STRUCTURED APPROACH TO BASIC

1

An Introduction to BASIC

OBJECTIVES

After studying this chapter, you will be able to

1. Describe the computer and its functions.
2. Describe the function and construction of a computer program.
3. Define keywords, commands, and statements.
4. Write simple BASIC programs using the keywords REM, PRINT, LPRINT, and END.
5. Use arithmetic operators in expressions.
6. Use the commands NEW, RUN, LIST, LLIST, DELETE, SAVE, and LOAD.
7. Add, delete, and change program lines.
8. Print program listings and program output on the printer.

Our lives are touched daily by computers. For some, using a computer is part of a day's work. For others, using a computer is a part of the educational process. For still others, computers are a hobby. Computers are in use everywhere—in businesses, schools, and homes.

WHAT IS A COMPUTER?

A **computer** is an information-processing machine that can accept data, make comparisons, perform computations, and produce an output of the results. Since it is electronic, it works accurately and tirelessly at high rates of speed. Computers process data, which is often referred to as input. **Input** (i.e., raw facts, numbers, characters, etc.) is entered into the computer and stored in its memory. The input is processed and becomes output. The **output**, therefore, is processed information that can be displayed on a screen, printed, or stored for future use. For example, a student's test scores during a given time period would be considered input if they were entered into a computer. If they were added together and averaged, this calculation would be the processing of the input. When displayed or printed, the average would be the output.

TOPIC 1.1 DEVELOPING A PROGRAM

In this section you will learn what a program is and how to write a simple program.

WHAT IS A PROGRAM?

Although some people think the computer has "intelligence," it can really do nothing without being directed step by step. These step-by-step instructions are referred to as a **program**. A person who writes a program is called a **programmer**.

Programs are usually keyed in (typed) from a keyboard and "remembered" by the computer. Once the instructions have all been entered the computer can carry them out quickly. If the computer is equipped with a storage device, the programs may be stored for future use. A **storage device** is an electronic unit that can write data on a magnetic disk or magnetic tape. The data or programs stored on these units can be "played back" into the computer's memory whenever needed. The most common storage device used is a **disk drive**.

A computer can only "understand" programs written in **machine language**. Programs written in machine language contain instructions using codes that have special meaning to the computer's electronic circuitry. Writing programs in machine language is very difficult and time consuming for the programmer. To avoid these problems, programmers generally use a high-level language. **High-level languages** use English-like instructions that the computer translates into machine language. An **interpreter** or **compiler** program does the translation. These translator programs are usually supplied by the manufacturer of the computer.

The computer language called **BASIC** (Beginner's All-purpose Symbolic Instruction Code) is a high-level language. BASIC can be used to write programs for almost all small computers as well as for many larger ones. BASIC uses certain English words, called **keywords**, that have a special meaning to the translator program of the computer.

In this text, each chapter concentrates on a number of keywords. The exact keywords used, as well as the way in which they are used, varies somewhat from one manufacturer's version of BASIC to another. This book explains keywords as they are used by the versions of BASIC supplied with the IBM Personal Computer family, as well as compatible machines using versions of Microsoft Corporation's GW-BASIC. Among the many compatible machines are the Tandy 1000 and 3000, Compaqs, and Zeniths. The Tandy Radio Shack Models III and IV use a slightly different version of BASIC, and the differences for these machines will be pointed out in the text as they occur. Appendix A contains a summary of the more commonly used keywords. The summary may be used as a reference when writing programs.

All computer programs consist of a series of steps. One of the best ways to learn how to program a computer is to study examples of various programs and then apply what has been learned to programming exercises and activities.

WRITING A SIMPLE PROGRAM

As indicated previously, a program is a sequence of instructions that tells the computer what to do. Each step in this sequence is known as a **statement**. Each statement begins with a line number. It is best to start with line number 10 and to increase each line number by 10. By doing this, additional lines needed to change the program may be inserted later.

Each statement in BASIC contains one or more keywords that have a special meaning to the computer. Before examining some of the keywords in depth, observe the following short program.

Example:

```
Line Number
|
|  Keyword
↓  ↓
10 REM PROG1
```

```
20 REM student name
30 REM THIS PROGRAM PRINTS A COUPLE OF LINES
40 REM
50 PRINT "HI!  I AM A FRIENDLY COMPUTER."
60 PRINT "I FOLLOW INSTRUCTIONS FROM A PROGRAM."
70 END
```

When the computer is instructed to execute the statements of this program, the following output will be produced:

Output:

```
HI!  I AM A FRIENDLY COMPUTER.
I FOLLOW INSTRUCTIONS FROM A PROGRAM.
```

Throughout this text, example programs and their output will be shown in a manner similar to this example. Each program will be shown on a shaded background, and most examples of output will be listed as shown here. Printed output will be shown on a computer printout page, and graphics will be shown on a display screen.

The preceding program illustrates three keywords that are used in almost all programs. They are explained in more detail in the following sections.

Using the Keyword REM

The keyword **REM** is a shortened form of the word REMark. It allows comments to be placed in a program. It may be placed on any line in the program where the programmer wishes to make comments. REM has no effect on the computer. In fact, the computer ignores any statement beginning with REM. Any character on the keyboard may be used in a REM statement. REM statements are useful for identifying a program, labeling different sections, or making explanations. In the preceding example program, note that REM statements were used on lines 10, 20, and 30 to indicate the name of the program, to identify the programmer who wrote it, and to describe what it does. The general form of the REM statement is as follows:

General Form: *line number* REM *text*

Example:
```
10 REM PROG2
::
::
70 REM THIS SECTION AVERAGES GRADES
```

In this text the general form of each new keyword will be illustrated in this manner. Notice that the zeros have a slash through them (Ø). This is done so they will not be confused with the letter O. The double colons (::) used between lines 10 and 70 indicate that some statements have been omitted.

If desired, the apostrophe may be used to indicate a remark rather than spelling out REM. Frequently, this abbreviated version of the keyword REM is used at the ends of program lines to describe what they do. When used in this manner, instructions before the keyword REM or ' are carried out, while everything after the REM or ' is ignored. Thus, the example program could be written as follows:

Example:

```
10 ' PROG1
20 ' student name
30 ' THIS PROGRAM PRINTS A COUPLE OF LINES
40 '
50 PRINT "HI!  I AM A FRIENDLY COMPUTER." ' This is a print line.
60 PRINT "I FOLLOW INSTRUCTIONS FROM A PROGRAM."
70 END
```

The output of the revised program will be exactly the same as before, since REM lines have no effect on the processing or output.

Using the Keyword PRINT

The keyword **PRINT** causes printing or output to appear on a **CRT** (cathode ray tube, which resembles a television screen) or other type of display.

General Form: *line number* PRINT *items to be printed*

Example: `50 PRINT "THIS LINE WILL BE PRINTED."`

Printing Literals. One of the items that can be printed is a literal. A **literal** is a message enclosed in quotation marks. In the example program on pages 4–5, the PRINT statements use literals.

Example:

```
50 PRINT "HI!  I AM A FRIENDLY COMPUTER."
```

Output:

```
HI!  I AM A FRIENDLY COMPUTER.
```

The PRINT statement will display any characters (including blanks) that have been keyed in between quotes. Quotation marks may not be used inside other quotation marks. If there is a need for quotation marks inside, use single quotation marks (apostrophes).

Example:

```
50 PRINT "'HELP!', SHE CRIED."
```

Output:

```
'HELP!', SHE CRIED.
```

If a blank line is desired, use a PRINT statement with nothing following it.

Example:

```
50 PRINT "THIS IS AN EXAMPLE
60 PRINT
70 PRINT "OF DOUBLE SPACING."
```

Output:

```
THIS IS AN EXAMPLE

OF DOUBLE SPACING.
```

Blank spaces may be keyed after the beginning quotation mark of a literal in order to move the printing to the right.

Example:

```
50 PRINT "THIS EXAMPLE SHOWS HOW"
60 PRINT "      BLANK SPACE"
70 PRINT "   MAY BE USED TO MOVE"
80 PRINT "  PRINTING TO THE RIGHT"
90 PRINT "TO GET DESIRED PLACEMENT."
100 END
```

Output:

```
THIS EXAMPLE SHOWS HOW
     BLANK SPACE
  MAY BE USED TO MOVE
 PRINTING TO THE RIGHT
TO GET DESIRED PLACEMENT.
```

Printing Constants. Another type of item that may follow the keyword PRINT is a constant. A **constant** is an actual number. It is not placed within quotation marks and may not include commas, dollar signs, or any other special characters; however, it may contain a minus sign to indicate a negative number.

Example:

```
50 PRINT 69.3
60 PRINT -331.54
```

Output:

```
 69.3
-331.54
```

Controlling Spacing. Combinations of literals and constants may appear after the keyword PRINT. The items may be separated by either commas or semicolons.

Controlling spacing with commas. If commas are used to separate print items, the results are printed in zones. Each zone is 14 spaces or characters, except the last one, which is shorter. The total number of zones depends on whether you are using a computer operating with a 40-column or 80-column display screen. As the following example demonstrates, using a comma to print items in zones is a method of setting up the output in columnar format.

Example:

```
50 PRINT "ANIMAL","KIND","SIZE"
60 PRINT "------","----","----"
70 PRINT "CHIHUAHUA","DOG","SMALL"
80 PRINT "COLLIE","DOG","LARGE"
90 PRINT "GUPPY","FISH","SMALL"
100 END
```

Output:

```
ANIMAL         KIND           SIZE
------         ----           ----
CHIHUAHUA      DOG            SMALL
COLLIE         DOG            LARGE
GUPPY          FISH           SMALL
```

In these lines, the commas between the literals cause the output to be aligned in columns. Each comma tells the computer to move to the next zone before printing. If the item to be printed contains more characters than will fit into a print zone, two zones will be used. If the program attempts to print more items than the number of zones available on a line, the output will wrap around (continue printing) on the next line.

Numbers can be spaced into zones with commas just as literals can.

Example:

```
50 PRINT -50,4,30
60 PRINT 3.5,80,-120
70 END
```

Output:

```
-50             4              30
 3.5            80            -120
```

Note that the numbers all start at the same position, rather than being aligned at the decimal point. However, also note that a space is reserved at the front of each number for a minus sign if one should be needed. Methods for aligning numbers at the decimal point will be introduced later in the text.

Controlling spacing with semicolons. When a semicolon is used to separate literals, no space is inserted between the printed items. The difference in printing literals with semicolons instead of commas can be seen easily by changing the commas of the previous example to semicolons as follows.

Example:

```
50 PRINT "ANIMAL";"KIND";"SIZE"
60 PRINT "------";"----";"----"
70 PRINT "CHIHUAHUA";"DOG";"SMALL"
80 PRINT "COLLIE";"DOG";"LARGE"
90 PRINT "GUPPY";"FISH";"SMALL"
100 END
```

Output:

```
ANIMALKINDSIZE
--------------
CHIHUAHUADOGSMALL
COLLIEDOGLARGE
GUPPYFISHSMALL
```

To see the effect on numbers when using semicolons, look again at the example program from page 9, with the commas changed to semicolons.

Example:

```
50 PRINT -50;4;30
60 PRINT 3.5;80;-120
70 END
```

Output:

```
-50  4  30
 3.5  80 -120
```

Unlike literals, the numbers do not run together when semicolons are used. Note that each number begins with either a space or a minus sign and is followed by a space. This automatic space after each number keeps them from running together.

Performing Calculations

One of the outstanding features of the computer is its ability to perform arithmetic rapidly and accurately. The easiest way to perform mathematical calculations is to write the desired computation following the keyword PRINT on a program line. Place the desired numeric values linked with one of the arithmetic symbols shown in Table 1-1. These symbols, which specify the kind of arithmetic to be done, are known as **operators**. The combination (formula) of values and operators states the problem and is referred to as an **expression**.

SYMBOL	MEANING	EXAMPLE	OUTPUT OF EXAMPLE
^ (carat)	Exponentiation	50 PRINT 5^2 (on IBM)	25
↑ (up arrow)	Exponentiation	50 PRINT 5^2 (on TRS, but displays as "[")	25
*	Multiplication	30 PRINT 6*3	18
/	Division	40 PRINT 54/9	6
+	Addition	10 PRINT 2+4	6
–	Subtraction	20 PRINT 12–5	7

Table 1-1 Arithmetic Operators Used in BASIC

Look at the following example:

Example:

```
50 PRINT 3+6-2
```

Output:

```
7
```

The computer knows that 3+6−2 is an expression because it was not enclosed in quotation marks. If the problem needs to be displayed in the output, it can be treated as a literal.

Example:

```
50 PRINT "THE ANSWER TO ";
60 PRINT "3+6-2 IS ";          ' ←—— Prints literal
70 PRINT 3+6-2                 ' ←—— Prints expression
80 END
```

Output:

```
THE ANSWER TO 3+6-2 IS  7
```

Lines 50 and 60 end with semicolons, causing the output to continue on one line. Line 70 contains an expression, and the results are calculated.

Changing the Order of Arithmetic Operations

When calculations are more complex than the examples in Table 1-1, the use of parentheses is important. If there are parentheses in an expression, operations inside the parentheses are performed first. If there are no parentheses, the computer performs calculations from left to right. First, it searches through the expression and computes any exponentiation operations. Then it starts again from left to right and computes all multiplication and division operations. Finally, all addition and subtraction operations are computed.

Following this fixed order of operations, note the difference made by parentheses in calculating the average of three test scores.

```
50 PRINT 76+80+99/3
```

Without parentheses the answer is 189, which obviously is not the correct average. The computer first divides 99 by 3 giving a result of 33, it then adds 76, 80, and 33 together.

```
50 PRINT (76+80+99)/3
```

With parentheses the answer is 85, which is the correct average. The computer first performs the addition within the parentheses and then divides the total by 3.

Using the Keyword END

The **END** statement causes the computer to stop executing a program. This statement is optional for the microcomputers covered by this text. However, it is a good habit to use it to indicate the end of each program.

General Form: *line number* END

Example: `200 END`

REVIEW QUESTIONS

1. What is a computer? (Obj. 1)
2. What is the difference between input and output? (Obj. 1)
3. What is a program? (Obj. 2)

4. Explain the difference between a program written in machine language and one written in a high-level language. (Obj. 2)
5. What is a keyword? (Obj. 3)
6. What is a statement? (Obj. 3)
7. Why is it desirable to increase each line number in a BASIC program by 10? (Obj. 4)
8. What is the purpose of the keyword REM? (Obj. 4)
9. What is a literal? Give an example of a statement that causes a literal to be displayed. (Obj. 4)
10. What is a constant? Give an example of a statement that causes a constant to be displayed. (Obj. 4)
11. Explain how the output of a program is different when a comma is used and when a semicolon is used. (Obj. 4)
12. Is the effect of spacing with the comma identical on all computers? (Obj. 4)
13. List the commonly used arithmetic operators and describe what they do. (Obj. 5)
14. In what order is arithmetic done? What is the effect of parentheses on the order? (Obj. 5)
15. What is the purpose of the END statement? (Obj. 4)

TOPIC 1.2 ENTERING AND USING A PROGRAM

The previous section introduced a simple program. This section introduces commands used for entering (typing) and running (executing) programs. A **command** is a keyword that tells the computer to take immediate action. To use a keyword as an immediate command, it is entered with no line number. Since commands have no line numbers, they are not a part of a program.

PROCEDURE FOR ENTERING AND RUNNING A PROGRAM

This section will acquaint you with the procedures used for entering and running a program.

Powering Up the Computer

Before a program can be keyed in, the computer must be turned on and made ready. This is sometimes known as powering up, or booting, the computer. Follow the instructions in your computer's owner's reference manual to get BASIC ready. Once BASIC is loaded into the computer's memory and is ready, follow the steps detailed here to enter and run programs.

Clearing the Computer's Memory

Before any program is keyed into the computer, the computer should be told to "forget" anything that may already be in its memory. The command **NEW** clears the computer's memory of any previously stored BASIC program and should always be used before a new program is entered. Simply key in the command and press the ENTER/RETURN key. The **cursor**, which usually is a dash, an underscore, or a solid block, marks the position on the screen where the next character will be displayed. As any character or space is keyed in, the cursor moves from left to right.

Entering and Executing a Program

Once the NEW command has been entered, the lines of a new program can be entered. Remember, each line must begin with a line number. Press the ENTER/RETURN key at the end of each line. Keying errors may be corrected before pressing ENTER/RETURN by backing up with the backspace key (or left arrow in TRS-80) and rekeying.

After keying a program into the memory of the computer, a command called **RUN** tells the computer to execute the program. Simply key in the word RUN and press the ENTER/RETURN key. Remember, do not key in a line number before the RUN command. If the command RUN is entered for the program on pages 4–5, the following output will appear:

Output:

```
HI!  I AM A FRIENDLY COMPUTER.
I FOLLOW INSTRUCTIONS FROM A PROGRAM.
```

RUN could be entered again, and the same output would appear because the program has been stored in the computer's memory. It will stay in memory until it is purposely altered, until it is removed with the NEW command, or until the machine is turned off.

MAKING CHANGES IN A PROGRAM

Changes may be made in a program when the programmer desires different results or needs to correct errors. If there is an error in the program (e.g., a misspelled keyword or a missing quotation mark), an error message will appear when the program is executed.

Error messages state the kind of error, such as the wrong usage or spelling of a keyword (these errors are commonly called syntax errors). The computer stops executing the program when an error is detected. The kind of error and the number of the line in which it occurred will be displayed on the screen. The IBM microcomputer will display the line containing the statement with the error. The TRS-80 computer will display only the number of the line containing the error; at this point, simply press ENTER/RETURN, and the remainder of the line containing the error will be displayed. If the error message that is displayed is not self-explanatory, refer to the BASIC reference manual supplied by the manufacturer of your computer in order to interpret the message. Any errors must be corrected before the program can be executed successfully. With either computer, the line can be corrected or reentered. This procedure is explained in the next section.

Listing a Program

To view part or all of a program, whether for error detection or any other reason,.the command **LIST** is used. Simply key in the command LIST and press ENTER/RETURN to display the entire program in the computer's memory. If the program is long and sections must be displayed one at a time, LIST may be followed by the range of line numbers to be displayed. For example, LIST 10-100 would display lines 10 through 100, and LIST 50 would display only line 50.

Adding Lines

New lines may be added to a program simply by keying them in. The line number assigned to the new line will control its placement in the program. For example, if a new line is to be placed between lines 30 and 40, the new one might be numbered 35. (The computer will automatically put the line in its proper place; it need not be physically keyed in between the two existing lines. In fact, program statements may be entered in any order; the computer will arrange the statements in numerical order.)

Deleting Lines

A single line may be deleted from a program simply by keying in the line number and pressing the ENTER/RETURN key. A group of consecutive lines (range) may be deleted by using the **DELETE** command. Key the command DELETE followed by the line number range. For example, the command DELETE 40-90 will remove all lines from 40 through 90.

Modifying Existing Lines

At this point, the simplest way to modify an existing program line on the TRS-80 is to reenter the line number and the changed line in its entirety. The new line simply replaces the old line. To make changes on the IBM and compatible computers, move the cursor (with the "arrow" keys) to any program line that is displayed on the screen. Strike the computer's INSERT key, then key in the character(s) to be inserted at the cursor location. When finished inserting, press the INSERT key again to turn insert mode off. Use the DELETE key to delete the character(s) at the cursor location; use the BACKSPACE key to delete the character(s) to the left of the cursor. Type over characters to change them to other characters. Once the desired changes have been made to a line, press the ENTER/RETURN key to record them as part of the program. Make sure the cursor is on the changed line when ENTER/RETURN is pressed in order to record the change(s).

OBTAINING HARD COPY

If your computer has a printer attached to it, **hard copy** output may be obtained—that is, output in printed form on paper. The hard copy may contain output from a program, or it may list the program lines themselves. Before attempting to obtain hard copy, make sure the printer is turned on and ready. If it has an on-line or ready light, make sure it is lit.

The keyword **LPRINT** will cause the output of a program to go to the printer instead of the display. Simply use the keyword LPRINT instead of PRINT any time output should go to the printer.

Example:

```
70 LPRINT "THESE LINES ARE TO BE PRINTED"
80 LPRINT "ON THE PRINTER."
```

To produce a program listing on the printer rather than on the display, simply use the command **LLIST** rather than LIST. If the program is long and sections must be listed one at a time, LLIST may be followed by a range of line numbers.

Example:

```
LLIST 1000-1999 ←——— Lists program lines 1000-1999 on the printer
```

SAVING A PROGRAM

When a program is entered into the memory of the computer, it stays there until the power goes off or it is purposely removed with the NEW command. If the program is needed for future use, it can be saved if a storage device is available. The storage device most commonly used is a disk drive (recording device) that uses a floppy diskette for storage. A **floppy diskette** is an oxide-coated plastic disk, usually 5 1/4 or 3 1/2 inches in diameter, enclosed in a protective jacket. It is used for magnetically storing data.

When preparing to save a program, recall the name given that program. This should have been done when the program was first started, and the name should appear in a REM statement. The maximum length for a name is eight characters. Always start the program name with a letter of the alphabet and use only letters and numbers in the name; spaces may not be used. While some special characters may be used, it is recommended that you stay with just letters and numbers; that way, you don't have to remember which symbols are acceptable and which are not.

The procedure to be used for saving a program on disk makes use of the **SAVE** command. If your computer has only one disk drive, the program is saved on that drive. If you have more than one disk drive and do not specify the one on which the program should be saved, it goes to the **default drive**—that is, the drive that is used when another disk drive is not designated. The default drive is usually drive A: (the left or top drive on most computers), but is known as drive 0 (the bottom drive) on the TRS-80.

Once a program has been keyed in, it may be saved. Simply key in the SAVE command and the program name within quotes and press ENTER/RETURN. Study the examples below, each of which assumes that we are saving a program we have named MYPROG.

Saving on the default drive: SAVE "MYPROG"

Saving on the second drive: SAVE "B:MYPROG"
(IBM and compatible)

SAVE "MYPROG:1"
(TRS-80 drive 1)

LOADING A PROGRAM

Later, when a program that has been saved is to be used, it must be loaded (copied) into the memory of the computer from the disk. The process is the same as saving, except that the command **LOAD** is used instead of SAVE. Once a program is loaded, it can be executed with the RUN command, displayed with LIST, or even altered if desired. For example, LOAD "MYPROG" loads the program into memory from the default disk, and RUN "MYPROG" loads and executes the program.

If the program to be loaded is not on the default drive, key the drive identification in front of the program name, such as LOAD "B:MYPROG" (or LOAD "MYPROG:1" on the TRS-80). Note that loading a program from disk erases any program that may have already been in memory. Therefore, if the program in memory is one you have just keyed in and wish to save, make sure you save it before loading another program.

REVIEW QUESTIONS

1. What is the function of the NEW command? (Obj. 6)
2. What is the function of the RUN command? (Obj. 6)
3. What is the function of the LIST command? (Obj. 6)
4. How do you list only part of a program? (Obj. 6)
5. How can a line be added to a program? (Obj. 7)
6. How can one or more lines be deleted from a program? (Obj. 7)
7. Describe how to modify or replace program lines. (Obj. 7)
8. What is meant by the term "hard copy"? (Obj. 8)
9. What keyword is used to obtain a hard copy of program output? (Obj. 8)
10. What is the command to obtain a hard copy of a program listing? (Obj. 8)
11. Describe the command to save a program. (Obj. 6)
12. Describe the command to load a program. (Obj. 6)

VOCABULARY WORDS

The following terms were introduced in this chapter:

BASIC
command
compiler
computer
constant
CRT
cursor
default drive
disk drive
error message
expression
floppy diskette
hard copy
high-level language
input
interpreter
keyword
literal
machine language
operator
output
program
programmer
statement
storage device

KEYWORDS AND COMMANDS

The following keywords and commands were introduced in this chapter:

DELETE
END
LIST
LLIST
LOAD
LPRINT
NEW
PRINT
REM
RUN
SAVE

PROGRAMS TO WRITE

Unless directed otherwise, begin all programming assignments with the following REMark lines. Actual program steps should begin with line 50.

```
10 REM program name
20 REM student name, chapter number, assignment number
30 REM description of program
40 REM
```

Program 1

Write a program that will print the following output:

```
PROGRAMMING A COMPUTER CAN BE FUN
```

Program 2

Write a program that will print the following output:

```
THIS IS THE OUTPUT OF THE FIRST

PROGRAM I HAVE DONE THAT MAKES

THREE LINES OF OUTPUT.
```

Program 3

Write a program that will print the output:

```
TUDBERRY'S IS HAVING A SALE!
```

Program 4

Write a program that will output the following lines. Use spaces within the quotation marks to properly line up the output so that the second and third lines are centered under the first.

```
THE EXECUTIVE FORUM INVITES
FRED R. MARBURY
TO ITS ANNUAL BARBECUE
```

Program 5

Write a program to output the names of salespersons in zone 1 and their cities in zone 2. Use commas to control the spacing. The data is as follows: ALBEMARLE, DETROIT; CANTON, ATLANTA; MILLER, SAN FRANCISCO; and WALLACE, NEW YORK.

Program 6

Write a program that will print the sum of the numbers 12 and 15.

Program 7

Write a program to compute and print the average of the grades 79, 96, 83, and 91.

Program 8

Write a program to print a list of the officers of a club. The name of the office belongs in zone 1, and the name of the officer belongs in zone 2. Use commas to control the spacing. The data is as follows: PRESIDENT, MARY MANN; SECRETARY, LEON BANKS; TREASURER, MICK MARTIN.

Program 9

Write a program that produces a table showing some sales made by a store. The output should resemble the following:

```
SALES REPORT

               QTY

STORE 1         12

STORE 2         53

STORE 3         21

TOTAL           86
```

Use commas to control spacing into columns. Let the program compute the total figure.

Program 10

Write a program to compute and print the area of different rectangles. The output should appear as follows, with spacing controlled by commas. Make sure the areas are computed by the program rather than being printed as constants. The formula for computing the area of a rectangle is area = length × width.

```
COMPUTATION OF AREAS

LENGTH         WIDTH          AREA

 10             5              50
 3              12             36
 40             4              160
```

2

The Design of Programs

> **OBJECTIVES**
>
> After studying this chapter, you will be able to
>
> 1. List and correctly use the steps in planning a simple program.
> 2. Describe and correctly use program documentation sheets.
> 3. Describe and correctly use spacing charts.
> 4. Describe and correctly develop program designs.
> 5. Describe and correctly use variables in programs.
> 6. Plan, code, and debug simple interactive programs.

In Chapter 1 you learned that a program is a series of steps to be followed by the computer in the processing of input in order to produce output. These steps must be written in the correct order if the program is to function properly. If all the steps are correct but are in the wrong order, the desired output will not be obtained. In this chapter you will learn more about successfully planning and writing programs.

TOPIC 2.1 PLANNING SIMPLE PROGRAMS

The following sections will introduce you to the planning process. As you study the sections, try to think of examples of your own to supplement those given in the text.

INTRODUCTION TO PROGRAM DESIGN

To improve productivity, as well as to help ensure the fewest errors, orderly planning must occur before a program is entered into the computer. The results of each step of the planning process should be documented by the use of forms. The first form you should use when working on any program is a program documentation sheet. A blank sheet is shown in Figure 2-1.

<table>
<tr><th colspan="4">PROGRAM DOCUMENTATION SHEET</th></tr>
<tr><td>Program:</td><td colspan="2">Programmer:</td><td>Date:</td></tr>
<tr><td colspan="4">Purpose:</td></tr>
<tr><td colspan="2">Input:</td><td colspan="2">Output:</td></tr>
<tr><td colspan="4">Data Terminator:</td></tr>
<tr><td colspan="4">Variables Used:</td></tr>
</table>

Figure 2-1 Program Documentation Sheet

The **program documentation sheet** is a form listing the name of the program, the name of the programmer, the date written, an explanation of the purpose of the program, the name and sources of input, what the output will be, the data terminator (if one is needed), and a list of variables and what they represent. These parts of the program documentation sheet will be filled in at appropriate points during the planning and writing of the program. Most of the items, however, will be self-explanatory once you are familiar with the terminology. The Purpose section should be a short but complete description of what the program does. The Input section should tell what kind of input data will be obtained as well as from where it will be obtained. The Output section should indicate what kind of output will be produced and whether the output will go to the display or to the printer. The sections on terminators and variables will be explained later.

At this point in your programming experience, it is suggested that you follow four steps when planning and writing a program. These steps will be used and developed more fully as you progress through the text.

Step 1: Plan the Desired Output and Identify the Required Input

Programs need to be planned rather than created by trial and error. You must first describe clearly the purpose of the program. Why are you writing it? What is it to do? What should the output be? How should the output be arranged? Once the output has been clearly defined, identify the input that will be necessary to produce the output and decide where the input will come from. Will the input data be written into the program, as it was in your Chapter 1 programs? Or will it be entered from the keyboard when the program is executed, as you will learn to do in this chapter? As these decisions are made in the planning process, much of the program documentation sheet can be completed.

As an example of this process, suppose that students at two universities are having a contest to see which group can develop the most fuel-efficient automobile. On the day of the contest, each vehicle's empty fuel tank will be filled and the amount of gas will be measured precisely. The cars then will be driven around a track until they run out of fuel. The vehicle getting the most miles per gallon will be declared the winner of the contest. Even though the gas mileage can obviously be calculated by hand or with a calculator, it is decided that a computer will be used to determine the winner.

In analyzing this problem, you realize that you have already specified the desired output. You need to know the miles per gallon for each vehicle, because that figure will determine the winner of the contest. You then decide that you would like the output arranged in table form to make it easier to read.

Once the output is determined, work backwards and decide what input is required to compute the desired output. In this case, miles per gallon can be computed by dividing the number of miles traveled by the number of gallons of gasoline consumed. Therefore, your program will require two inputs for each vehicle: (1) the number of miles traveled and (2) the number of gallons of gasoline used. Do not write the input data into the program as was done in Chapter 1; instead, the data should be obtained from the keyboard during execution of the program. The program can ask the user for the data and store that information in the computer's memory until it is needed. A program such as this one gets data from the user during execution and is known as an **interactive program**.

As these decisions are reached, the program documentation sheet should be partially completed. Examine Figure 2-2 and study the items that have been completed so far. We have named the program C2E1, standing for Chapter 2, Example 1. This is a practice we will continue throughout the text in naming example programs. Other parts of the sheet are filled in with the decisions made in planning the program.

Now, design the table of output in more detail. To do this, use a form called a **spacing chart**. This chart contains rows and columns for planning the format of the output. The completed chart (see Figure 2-3) shows where each item should be placed when the output is produced. Note that the headings of the table have been written just as they will appear. The data, however, have not been written in. Instead, the spaces in which alphabetic data will appear have been marked off with reverse slashes (\), while the spaces for numeric data have been marked off with number signs (#). Note that only one line of data from the spacing chart has been filled in. The symbols drawn below each column show that the actual report will be longer than one line. It would be inefficient to keep repeating the line showing the spacing, especially if the table to be produced would contain many lines.

As the program planner, you must decide where each item of the output should appear by indicating its location on the spacing

<table>
<tr><th colspan="3">PROGRAM DOCUMENTATION SHEET</th></tr>
<tr><td>Program: C2E1</td><td>Programmer: STUDENT NAME</td><td>Date: 1-12-xx</td></tr>
<tr><td colspan="3">Purpose: Determine winner of fuel-efficient vehicle contest.</td></tr>
<tr><td colspan="2">Input: Name, miles traveled, and gallons used for each vehicle. Data to be entered from keyboard as program is executed.</td><td>Output: A miles-per-gallon figure for each contest entrant, with output going to the display.</td></tr>
<tr><td colspan="3">Data Terminator:</td></tr>
<tr><td colspan="3">Variables Used:</td></tr>
</table>

Figure 2-2 Partially Completed Program Documentation Sheet

chart. Make the output look neat, well organized, and easy to read. Also, be careful that you do not plan for more columns or lines than are available on the display or printer being used. Most displays will contain either 24 or 25 lines and either 40 or 80 columns. Since the same brand and model of computer may vary

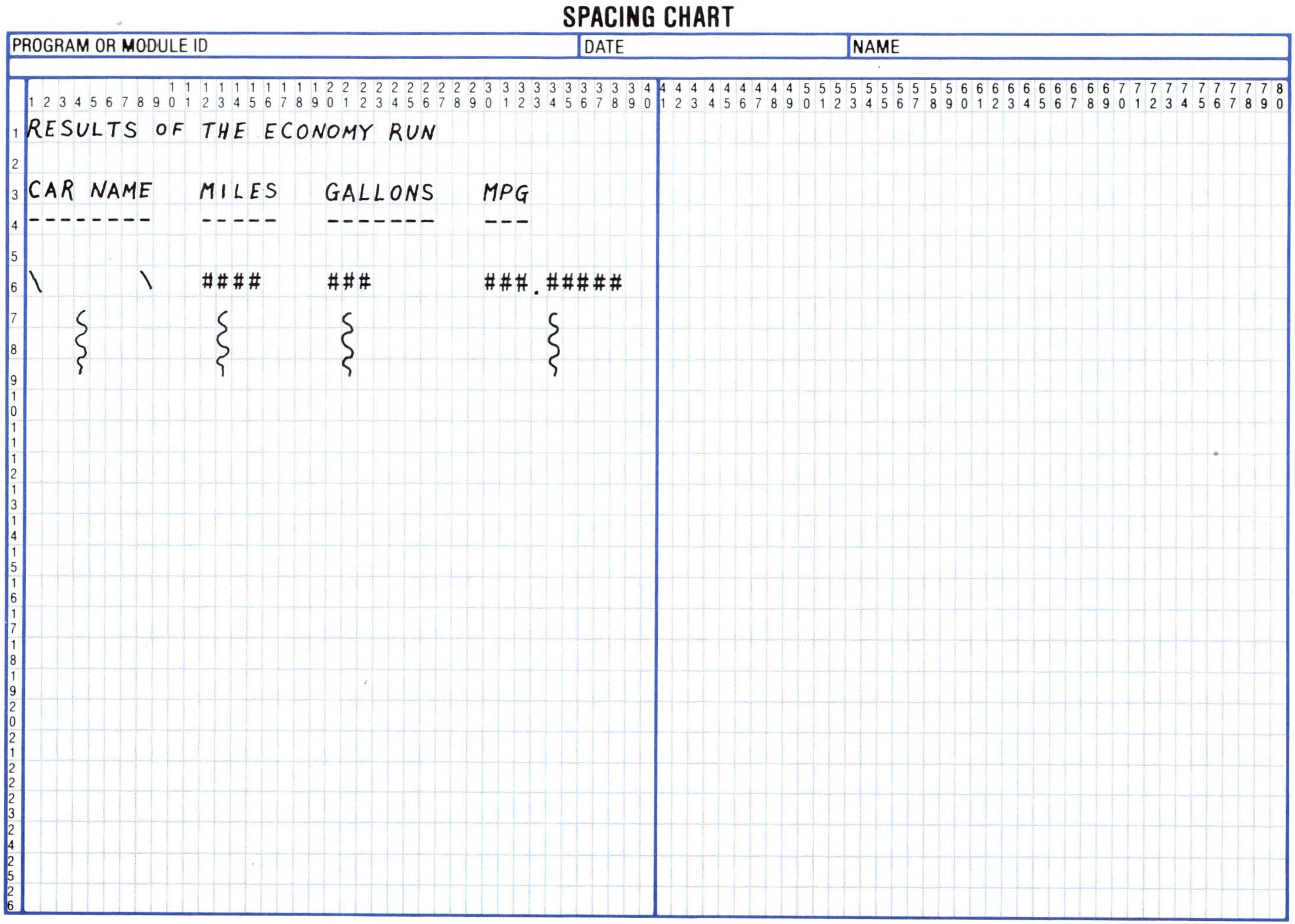

Figure 2-3 Spacing Chart

in the number of columns on the screen display, it is best to check with your instructor about the computer you are using.

Step 2: Plan the Processing Steps

Once the desired output and required input have been determined and documented on the program documentation sheet and spacing chart, plan the processing steps required to get from the input to the output. In writing these steps, it is easier to think and plan in English than in a computer language. These English language steps are referred to as the **program design**. After the planning is completed, the steps of the program design are translated into the exact language required by the computer.

Continuing with our example of finding the most fuel-efficient automobile, the processing steps might resemble the following list. Remember that these steps must be logically analyzed so that they will be in the right order (e.g., the input must be obtained before any computations can be done). For now, write the steps on plain paper.

1. Clear the computer's display.
2. Get the name, miles traveled, and gallons used by Car A and store the data in memory.
3. Get the name, miles traveled, and gallons used by Car B and store the data in memory.
4. Calculate and store in memory the miles per gallon for Car A.
5. Calculate and store in memory the miles per gallon for Car B.
6. Clear the display so the report starts on a clean screen.
7. Print the items on the report using the spacing chart as the guide.

Once you have completed the steps of the program design, your instructor may suggest that you have someone else go over the steps with you to try to find any logic errors that may have been made. **Logic errors** are errors in the sequence of instructions or the actions to be taken based on those instructions.

Step 3: Code the Program

Coding a program means writing its steps in a language acceptable to the computer. For this text, that language is BASIC. To code a program, each step of the program design is translated into one or more steps in BASIC. The translation may be done on paper; however, if enough computer time is available, the translation may be done directly at the computer. In other words, you would read each step of the program design and mentally translate it into BASIC as you enter the lines into the computer. As the translation is made, use as many REM statements as desired. Remember to use REM statements for identification (as shown on pages 4–5) at the beginning of the program. Also, insert remarks to document particular parts of a program or to describe the action of any program lines that are not self-explanatory.

If the translation to BASIC is made on paper, your instructor may want to check the coding with you before you enter the program into the computer, or the instructor may prefer that you and another student check the code together. This will help identify lines that have errors, which will enable you to correct them before keying them in and wasting computer time.

Step 4: Test the Program and Correct Errors

As soon as the program is entered into the computer, you should save it. Next, you should test the program to be sure it performs the desired task. Anything that causes a program not to perform as expected is known as a program **bug**. (Referring to problems as bugs started in the early days of computing, when difficulties in running programs on a particular computer were caused by an insect lodged in the circuits of the computer.) If you have followed the steps suggested for planning and coding the program, any program problems you find will most likely be syntax errors. **Syntax errors** are errors caused by not following the rules of the computer language (e.g., misspelling a keyword or forgetting a quotation mark where required). Syntax errors are frequently caused by making errors when keying in the program.

Continue to test the program, making necessary corrections, until it operates as planned. This process of testing and correcting a program is known as **debugging** (see Appendix B for a further discussion of debugging).

Once the program is working correctly, save it again. Next, print a hard copy listing of the program and attach it to the other documentation of the program. Remember that a good program has good documentation.

REVIEW QUESTIONS

1. Why is it important to plan a program before beginning to code it? (Obj. 1)

2. What are the steps in planning and coding a program? (Obj. 1)
3. What kinds of information are contained on a program documentation sheet? (Obj. 2)
4. What is the purpose of a spacing chart? (Obj. 3)
5. Describe how to complete a spacing chart. (Obj. 3)
6. What is a program design? (Obj. 4)
7. Why is a program design written in English rather than a computer language? (Obj. 4)
8. What kinds of errors are most likely to be found when a program is keyed into the computer and executed? (Obj. 1)

TOPIC 2.2 CODING FROM PROGRAM DESIGNS

As indicated in Topic 2.1, the steps from the program design are converted into code that can be understood by a computer using the BASIC language. In Topic 2.2, we will examine the program design developed in Topic 2.1 for the fuel-efficient automobile contest. You will see how to convert each step into BASIC. Since some of the steps require the use of keywords you have not yet learned, we will introduce those keywords as they are needed.

Before we begin, reexamine the seven-step program design as we developed it earlier. Make sure you understand what must be done in each step, but do not be concerned if you do not yet know how to make the computer carry out each step.

TRANSLATING ENGLISH INTO BASIC

Each of the steps from the program design will be reprinted in the following sections. After each step, there will be a discussion of how to code the step from English into BASIC. Remember, however, that we have decided to begin each program with four standard REMark lines for identification purposes. Therefore, let's write those first as follows, using the apostrophe to stand for REM:

Example:

```
10 ' C2E1
20 ' STUDENT NAME, CHAPTER 2, EXAMPLE 1
30 ' DETERMINES WINNER OF FUEL-EFFICIENT VEHICLE CONTEST
40 '
```

Now, let's code the steps of the program as defined in the program design.

Step 1: Clear the Computer's Display

By clearing (erasing) the computer's display, you will ensure that the program begins execution on a fresh screen. There will be no "leftover" output of any kind on the display. The screen is cleared with one simple statement, **CLS**. In this example, line 50 is used as the next line in ongoing code for our program.

General Form: *line number* CLS

Example: `5Ø CLS`

Step 2: Get the Name, Miles Traveled, and Gallons Used by Car A and Store the Data in Memory

A knowledge of variables is required to obtain the information requested in step 2. The term **variable** refers to a named storage location in the computer's memory. You might want to think of each of the variables as a "mailbox" in the computer's memory. The program "writes" the name of the "occupant" on the mailbox, then delivers "mail" to the box or retrieves "mail" from the box as required. The name of the variable is determined by the programmer and assigned by the program. The computer then stores data in the assigned location denoted by the variable name. The storage location is referred to as a variable because the data stored there varies dependent upon what the program puts into the location from time to time.

For this step of the program design, we must have variables for the name of the first car, its miles traveled, and its gallons consumed. To make it easier to remember which variables represent the first car, use a common letter to begin all the variable names. This example will use the variable names ACAR$, ADIST, and AGAL. ACAR$ will be the name of the A (or first) car. Note that BASIC requires that the name of variables used for nonnumeric data end with a dollar sign. (Think of the $ as standing for an *S* indicating a **string** or group of characters.) ADIST will be the miles traveled for the A car. AGAL will be the number of gallons of fuel used by the A car. As soon as the variables are named, write them on the program documentation sheet. If the contents of the variable are not apparent from its name, write a description of the contents next to the name on the documentation sheet.

Once the variable names are chosen, the next step is for the program to ask for the data, which will be entered on the keyboard, and store it into these variables (mailboxes). BASIC uses the keyword **INPUT** to do this.

General Form:
line number INPUT "*prompt*";*variable name(s)*

Example:

```
60 INPUT "NAME OF THE FIRST CAR";ACAR$
70 INPUT "NUMBER OF MILES TRAVELED";ADIST
80 INPUT "NUMBER OF GALLONS USED";AGAL
```

When the program is executed, the effect of the INPUT statement is as follows:

1. The **prompt** (the words between quotes) is printed on the display. A question mark is automatically printed at the end of the prompt. If desired, the programmer may omit the prompt part of the INPUT statement; if that is done, however, the operator will have to guess which information to key in when the program is executed.
2. The computer waits for the user to respond. The user keys the input data on the keyboard.
3. When the user presses ENTER/RETURN, the computer stores the keyed data in the named variable.

Examine Figure 2-4 to see how this interaction looks on the screen. The part displayed by the program is printed in regular print, while the part keyed in by the operator is printed in bold (in actuality, all data would look the same on the screen). The table at the right of the screen shows the contents that would be stored under each variable name as the three input statements are executed; nothing is output to the screen as the storage takes place.

If desired, more than one variable name may be included on the INPUT line. In this case, the variable names must be separated by commas in the program. Also, the user must enter the equivalent number of items of data, separating them with commas. By doing

```
NAME OF THE FIRST CAR?   STATE

NUMBER OF MILES TRAVELED?   140

NUMBER OF GALLONS USED?   1.17
```

Variable Name	Contents
ACAR$	STATE
ADIST	140
AGAL	1.17

Figure 2-4 Illustration of Input Interaction for Car A

this, the three input lines in Figure 2-4 could be reduced to one with the code from the following example:

Example:

```
60 INPUT "CAR A'S NAME, MILES, GALLONS";ACAR$,ADIST,AGAL
```

Examine Figure 2-5 to see how the interaction with the program line would appear during program execution. (If using a 64-column or 40-column display, the input data will "wrap around" to the next line as the operator keys it in.)

```
CAR A'S NAME, MILES, GALLONS?   STATE,140,1.17
```

Figure 2-5 Input Interaction with Three Variables on One Line

While it is acceptable to use multiple variables within one input statement, it is recommended procedure to use a separate input statement for each variable.

Step 3: Get the Name, Miles Traveled, and Gallons Used by Car B and Store the Data in Memory

This step is identical to the previous one, except that the data used will be for the second car. Therefore, the steps can be the same, but different variable names must be used. If we used the same variable names as before, the data for the second car would "replace" the data for the first car, and the first car's data would be lost forever. Since we started the first car's variable names with the letter A, let's start the second car's variable names with the letter B. This will result in the following three program lines.

Example:

```
90 INPUT "NAME OF THE SECOND CAR";BCAR$
100 INPUT "NUMBER OF MILES TRAVELED";BDIST
110 INPUT "NUMBER OF GALLONS USED";BGAL
```

Examine Figure 2-6 to see how this interaction looks on the screen. As with Figure 2-4, the part displayed by the program is printed in regular print, while the part keyed in by the operator is printed in bold (in actuality, all data would look the same on the screen). The table at the right of the screen shows the contents that would be stored under each variable name as the three input statements are executed; nothing is printed on the screen as the storage takes place.

```
NAME OF THE SECOND CAR?    TECH

NUMBER OF MILES TRAVELED?   193

NUMBER OF GALLONS USED?   1.21
```

Variable Name	Contents
BCAR$	TECH
BDIST	193
BGAL	1.21

Figure 2-6 Illustration of Input Interaction for Car B

Step 4: Calculate and Store in Memory the Miles Per Gallon for Car A

To calculate the miles per gallon, use the division operator (/) to divide the miles driven by the number of gallons of fuel used. Once the computation is made, the result must be stored in a variable in the computer's memory. A good variable name is AMPG, short for Car A's miles per gallon. The keyword **LET** will compute the data, create the previously unused variable, and store the data in it.

General Form:
line number LET *variable name* = *number, variable, or expression*

Example: `120 LET AMPG=ADIST/AGAL`

Results of this program line are as follows:

Variable Name	Containing
ADIST	140

is divided by

Variable Name	Containing
AGAL	1.17

giving a result of 119.6581, which is stored as

Variable Name	Containing
AMPG	119.6581

If keyword LET is omitted, the exact same action will be taken by the computer.

Example:

```
120 AMPG=ADIST/AGAL
```

In addition to performing a computation and putting the answer in a variable, you may use a constant, literal, or another variable name to the right of the equal sign. Whatever data you specify to the right of the equal sign will be stored in the variable name on the left of the equal sign. Any variables you use on the right of the equal sign will be unchanged by the LET statement.

In performing these operations with the LET statement, the variable types used must match. That is, if a numeric variable, expression, or data appears on the right of the equal sign, the variable on the left must be numeric; if a character variable or literal appears on the right of the equal sign, the variable on the left must be a string variable.

Step 5: Calculate and Store in Memory the Miles Per Gallon for Car B

This step mirrors step 4 except that data for the second car is used. Therefore, for miles per gallon use a variable name of BMPG. Use the variables beginning with B to the right of the equal sign to designate the second car's input data.

Example:

```
130 LET BMPG=BDIST/BGAL
```

Results of the program line are as follows:

Variable Name	Containing
BDIST	193

is divided by

Variable Name	Containing
BGAL	1.21

giving a result of 159.5041, which is stored as:

Variable Name	Containing
BMPG	159.5041

Step 6: Clear the Display So the Report Starts on a Clean Screen

To clear the screen again, use the same keyword, CLS, as before. In this case, the lines that were used for the input of data will be removed from the display so the report will start on a clean screen.

Example:

```
140 CLS
```

Step 7: Print the Items on the Report, Using the Spacing Chart as the Guide

At this point in the program, all the data has been entered, all the computations have been done, and all results have been stored in variables. All that remains is to print the final results, which will be done with PRINT statements. Recall from the spacing chart in Figure 2-3 that the columns were not the distance apart that is automatically provided by separating the items to print with commas. Therefore, you need to use either the **TAB** (short for *tabulate*) function or the **SPC** (short for *space*) function in some of the PRINT statements.

The TAB function moves the starting point to a particular column number before printing.

> **General Form:** TAB(*column number*)

If the program says to tab to column 27, the cursor moves *forward* to column 27 before printing. In coding programs, therefore, always be sure the designated column is *greater than* the current cursor position. Otherwise, on some computers (TRS-80) the tab will be ignored; on others (IBM) the cursor will go *forward* to the following line before printing at the designated tab position.

Note that the TAB function is not a complete program statement. It is always placed within a PRINT statement at any point where the cursor should move forward. Separate the TAB function from other items on the PRINT line with semicolons. If you use commas, one of the commas may cause the computer to jump to the next preset print zone, thereby skipping over your desired tab column.

With the knowledge you now have about the TAB function, see how the printing of the fuel-efficient automobile report might be coded. Be sure to refer to the spacing chart from Figure 2-3 as you study the program lines. Note that items are printed just as they were planned on the chart.

Example:

```
150 PRINT "RESULTS OF THE ECONOMY RUN"
160 PRINT
170 PRINT "CAR NAME   MILES   GALLONS   MPG"
180 PRINT "--------   -----   -------   ---"
190 PRINT
200 PRINT ACAR$;TAB(12);ADIST;TAB(20);AGAL;TAB(30);AMPG
210 PRINT BCAR$;TAB(12);BDIST;TAB(20);BGAL;TAB(30);BMPG
220 END
```

Observe that lines 200 and 210 are alike except that one prints the data for the first car, while the other prints the data for the second car. Figure 2-7 shows the output that would appear on the screen when the program is executed.

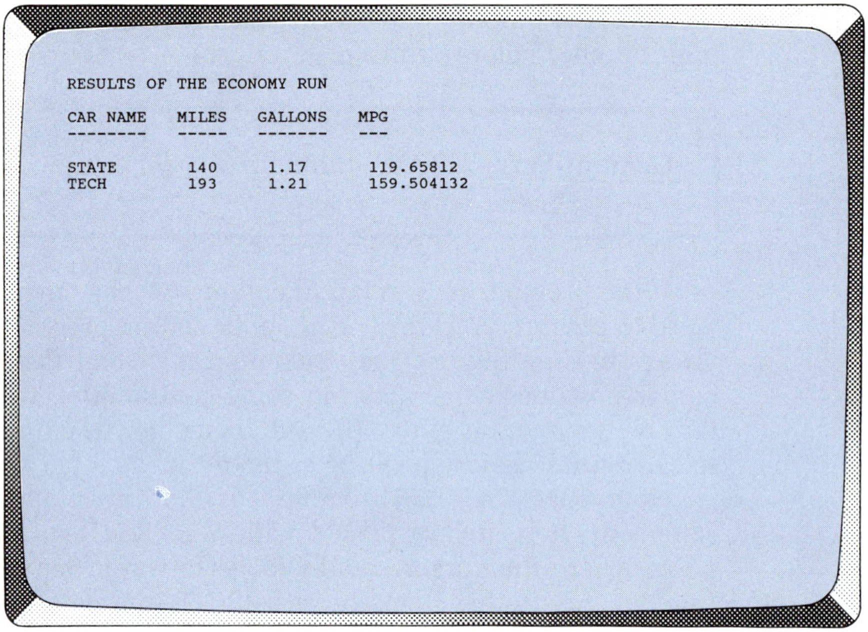

Figure 2-7 Output of Program Run

Another function that can be used in a PRINT statement is the SPC function. This function is similar to the TAB function, except where the TAB function moves to the specified column number, the SPC function moves forward the specified number of *spaces* from wherever the cursor is located. In later chapters, you will learn other uses for the SPC function.

REVIEWING THE COMPLETE CODED EXAMPLE

We have now gone through the entire program design for the example, coding each step into BASIC. To reinforce what you have learned, review the program in its entirety. Examine the program design and see how each step appears in the finished program. Note that an END statement has been added as line 220, indicating the termination of the program. The complete program follows:

Example:

```
10 ' C2E1
20 ' STUDENT NAME, CHAPTER 2, EXAMPLE 1
30 ' DETERMINES WINNER OF FUEL-EFFICIENT VEHICLE CONTEST
40 '
```

```
50 CLS
60 INPUT "NAME OF THE FIRST CAR";ACAR$
70 INPUT "NUMBER OF MILES TRAVELED";ADIST
80 INPUT "NUMBER OF GALLONS USED";AGAL
90 INPUT "NAME OF THE SECOND CAR";BCAR$
100 INPUT "NUMBER OF MILES TRAVELED";BDIST
110 INPUT "NUMBER OF GALLONS USED";BGAL
120 LET AMPG=ADIST/AGAL
130 LET BMPG=BDIST/BGAL
140 CLS
150 PRINT "RESULTS OF THE ECONOMY RUN"
160 PRINT
170 PRINT "CAR NAME   MILES   GALLONS   MPG"
180 PRINT "--------   -----   -------   ---"
190 PRINT
200 PRINT ACAR$;TAB(12);ADIST;TAB(20);AGAL;TAB(30);AMPG
210 PRINT BCAR$;TAB(12);BDIST;TAB(20);BGAL;TAB(30);BMPG
220 END
```

MORE ABOUT VARIABLE NAMES

Earlier in this topic, you were introduced to variable names. There are additional rules you need to follow, however, when thinking up variable names for use with your particular computer. Variable names should begin with a letter. It is also a good practice to use nothing but letters and numbers in variable names, although you can use a limited number of symbols as a part of a name. If you do not use symbols, your programs are more "transportable" from one version of BASIC to another. Also, you do not have to remember which symbols can be used and which ones cannot be used.

The maximum length allowed for variable names differs with computers. On the IBM and compatibles (but not TRS-80 Model III), variable names can be up to 40 characters long. With these machines you should use fully descriptive names in your programs. For example, not using a variable name of P when you can spell out PAYMENT will make the program much easier to understand.

The TRS-80 Model III computer looks at only the first two characters of variable names, even though you are allowed to key in additional characters. Therefore, if you key in more than two characters, make sure the first two characters of each variable name are unique. Our example program for this chapter demonstrates this. Perhaps it would have made more sense to call the variables for the car names CAR1$ and CAR2$. However, on the TRS-80 Model III, CAR1$ and CAR2$ would be considered the same variable because the first two characters (CA) of the variable names are the same. This would cause the data for the first car to be replaced by the data for the second car, and both data lines of the printout would be the same. However, by using the variable names ACAR$ and BCAR$, the first two letters were kept unique while at the same time the names were long enough to be easily understood.

One additional caution is in order when using longer variable names. Be careful not to attempt to use a keyword as a variable name. For example, REM cannot be used as a variable since it is a keyword. On the IBM and compatibles, variables may *contain* embedded keywords; therefore, *REM*AINDER could be used as a variable name. However on the TRS-80 Model III, you may not use a variable name that includes an embedded keyword (e.g., *REM*AINDER could not be used since REM is a keyword). See Appendix A for a list of reserved keywords.

The following chart summarizes examples of valid and invalid variable names:

VARIABLE NAME	STATUS
A	Valid, but not recommended since it is hard to associate the name with the variable's contents
CART	Valid
CABLE	Valid, but could not be used on the TRS-80 Model III in the same program with CART, since the two beginning letters are the same and the computer would consider them the same variable. May be used with CART or other "first-two-letters-alike" variables on IBM and compatibles.
REM	Invalid, because REM is a keyword
REMAINDER	Valid on IBM and compatibles; invalid on TRS-80 Model III, because a keyword is embedded in the name
AMT1988	Valid

VARIABLE NAME	STATUS
1988AMT	Invalid, because it does not begin with a letter
RATE@	Invalid, because it contains an invalid special symbol

Remember that any valid variable name *without* a dollar sign at the end is a numeric variable and can only store digits and the decimal point. Any valid variable name may have a dollar sign added at the end, making it a string or character variable capable of holding any characters, including numbers. However, you cannot do arithmetic with numbers stored in a string variable.

REVIEW QUESTIONS

1. Describe the process of coding a program. (Obj. 6)
2. What is a variable? (Obj. 5)
3. What are the rules for naming variables? How are numeric and nonnumeric variables distinguished? (Obj. 5)
4. Name and describe the statement used to clear the screen on the computer you are using. (Obj. 6)
5. Describe the use of the INPUT statement. (Obj. 6)
6. Describe the use of the LET statement. (Obj. 6)
7. What is the role of the TAB function? Explain how to use the TAB function. (Obj. 6)
8. What are the similarities and differences between the TAB function and the SPC function? (Obj. 6)

VOCABULARY WORDS

The following terms were introduced in this chapter:

bug
debugging
interactive program
logic errors
program design
program documentation sheet
prompt
spacing chart
string
syntax errors
variable

KEYWORDS AND COMMANDS

The following keywords and commands were introduced in this chapter:

CLS	LET	TAB
INPUT	SPC	

PROGRAMS TO WRITE

For each of the following programs, prepare a program documentation sheet and program design. For all programs whose output will be arranged in columns, also prepare a spacing chart. Ask your teacher for the blank forms. Next, code the program design into BASIC, execute the program, and debug it. In some of the programs, the output may not be as organized as you would like, since you do not yet know how to line up numbers at the decimal points or how to specify the number of decimals to include in an answer. With some numbers, you may also see that the computer stores the number a little inaccurately. For example, on occasion you might store the number 4.95 and see 4.949999 when the stored value is printed. For now, just tolerate these imperfections. You will learn how to deal with them in later chapters.

Program 1

Write a program that will calculate and print the amount of sales tax on a purchase. The program should request the purchase amount from the keyboard and then compute the tax at 5 percent of the purchase amount. The output should be in the following form: THE SALES TAX IS $xx.xx. Use a purchase amount of $321.64 to test the program.

Program 2

Write a program that will calculate and print the amount of gross pay earned by an employee. The program should ask the operator for the number of hours worked and the hourly rate of pay. It should then compute the result by multiplying the hours times the rate. The output may be in the form of a single line. Test your program using data of 37 hours at $6.17 per hour.

Program 3

Write a program that will calculate and print the area of a circle. The program should request from the operator the radius of the circle. The output may be displayed on a single line. Use a radius of 4 in testing the program. Remember that the formula for the area of a circle is π (roughly 3.14) times the radius squared.

Program 4

Write a program that asks the user for the number of persons who attended a lecture on Monday night, on Tuesday night, and on Wednesday night. The program should produce output showing the attendance each night as well as the average attendance figure. Test the program using an attendance figure of 974 on Monday night, 1,145 on Tuesday night, and 1,019 on Wednesday night.

Program 5

This program should produce a sales slip for the purchase of a single item in Wyler's Store. The program should ask for the quantity of the item purchased and for the price for each unit. It should then compute the cost by multiplying the quantity by the unit price. The output should be arranged in columns similar to the following:

```
**** WYLER'S STORE ****

QTY  PRICE     AMOUNT

XXX  XXXXXX    XXXXXXX
```

Test the program using a quantity of 12 items at a price of $7.91 each.

Program 6

Prepare a program that calculates and prints unit prices for two competing packages of a similar product. The input, which consists of a price and package size (number of units) for each of two products, should be obtained from the keyboard. The unit price is calculated by dividing the price by the number of units. Print the output in a form similar to the following:

```
UNIT PRICE FOR PKG. 1:   $XXXXXXX
UNIT PRICE FOR PKG. 2:   $XXXXXXX
```

For test data, use a package that costs $5.18 and contains 16 ounces and a package that costs $4.59 and contains 12 ounces.

Program 7

Write a program that requests a number from the user, prints the number, the number's square, and the number's cube.

(Remember that the square of a number is computed as *number* times *number*, while the cube is calculated as *number* times *number* times *number*.) Use the column headings NUMBER, SQUARE, and CUBE and the example number 3 for test data.

Program 8

This program should compare the performance of two teams by calculating each team's percentage of wins for the season. Input from the keyboard should consist of the name of each team, its number of wins, and its number of losses. The output should be in columns headed TEAM, WINS, LOSSES, and PERCENT. Test data for the Cardinals is 12 wins and 3 losses; for the Redbirds, the data is 7 wins and 8 losses.

Program 9

With some loans, the interest is figured monthly. That is, the amount owed at the beginning of the month is multiplied by the monthly interest rate (the annual rate divided by 12). This gives a monthly interest figure that is added to the beginning balance. The payment made that month is then subtracted from the total, giving an ending balance. Write a program to accept as input the borrower's name, the balance owed at the beginning of the month, and the amount paid. The interest rate should be written into the program as a constant 14.5 percent annual rate. The program should print in columns the borrower's name, beginning balance, payment amount, and ending balance. Try the program using Sid Martin as the borrower, with a beginning balance of $347.18 and a payment amount of $75.

Program 10

As part of their work, an engineering firm must, at times, compare the volumes of two different cylindrical tanks used in a particular manufacturing application. Write a program that will ask the user for the radius and depth for each of the two tanks and then print a report showing the volumes of the tanks. To compute the volume of a cylinder, multiply the area of the cylinder's cross-section by its height; all measurements must be in the same units. For example, if measurements are in feet, the volume will be expressed as cubic feet. Use test data of a two-foot radius and six-foot height for the first tank; a three-foot radius and five-foot height for the second tank.

3

The Use of Structure

OBJECTIVES

After studying this chapter, you will be able to

1. Define structured programming.
2. Describe what is meant by top-down design.
3. Define a hierarchy chart.
4. State the difference between a main module and a submodule.
5. Explain how program designs are prepared for modules.
6. List the steps in coding a modular program.
7. Plan and code modular programs.

In Chapter 1 you learned the definition of a computer program. In Chapter 2 you learned about some methods of planning and documenting programs. In this chapter you will learn about the recommended procedure for developing programs. A series of steps designed to make programming as easy and effective as possible include: (1) planning the program; (2) coding the program; and (3) testing the program. Planning of the program is discussed in Topic 3.1, while the coding and testing phases are covered in Topic 3.2.

TOPIC 3.1 PLANNING A STRUCTURED PROGRAM

The recommended method of program development is called structured programming. **Structured programming** is defined as breaking a program into segments or modules, each performing a separate and specific function and executed in a logical order. The planning of a structured program involves the use of a procedure known as top-down design and includes the preparation of a hierarchy chart and module documentation sheets. These forms explain and document the design of the program.

TOP-DOWN DESIGN

Top-down design of a program means that you begin by defining the overall purpose of the program and work your way down to more detailed levels of the design. The first step in top-down design is to define the problem. You did this in Chapter 2 when you wrote the purpose of a program on a program documentation sheet. From this statement of the problem, you gradually refine the definition of the program, adding more detail at each step.

As soon as the planning of the program proceeds far enough to allow it, you should prepare a spacing chart. This chart will be your definition of what the output will look like. If necessary, you may use spacing charts to define more than one output. From this definition of the output, you can determine what inputs and processing are necessary to achieve the desired output.

HIERARCHY CHART

The next step in top-down design is preparation of a **hierarchy chart**, which is a diagram that shows the relationship between the different functions to be performed by a program. The hierarchy chart is a series of boxes (see Figure 3-1). The top box is used to write the overall name of the problem, while each of the underlying boxes gives the name of one function to be performed by the program. The hierarchy chart thus follows the idea of top-down design, starting as it does with the overall problem and progressing downward to the detailed functions. The connecting lines show the relationship between the functions. Each of the functions is known as a **module**, meaning it is a part of the whole program. Let's go back and use the example program from Chapter 2 to illustrate the process of preparing a hierarchy chart. Remember that the program's purpose was to compute miles per gallon to find the most fuel-efficient automobile.

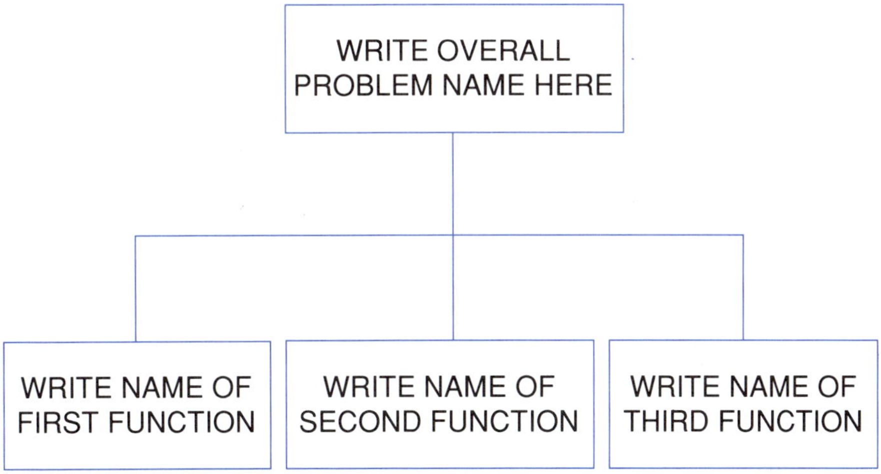

Figure 3-1 Arrangement for Writing a Hierarchy Chart

The overall program you have decided to write can be labeled as the fuel-efficiency program; this is the statement of the overall problem. Show this by drawing a box and writing the title of the overall problem inside it. This first box is known as the **main module** or **control module** because it controls the operation of the problem (see Figure 3-2).

Figure 3-2 First Step in the Hierarchy Chart

Once the top block (representing the main module) has been drawn and labeled with the name of the entire project, details can be added to the plan. Think about what functions must be performed by the program. Each of these functions is also designated as a module. Since they operate under the control of the main module, each function is called a **submodule**. One function (submodule) of the present program is to get the data; without this function, the program would be totally useless. A box representing this function is added below the main module (see Figure 3-3).

Calculations must be made from the inputted data in order to arrive at the miles-per-gallon figures. These calculations represent

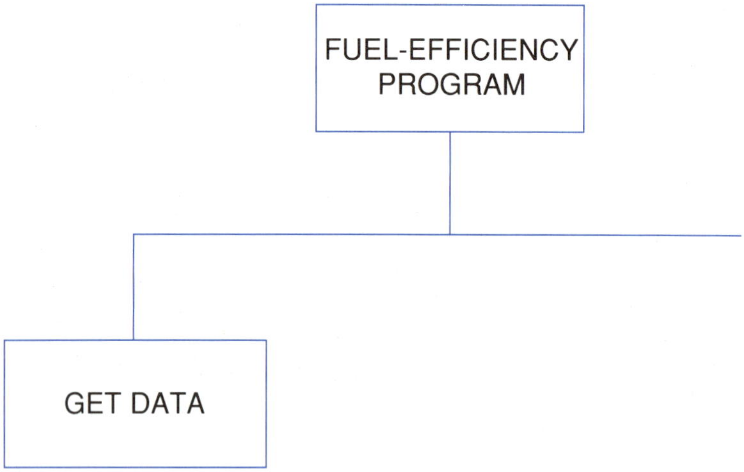

Figure 3-3 Hierarchy Chart with the Get Data Module Added

another function and another submodule of the program. Add this submodule to the hierarchy chart as shown in Figure 3-4.

The last function of the program is that it must be able to print the results. Addition of this submodule will complete the hierarchy chart (see Figure 3-5).

Each of the boxes on the hierarchy chart represents one module of the final program. Each of these modules performs its particular

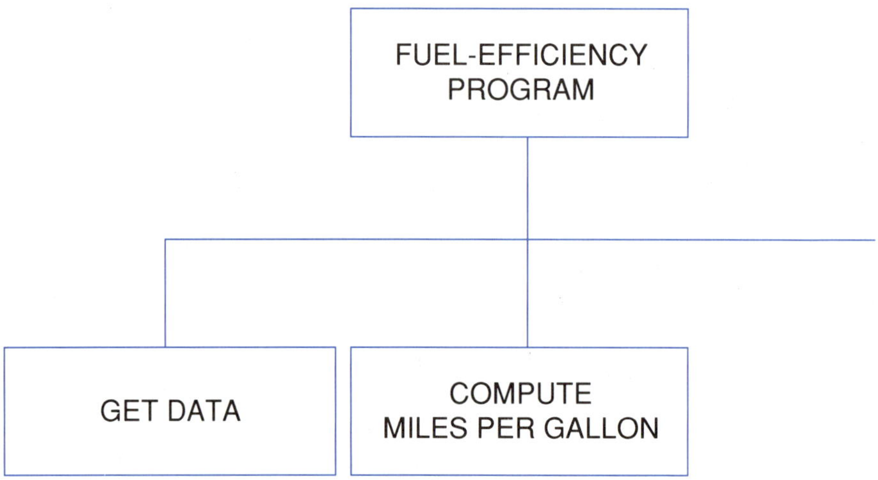

Figure 3-4 Hierarchy Chart with the Compute Miles Per Gallon Module Added

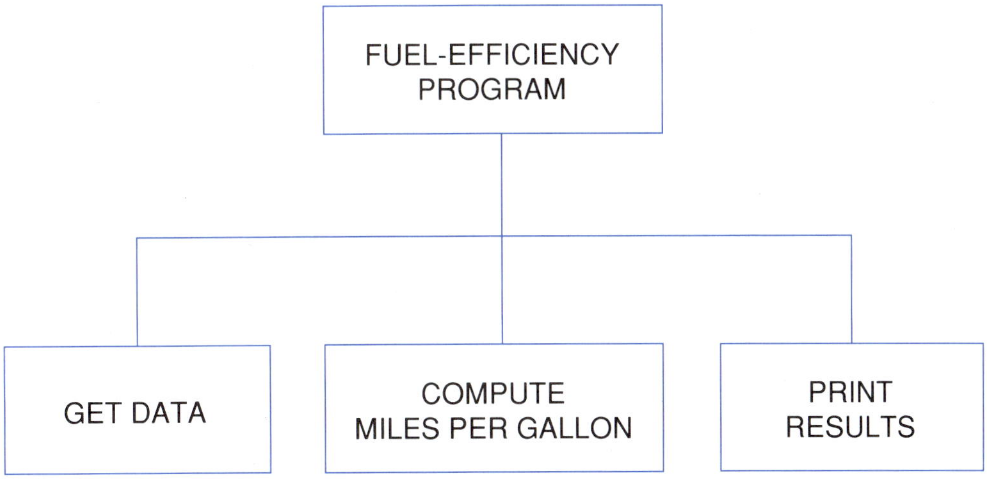

Figure 3-5 Complete Hierarchy Chart

work when it is called (instructed to do so) by the main module above it. This process works in much the same way as a general contracting business. The general contractor hires various people to work on a house. This contractor is equivalent to the main (control) module of the hierarchy chart, and each of the workers hired is equivalent to one of the submodules. Each worker does a particular job, such as plumbing or electrical wiring, when instructed to do so by the general contractor.

PROGRAM DESIGN

Once the hierarchy chart with its main module and submodules has been completed, the next step is to prepare the program design. This design is different from the one used in Chapter 2 however. Instead of one overall design, there is a separate design for each of the modules identified in the hierarchy chart. Also, we will begin using a special **module documentation sheet** (see Figure 3-6) to write the program design. Note that the form includes spaces to write the program name, module name, module lines, and module description as well as the program design. As the module documentation sheets are prepared, complete all spaces except the one for the module lines. The assignment of module lines will be explained later.

The module documentation sheet is always done for the main module first and indicates the order in which the other modules

MODULE DOCUMENTATION SHEET	
Program:	Module: Lines:
Module Description:	
Module Function (Program Design):	

Figure 3-6 Module Documentation Sheet

are to do their work. Note, however, that the main module can also perform processing functions. Study the program design for the main module of our example program (see Figure 3-7). Note that in step 1 the main module itself is clearing the display screen. In steps 2, 3, and 4 the main module is controlling the submodules by calling upon them to perform their processing functions.

Note that the steps in Figure 3-7 define everything the program must do; however, they do not include all the details of how to do it. These details will be included in the documentation for the submodules. In planning the submodules, the following rules should be observed. They will help make the program much easier to understand.

1. Each module will perform one logical function.
2. Each module will do its work when instructed or called by the module above it (main module) on the hierarchy chart.

MODULE DOCUMENTATION SHEET	
Program: C3E1	Module: MAIN Lines:
Module Description: Main Module	
Module Function (Program Design): 1. Clear the display. 2. Call the Get Data module. 3. Call the Compute Miles Per Gallon module. 4. Call the Print Results module.	

Figure 3-7 Module Documentation Sheet for Main Module

3. Upon completion of its task, each module will return control to the module that called it. That is, the submodule will tell the module above it (main module) that its work is done. The module above then will continue with its next instruction.
4. There will be only one way in and one way out of each module. That is, each module always starts working with its first program line and stops working with its last program line.
5. No module will make a decision that must be followed by any module above it on the hierarchy chart. Submodules may send results back to the module above, with the module above choosing different courses of action based on the results.

Using these rules, a documentation sheet is prepared for each of the submodules. Study the program documentation sheets in Figures 3-8 through 3-10.

Once the program designs are complete for all modules, you are ready to proceed to the coding process as described in the next topic.

<table>
<tr><th colspan="2">MODULE DOCUMENTATION SHEET</th></tr>
<tr><td>Program: C3E1</td><td>Module: GET DATA
Lines:</td></tr>
<tr><td colspan="2">Module Description: Requests entry of data from the keyboard and stores it in variables.</td></tr>
<tr><td colspan="2">Module Function (Program Design):
1. Get the name, distance, and gallons of fuel for the first car and store them in variables.
2. Get the name, distance, and gallons of fuel for the second car and store them in variables.</td></tr>
</table>

Figure 3-8 Module Documentation Sheet for the Get Data Module

<table>
<tr><th colspan="2">MODULE DOCUMENTATION SHEET</th></tr>
<tr><td>Program: C3E1</td><td>Module: COMPUTE MILES PER GALLON
Lines:</td></tr>
<tr><td colspan="2">Module Description: Calculates miles per gallon for both automobiles and stores the results in variables.</td></tr>
<tr><td colspan="2">Module Function (Program Design):
1. Compute the miles per gallon for the first car by dividing its distance by its gallons. Store the result in a variable.
2. Compute the miles per gallon for the second car by dividing its distance by its gallons. Store the result in a variable.</td></tr>
</table>

Figure 3-9 Module Documentation Sheet for the Compute Miles Per Gallon Module

MODULE DOCUMENTATION SHEET	
Program: C3E1	Module: PRINT RESULTS Lines:
Module Description: Prints output based on spacing chart.	
Module Function: 1. Clear the display. 2. Print report headings. 3. Print the results for each of the two cars.	

Figure 3-10 Module Documentation Sheet for the Print Results Module

REVIEW QUESTIONS

1. What is structured programming? (Obj. 1)
2. What are the three primary steps in planning a structured program? (Obj. 1)
3. Describe what is meant by top-down design. (Obj. 2)
4. What is a hierarchy chart? (Obj. 3)
5. Explain how to prepare a hierarchy chart. (Obj. 3)
6. Explain the differences in the roles of the main module and the submodules of a program. (Obj. 4)
7. What rules are to be followed in planning the functions of a program module? (Obj. 5)
8. How are program designs prepared for a modular program? (Obj. 5)
9. What rules should be followed in planning submodules of a program? (Obj. 5)

TOPIC 3.2 CODING AND TESTING A STRUCTURED PROGRAM

Once a program is planned as discussed in the preceding section, the next step is to code it—that is, write the actual program lines. The coding of a modular or structured program is generally broken into several steps.

1. Assign line number ranges to the main module and each of the submodules.
2. Code the main module.
3. Create stub submodules (coded in abbreviated form).
4. Test the main module.
5. Completely code and test the submodules one at a time.

The example program used in this chapter is so simple that some of these steps may seem unnecessary. However, as programs become more complex, you will appreciate the benefits of this structured approach. Following the suggested steps will result in faster program completion and fewer errors. These steps are discussed in the following sections, still using the example from Topic 3.1.

ASSIGNING LINE NUMBER RANGES

Since the main module and all the submodules will be in the computer's memory at the same time, they must be assigned line number ranges that do not overlap. For the example, the following assignments are used:

LINE NUMBER RANGE	MODULE
10-999	Main
1000-1999	Get Data
2000-2999	Compute Miles Per Gallon
3000-3999	Print Results

There are no rules for making these line number assignments. However, the lowest line number range should be assigned to the main module. Each submodule should start with an even thousand number. Be sure to make the ranges large enough to contain all possible required program lines. Once the line number ranges are assigned, write them on the appropriate module documentation sheets after the "Lines:" heading.

WRITING THE MAIN MODULE

As indicated earlier, the main module controls the operation of the other modules by making sure that they have the proper data available and that they carry out their function at the proper time. In coding the main module (and the submodules later), the module documentation sheets should be precisely followed.

On the module documentation sheet for the main module, several steps involve instructing a submodule to perform its work. This instruction is given by using the keyword **GOSUB** in the main module. GOSUB is the abbreviation of GO to SUBroutine. In the vocabulary of the BASIC language, each submodule is known as a subroutine. The keyword **RETURN** is used at the end of each submodule to return control of the computer to the statement following the GOSUB that called the submodule. Note that when used as a keyword, RETURN is spelled out. It is not the same as the ENTER or RETURN key. Here is the general form of the two keywords. To instruct a submodule to perform its task, the general form is as follows:

General Form: *line number* GOSUB *line number*

Example: `50 GOSUB 1000`

To transfer control from a submodule back to the calling module, the general form is as follows:

General Form: *line number* RETURN

Example: `1999 RETURN`

Here is the coding of the main module of the example program. Note that each step from the module documentation sheet (see Figure 3-6) is converted to one or more lines of BASIC code. The step numbers from the module documentation sheet are shown to the right to help show this relationship. REM statements (denoted by the ' form) have also been used on program lines to explain the action that is taking place. Note that a colon (:) is used to separate two statements on the same line. A "box" of asterisks is used to make it easy to see where the actual work of the module begins. The keyword RETURN will be used later in coding the submodules.

Example:

```
10 ' C3E1
20 ' STUDENT NAME, CHAPTER 3, EXAMPLE 1
30 ' DETERMINES WINNER OF FUEL-EFFICIENT VEHICLE CONTEST
40 '
50 ' ******************************
60 ' * MAIN MODULE                *
70 ' ******************************
80 CLS  <---------------------------------------------- 1
90 GOSUB 1000        ' GET DATA MODULE <--------------- 2
100 GOSUB 2000       ' COMPUTE MILES PER GALLON MODULE <-- 3
110 GOSUB 3000       ' PRINT RESULTS MODULE <---------- 4
999 END
```

STUBBING IN THE SUBMODULES

Stubbing in the submodules means coding the submodules in skeleton form. Each of the skeletons consists of REM lines to identify the module on a program listing, a PRINT statement to display the module function, and a RETURN statement at the end of the module to send control back to the main module.

The stubbed-in submodules for the example program follow. Note that they use the line number ranges assigned earlier. The asterisks are used on the REM lines to make the beginning of each module easy to spot on a program listing. Note also that the RETURN statement is always on the very last line of the assigned line number range.

Example:

```
1000 ' ******************************
1010 ' * GET DATA                   *
1020 ' ******************************
1030 PRINT "GET DATA MODULE"
1999 RETURN
2000 ' ******************************
2010 ' * COMPUTE MILES PER GALLON   *
2020 ' ******************************
2030 PRINT "COMPUTE MILES PER GALLON MODULE"
2999 RETURN
3000 ' ******************************
3010 ' * PRINT RESULTS              *
3020 ' ******************************
3030 PRINT "PRINT RESULTS MODULE"
3999 RETURN
```

TESTING THE MAIN MODULE

Once the main module and the stubbed-in submodules have been entered into the computer, the main module should be tested. This is done simply by running the program. The results outputted by the PRINT statements in the submodules indicate whether the program is functioning properly. For example,

1. If the messages are printed in the order in which the submodules should do their work, the GOSUB statements in the main module are in the proper order.
2. If the messages are printed in the wrong order, the GOSUB statements in the main module are not being executed in the proper order.
3. If any message is missing, the main module is not executing a GOSUB statement transferring control to that particular module.
4. If any work designated for performance by the main module is not done, that is an indication that the coding for that work is incorrect.
5. If the module messages are repeated, the main module may be missing an END statement.

If any of these problems occur during testing, the main module must be corrected and the test repeated.

The proper output of a test run of the example program's main module is shown in Figure 3-11. Remember that the main module and the stubbed-in submodules have both been entered into the computer before running the program for this test.

```
(Screen clear)

GET DATA MODULE
COMPUTE MILES PER GALLON MODULE
PRINT RESULTS MODULE
```

Figure 3-11 Output from Main Module Test

CODING AND TESTING THE SUBMODULES

As soon as the main module has passed its tests, each submodule should be completely coded and tested. First, remove the PRINT line that was placed in the module for test purposes. Then add the lines (code) to do the module's assigned work. The only rule for determining which module to code first is that of logic. If you examine the example program's design, you will note that no processing may be done until the input data is obtained. Therefore, it is logical to code the Get Data module first. Logic then proceeds to the Compute Miles Per Gallon module and then to the Print Results module.

Get Data Module

The complete coding for the Get Data module follows. As with the main module, one or more lines of BASIC are written for each step on the module documentation sheet. The step numbers from the module documentation are shown to the right of the program lines.

Example:

```
1000 ' ******************************
1010 ' * GET DATA                   *
1020 ' ******************************
1030 INPUT "NAME OF THE FIRST CAR";ACAR$ ←————————— 1
1040 INPUT "NUMBER OF MILES TRAVELED";ADIST ←—————— 1
1050 INPUT "NUMBER OF GALLONS USED";AGAL ←————————— 1
1060 INPUT "NAME OF THE SECOND CAR";BCAR$ ←———————— 2
1070 INPUT "NUMBER OF MILES TRAVELED";BDIST ←—————— 2
1080 INPUT "NUMBER OF GALLONS USED";BGAL ←————————— 2
1999 RETURN
```

The Get Data module should be entered into the computer along with the main module and the remaining stubbed-in submodules. Then the program should be executed to determine if there are any errors in the newly entered module. If the module has been coded and entered correctly, no error message will appear. The proper questions should be asked on the display, and the operator should be allowed to key in responses. Since there is no printout capability entered into the computer yet, there is no direct way to determine whether the data is correctly stored in the variables after the Get Data module is executed. However, due to the interactive nature of BASIC, the variables can be examined. Note that the variables for the first car are ACAR$, ADIST, and AGAL. Those for the second car are BCAR$, BDIST, and BGAL. These variables will still have values in them immediately after the program has been run. Therefore, if you enter a PRINT statement with no line number, the contents of the variables can be displayed, and you can see if they are correct. For example, you can enter PRINT ACAR$ and press the ENTER/RETURN key to display just the contents of this variable. To display the contents of more than one variable at the same time, just place more than one variable name after the keyword PRINT, separating the variables with commas (e.g., PRINT ACAR$,ADIST,AGAL).

Compute Miles Per Gallon Module

Once the Get Data module passes its test, the Compute Miles Per Gallon module can be coded as shown here. The steps from the module documentation sheet are shown to the right.

Example:

```
2000 ' ******************************
2010 ' * COMPUTE MILES PER GALLON   *
2020 ' ******************************
2030 LET AMPG=ADIST/AGAL  <-------------------- 1
2040 LET BMPG=BDIST/BGAL  <-------------------- 2
2999 RETURN
```

After entering this module, the program should again be run. As with the Get Data module, there will be no printout. However, if you enter PRINT AMPG,BMPG and press the ENTER/RETURN key after the program is executed, the contents of the result variables will be printed. You can thus verify whether the computations were done correctly.

Print Results Module

The Print Results module that follows is coded from the module documentation sheet in Figure 3-10. It uses data that has been placed in variables by preceding modules of the program.

Example:

```
3000 ' ******************************
3010 ' * PRINT RESULTS              *
3020 ' ******************************
3030 CLS  <------------------------------------ 1
3040 PRINT "RESULTS OF THE ECONOMY RUN"  <----- 2
3050 PRINT  <---------------------------------- 2
```

```
3060 PRINT "CAR NAME    MILES    GALLONS    MPG" ← 2
3070 PRINT "--------    -----    -------    ---" ← 2
3080 PRINT ← 2
3090 PRINT ACAR$;TAB(12);ADIST;TAB(20);AGAL;TAB(30);AMPG ← 3
3100 PRINT BCAR$;TAB(12);BDIST;TAB(20);BGAL;TAB(30);BMPG ← 3
3999 RETURN
```

With the Print Results module coded, the entire program is complete. Thus, when the program is executed, the accuracy can be checked by reading the output. If the previous modules were properly tested as they were completed, any error occurring at this point will be isolated in the Print Results module.

Here is the entire program as coded in the preceding sections; note that the END statement in line 999 makes the program end at the proper point rather than "falling" into the first subroutine again after all the work is completed:

Example:

```
10 ' C3E1
20 ' STUDENT NAME, CHAPTER 3, EXAMPLE 1
30 ' DETERMINES WINNER OF FUEL-EFFICIENT VEHICLE CONTEST
40 '
50 ' ******************************
60 ' * MAIN MODULE                *
70 ' ******************************
80 CLS
90 GOSUB 1000                ' GET DATA MODULE
100 GOSUB 2000               ' COMPUTE MILES PER GALLON MODULE
110 GOSUB 3000               ' PRINT RESULTS MODULE
999 END
1000 ' ******************************
1010 ' * GET DATA                   *
1020 ' ******************************
1030 INPUT "NAME OF THE FIRST CAR";ACAR$
1040 INPUT "NUMBER OF MILES TRAVELED";ADIST
1050 INPUT "NUMBER OF GALLONS USED";AGAL
1060 INPUT "NAME OF THE SECOND CAR";BCAR$
1070 INPUT "NUMBER OF MILES TRAVELED";BDIST
1080 INPUT "NUMBER OF GALLONS USED";BGAL
1999 RETURN
```

```
2000 ' *****************************
2010 ' * COMPUTE MILES PER GALLON   *
2020 ' *****************************
2030 LET AMPG=ADIST/AGAL
2040 LET BMPG=BDIST/BGAL
2999 RETURN
3000 ' *****************************
3010 ' * PRINT RESULTS             *
3020 ' *****************************
3030 CLS
3040 PRINT "RESULTS OF THE ECONOMY RUN"
3050 PRINT
3060 PRINT "CAR NAME   MILES   GALLONS   MPG"
3070 PRINT "--------   -----   -------   ---"
3080 PRINT
3090 PRINT ACAR$;TAB(12);ADIST;TAB(20);AGAL;TAB(30);AMPG
3100 PRINT BCAR$;TAB(12);BDIST;TAB(20);BGAL;TAB(30);BMPG
3999 RETURN
```

REVIEW QUESTIONS

1. What steps should be followed in coding a modular program? (Obj. 6)
2. How can the main module be tested before the submodules are coded? (Obj. 6)
3. What determines the order in which submodules are coded and tested? (Obj. 6)
4. What is the function of the keyword GOSUB? How should it be coded? (Obj. 7)
5. What is the function of the keyword RETURN? Where should it be used? (Obj. 7)

VOCABULARY WORDS

The following terms were introduced in this chapter:

control module
hierarchy chart
main module
module
module documentation sheet
stubbing in
structured programming
submodule
top-down design

KEYWORDS

The following keywords were introduced in this chapter:

GOSUB RETURN

PROGRAMS TO WRITE

For program assignments 1 through 10, perform the following steps. Note: Many of the steps may seem like extra work if a program is simple; however, getting in the habit of following these steps will prove valuable when writing more complicated programs.

1. Begin a program documentation sheet by writing the name of the program, your name, and the purpose of the program.
2. Prepare a hierarchy chart. For the program assignments that follow, the submodules will be similar for all programs. That is, one submodule should get the data, one should do the computations, and one should print the results.
3. Prepare a spacing chart when appropriate.
4. Complete a module documentation sheet for each module.
5. Code the main module. Remember to use REM statements as illustrated in the example program in the chapter whenever appropriate.
6. Stub in all the submodules. Use REM statements as illustrated in the example program in the chapter. Be sure the RETURN statement is on the last line of the assigned line number range.
7. Key in and execute the program to test the main module's operation. If any corrections are necessary in the main module, make them before proceeding.
8. Complete the coding of the submodules one at a time so that they perform the desired actions. Code the submodules in a logical order so that the operation of each may be tested as soon as it is finished.

Programs 1 through 4

Rewrite Programs 1 through 4 from Chapter 2 so that they are in modular form. Using programs with which you are already familiar will help make your first use of structured programs easier.

Program 5

County governments generally collect a property tax based on the value of real estate owned. Assume that in one county property tax is computed at a set rate times a dollar amount called the assessed valuation. The assessed valuation is 40 percent of the market value of the property. As an example, assume you own a house with a market value of $100,000. The assessed valuation would be 40 percent of this amount, or $40,000. If the tax rate is $0.025, the tax is found by multiplying .025 times $40,000. Write a program that will ask the user to input the market value and tax rate, compute the assessed valuation by multiplying the market value by 40 percent, compute the amount of the tax, and display the tax amount. The output need not be arranged in columns. In planning the program, have the main module clear the screen, display a description of what the program does, and call the necessary submodules. To test the program, use a market value of $100,000 with a tax rate of $0.025.

Program 6

Frequently, different divisions of a business are given sales quotas or goals for each quarter or year. At the end of the period, actual performance is compared with the quota or goal. A percentage is usually computed to show the magnitude by which the division exceeded or failed to meet its goal. For this program, assume a business has two divisions (divisions A and B). The program should ask for the quota and actual performance for each division and then calculate and print output arranged as follows:

```
      SALES PERFORMANCE COMPARISON

  DIV   QUOTA   PERFORMANCE   PERCENT

   #    #####     #####        ######
```

In planning the program, have the main module clear the screen, display a description of what the program does, and call the necessary submodules. For test purposes, use a quota of $46,000 and a performance of $47,851 for division A. For division B, use a quota of $42,000 and a performance of $39,658.

Program 7

Using inputs of the length and width of a room, this program should compute the number of square feet in the room by multiplying the length times the width. The output should be arranged in three columns headed LENGTH, WIDTH, and AREA. The LENGTH should begin at the left of the display, the WIDTH should begin at column 10 of the display, and the AREA should begin at column 20 of the display. In planning the program, have the main module clear the screen, display a description of what the program does, and call the necessary submodules. Test the program using a length of 20 feet and a width of 15 feet.

Program 8

Car performance enthusiasts sometimes like to compare the output per liter of displacement for various auto engines. Write a program to help them compare any two engines. The input should be the name of the engine, its liters of displacement, and its horsepower. After printing a heading of HORSEPOWER COMPARISONS, the program should print the output in columns headed ENGINE, LITERS, HP, and HP PER LITER. HP (horsepower) PER LITER is computed by dividing the horsepower by the number of liters. In planning the program, have the main module clear the screen, display a description of what the program does, and call the necessary submodules. Test the program using data for an SV500 engine (5 liters displacement, 145 horsepower) and an HVI5 engine (4.8 liters, 132 horsepower).

Program 9

A lawn care company uses liquid chemicals to treat its customer's lawns. Usually they spray on fertilizer, weed killer, and insecticide. The customer is charged based on the number of gallons of chemicals applied. Write a program to accept as input the number of gallons of each chemical used. The program should then compute the amount owed and print an invoice. The amounts for fertilizer, weed killer, and insecticide should each be printed on a separate line, followed by a line for the total owed. The price per gallon of insecticide remains fairly constant. Therefore, near the beginning of the main module assign the current prices to variables. Then use the variables in the computation module. The data for testing the program should be $6.54 per gallon (5 gallons) for fertilizer, $4.18 per gallon (2 gallons) for weed killer, and $9.47 per gallon (2.5 gallons) for insecticide.

Program 10

The amount of fuel required by an airplane flying from one place to another depends on several factors. Assume that the aircraft will burn a given number of gallons of fuel per hour when flying at a given speed through the air. If flying into a head wind, the speed over the ground will be less than the airspeed. If flying with a tail wind, the speed over the ground will be greater than the airspeed. Write a program that will request as input the miles to be flown, the gallons of fuel to be burned per hour, the plane's airspeed, and the speed of the wind. The operator should be prompted to enter positive numbers for tail winds and negative numbers for head winds. The program should determine and display the number of gallons of fuel required to fly the number of miles indicated. Run the program using two different sets of test data. First, use 850 miles, 6 gallons per hour, airspeed of 95 miles per hour, and a tail wind of 15 miles per hour. Next, use 340 miles, 10 gallons per hour, airspeed of 170 miles per hour, and a head wind of 10 miles per hour.

PROJECT 1—WRITING AN INVOICING PROGRAM

This is the first of six projects you will be completing. There is one at the conclusion of each part of the text. The project for each part is not necessarily more difficult than the programming assignments for the chapters. Instead, each project gives you an opportunity to more fully integrate what you have learned.

For this project, you will be writing an invoicing program. An invoice is a written statement of what is purchased by a customer. It is given to the customer as a record of the purchase, and a copy is usually kept by the business for its records. Invoices may be produced in almost any shape and size, and they may be arranged in any way desired by the business. However, it is important that the invoice contain information about the name of the business making the sale; the date of the sale; the quantity, description, and prices of the items purchased; a subtotal; the amount of sales tax, if any; and the total of the sale including the tax.

The invoice program you will plan and write for this project should have the name of the business stored as a constant within the program. All other input data should be requested from the keyboard. Since you do not yet know how to handle a varying number of items, write the program so that each invoice is for three different items. The quantity of each of these items, however, should be entered from the keyboard. Write in a constant 5 percent as the sales tax rate. While input is to be done with the keyboard, output of the program should be routed to the printer if one is available.

Follow the rules for good structured programming as you plan, code, and test the program. The invoices produced by your program should be similar to the following:

WALLY'S TIRE STORE **DATE**

QTY	ITEM	PRICE	AMOUNT
2	Custom 431	90	180
2	Valve stems	4.25	8.50
2	Balance	10	20
		Subtotal	208.50
		Tax	10.425
		Total	218.925

Note that the columns of numbers need not line up perfectly at the decimal point, as you have not yet learned that step. Note also that there may be more than two decimal places in some numbers. This, too, is acceptable at this point. You will learn how to remedy the problem in later chapters.

PART TWO
STRUCTURED PROGRAM CONTROL

4

Decision Making in Programs

OBJECTIVES

After studying this chapter, you will be able to

1. Describe the importance of programs that can make decisions.
2. Describe how menus may be used in programs.
3. Explain the procedure for planning programs that make decisions.
4. Explain the use of the BASIC keywords used in decision making.
5. Plan and code programs that make decisions.

In previous chapters you wrote programs that used only sequential steps. That is, each statement was executed sequentially (one after the other) from the beginning of the program to the end, and the program terminated at that point. Frequently, however, it is desirable for some of the steps in a program to be executed in other than sequential order. For example, some of the steps might need to be executed under certain circumstances, while some steps should be executed under different circumstances or may need to be repeated. To make these varying execution paths possible, control structures are used. A **control structure** is defined as any one of several different methods used to control the order in which program steps are executed. The use of such a method enables a program to make decisions and take different actions, thus making it much more useful. For example, an airline's reservation system takes different steps depending on the type of ticket desired. If you want a full-price ticket, all the system must do is determine if there is an available seat; if you want a discount ticket for which a predetermined limit of seats is available, the program must check the number of seats remaining for that particular ticket type.

TOPIC 4.1 CONCEPTS OF ALTERNATIVE ACTIONS

In this chapter you will learn about three kinds of control structures—the decision structure, the enhanced decision structure, and the case structure. In the next chapter, you will learn about a fourth type—the controlled loop. When programming, you should always use combinations of these generally accepted control structures.

THE DECISION STRUCTURE

The first control structure for taking alternative actions is used in situations in which the number of alternatives is limited. It is known as the decision structure. The **decision structure** simply says that the computer should take a specified action if a specified condition is true. This structure is easily stated in English, and there are many examples of it in everyday life. The following examples have nothing to do with programming computers, but they will help you understand the concept.

IF the car door is locked, THEN unlock it.

IF the steak is done, THEN take it off the grill.

IF the tire is flat, THEN change it.

Now, look at some examples that would more likely be programmed for the computer:

IF the sales tax rate is 5 percent, THEN calculate the sales tax by multiplying the amount times 5 percent.

IF the temperature is less than or equal to 32 degrees, THEN print "IT IS FREEZING".

IF the average is greater than 89 percent and the number of courses being taken is five or greater, THEN print "YOU MADE THE DEAN'S LIST".

IF the requirements for dean's list (average greater than 89 percent and at least five courses being taken) have not been met, THEN print "YOU DID NOT MAKE THE DEAN'S LIST".

IF the applicant's age is greater than or equal to 19 years (or if the applicant's age is greater than or equal to 16 years and the applicant has completed driver training), THEN perform the driver's licensing procedure.

Note that all the examples have the same structure and state that some action should be taken under a certain condition. Each of these examples could be part of the program design for a computer program. Each example begins with the word IF followed by some relationship and the word THEN. The last thing on the line is an action to be taken if the relationship is true. In all the examples, if the relationship is true, the action is taken. Otherwise, the action is not taken. The decision control structure is stated in the BASIC language with the **IF . . . THEN** statement as follows:

> **General Form:** IF *logical condition* THEN *action to take*

The relationship that appears between IF and THEN can be stated with one or more operators or symbols. These operators are divided into two groups called relational operators and logical operators.

Relational Operators

Relational operators allow the computer to compare one value with another (see the list of relational operators in Table 4-1).

MEANING	COMMON SYMBOL
Equal to	=
Not equal to	<>
Less than	<
Greater than	>
Less than or equal to	<=
Greater than or equal to	>=

Table 4-1 Relational Operators

Now that you have examined the symbols most commonly used to represent the different relations, the following paragraphs will describe how some of the earlier examples can be rewritten using the relational operator symbols. First, the example will be repeated in its original form and then you will be shown how to rewrite it.

> IF the sales tax rate is 5 percent, THEN calculate the sales tax by multiplying the amount spent times 5 percent.

This statement says "IF the sales tax *is* 5 percent". The word "is" implies is equal to. Therefore, the statement may be rewritten using the relational operator equal to. When rewritten, the statement is

> IF the sales tax rate = 5 percent, THEN calculate the sales tax by multiplying the amount times 5 percent.

Examine the second example used earlier:

> IF the temperature is less than or equal to 32 degrees, THEN print "IT IS FREEZING".

In this example, the relationship states that the temperature may be either equal to 32 degrees or less than 32 degrees. In either case, the relationship will be considered true. Therefore, the statement may be rewritten using the less than or equal to symbol as follows:

> IF the temperature <= 32, THEN print "IT IS FREEZING".

Note that in rewriting both of these examples, we have simply substituted a symbol for one or more English words in the statement.

Logical Operators

Logical operators logically effect one or more relations (see Table 4-2 for a list of logical operators).

Again, by referring to some of the previous examples, we can see how these operators may be used. For instance, the third example stated:

> IF the average is greater than 89 percent and the number of courses being taken is five or greater, THEN print "YOU MADE THE DEAN'S LIST".

This statement can easily be rewritten using logical operators as follows:

OPERATOR	EFFECT
AND	Used to connect more than one relationship in the same IF . . . THEN statement. *All* statements connected with ANDs must be true in order for the overall relation expressed in the IF . . . THEN statement to be true.
OR	Also used to connect more than one relationship in the same IF . . . THEN statement. However, when relationships are connected with OR, only *one* of the connected statements must be true for the overall relation expressed in the IF . . . THEN statement to be true.
NOT	Used to reverse the effect of any relational operator.

Table 4-2 Logical Operators

> IF the average > 89 percent AND the number of courses being taken >= 5, THEN print "YOU MADE THE DEAN'S LIST".

Note that the word *AND* as used in the original version is still there. It is shown in capital letters to indicate that it is a logical operator.

The logical operator NOT is used much less frequently than AND and OR. As an illustration, however, let us rewrite another example from earlier in the chapter. The example in its original form reads:

> IF the requirements for the dean's list (average greater than 89 percent and at least five courses being taken) have not been met, THEN print "YOU DID NOT MAKE THE DEAN'S LIST".
>
> Rewritten using the NOT logical operator, this statement reads:
>
> IF NOT (average greater than 89 percent AND number of courses >= 5), THEN print "YOU DID NOT MAKE THE DEAN'S LIST".

Note that the NOT operator simply "turned around" whatever result would otherwise have been obtained. Assume that a student with an average of 81 percent was enrolled in five courses. This data would not meet the stated criteria. Therefore, no action would be taken. NOT, however, turns the false into true, meaning that action is taken in the printing of the "no dean's list" message. The parentheses were used to make sure the entire relation between them was done *before* the NOT was applied.

Now, let's examine the last example. In original form it reads:

> IF the applicant's age is greater than or equal to 19 years (or if the applicant's age is greater than or equal to 16 years and the applicant has completed driver training), THEN perform the driver's licensing procedure.

Rewriting the statement using operator symbols can lead to the following:

> IF the applicant's age >= 19 OR the applicant's age >= 16 AND the applicant has completed driver training, THEN perform the driver's licensing procedure.

With so many operators, which one is executed first? As a general rule, the relational operators are performed *before* the logical operators. As with arithmetic operations, however, parentheses can be used to ensure that the desired operations are done first. By using parentheses, the example can be rewritten to work properly as follows:

> IF (the applicant's age >= 19) OR (the applicant's age >= 16 AND the applicant has completed driver training), THEN perform the driver's licensing procedure.

With this latest rewrite, the parentheses totally enclose each of the two conditions under which a person may obtain a driver's license. This means that all other comparisons are done first, and finally a decision is made as to whether either of the two licensing conditions has been met.

THE ENHANCED DECISION STRUCTURE

In one of the previous examples, we printed one message if requirements for the dean's list were met and a different message if the requirements were not met. This took two statements, one for each condition. For statements such as this (with two possible outcomes), the **enhanced decision structure**, which is an extension of the decision structure, may be used. Instead of containing one action that is taken if the relationship is true, it contains two actions. One action is taken if the relationship is true, the other action is taken if the relationship is false. In a program design, this enhanced decision structure can be written in English with the words **IF . . . THEN . . . ELSE**. The second action follows the word ELSE. If the relationship is true, the action after THEN is taken. If the relationship is false, the action after ELSE is taken. By using IF . . . THEN . . . ELSE, the dean's list example can be rewritten in one statement as follows:

> IF the average > 89 percent AND the number of courses being taken >= 5, THEN print "YOU MADE THE DEAN'S LIST" ELSE print "YOU DID NOT MAKE THE DEAN'S LIST".

THE CASE STRUCTURE

When there are several alternative actions possible, the **case structure** is used to indicate the one to take. One common example of the use of the case structure is a computer program's menu. A **menu** shows a list of possible alternatives on the screen and asks the user to select the desired one. For example, the menu for a mailing list program might appear as shown in Figure 4-1.

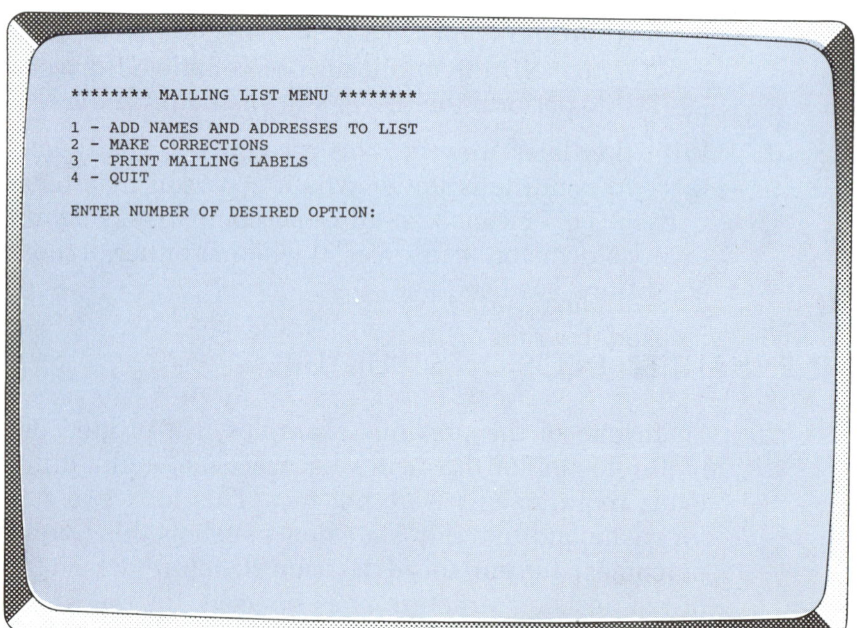

Figure 4-1 Mailing List Menu

The program to create this menu clears the screen, prints the list of choices, and then pauses for the user to input his or her choice. Once the choice is made, the computer branches to different modules of the program to handle the appropriate actions or functions. Written in English as a program design, the case structure for handling the menu might appear as follows (this assumes that the user's choice has been entered and stored):

CASE

User's choice = 1 perform data entry module processing.

User's choice = 2 perform data correction module processing.

User's choice = 3 perform print mailing labels module processing.

User's choice = 4 perform shutdown module processing.

END CASE

With the case structure, the number of different actions that may be taken depends on the circumstances. The value that determines the action might be input from the keyboard as in this example, or it might be the result of various computations performed by the program.

REVIEW QUESTIONS

1. How does the ability to take alternative actions increase the usefulness of the computer? (Obj. 1)
2. In planning programs, what three control structures may be used in writing a program design for making decisions? (Obj. 3)
3. What are the differences between the decision structure, the enhanced decision structure, and the case structure? (Obj. 3)
4. How can the decision structure be expressed in English as part of a program design? (Obj. 3)
5. How can the enhanced decision structure be expressed in English as part of a program design? (Obj. 3)
6. How can the case structure be expressed in English as part of a program design? (Obj. 3)
7. What is the purpose of a menu? (Obj. 2)

TOPIC 4.2 PROGRAMMING ALTERNATIVE ACTIONS

In Topic 4.1 you learned about the decision structure, the enhanced decision structure, and the case structure. In this topic, you will learn how to implement these structures in programs using the BASIC language.

CODING THE DECISION STRUCTURE

The discussion of the decision structure in Topic 4.1 described how to use the English words IF and THEN to write a program design. These same words are used in BASIC as keywords to implement the decision structure. Therefore, there can be a direct translation of the program design into BASIC language. The general form of the BASIC statement is

General Form: *line number* IF *relationship* THEN *action*

For examples of this statement, let's look at the examples used earlier. For each of them, the text will list the program design statement, followed by the BASIC code. In each example, it is assumed that values have already been placed in variables by preceding program steps.

Example 1

Program Design: IF the sales tax rate is 5 percent, THEN calculate the sales tax by multiplying the amount times 5 percent.

Code:
```
300 IF PCTTAX=5 THEN TAX=AMT*.05
```

Example 2

Program Design: IF the temperature is less than or equal to 32 degrees, THEN print "IT IS FREEZING".

Code:
```
300 IF TEMP<=32 THEN PRINT "IT IS FREEZING"
```

Example 3

Program Design: IF the average is greater than 89 percent and the number of courses being taken is five or greater, THEN print "YOU MADE THE DEAN'S LIST".

Code:
```
300 IF AVG>89 AND COURSES>=5 THEN PRINT "YOU MADE THE DEAN'S LIST"
```

Example 4

Program Design: IF the requirements for honor roll (average greater than 89 percent and at least five courses being taken) have not been met, THEN print "YOU DID NOT MAKE THE DEAN'S LIST".

Code:
```
300 IF NOT (AVG>89 AND COURSES>=5) THEN PRINT "YOU DID NOT MAKE
    THE DEAN'S LIST"
```

Example 5

Program Design: IF the applicant's age is greater than or equal to 19 years or the applicant's age is greater than or equal to 16 years and the applicant has completed driver training, THEN perform the driver's licensing procedure.

Code:
```
300 IF AGE>=19 OR (AGE>=16 AND DRIVTR$="Y") THEN GOSUB 1000
```

In this last example, note that we have used a GOSUB. This assumes that the submodule that actually prints a driver's license is located in the program beginning at line 1000. Anytime multiple steps must be taken as a result of the IF . . . THEN statement, a submodule should be used to contain the steps. Note also that the variable DRIVTR$ was used to indicate whether driver training had been taken, with the dollar sign ($) at the end indicating that it is a string variable. A numeric variable could have been used instead, if desired. This is possible because BASIC interprets zero as false and a nonzero value as true. Therefore, you could use the variable name of DRIVTR, with a 0 stored in it for persons not having driver training, while a 1 could be placed in it for persons who have received driver training. In this case, you could omit the equal sign, writing the decision structure as follows:

Code:

```
300 IF AGE>=19 OR (AGE>=16 AND DRIVTR) THEN GOSUB 1000
```

CODING THE ENHANCED DECISION STRUCTURE

To code this same example using the enhanced decision structure, simply add the keyword **ELSE** and the accompanying action to an IF . . . THEN statement. The general form is:

General Form:
line number IF *relationship* THEN *action* ELSE *alternate action*

Example:

```
300 IF AVG>89 AND COURSES>=5 THEN PRINT "YOU MADE THE DEAN'S LIST"
    ELSE PRINT "YOU DID NOT MAKE THE DEAN'S LIST"
```

CODING THE CASE STRUCTURE

The BASIC statement known as **ON . . . GOSUB** is often used in coding the case structure. This statement can make a choice between several different modules (subroutines) based on a numeric value. Its form is as follows:

General Form:
line number ON *numeric expression* GOSUB *line1,line2 . . . lineN*

Example: `90 ON C GOSUB 1000,2000,3000`

In this example, it is assumed that the numeric variable C has had a value of 1, 2, or 3 placed in it by a previous program line. If its value is 1, the program will GOSUB to the module beginning with line 1000. If its value is 2, the program will GOSUB to the module beginning with line 2000. If its value is 3, the program will GOSUB to the module beginning with line 3000. After branching to the selected module and encountering a RETURN statement, the program returns to the statement following the ON . . . GOSUB statement. If the value in the numeric variable is greater than the number of program lines listed, the program does not perform a GOSUB. Instead, the next statement is executed. Note that we have used lines 1000, 2000, and 3000 as this numbering matches our guidelines for constructing modules. However, any line numbers to which the programmer would like to transfer control can be used. RETURN statements must be used to transfer control back to the GOSUB statement when the chosen processing is finished. Control comes back to the next statement after the GOSUB statement from which it left.

Example Programs

To illustrate the use of the decision structure, enhanced decision structure, and case structure, we will use two programs. Example Program 1 shows the use of the decision structure and enhanced decision structure; Example Program 2 uses the case structure.

Example Program 1—The Car Dealer's Helper. This program will compute sales tax on automobiles sold by a dealer. The dealer delivers cars in several different counties. One county has a sales tax rate of 6 percent, while all the others have a rate of 5 percent. Therefore, the program must make a decision as it computes the sales tax. Study the program documentation sheet as shown in Figure 4-2.

PROGRAM DOCUMENTATION SHEET		
Program: C4E1	Programmer: STUDENT NAME	Date: 4-14-xx
Purpose: Computation of sales tax at either of two rates, depending on the county.		
Input: County name and sale amount from keyboard.	Output: Amount of sales tax displayed on screen.	
Data Terminator: None.		
Variables Used: All names are self-explanatory.		

Figure 4-2 Program Documentation Sheet

The steps in the program design are as follows:

1. Clear the screen.
2. Get amount of sale from keyboard.
3. Get county of sale from keyboard.
4. If county is "HART" then set tax rate to 6 percent, else set tax rate to 5 percent.
5. Compute and print the sales tax amount.

Here is the BASIC code, translated directly from the preceding five-step program design. As you study the code, examine the corresponding step of the program design.

Example:

```
10 ' C4E1
20 ' STUDENT NAME, CHAPTER 4, EXAMPLE 1
30 ' COMPUTES AUTO DEALER'S SALES TAX
40 '
50 CLS
60 PRINT "THIS PROGRAM COMPUTES AUTO DEALER'S SALES TAX"
70 PRINT
80 INPUT "WHAT IS THE SALE AMOUNT";AMOUNT
90 INPUT "WHAT IS THE COUNTY";COUNTY$
100 IF COUNTY$="HART" THEN TAXPCT=.06 ELSE TAXPCT=.05
110 PRINT
120 PRINT "SALES TAX IS $";AMOUNT*TAXPCT
130 END
```

Example Program 2—Rental Car Driving Instructions. You have been employed to write a program for a car rental agency. The purpose of the program is to give instructions to car renters for getting from the airport to popular nearby hotels. The program is to display a menu listing the hotels. When the operator selects a hotel, the driving instructions are displayed. The instructions for each hotel are contained in separate submodules. Figure 4-3 shows how the menu screen appears.

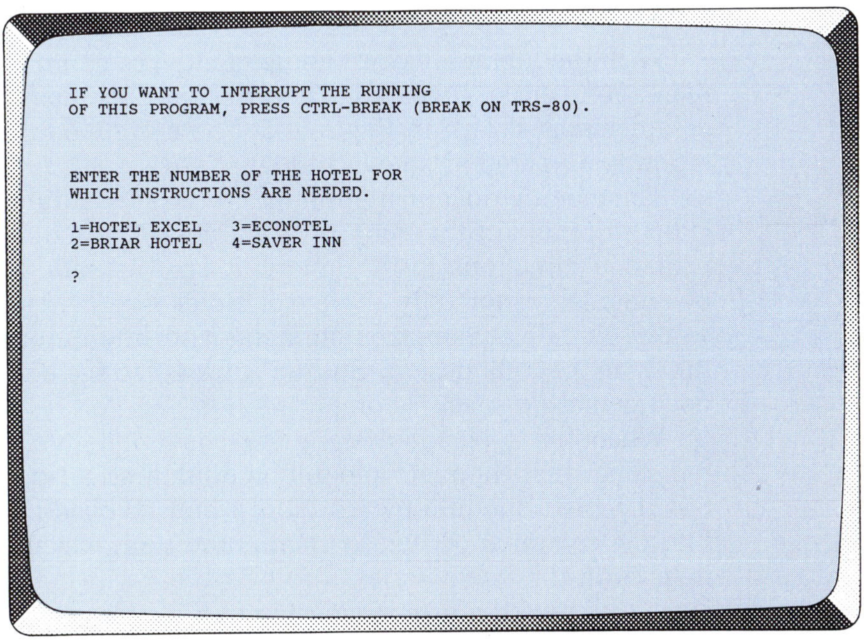

Figure 4-3 Menu Screen of Driving Instruction Program

The first step in planning the program is to prepare a hierarchy chart (see Figure 4-4). Note that the chart contains a main module plus a submodule for each hotel.

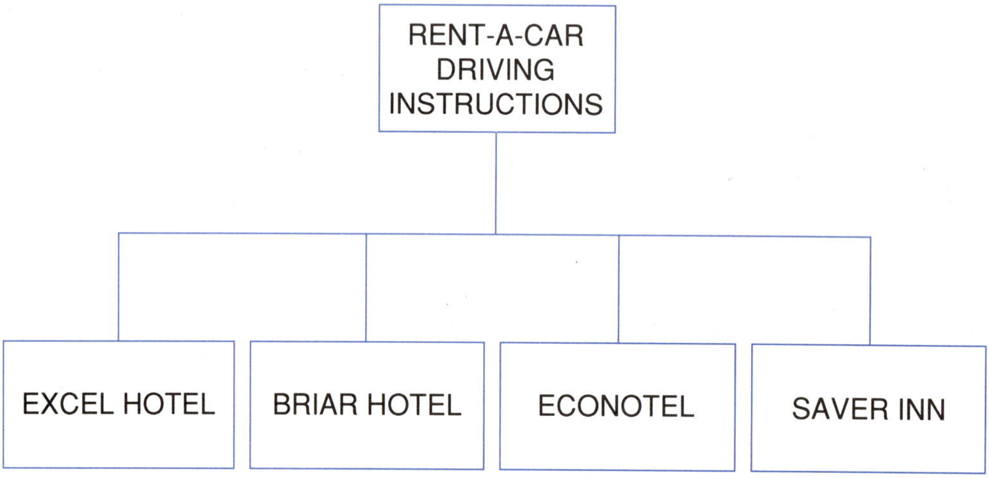

Figure 4-4 Hierarchy Chart for Car Rental Program

With the hierarchy chart complete, the remainder of the documentation can be prepared. The program documentation sheet is completed as shown in Figure 4-5. The main module's documentation is prepared as shown in Figure 4-6.

The module documentation for all the submodules in this program will contain the same program design. It will simply say to print the directions to the hotel. As an illustration, the module documentation for only the Excel Hotel is provided. The others would contain the appropriate name and line number range, but the same program design. Study Figure 4-7 to see how the module documentation sheet is completed.

When the program designs are converted into BASIC code, remember that the main module is done first. Also, remember to test the main module by entering it and stubbed-in submodules into the computer. When the main module is executing properly, then code the submodules. Here is the entire program in final form. Compare the program design to the code on p. 84.

PROGRAM DOCUMENTATION SHEET		
Program: C4E2	Programmer: STUDENT NAME	Date: 2-6-xx
Purpose: Print driving instructions to nearby hotels for car renters.		
Input: Operator's choice of hotel.	Output: Driving instructions.	
Data Terminator: None.		
Variables Used: All are self-explanatory.		

Figure 4-5 Program Documentation Sheet for Driving Instructions

MODULE DOCUMENTATION SHEET	
Program: C4E2	Module: MAIN Lines: 10-999
Module Description: Main Module	
Module Function (Program Design): 1. Clear the screen. 2. Display menu of hotels to which instructions are available. 3. Get operator's choice of hotel. 4. Depending on which hotel is chosen, perform one of the modules that prints driving instructions. 5. Pause until user is ready to continue. 6. Repeat the above instructions.	

Figure 4-6 Main Module Documentation

MODULE DOCUMENTATION SHEET	
Program: C4E2	Module: EXCEL Lines: 1000-1999
Module Description: Print instructions to the Excel Hotel.	
Module Function (Program Design): 1. Print instructions explaining how to drive from the airport to the Excel Hotel.	

Figure 4-7 Example of Submodule Documentation

Example:

```
10 ' C4E2
20 ' STUDENT NAME, CHAPTER 4, EXAMPLE 2
30 ' PRINTS DRIVING INSTRUCTIONS
40 '
50 ' ********************************
60 ' * MAIN MODULE                  *
70 ' ********************************
80 CLS
90 PRINT "IF YOU WANT TO INTERRUPT THE RUNNING"
100 PRINT "OF THIS PROGRAM, PRESS CTRL-BREAK (BREAK ON TRS-80)."
110 PRINT
120 PRINT
130 PRINT
140 PRINT "ENTER THE NUMBER OF THE HOTEL FOR"
150 PRINT "WHICH INSTRUCTIONS ARE NEEDED."
160 PRINT
170 PRINT "1=HOTEL EXCEL   3=ECONOTEL"
180 PRINT "2=BRIAR HOTEL   4=SAVER INN"
190 PRINT
200 INPUT HOTEL
210 CLS
```

```
220 ON HOTEL GOSUB 1000,2000,3000,4000
230 PRINT
240 INPUT "PRESS RETURN TO CONTINUE...";Z$
250 GOTO 80
999 END
1000 ' ******************************
1010 ' * HOTEL EXCEL                *
1020 ' ******************************
1040 PRINT "FOR THE HOTEL EXCEL, TURN LEFT ON"
1050 PRINT "SIMPSON.  GO THREE BLOCKS, THEN TURN"
1060 PRINT "RIGHT ON BYRD TO THE HOTEL."
1999 RETURN
2000 ' ******************************
2010 ' * BRIAR HOTEL                *
2020 ' ******************************
2040 PRINT "FOR THE BRIAR HOTEL, TURN RIGHT ON"
2050 PRINT "BROAD.  GO THREE MILES.  THE HOTEL"
2060 PRINT "IS ON YOUR LEFT."
2999 RETURN
3000 ' ******************************
3010 ' * ECONOTEL                   *
3020 ' ******************************
3040 PRINT "FOR THE ECONOTEL, TURN RIGHT ON BROAD."
3050 PRINT "GO TWO MILES, TURN RIGHT ON MAYFIELD."
3060 PRINT "HOTEL IS ONE MILE ON THE LEFT."
3999 RETURN
4000 ' ******************************
4010 ' * SAVER INN                  *
4020 ' ******************************
4040 PRINT "FOR THE SAVER INN, TURN RIGHT ON"
4050 PRINT "BROAD.  GO ONE MILE AND TURN RIGHT"
4060 PRINT "ON SMITH.  HOTEL IS ON LEFT."
4999 RETURN
```

As the prompt in line 100 indicates, the program can be terminated on the IBM by holding down the CTRL key and pressing the BREAK key. On the TRS-80, pressing the BREAK key will stop execution.

Notice that the input statement on line 200 has no prompt message. This is because adequate instructions have already been given in the print statements above it.

Also notice in line 250 of the program that the keyword **GOTO** is used. The purpose of the GOTO statement is to transfer control to another line. The general form of the GOTO statement is

> **General Form:** *line number* GOTO *line number*
>
> **Example:** `250 GOTO 80`

In this program, line 80 is executed immediately after line 250. After the user selects a hotel and receives instructions, the screen is cleared and the menu is redisplayed. The user can print as many sets of instructions as desired.

The keyword GOTO should be used as little as possible when coding a program. Excessive use of GOTOs makes it very difficult to follow the sequence of instructions in a program.

Observe that the keyword INPUT is used in the main module (line 240) to cause the computer to pause until the operator is ready to continue. If there were no pause, the driving instructions would appear on the screen and then immediately disappear as the main module returned to the CLEAR SCREEN statement.

REVIEW QUESTIONS

1. What BASIC keywords are used in coding the decision structure? Describe the way statements are written using these words. (Obj. 4)
2. Which control structure (decision, enchanced decision, or case) is easiest to translate directly from a program design into BASIC code? Why? (Obj. 4)
3. Describe the difference between the IF . . . THEN keywords and the ON . . . GOSUB keywords. (Obj. 4)
4. Describe how the ON . . . GOSUB functions. (Obj. 4)

VOCABULARY WORDS

The following terms were introduced in this chapter:

case structure
control structure
decision structure
enhanced decision structure
logical operator
menu
relational operator

KEYWORDS

The following keywords were introduced in this chapter:

GOTO
IF . . . THEN
IF . . . THEN . . . ELSE
ON . . . GOSUB

PROGRAMS TO WRITE

For each of the following programming assignments, prepare a program documentation sheet, hierarchy chart (for modular programs), and module documentation sheets or program design before coding the program.

Program 1

Write a program that computes interest on money for one year. The amount invested (the principal) should be entered from the keyboard. If the amount is less than $2,500, interest should be calculated as the amount times 8 percent. If the amount is $2,500 or more, the interest should be calculated as the amount times 10 percent. The formula for calculating the interest is as follows: interest = principal * rate. First, use sample data of $2,499.99 and then $2,500. Using these two numbers will demonstrate that the change in interest rate is occurring at the correct point.

Program 2

A bank charges a fee of $10 per month if a depositor's balance falls below $500. Write a program that gets the balance from the keyboard and then prints a statement telling whether a fee is due. First, use sample data of $499.99 and then $500. Like the previous program, this will determine if the decision point is operating correctly.

Program 3

Write a program that asks the user to input three angles. If the three angles do not add up to 180 degrees, the message "This is not a triangle" should print. If the angles add up to 180 degrees and one of them is 90 degrees, then the message "This is a right triangle" should print; otherwise, the message "This is a triangle" should print. Test the program with angles 90, 40, and 50; 30, 40, and 50; and 80, 50, and 50.

Program 4

Assume that a person who eats less than 2,000 calories per day will lose weight, while a person who eats 2,000 or more calories will gain weight. Write a program that asks the user to input the number of calories eaten in a day. The program should then print a statement telling whether the person will lose or gain weight, based on the calories consumed. In testing the program, first use 1,999 calories as data and then use 2,000 calories.

Program 5

A popular magazine offers subscriptions at a basic rate of $20 per year. However, if a subscriber renews for a two-year period, there is a 10 percent discount. If the renewal is for three years, there is a 20 percent discount. Write a program that gets the number of years (1, 2, or 3) from the keyboard and then prints the price of the subscription. Run the program at least three times to test each of the three subscription periods and rates.

Program 6

If the amount of a purchase is under $1,000, a business gives no discount. For a purchase of $1,000 or more but less than $2,000, it gives a 5 percent discount. Buyers purchasing $2,000 or more get a 7 percent discount. Write a program that will get the amount of purchase from the keyboard, compute and subtract the discount, and print the amount that must be paid by the customer. In testing, run the program with data that will verify all the discount change points (i.e., purchases of $999.99, $1,000, $1,999.99, and $2,000).

Program 7

Write a program that computes the perimeter of a rectangle or the perimeter of a circle, depending on the desire of the user. The perimeter of a rectangle is computed by adding the length and width and multiplying by two. The perimeter of a circle is computed by multiplying its diameter by π (approximately 3.14). To test the program, use a rectangle with a length of 4.5 inches and a width of 3.75 inches; use a circle with a 9.75-inch diameter.

Program 8

Write a program to determine which person soliciting funds for a charity has raised the most money. The program should ask for the name of a person and the amount collected. It should then compare this figure with the highest amount previously entered. If the new figure is higher, the figure and the name of the person should be stored as the highest values. Once the user has entered the data for all the fund raisers, the program should print out the name and amount of the most successful person. For sample data, use the following: Carmichael, \$2,714; Darwell, \$1,296; Mescon, \$4,873; and Zombec, \$3,298.

Program 9

A store sells appliances either with or without a service contract. If a service contract is purchased, the store will repair anything that goes wrong for a year after the warranty expires. Write a program that asks the operator for the name of the customer, the model number and description of the appliance, the selling price, and the price of the service contract. If there is no service contract, an amount of zero is entered as the service contract price. If no service contract is purchased, the program should print only an invoice (output showing the customer's name, appliance model number, description, and price). If a service contract is purchased, a certificate showing the invoice data and a comment denoting the existence of the service contract should also be printed. Set up each of the print operations as a separate module in the program. As sample data, use Martin Brewer with a purchase of \$350 and a service contract of \$80. Also, use Susan Sampford with a purchase of \$275 and no service contract.

Program 10

Write a program that computes the areas of rectangles, right triangles, and circles. Use a menu that gives the user a choice of the three. Have a separate module for each kind of computation.

The formulas are as follows: area of rectangle = length * width; area of right triangle = base * side * .5; and area of circle = 3.14 * radius ^ 2. For testing the program, use the following sample data: a rectangle of 12 by 3, a triangle of 4 by 8, and a circle with a radius of 10.

5

Controlled Loops

OBJECTIVES

After studying this chapter, you will be able to

1. Define a controlled loop.
2. Describe the importance of controlled loops.
3. Describe the two kinds of controlled loops.
4. Explain how to use BASIC keywords in controlled loops.
5. Plan and code programs that use controlled loops.

In this chapter you will learn about another control structure. With the explanation of the additional structure, you now will be familiar with the control structures needed to write almost any program.

TOPIC 5.1 INTRODUCTION TO CONTROLLED LOOPS

Remember from Chapter 4 that a control structure is used to control the sequence in which the instructions of a program are executed. In Chapter 4 you learned how to use the decision structure, the enhanced decision structure, and the case structure to cause a program to execute alternate instructions depending on the circumstances. In this chapter you will learn about a control structure that causes the computer to repeat a sequence of instructions. This structure is known as a **loop** or **controlled loop**. The ability to repeat sequences of instructions gives a tremendous amount of power to a computer program and makes programming much easier and less time consuming. Without this ability, sets of instructions frequently would have to be written repeatedly. Loops can be classified as either Do . . . Until loops or Do . . . While loops.

DO . . . UNTIL LOOPS

A **Do . . . Until loop** repeats a series of steps until a condition in the program becomes true. For example, the multiplication table that follows may be printed using a Do . . . Until loop. The program to do this may be written to print one line each time a loop is repeated. The first time the steps are executed, the 9 × 1 line is printed. The second time through the loop, the 9 × 2 line is printed. This continues until the maximum value of 9 is reached. That is, the loop does its work until the prescribed condition is reached.

```
9 X 1 =  9
9 X 2 =  18
9 X 3 =  27
9 X 4 =  36
9 X 5 =  45
9 X 6 =  54
9 X 7 =  63
9 X 8 =  72
9 X 9 =  81
```

Written in English, a description of what happens in printing the table is as follows:

> Multiply the value in the variable by 9, and print the result. Add 1 to the value stored in the variable. If the new value is greater than 9 then quit; otherwise, repeat the actions.

DO . . . WHILE LOOPS

A **Do . . . While loop** is the opposite of a Do . . . Until loop. A Do . . . While loop starts off with the prescribed condition true and continues until the condition becomes false. A Do . . . While loop might be used to input and process data. The condition would be stated in English as "do processing while there is more data being inputted." This means keep repeating the loop as long as data is available. As an example, a Do . . . While loop could be used to repeat the inputting of data as long as a cashier wanted to continue entering purchases.

REVIEW QUESTIONS

1. What is meant by a looping structure? (Obj. 1)
2. Why are looping structures important? (Obj. 2)
3. What is a Do . . . Until loop? (Obj. 3)
4. What is a Do . . . While loop? (Obj. 3)
5. Describe one application of a Do . . . Until loop. (Obj. 3)
6. Describe one application of a Do . . . While loop. (Obj. 3)

TOPIC 5.2 CODING CONTROLLED LOOPS

In this topic, you will learn how to code Do . . . Until and Do . . . While loops using the BASIC language.

CODING THE FOR . . . NEXT LOOPS

Although there are no keywords Do . . . Until, the keywords FOR and NEXT may be used to set up Do . . . Until loops. Loops set up in this fashion execute repeatedly until the specified condition for ending the loop becomes true.

Using FOR and NEXT

The syntax for the FOR . . . NEXT loop is as follows: A statement containing the keyword **FOR** is the beginning of the loop. A statement containing the keyword **NEXT** is the end of the loop. All statements between the FOR and NEXT are performed each time the loop is repeated. The two keywords will be explained separately and then used in an example program.

General Form:
line number FOR *numeric variable*=*initial value* TO *final value*

Example: `50 FOR COUNT=1 TO 9`

The numeric variable named after FOR is a counter variable. In the example, we have called it COUNT. Any valid numeric variable name may be used, however. The value of the counter changes each time the loop is repeated. In the example, COUNT begins with the value of 1 and stops with 9. The word **TO** tells the computer to repeat the loop until the prescribed condition (the final value of 9) has been exceeded.

The NEXT statement is followed by the same counter numeric variable name as was used in the FOR statement.

General Form: *line number* NEXT *numeric variable*

Example: `70 NEXT COUNT`

The NEXT statement tells the computer to loop back to the FOR statement. On the TRS-80, it also increments the counter variable and then checks to see if the final value exceeds the value given in the FOR statement. If the final value has not been exceeded, the loop is repeated. On the IBM computer, the counter variable is incremented by the FOR statement. This slight difference in implementation means that a FOR . . . NEXT loop will always be executed at least once on the TRS-80, even if the beginning value of the counter has already exceeded the final value. On the IBM, the loop will not be executed at all if the initial value of the counter exceeds the ending value.

The multiplication table used as a previous example may be programmed using a FOR . . . NEXT loop in the following manner.

Example:

```
10 ' C5E1
20 ' STUDENT NAME, CHAPTER 5, EXAMPLE 1
30 ' PRINTS MULTIPLICATION TABLE
40 '
50 FOR COUNT=1 TO 9
60    PRINT "9 X";COUNT;"= ";9*COUNT
70 NEXT COUNT
80 END
```

Lines 50 through 70 form a FOR . . . NEXT loop. The BASIC statements within this loop are repeated nine times as the value of COUNT increases from 1 to 9. Each time through the loop, the computer adds 1 to variable COUNT and checks it against the limit, which is 9 in this example. When the value of COUNT is greater than the limit, the computer continues execution with the program line that follows the NEXT statement.

After the loop has been executed, the value stored in the counter variable can be used in other calculations, but it will have a value one step beyond the limit (a value of 10 in this case). However, normally nothing should be done within the loop to change the value of the counter variable. For example, changing the value of the counter with a LET or INPUT statement may cause the loop to be altered, thereby yielding undesired results.

When writing BASIC code and entering a program, the statement or statements within the loop should be indented as shown in the example above. The computer does not require this, but it is a good programming practice. This easily identifies a loop and the statements within it. Make the indention by using the space bar or TAB key.

Using the STEP Option in a FOR . . . NEXT Loop

When using a FOR . . . NEXT loop, the value in the numeric counter variable will always be incremented by 1 unless otherwise indicated. However, if desired, you can change the value of the "step" by which the counter is incremented by adding the keyword **STEP** and the desired increment value at the end of the FOR statement.

General Form:
line number FOR *numeric variable = initial value* TO *final value* STEP *increment value*

Example:
```
50 FOR X=0 TO 25 STEP 5
```

In the example, the initial value of X will be set to 0 at the beginning but will be incremented by 5 each time the loop is repeated. Look at how this may be used within a program to count by fives.

Example:

```
10 ' CSE2
20 ' STUDENT NAME, CHAPTER 5, EXAMPLE 2
30 ' COUNTS BY FIVES
40 '
50 FOR X=0 TO 25 STEP 5
60    PRINT X
70 NEXT X
80 END
```

Output:

```
0
5
10
15
20
25
```

The increment need not be a positive whole number. It can be a decimal or a negative number. If it is a negative number, the counter variable decreases each time the loop is executed. Therefore, under this circumstance, the initial value must be larger than the final value. The following example counts down from 5 to 1.

Example:

```
10 ' CSE3
20 ' STUDENT NAME, CHAPTER 5, EXAMPLE 3
30 ' COUNTS BACKWARDS
40 '
50 FOR LOOPER=5 TO 1 STEP -1
60    PRINT LOOPER
70 NEXT LOOPER
80 END
```

Output:

```
5
4
3
2
1
```

Using Variables in FOR . . . NEXT Loops

Up to this point the starting and ending values in all of the FOR . . . NEXT loops have been expressed as numeric constants. The values may also be expressed as numeric variables, but they must be assigned *before* the FOR statement is executed. This can be done with any BASIC keyword that can place a value into a variable. For example, LET or INPUT might be used. The following example illustrates how all of the values in the FOR . . . NEXT loop may be variables with values that are obtained from INPUT statements.

Example:

```
10 ' CSE4
20 ' STUDENT NAME, CHAPTER 5, EXAMPLE 4
30 ' COUNTS ANY DESIRED RANGE
40 '
50 PRINT "THIS PROGRAM COUNTS."
60 INPUT "WHERE DO YOU WISH TO BEGIN";START
70 INPUT "WHERE DO YOU WISH TO END";QUIT
80 INPUT "BY WHAT INCREMENT";NCRE
90 PRINT
100 FOR COUNT=START TO QUIT STEP NCRE
110     PRINT COUNT;
120 NEXT COUNT
130 END
```

Output:

```
THIS PROGRAM COUNTS.
WHERE DO YOU WISH TO BEGIN? 20 <———— User inputs 20
WHERE DO YOU WISH TO END? 50 <———— User inputs 50
BY WHAT INCREMENT? 5 <———— User inputs 5

 20  25  30  35  40  45  50
```

Assigning Values with Expressions

Through the use of expressions, calculations may be made. The result of these calculations may be assigned as the beginning, ending, or incremental value in the FOR . . . NEXT loop, as the following example indicates.

Example:

```
10 ' CSE5
20 ' STUDENT NAME, CHAPTER 5, EXAMPLE 5
```

```
30 ' LOOPS WITH CALCULATED VALUES
40 '
50 J=3
60 FOR F=J TO J*5 STEP J/1.5
70    PRINT F;
80 NEXT F
90 END
```

Mentally doing the calculations, you can see that the counter F will begin with a value of 3 and will continue to be incremented until it exceeds 15, which is the ending value. The step value will be 3 divided by 1.5, which equals 2.

Writing Nested Loops

One loop may be written within another loop. These two loops are then known as **nested loops**. Each loop in the nested loop pair must have its own FOR and NEXT statements. The first loop is referred to as the **outer loop**, while the second loop is referred to as the **inner loop**. The outer loop and inner loop cannot have the same counter variable.

The nested loops cannot overlap. The inner loop must be totally inside the outer loop. This is usually indicated visually by indenting the inner loop within the outer loop as shown in the example, although the program will run properly without the indention. For each time the outer loop is executed, the inner loop will run through its repetition cycle. Arrows point to the beginning and ending of each loop in the following example.

Example:

```
10 ' C5E6
20 ' STUDENT NAME, CHAPTER 5, EXAMPLE 6
30 ' ILLUSTRATES NESTED LOOPS
40 '
50 FOR A=1 TO 3                          <----------+
60    PRINT "THIS IS AN OUTER LOOP"                 |
70    FOR B=1 TO 2                   <---+          |  Outer
80       PRINT "   THIS IS AN INNER LOOP"|  Inner   |  Loop
90    NEXT B                         <---+  Loop    |
100 NEXT A                               <----------+
110 END
```

Note that the words "THIS IS AN OUTER LOOP" will be printed each time the outer loop executes. The words "THIS IS AN INNER LOOP" will be printed each time the inner loop executes. Upon examining the output, you will see that for each execution of the outer loop, there are two executions of the inner loop.

Output:

```
THIS IS AN OUTER LOOP
   THIS IS AN INNER LOOP
   THIS IS AN INNER LOOP
THIS IS AN OUTER LOOP
   THIS IS AN INNER LOOP
   THIS IS AN INNER LOOP
THIS IS AN OUTER LOOP
   THIS IS AN INNER LOOP
   THIS IS AN INNER LOOP
```

CODING THE WHILE . . . WEND LOOPS

A Do . . . While loop in IBM compatibles may be coded with the WHILE . . . WEND keywords. (There is no WHILE . . . WEND loop on the TRS-80.) On IBM computers, a **WHILE** statement indicates the beginning of the loop, and **WEND**, which is short for While End, marks the end of the loop. All statements between the WHILE and the WEND are repeated each time the loop is executed. The execution continues as long as an expression following WHILE remains true.

General Form: *line number* WHILE *expression*

Example: `50 WHILE CHOICE$="Y"`

General Form: *line number* WEND

Example: `90 WEND`

If the expression in the WHILE statement is true, the statements in the loop are executed until the WEND statement is reached.

When the WEND statement is reached, the computer loops back to the WHILE statement, where the expression is checked again. If the expression is still true, the statements in the loop are executed again. Unlike a FOR . . . NEXT loop, a WHILE . . . WEND loop does no counting. Therefore, there must be a statement inside the loop that will change the value of the expression in the WHILE statement. Otherwise, the expression will remain true, and the program will loop continuously.

As an example, consider a program that will compute the average number of points scored by various players in four basketball games. The execution of the program will continue as long as there are additional players for whom points are to be averaged. The program design is as follows:

1. Set choice variable to "Y"
2. While choice = "Y"
   a. Get four point scores from keyboard.
   b. Calculate and print the average score.
   c. Get user's choice (Y or N) on whether to continue with another player.

Converting this program design to BASIC code on the IBM gives the following result.

Example:

```
10 ' CSE7
20 ' STUDENT NAME, CHAPTER 5, EXAMPLE 7
30 ' AVERAGES PLAYER'S SCORES IN GAMES
40 '
50 CHOICE$="Y"
60 WHILE CHOICE$="Y"
70    PRINT "ENTER FOUR SCORES, SEPARATED BY COMMAS"
80    INPUT S1,S2,S3,S4
90    PRINT "THE AVERAGE PER GAME IS ";(S1+S2+S3+S4)/4
100   INPUT "CONTINUE (Y OR N)";CHOICE$
110 WEND
120 END
```

Converting this program design to BASIC code on the TRS-80 gives the following result.

Example:

```
10 ' C5E7
20 ' STUDENT NAME, CHAPTER 5, EXAMPLE 7
30 ' AVERAGES PLAYER'S SCORES IN GAMES
40 '
50 CHOICE$="Y"
60 IF CHOICE$ <> "Y" THEN GOTO 120
70     PRINT "ENTER FOUR SCORES, SEPARATED BY COMMAS"
80     INPUT S1,S2,S3,S4
90     PRINT "THE AVERAGE PER GAME IS ";(S1+S2+S3+S4)/4
100    INPUT "CONTINUE (Y OR N)";CHOICE$
110 GOTO 60
120 END
```

CONCLUDING EXAMPLE PROGRAM

As one last example of the use of controlled loops, consider a program that calculates temperature conversions. When the program is executed, it presents a menu as follows:

The program is planned with two functions—Fahrenheit to Celsius conversion and Celsius to Fahrenheit conversion. Therefore, its hierarchy chart is constructed as shown in Figure 5-1.

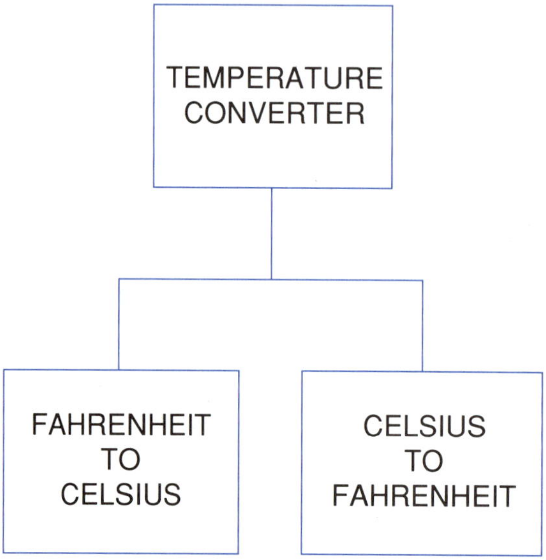

Figure 5-1 Hierarchy Chart for Temperature Conversion Program

Now, study the program documentation sheet in Figure 5-2 and the module documentation sheets in Figures 5-3 through 5-5.

Coding from the program designs results in the following program on the IBM:

Example:

```
10 ' CSE8
20 ' STUDENT NAME, CHAPTER 5, EXAMPLE 8
30 ' TEMPERATURE CONVERTER PROGRAM
40 '
50 ' ********************************
60 ' * MAIN MODULE                  *
70 ' ********************************
80 WHILE CHOICE<>3
90 CLS
100    PRINT "TEMPERATURE CONVERTER PROGRAM"
110    PRINT
120    PRINT "1 - FAHRENHEIT TO CELSIUS"
130    PRINT "2 - CELSIUS TO FAHRENHEIT"
140    PRINT "3 - QUIT"
```

continued on p. 103

PROGRAM DOCUMENTATION SHEET		
Program: C5E8	Programmer: STUDENT NAME	Date: 2/7/xx
Purpose: To produce a table showing Fahrenheit to Celsius or Celsius to Fahrenheit conversions.		
Input: Start, stop, increment, and kind of conversion entered from keyboard.	Output: Table of desired conversion printed on screen.	
Data Terminator: None		
Variables Used: START = Starting temperature QUIT = Ending temperature NCRE = Increment value CHOICE = User's specification of conversion option FAHRENHEIT = Counter CELSIUS = Counter		

Figure 5-2 Program Documentation Sheet

```
150    PRINT
160    INPUT CHOICE
170    CLS
180    ON CHOICE GOSUB 1000,2000
190 WEND
999 END
1000 ' ******************************
1010 ' * FAHRENHEIT TO CELSIUS      *
1020 ' ******************************
1030 INPUT "STARTING FAHRENHEIT TEMPERATURE";START
1040 INPUT "ENDING FAHRENHEIT TEMPERATURE";QUIT
1050 INPUT "INCREMENT VALUE";NCRE
1060 CLS
1070 PRINT "FAHRENHEIT","CELSIUS"
```

continued on p. 105

MODULE DOCUMENTATION SHEET	
Program: C5E8	Module: MAIN Lines: 10-999
Module Description: Main Module	

Module Function (Program Design):

1. As long as user's choice is to continue:
   a. Clear the screen.
   b. Get user's menu choice.
   c. Perform the chosen module.

Figure 5-3 Documentation for Main Module

MODULE DOCUMENTATION SHEET	
Program: C5E8	Module: FAHRENHEIT TO CELSIUS Lines: 1000-1999
Module Description: Converts Fahrenheit to Celsius	

Module Function (Program Design):

1. Get starting temperature, ending temperature, and increment from keyboard.
2. Print a conversion table, beginning at the starting temperature and continuing through the ending temperature, incrementing the table as specified by the user. The formula to convert Fahrenheit to Celsius is 5/9*(Fahrenheit−32).

Figure 5-4 Documentation for Fahrenheit to Celsius Model

MODULE DOCUMENTATION SHEET	
Program: C5E8	Module: CELSIUS TO FAHRENHEIT Lines: 2000-2999
Module Description: Converts Celsius to Fahrenheit	
Module Function (Program Design): 1. Get starting temperature, ending temperature, and increment from keyboard. 2. Print a conversion table, beginning at the starting temperature and continuing through the ending temperature, incrementing the table as specified by the user. The formula to convert Celsius to Fahrenheit is 9/5*Celsius+32.	

Figure 5-5 Documentation for Celsius to Fahrenheit Model

```
1080 FOR FAHRENHEIT=START TO QUIT STEP NCRE
1090    PRINT FAHRENHEIT,5/9*(FAHRENHEIT-32)
1100 NEXT FAHRENHEIT
1110 PRINT
1120 INPUT "PRESS RETURN TO CONTINUE . . . ";Z$
1999 RETURN
2000 ' ******************************
2010 ' * CELSIUS TO FAHRENHEIT      *
2020 ' ******************************
2030 INPUT "STARTING CELSIUS TEMPERATURE";START
2040 INPUT "ENDING CELSIUS TEMPERATURE";QUIT
2050 INPUT "INCREMENT VALUE";NCRE
2060 CLS
2070 PRINT "CELSIUS","FAHRENHEIT"
2080 FOR CELSIUS=START TO QUIT STEP NCRE
2090    PRINT CELSIUS,9/5*CELSIUS+ 32
2100 NEXT CELSIUS
2110 PRINT
2120 INPUT "PRESS RETURN TO CONTINUE . . . ";Z$
2999 RETURN
```

Coding from the program design results in the following on the TRS-80 main module; the submodules on the TRS-80 are the same as on the IBM.

Example:

```
10 ' C5E8
20 ' STUDENT NAME, CHAPTER 5, EXAMPLE 8
30 ' TEMPERATURE CONVERTER PROGRAM
40 '
50 ' ***********************************
60 ' * MAIN MODULE                     *
70 ' ***********************************
80 IF CHOICE = 3 THEN GOTO 999
90    CLS
100     PRINT "TEMPERATURE CONVERTER PROGRAM"
110     PRINT
120     PRINT "1 - FAHRENHEIT TO CELSIUS"
130     PRINT "2 - CELSIUS TO FAHRENHEIT"
140     PRINT "3 - QUIT"
150     PRINT
160     INPUT CHOICE
170     CLS
180     ON CHOICE GOSUB 1000,2000
190 GOTO 80
999 END
```

REVIEW QUESTIONS

1. Explain the difference in constructing a FOR . . . NEXT loop and a WHILE . . . WEND loop. (Obj. 4)
2. How can the numeric counter variable in a FOR . . . NEXT loop be incremented by a value other than one? (Obj. 4)
3. How can the BASIC FOR . . . NEXT loop be made to count backwards? (Obj. 4)
4. What is a nested loop? (Obj. 4)
5. Explain the difference between an inner loop and an outer loop. (Obj. 4)
6. What is the advantage of using INPUT to assign values to FOR . . . NEXT variables? (Obj. 4)

VOCABULARY WORDS

The following terms were introduced in this chapter:

controlled loop	inner loop	outer loop
Do . . . Until loop	loop	WHILE . . . WEND loop
Do . . . While loop	nested loop	

KEYWORDS

The following keywords were introduced in this chapter:

FOR	STEP	WEND
NEXT	TO	WHILE

PROGRAMS TO WRITE

For each of the assignments, complete appropriate documentation before coding the program.

Program 1

A business puts three prices on each of its items of merchandise. The first price is the list price and is the amount a customer pays if using a bank charge card. The second price is a discount of 2 percent and is the amount a customer pays if using the store's own charge card. The third price is a discount of 4 percent and is the amount a customer pays when paying with cash. Write a program into which the list price is entered. The computer then will use a FOR . . . NEXT loop to calculate and print all three prices with one formula. The counter variable will be used in the formula. Assume that the output going to the screen is to be printed on a price tag. For sample data, use list prices of $43.18, $57.49, and $98.31.

Program 2

Assume that in your state sales tax is collected on the whole dollar amount of a sale—that is, the cents are dropped before figuring the tax. Write a program that will print a sales tax table for each dollar amount from $1 through $20, at a rate of 5 percent.

Program 3

Write a program that will print a table of numbers and their squares, starting with 1 and continuing through 20.

Program 4

Your organization is producing a play, the tickets for which cost $9.75 each. Write a program that will print a table showing ticket prices in multiples of $9.75. For example, if someone wants to buy 3 tickets, you look up 3 in the first column of the table and find the corresponding price in the second column. For sample data use ticket quantities from 1 to 12.

Program 5

A business pays its salesperson a commission. Write a program that will ask for the amount of sales for each day of the week and will add the sales together as it goes. The total sales for the week should then be multiplied by 7 percent to get the amount of commission, which should then be printed. Test and debug the program with sales amounts for five days of $1,548, $1,893, $931, $1,583, and $899.

Program 6

Assume that your money is invested in an account that draws interest compounded annually. That is, at the end of each year the amount invested (principal) is multiplied by the interest rate, and that interest amount is added to the principal. Write a program that will get the amount invested, the interest rate, and the number of years from the keyboard. It should then produce a printout showing how much money will be on hand at the end of each year. For one run of the program, use an investment of $1,000 for four years at 9 percent interest.

Program 7

Write a program that will print multiplication tables, beginning and ending with any desired number, and will multiply that number by 1 through 12. Use nested loops to construct the program. Test the program with tables from 1 to 4 (1*1 . . . 1*12 to 4*1 . . . 4*12) and from 6 to 8 (6*1 . . . 6*12 to 8*1 . . . 8*12).

Program 8

You need a modification of Program 4. The number of children's tickets desired by a patron should be printed across the top of the table, while the number of adult tickets desired by the same patron should be printed on the left side of the table. At the intersection of the top and side quantities, the printout should contain the amount of money to be collected. For purposes of producing the printout, assume a ticket price of $9.75 per adult and $5.25 per child. The table should contain data for up to four children's tickets and four adults' tickets.

Program 9

Modify Program 6 to handle different compounding periods. There should be three submodules in the revised program. One submodule handles interest compounded quarterly, one handles interest compounded every six months, and the third handles interest compounded annually. The printout should resemble the table from Program 6, showing only the amount of money on hand at the end of each compounding period. Use a menu to enable the operator to choose the compounding period. As sample data, use an investment of $2,000 at 12 percent for each compounding period. Compare the different amounts earned for each compounding method.

Program 10

An engineering firm needs a program to compute the volume of material that will flow through a conduit of a particular size and shape at varying speeds of flow. The program should contain a menu that allows the engineer a choice of obtaining figures for a tubular conduit or a conduit with a rectangular cross section. Output should consist of a table that lists the volume of material per minute for each of the requested flow rates. When the program is executed, the following items should be input from the keyboard:

1. The dimensions of the conduit
2. The minimum and maximum speed of flow (in feet per second) to be used in printing the table
3. The flow speed increment to be used in printing the table

In computing the flow, calculate the area of a cross section of the conduit, expressing your result in square feet. This figure multiplied by the flow speed will give the cubic feet per second. Multiply this by 60 to convert to cubic feet per minute. First, use sample data of a 6-by-8-inch rectangular conduit with flows of 2 to 10 feet per second and a flow speed increment of 2. Next, use a tubular conduit with a 2.5 inch radius, flows of 2 to 10 feet per second, and a flow speed increment of 2. Experiment with several additional program runs, all using the same flow rates. Try to find a size of rectangular conduit and a size of tubular conduit that will produce nearly the same flow volume.

PROJECT 2—WRITING A TRACTOR PULL PROGRAM

As you do with all your programs, complete the appropriate documentation before coding the program for Project 2. You will need a program documentation sheet, a spacing chart, and module documentation sheets.

For this project, assume you are the operator of the Deep West Tractor Pull. A tractor pull is a sporting event in which competitors use custom-made tractors to pull a heavily weighted sled as far as possible. There are different classes of competition for tractors of different horsepower and design.

Three classes of tractors pull in each competition. All the class 1 tractors pull first, followed by class 2, and finally class 3. Each of the tractors in a class is given a number. The first driver in each class to qualify is given number 1, the second to qualify is given number 2, and so on. The maximum number of entrants in each class is 20.

The pulling track is a dirt strip 300 yards long. It is equipped with markers on the sidelines indicating distance. Laser devices help produce a precise measurement of the distance each tractor pulls the sled. This distance and the name of the driver are recorded on the official pull results.

The results of the day's pull are to be printed by your computer. If a printer is available, the report should be on paper. If no printer is available, you will have to print to the screen. Keep in mind, however, that if you use the screen, the input prompts and input will be intermixed with the output. The following illustration shows the general form the output report should take; your program's output need not be exactly the same.

```
DEEP WEST TRACTOR PULL

CLASS 1
ENTRANT      DISTANCE
-------      --------

 1 SMITH      131.1
 2 BROWN      117
 3 MYERS      139.83

CLASS 2
ENTRANT      DISTANCE
-------      --------

 1 ABEL       149.12
 2 MARKS      97.31
 3 BURTON     148.93

CLASS 3
ENTRANT      DISTANCE
-------      --------

 1 MIMMS      254.12
 2 DILL       239.32
```

As each driver takes his or her tractor down the strip, the data is entered into the computer. The program asks for the required data in order—that is, the computer begins with class 1 and asks for the information for class 1, entrant 1, followed by data for class 1, entrant 2. When the operator indicates that there are no more class 1 entrants, the computer proceeds to class 2, entrant 1, and so on. The data entered by the operator should include the entrant's name and the distance pulled. As soon as the data for each entrant is entered, the printer should print a line of output. Note that headings must also be printed at the appropriate times.

In setting up the program, you may decide to have a module for printing headings, a module for inputting data, and a module for printing a line on the report. You may want the operator to enter

"END" for the entrant's name to indicate that there are no more tractors in that class, or you may want to ask the operator whether there are any more tractors in that class. In either case, make sure your program lets the operator know what action to take. To test your program, use the data from the preceding sample output.

PART THREE
BUILDING EFFECTIVE PROGRAMS

6

Data Storage Within Programs

> **OBJECTIVES**
>
> After studying this chapter, you will be able to
>
> 1. Give the advantages and disadvantages of storing data within a program.
> 2. Describe some applications for which storing data within a program is appropriate.
> 3. Explain how data stored in a program is used.
> 4. Describe the use of BASIC keywords for storing data within a program.
> 5. Plan and code programs that store data.

TOPIC 6.1 USING DATA STORED IN PROGRAM STATEMENTS

In previous lessons, you have used the INPUT statement to get data from the keyboard for use by a program. When you use the INPUT statement, data is entered each time the program is executed. With some programs, however, much of the data needed is the same every time the program is executed. For such programs, the data that is to be used each time the program is executed may be read from special DATA statements stored within the program itself.

The storage of data in program statements is ideal for some applications, but it is not always the best solution. Data that changes frequently should not be stored in program statements, since the program would have to be changed frequently. Also, programs that require large quantities of data should not store it in DATA statements in the program. For these programs, more effective and efficient methods are available. These methods, which involve the separate storage of data on a disk or other medium, will be discussed in Chapters 12 and 13 of this text.

WHEN IS STORAGE OF DATA IN PROGRAM STATEMENTS APPROPRIATE?

Data stored in program statements becomes a part of the program itself. Therefore, one or more lines of the program must be changed if the data ever changes. This limitation means that data stored within a program should be relatively unchanging. If data used by a program is likely to change each time the program is run, the data should be obtained from the keyboard rather than from program statements.

TERMINATING WITHIN-PROGRAM DATA

When writing a program in which data is stored in program statements, the programmer frequently does not know how many items of data may eventually be included. Because of the likelihood that the number of data items will change, there must be some way to indicate when the end of data has been reached. The easiest method is to simply let the program run out of data. However, when this happens the program stops execution and an error message is displayed. To detect when the end of data is reached, a data terminator is used. A **data terminator** is nothing more than a dummy data item that is added at the end of the actual data. Frequently, if the stored data is string/character data, you may want to always add a last data item called EOD, which is short for "end of data." If the data is numeric, use a numeric data terminator that is completely different from any possible data item (e.g., 0, 9999, or -1).

Since the terminator will always be placed at the end of the actual data, your program can check each new data item it reads to see whether it is the terminator. If it is the terminator, data reading can be stopped. If it is not the terminator, data reading can continue. Even after data reading stops, other processing may be necessary.

REUSING WITHIN-PROGRAM DATA

With some programs, the reuse of stored data during the same program run is desirable. For example, suppose you are using a program that will look up phone numbers and display them on the screen. You may not want to rerun the program from the beginning for each number you want to look up. Therefore, the program may be written so that it will start rereading data beginning with the first item, rather than going to the next item following the one with which it quit reading on the previous lookup. When a program is written in this fashion, DATA statements may be reread as many times as desired.

REVIEW QUESTIONS

1. Describe why the storage of data within a program is preferable to using constants or literals in the program. (Obj. 1)
2. What are the advantages and disadvantages to using DATA statements in a program? (Obj. 1)
3. List the similarities and differences between getting data from the keyboard and getting data from storage within a program. (Obj. 3)
4. How does a program know when it has read all the data? (Obj. 3)
5. How many times may stored data be used during a program run? (Obj. 3)

TOPIC 6.2 PROGRAMMING WITH READ AND DATA STATEMENTS

Recall from Topic 6.1 that a program obtains data from a program DATA statement in much the same way that it gets data from the keyboard. Rather than using the keyword INPUT, however, the keyword **READ** is used. It tells the computer to examine **DATA** statements in the program and assign the values it finds there to variables. Therefore, one or more DATA statements must exist in a program that uses the READ statement. The following example illustrates how this process works:

Example:

```
10 ' C6E1
20 ' STUDENT NAME, CHAPTER 6, EXAMPLE 1
30 ' COMPUTES AND PRINTS AREA OF RECTANGLE
40 '
50 READ LGTH,WDTH
60 PRINT LGTH,WDTH,LGTH*WDTH
70 END
80 DATA 12,10
```

Here is how the output will look when the program is executed:

Output:

```
12              10              120
```

Except for the source of data, line 50 in this example functions just as an INPUT statement would. While the INPUT statement would get its data from the keyboard, the READ statement gets its data from the DATA statement. Note that the two variables in the READ statement are numeric. Note, too, that the two items in the DATA statement are also numeric. Thus, the type of data (numeric or string) in the DATA statement matches the type of variable(s) in the READ statement.

USING THE KEYWORD DATA

DATA statements are not actually executed when the program runs. Instead, they inform the computer that the items are to be stored in memory until the program is ready to process them by use of the READ statement. Because they are never actually executed, DATA statements may be placed anywhere in a program. It is good practice, however, to place all the DATA statements after the actual end of the program. Note in the previous example, the DATA statement appeared as line 80, after the end of the program. The advantage of doing this is that plenty of space is left for adding additional data as needed. If several DATA statements are used, they are usually placed on consecutive program lines, although they can be scattered throughout a program. In any case, the DATA statements are read in the sequence in which they physically appear (top to bottom) in the program.

Regardless of where DATA statements are located within a program, each of them must begin with a line number and the keyword DATA.

General Form: *line number* DATA *item list*

Examples:

```
500 DATA MELINDA,6.25
510 DATA WYLIE,5.93
```

The items in the DATA statements will be read sequentially, starting with the first item in the first DATA statement and ending with the last item in the last DATA statement. The items in a DATA statement must be separated by commas.

Items in a DATA statement may be either numeric or character in nature. Remember, though, that the type of data must agree with the type of variables used in the READ statement. That is, any data can be read into a character or string variable, but only numbers may be read into numeric variables. If an item of data contains a comma, the item must be enclosed in quotes in the DATA statement. For example, suppose someone's last and first name, separated by a comma, are to be read into a variable called NAM$. The name in the DATA statement would read "SMITH, ANTHONY". Since the comma is usually used to separate items read into different variables, the name must be enclosed in quotation marks to let the computer know that it is to be placed into one variable, not two. Also, if the character data begins with a leading blank, it must be enclosed in quotes.

USING THE KEYWORD READ

The READ statement instructs the computer to read one or more values from a DATA statement for assignment to the named variable or variables.

General Form: *line number* READ *variable name(s)*

Example:

```
90 READ NAM$,HRLY
```

In this example, the first item (a string) in the first DATA statement is assigned to the variable NAM$. The second item (a numeric value) in a DATA statement is assigned to the variable HRLY. There must always be enough data to supply a value for each of the variables following the keyword READ. If there are two variable names following READ but only one item of data, for example, an error will result.

Example of Using READ and DATA in a Loop

In the first example program in this chapter (see p. 117), only one set of data was read and calculated. In most applications using READ and DATA statements, several data items will be used, and a loop will be created to read all the data items.

Example:

```
10 ' C6E2A
20 ' STUDENT NAME, CHAPTER 6, EXAMPLE 2A
30 ' CALCULATES AND PRINTS AREA OF RECTANGLES
40 '
50 READ LGTH,WDTH
60 PRINT LGTH,WDTH,LGTH*WDTH
70 GOTO 50
80 END
90 DATA 9,7,6,8,10,5
```

Output:

```
 9             7             63
 6             8             48
 10            5             50
Out of DATA in 50
```

This is how the data was read each time through the loop in the preceding example.

First time through:

```
50 READ LGTH,WDTH

90 DATA 9,7,6,8,10,5
```

Second time through:

```
50 READ LGTH,WDTH

90 DATA 9,7,6,8,10,5
```

Third time through:

```
50 READ LGTH,WDTH

90 DATA 9,7,6,8,(10),(5)
```

Fourth attempt:

```
50 READ LGTH,WDTH

90 DATA 9,7,6,8,10,5 [NO DATA]
```

On the fourth attempt, the message "Out of DATA in 50" appeared. When there are more attempts to read than there are data items, an out-of-data error occurs, the program terminates, and an error message appears. It is important to note that, while the READ statement may contain the appropriate number of variable names desired, the number of items in the DATA statement(s) must be a multiple of the number of variable names in the READ statement. For example, in the previous program, the READ statement contains two variable names. Therefore, the number of items in the DATA statement(s) must be a multiple of two, which six is.

To prevent the error from occurring when the program runs out of data, a terminator may be used. Since none of the data can be less than zero in this example, a negative number makes a good terminator. Remember that a terminator is a dummy data item or items that would never occur among the actual data. Here is how the program may be modified to use terminators. There must be two terminator items in this program since two data items are read at a time. If only one terminator was used, the program would still stop executing with an error message. Note the IF . . . THEN statement in line 60, which checks to see if the terminator has been read:

Example:

```
10 ' C6E2B
20 ' STUDENT NAME, CHAPTER 6, EXAMPLE 2B
30 ' CALCULATES AND PRINTS AREA OF RECTANGLES
40 '
50 READ LGTH,WDTH
60 IF LGTH<0 THEN 90 ' GOES TO END WHEN TERMINATOR IS DETECTED
70 PRINT LGTH,WDTH,LGTH*WDTH
80 GOTO 50
90 END
100 DATA 9,7,6,8,10,5,-1,-1
```

Output:

```
9           7           63
6           8           48
10          5           50
```

Example Program 1

As a more complex example, let's consider a program that might be used by a meteorologist for averaging low and high temperatures. Suppose that Farley Forecasting Service is using the computer to help find the average temperature for various cities. The program is simple enough that it does not require the use of different modules. Therefore, the program documentation sheet can be developed as shown in Figure 6-1. Study the documentation carefully and make sure you can follow the logic.

PROGRAM DOCUMENTATION SHEET		
Program: C6E3	Programmer: STUDENT NAME	Date: 2-18-xx
Purpose: To calculate average temperatures for selected cities.		
Input: City names from DATA statements; temperatures from keyboard.	Output: Average temperatures on screen.	
Data Terminator: City name of EOD		
Variables Used: CITY\$ LOW HIGH		

Figure 6-1 Documentation Sheet for Temperature Averaging Program

The program design is as follows:

1. Clear the screen and print the opening message.
2. As long as there is still data:

   a. Read a city name from data.
   b. If the city name is the data terminator, then exit loop.
   c. Display the city name.
   d. Get the city's low and high temperature for the day from keyboard entry.
   e. Calculate and print the average temperature for the day.
3. End of program.

Using the program design, the following code was developed. Study how each step from the program design was converted into BASIC code. Note that a city name of EOD was used as the data terminator and that the low and high temperatures for each city were input from the keyboard.

Example:

```
10 ' C6E3
20 ' STUDENT NAME, CHAPTER 6, EXAMPLE 3
30 ' CALCULATES AVERAGE TEMPERATURES
40 '
50 CLS
60 PRINT "THIS PROGRAM CALCULATES THE AVERAGE"
70 PRINT "TEMPERATURE FOR VARIOUS CITIES. "
80 PRINT
90 WHILE CITY$<>"EOD" ' REPLACE WITH REM STATEMENT ON TRS-80 MODEL III
100     READ CITY$
110     IF CITY$="EOD" THEN 200 ' EXIT THE LOOP; USE GOTO 210 ON TRS-80
120     PRINT "ENTER DATA FOR ";CITY$
130     INPUT "LOW TEMPERATURE TODAY";LOW
140     INPUT "HIGH TEMPERATURE TODAY";HIGH
150     PRINT
160     PRINT "THE AVERAGE TEMPERATURE FOR"
170     PRINT CITY$;" WAS ";(LOW+HIGH)/2
180     PRINT
190     PRINT
200 WEND:' REPLACE WITH A 'GOTO 100' FOR TRS-80 MODEL III
210 END
220 DATA BALTIMORE,DALLAS
230 DATA LOS ANGELES,SEATTLE
240 DATA EOD
```

Here is an example run of the program. The data entered by the user is shown in bold.

Output:

```
THIS PROGRAM CALCULATES THE AVERAGE
TEMPERATURE FOR VARIOUS CITIES.

ENTER DATA FOR BALTIMORE
LOW TEMPERATURE TODAY? 20
HIGH TEMPERATURE TODAY? 30

THE AVERAGE TEMPERATURE FOR
BALTIMORE WAS  25

ENTER DATA FOR DALLAS
LOW TEMPERATURE TODAY? 50
HIGH TEMPERATURE TODAY? 70

THE AVERAGE TEMPERATURE FOR
DALLAS WAS  60

ENTER DATA FOR LOS ANGELES
LOW TEMPERATURE TODAY? 70
HIGH TEMPERATURE TODAY? 78

THE AVERAGE TEMPERATURE FOR
LOS ANGELES WAS  74

ENTER DATA FOR SEATTLE
LOW TEMPERATURE TODAY? 48
HIGH TEMPERATURE TODAY? 56

THE AVERAGE TEMPERATURE FOR
SEATTLE WAS  52
```

Example Program 2

When the items from DATA statements are to be reread during a program run, use the keyword RESTORE. **RESTORE** tells the program to go back to the beginning of the first DATA statement in the program. Therefore, when the next READ instruction is executed, the first data item in the list will be read. The keyword RESTORE should be used whenever the program needs to go back to the beginning of the data.

General Form: *line number* RESTORE

Example: `270 RESTORE`

To see how data may be reread with BASIC, examine a simple directory program. When the name of any county in the state is input from the keyboard, this program will supply the name of the county seat, the number of square miles, and the population. So that we don't have to enter too much data, we will assume this state has only five counties. The number of counties is not likely to change, but we will write the program to handle that possibility.

Study the program documentation sheet in Figure 6-2 and the module documentation sheets in Figures 6-3 through 6-5. Note that the number of counties to be handled is set in a variable at the beginning of the program. This variable is then used to control the number of times the loop is executed. By doing this, the number can be easily changed later, if necessary—that is, one program line will change rather than changing a constant in the line that sets up the loop. In this example, the value is used only once. However, when the same value is used several times in a program, this technique becomes even more valuable.

From the module function, the following program is coded:

Example:

```
10 ' C6E4
20 ' STUDENT NAME, CHAPTER 6, EXAMPLE 4
30 ' LOOKS UP AND PRINTS DATA FOR DESIRED COUNTIES
40 '
50 ' ********************************
60 ' * MAIN MODULE                  *
70 ' ********************************
80 QTY=5    ' NUMBER OF COUNTIES
90 Z$="Y"
100 WHILE Z$="Y" 'REPLACE WITH REM STATEMENT ON TRS-80 MODEL III
110    CLS
120    GOSUB 1000    ' GET INPUT DATA
130    GOSUB 2000    ' LOOK UP DATA AND PRINT
140    INPUT "DO YOU WANT TO CONTINUE (Y/N)";Z$
```

continued on p. 125

PROGRAM DOCUMENTATION SHEET		
Program: C6E4	Programmer: STUDENT NAME	Date: 2-18-xx

Purpose: To look up and print information about counties within the state.

Input: County names and county data from DATA statements. Desired county from the keyboard.	Output: Name of county seat, square miles, and population displayed on screen.

Data Terminator: None

Variables Used:

DESIRED$ = Name of county
QTY = number of counties
PLACE$ = county read from DATA
CITY$ = county seat read from DATA
SQMI = square miles
PEOPLE = population
N = loop counter

Figure 6-2 Documentation Sheet for Temperature Averaging Program

```
150 WEND:'REPLACE WITH 'IF Z$='Y' THEN 100' ON TRS-80 MODEL III
999 END
1000 ' ******************************
1010 ' * GET INPUT DATA             *
1020 ' ******************************
1030 PRINT "ENTER THE NAME OF THE COUNTY"
1040 PRINT "FOR WHICH YOU WISH TO KNOW THE"
1050 INPUT "INFORMATION:  ";DESIRED$
1999 RETURN
```

continued on p. 126

MODULE DOCUMENTATION SHEET	
Program: C6E4	Module: MAIN Lines: 10-999
Module Description: This is the main module.	
Module Function (Program Design): 1. Store number of counties in a variable. 2. As long as user wants to continue: a. Clear the screen. b. Perform Get Data Module. c. Perform Lookup and Print Module.	

Figure 6-3 Module Documentation for Main Module

```
2000 ' *******************************
2010 ' * LOOK UP DATA AND PRINT      *
2020 ' *******************************
2030 PRINT
2040 RESTORE
2050 FOR N=1 TO QTY
2060    READ PLACE$,CITY$,SQMI,PEOPLE
2070    IF PLACE$=DESIRED$ THEN PRINT "COUNTY SEAT IS ";CITY$
2080    IF PLACE$=DESIRED$ THEN PRINT "SQUARE MILES ARE ";SQMI
2090    IF PLACE$=DESIRED$ THEN PRINT "POPULATION IS ";PEOPLE
2100    IF PLACE$=DESIRED$ THEN 2140  ' EXIT SEARCH LOOP
2110 NEXT N
2120 PRINT "NOT FOUND. "    ' CONTROL WILL COME HERE ONLY IF COUNTY
2130                        ' IS NOT FOUND.
2140 PRINT
2999 RETURN
5000 DATA ARGO,THOMASTON,114,52398,GORDON,COLLEGE STATION,2532,45898
5010 DATA MILLER,GRANTSTOWN,532,312432,NEWTON,SMITHVILLE,1323,14321
5020 DATA TOLIVAR,BRYANTSBURG,971,73892
```

MODULE DOCUMENTATION SHEET	
Program: C6E4	Module: GET DATA Lines: 1000-1999
Module Description: This module gets the input data.	
Module Function (Program Design): 1. Get county name from keyboard.	

Figure 6-4 Module Documentation for Get Data Module

MODULE DOCUMENTATION SHEET	
Program: C6E4	Module: LOOKUP AND PRINT Lines: 2000-2999
Module Description: This module looks up a county seat and displays its name.	
Module Function (Program Design): 1. Set the data pointer back to the beginning of the data. 2. Do . . . Until all counties are read: a. Read a county name, county seat, square miles, and population. b. If the county name matches the one entered from the keyboard, print the data that was read and exit the loop. c. If the county entered from the keyboard was not found, print a "not found" message.	

Figure 6-5 Module Documentation for Lookup and Print Module for the County Seat Program

Here is a sample run of the program. Data entered by the user is shown in bold.

```
ENTER THE NAME OF THE COUNTY
FOR WHICH YOU WISH TO KNOW THE
INFORMATION:  ? GORDON

COUNTY SEAT IS COLLEGE STATION
SQUARE MILES ARE  2532
POPULATION IS  45898

DO YOU WANT TO CONTINUE (Y/N)? Y                (Screen clears)

ENTER THE NAME OF THE COUNTY
FOR WHICH YOU WISH TO KNOW THE
INFORMATION:  ? LUMPKIN

NOT FOUND.

DO YOU WANT TO CONTINUE (Y/N)? Y                (Screen clears)

ENTER THE NAME OF THE COUNTY
FOR WHICH YOU WISH TO KNOW THE
INFORMATION:  ? TOLIVAR

COUNTY SEAT IS BRYANTSBURG
SQUARE MILES ARE  971
POPULATION IS  73892

DO YOU WANT TO CONTINUE (Y/N)? N
```

REVIEW QUESTIONS

1. What keywords are used to store and read data within a program? (Obj. 4)
2. How are the keywords INPUT and READ alike? How are they different? (Obj. 4)
3. What kind of relationship is necessary between variables in a READ statement and the data in a DATA statement? (Obj. 4)
4. What determines which data item will be read whenever a READ statement is used in a program? (Obj. 4)
5. What keyword is used to tell the computer to start over at the beginning of the data stored in DATA statements? (Obj. 4)

VOCABULARY WORD

The following term was introduced in this chapter:

data terminator

KEYWORDS

The following keywords were introduced in this chapter:

DATA READ RESTORE

PROGRAMS TO WRITE

Prepare the appropriate documentation for each program before coding it. When working on modular programs, remember to test the main module first with stubbed-in submodules.

Program 1

Write a program that reads the names of items and their prices from DATA statements and prints them. The following data should be used: EQUALIZER, $432.12; SPEAKERS, $479.45; and TAPE DECK, $319.95.

Program 2

Write a program for use by a bank when talking to customers about investing their money. The bank has three different kinds of accounts in which a person may invest money for one year. The program should store the three interest rates of 5.25 percent, 6.0 percent, and 7.5 percent in DATA statements. The principal to be invested should be obtained by the program with an INPUT statement. The principal and interest at each of the three rates should be calculated as PRINCIPAL * RATE * TIME (in years) and printed. Print the appropriate column headings before beginning to read the data and perform the calculations. To test your program, use principals of $1,000, $2,500, $4,600, and $5,200 for one-year periods.

Program 3

Suppose you want to find the value of numbers raised to the powers of 2, 3, and 5. Write a program that obtains a number by means of an INPUT statement, reads from DATA statements the three powers, and calculates and prints the answers. Use the following input data: 2, 24, 3, 15, 1.5, 10, and 78.

Program 4

A report is needed to calculate the percentage of correct answers given by participants in an academic bowl. In this game show event, students try to beat the competition by answering more questions correctly. Each player's name, number of questions attempted, and number of questions answered correctly, is in a DATA statement. For each player, the program should read the data, calculate the percentage of correct answers by dividing the number of correct answers by the number of attempts, and print a line of output. The output of the report should resemble the following:

```
NAME        TRIED      CORRECT  PERCENT

BRYANT       12          6        XXX
GOLD         18          8        XXX
SMITH        6           1        XXX
WYATT        10          2        XXX
```

Program 5

The credit department of a store has decided to use the computer to approve or turn down customers' requests to purchase on credit. To do this, the store has created a program that stores the customer numbers and names for those with charge accounts. Immediately following each name, it stores the word YES or the word NO to tell whether the customer will be allowed to charge anything else. When a customer wants to charge something, the clerk enters the customer's number into the computer. The computer reads DATA statements until it finds the number and then prints out the name of the customer and the YES or NO to indicate whether the charge may be made. To test the program, use the following data: 389, JOHN SMITH, YES; 321, MYRTLE VANN, NO; 931, WILLENE WYLIE, YES; and 313, FREDERICK FROMM, NO. When testing the program, try all the customer numbers in random order, and enter some customer numbers that don't exist. An appropriate "not found" message should be printed when a nonexistent number is entered.

Program 6

A small business plans to use the computer to calculate the gross pay of its employees. The employees' names and hourly pay rates are stored in DATA statements within the program. As the program runs, each employee's name is printed by the program, and the number of hours worked is requested. The program then calculates the gross pay by multiplying the hours worked times the employee's hourly rate and prints the amount on the screen. In writing the program, plan a data input module, a computation module, and a printout module. For testing the program, use the following data in the program: Burgess, Wylene, $4.95; Myers, Viola, $3.75; Smith, Frank, $4.50; and Zoe, Peter, $3.75. When running the program, enter hours of 40 for Burgess, 38 for Myers, 40 for Smith, and 39 for Zoe.

Program 7

A program stores automobile names and their gas mileage figures in DATA statements. It reads this data and produces a bar graph showing the mileage for each auto. The data should be: CARIBOU, 11; ECONODEER, 24; GAZELLE, 17; MOOSEMOBILE, 5. The output should appear on the screen as follows:

```
EPA GAS MILEAGE, 19--

                             1         2         3
CAR                     . . . . 0 . . . . 0 . . . . 0

CARIBOU                 XXXXXXXXXXX
ECONODEER               XXXXXXXXXXXXXXXXXXXXXXXX
GAZELLE                 XXXXXXXXXXXXXXXXX
MOOSEMOBILE             XXXXX
```

In addition to the loop that repeats four times to read the data for the four different cars, you may also want to use a loop to print the correct number of Xs to produce each bar of the graph.

Program 8

You have invented a new party game, a computer-controlled scavenger hunt. You enter into the program the names of seven items the guests should find. Then, a guest enters the day of the week (1 through 7) on which his or her birthday occurs this year. That number determines the object that the guest and a partner must find and photograph before returning to your party. When the day of the week is entered into the computer, the program reads that many items from the DATA statements by means of a loop and then prints the description of the object to be found. The objects are: a purple cow, a large clock with orange hands, Crooked Street, a parked Maserati, a horse with foal, a banyan tree, and a sign with a palindrome on it.

Program 9

Modify Program 6 to make it more useful. To the data for each employee, add a rate for calculating the income tax deduction. (This is a simplification of how withholding tax is actually calculated.) Also, compute the deduction for social security (FICA) at 7.05 percent of gross pay. Once the computations have been done, print a check stub and check on the screen. If a printer is available, you may use it to print the stub and check. The layout of the stub and check should resemble the following:

```
PAYCHECK STUB FOR employee
DATE:  date

HOURS:  hours RATE:  rate
GROSS PAY:    gross pay
INCOME TAX:   income tax amount
FICA:         FICA amount

NET PAY:      net pay amount

----------------------------------------
```

```
                    date

PAY TO THE
ORDER OF employee          $amount


                ---------------------------
                SIGNED
```

The data for the program, with the added withholding rate, is: Burgess, Wylene, $4.95, .15; Myers, Viola, $3.75, .12; Smith, Frank, $4.50, .14; and Zoe, Peter, $3.75, .11. When running the program, enter hours of 40 for Burgess, 38 for Myers, 40 for Smith, and 39 for Zoe.

Program 10

Design a logo that may be created by printing letters in a grid with 15 letters across, and 7 letters down. This logo may be your initial, a school mascot, or some other symbol. In a program, represent the logo on DATA statements as sequences of 1s and 0s. Each place there should be a letter in the logo, place a 1 in the DATA statement. Each place there should be a blank space, place a 0 in the DATA statement. Examine the following example logo:

```
VVV         VVV
VVV         VVV
 VVV       VVV
  VVV     VVV
   VVV   VVV
    VVV VVV
     VVVVV
```

The DATA statement for the first line of this logo might appear as:

```
500 DATA 1,1,1,0,0,0,0,0,0,0,0,0,1,1,1
```

The program should read the lines of data and print the logo on the screen. At the beginning of the run, the program should request the user to enter the letter or symbol from which the logo should be printed.

7

Improved Data Input Routines

OBJECTIVES

After studying this chapter, you will be able to

1. Describe what is meant by data validation.
2. Explain why good prompts are important.
3. Describe seven data validation methods.
4. Plan and write the BASIC code for data validation routines.

TOPIC 7.1 CHARACTERISTICS OF RELIABLE DATA ENTRY

If the data that is input into the computer is inaccurate, the output will also be inaccurate. There are several techniques the programmer can use to help ensure the accuracy of data. Several of these techniques are discussed in this topic.

USE OF GOOD PROMPTS

One way to ensure data accuracy is to use good prompts—that is, make sure the operator knows what kind of information is needed by the program. Suppose you are using an unfamiliar program and the prompt "NUMBER?" appears on the screen. You obviously have no way of knowing what kind of number is to be input. If you are familiar with what the program is to do and you know only one number is required, you may be able to successfully use the program. However, even if you are familiar with the program, if it must ask for several different numbers during the run, you would find it difficult to know which number is being requested at a particular time.

As an example, consider a program that helps register students for courses. The input includes the student's name, the student's number, and the number of the course being requested. Now, examine the following examples of bad and good prompts. Think about how much easier data entry would be with the more descriptive prompts.

Poor Prompt: NAME?

Good Prompt: STUDENT'S NAME?

Poor Prompt: NUMBER?

Good Prompt: STUDENT'S NUMBER?

Poor Prompt: COURSE?

Good Prompt: COURSE NUMBER?

USE OF DATA VALIDATION

In addition to using good prompts, a program will frequently use data validation. **Data validation** is a procedure whereby the program checks the data after entry to try to determine whether the data is good. The procedures for checking data for errors are frequently known as **error traps** (or error checking). Whenever an error trap detects invalid data, the program should output a message identifying the error and should ask the operator to reenter the correct data.

Different applications have various ways of checking input data. The following are some of the commonly used methods of data validation.

1. Check to ensure that the data is within a range (between limits). If a company's sales staff have assigned numbers between 11 and 99, for example, then numbers less than 11 or greater than 99 are out of range and should not be accepted.
2. Check to ensure that "choice" questions are indeed answered with a valid choice. The most common example of this is when a program asks the user a "yes or

no" question. For example, for a question that asks "Do you want to continue (Y/N)?", any response other than "Y" or "N" is invalid. Another example occurs when a program menu asks a user to enter A to add names, C to change names, or P to print. Any choice other than "A", "C", or "P" is invalid.

3. Make sure that the program will accept all desired characters. For example, you may want the user to be able to enter commas to separate first and last names. Yet, unless special provision is made in the program code, it may refuse to accept the commas.
4. Check to ensure that character data is of a valid length. This check involves two activities. The first is to ensure that the operator has indeed entered data rather than just pressing the ENTER/RETURN key. The second is to ensure that the length of the data entered is within the range that can be handled by the program. For example, you may have allowed 25 spaces for a name when planning the spacing chart. Therefore, the program should make sure that no name shorter than 1 character or longer than 25 characters is entered.
5. Check to ensure that the data entered is the correct type. It is especially important that only numeric data be entered whenever numbers are expected.
6. Check to ensure appropriateness. For example, in a ticket reservation system, if the event is not being held on the date for which a ticket is requested, the date requested is invalid. The computer should call attention to the error and refuse to accept the data.
7. Check to ensure that the data is on a list of possible values (words or numbers). For example, if flight numbers are being entered, a list of valid flight numbers can be included in the program. The currently entered flight number may be compared with the list to see that it is a valid number.

While an error trap may be constructed to catch invalid data, there is no such thing as an error trap that can guarantee that only the correct data is entered. Therefore, the user will need to proofread the keyed entry as it appears on the screen. If desired for an application, the computer can be programmed to ask "Is this correct?" The user must then reply "Y" (or "yes") before the program will continue execution.

REVIEW QUESTIONS

1. What is meant by data validation? (Obj. 1)
2. What is the main characteristic of a good prompt? (Obj. 2)
3. Give some examples of good and poor prompts. (Obj. 2)
4. List and describe seven methods of data validation. (Obj. 3)
5. Which method of data validation do you think would be least effective? Why? (Obj. 3)
6. Which method of data validation do you think would be most effective? Why? (Obj. 3)

TOPIC 7.2 USING DATA ENTRY ROUTINES

In this topic, we will consider how to accomplish each of the data validation routines described in Topic 7.1. You will also learn how to code them in BASIC.

ENSURING THAT DATA IS WITHIN A RANGE

There are many examples that require data to be within a particular range. For example, if a program is used for registering students, freshmen may be entered as class 1, sophomores as class 2, juniors as class 3, and seniors as class 4. Therefore, any class number less than 1 or greater than 4 is invalid and should be rejected. The program design for doing this is quite simple. Just use IF . . . THEN or WHILE . . . WEND statements to check the entered data. (WHILE . . . WEND is not an option for use with the TRS-80 Model III.) Study the following example, which uses an IF . . . THEN statement.

Example:

```
210 INPUT "CLASS (1,2,3,OR 4): ";CLASS
220 IF CLASS<1 OR CLASS>4 THEN PRINT "REENTER":GOTO 210
```

This second example uses a WHILE . . . WEND statement.

Example:

```
210 CLASS=0
220 WHILE CLASS<1 OR CLASS>4
230     INPUT "CLASS (1,2,3,OR 4): ";CLASS
240 WEND
```

ENSURING THAT QUESTIONS ARE ANSWERED WITH A VALID CHOICE

Programs should be designed so that if the user gives an unexpected response to choice questions, the computer will not produce incorrect results. It is not safe, for example, to assume that a non-yes response is a no response. Instead, the operator may have accidentally hit a wrong key. There are several methods that may be used to check validity. These will be discussed in the following paragraphs.

Using IF . . . THEN to Validate a Choice

One method of checking to see if a choice is valid is to use an IF . . . THEN statement. If a correct response is not entered, the program should simply go back to the INPUT line and require the user to reenter the correct choice. The program design for such a method is as follows:

1. Get the user's choice from the keyboard.
2. Check the user's choice to see whether it is valid. If it is not, go back to step 1 for reentry of the data.

Now study the following example of the program design as coded:

Example:

```
210 INPUT "CONTINUE (Y/N)";CHOICE$
220 IF CHOICE$<>"Y" AND CHOICE$<>"N" THEN 210
```

Line 210 asks for, and accepts, the input from the keyboard. Line 220 then checks for validity. If the entered choice is not "Y" and it is not "N", then the data item is invalid and should be reentered. Therefore, program control is sent back to line 210, which repeats the INPUT statement.

Using WHILE . . . WEND to Validate a Choice

By using WHILE . . . WEND, you can perform this same error trap in a more structured fashion (this is not an option for use with the TRS-80 Model III):

Example:

```
210 CHOICE$=""
220 WHILE CHOICE$<>"Y" AND CHOICE$<>"N"
230     INPUT "CONTINUE (Y/N)";CHOICE$
240 WEND
```

Note that this method has constructed the error trap without using a GOTO. The first step is to make sure the variable CHOICE$ does not accidentally have a leftover Y or N in it. This is done by placing any nonvalid character in the variable; we used a null character—that is, two quotation marks with nothing between them. This has the effect of putting a "nothing" character in the variable. A loop was then constructed that will continue to operate as long as a nonvalid character is in the variable. Once a valid character is in the variable, the loop exits.

Handling Only the Desired Portion of a Response

In response to prompts such as "Do you want to continue?", which are answered with a yes or no choice, the user may enter only the first letter of the response or the entire word. Even if the prompt designates that only Y or N should be entered, experience shows that some operators will enter the entire word. To validate the input under such circumstances, you may want to examine only the desired number of characters, ignoring the others. This can be accomplished by use of the LEFT$ function.

**LEFT$** is short for "left string." The LEFT$ function is used to examine characters beginning at the left of string data. For example, the function could be used to examine just the first three characters of a string, as shown in the following example.

General Form: LEFT$(*string data,number of characters*)

Example: `240 PRINT LEFT$("CATERPILLAR",3)`

Output: `CAT`

The LEFT$ function may be used as part of a PRINT statement, a LET statement, or a logical statement. The data may be in the form of literals, variables, or expressions. When used to check the response to a request for input, the following program lines can be used. (This is based on the example used earlier to verify a Y or N response.) Now, however, line 220 examines all the characters that have been input into the variable CHOICE$, takes the first character, and stores it back in CHOICE$. Therefore, if CHOICE$ has more than one character in it, all the excess ones are effectively discarded.

Example:

```
210 INPUT "CONTINUE (Y/N)";CHOICE$
220 CHOICE$=LEFT$(CHOICE$,1)
230 IF CHOICE$<>"Y" AND CHOICE$<>"N" THEN 210
```

Handling More Than Two Valid Responses

The previous examples handled inputs with only two possible answers. How are situations with more than two answers checked? One method is to use additional conditions in the IF . . . THEN statement. Suppose we have a menu with possible choices of A, C, and P. Three conditions could be combined in one IF . . . THEN statement:

Example:

```
120 INPUT "CHOICE";CHOICE$
130 IF CHOICE$<>"A" AND CHOICE$<>"C" AND CHOICE$<>"P" THEN 120
```

Line 120 gets the user's input, while line 130 makes sure the input is one of the three valid choices. These lines would be followed by statements that handle the processing required for each of the three choices.

In a second method, a new statement may be used to check for validity. This statement is the function known as **INSTR**, which stands for "in string." It determines whether one string is contained in another string.

General Form:
line number numeric variable=INSTR(*start position, string to search, string to find*)

Example: `130 L=INSTR(1,"ACP",CHOICE$)`

As can be seen from the general form, the data with which this function works must be string or character data. The answer given by the function is a number. The search starts with the character number indicated by the start position, which is 1 in the example. If the variable CHOICE$ contains the letter "A", a 1 will be placed in variable L since the A is the first letter of "ACP". If CHOICE$ contains a "C", a 2 will be placed in variable L since the C is the second letter of "ACP". If the letter "P" is contained in CHOICE$, variable L will contain a 3. If neither A, C, or P is contained in the variable CHOICE$, L will contain a zero.

The simple rule for the INSTR function is as follows. If the string being searched for is found, the function gives the beginning location. If the string being searched for is not found, the function gives a zero. When using this function, the check for validity of input data can be done as shown here:

Example:

```
120 INPUT "CHOICE";CHOICE$
130 L=INSTR(1,"ACP",CHOICE$)
140 IF L=0 THEN 120
```

When the start position is one, as in the example, the number specifying the start position may be omitted. This will produce the following variation of the error checking code:

Example:

```
120 INPUT "CHOICE";CHOICE$
130 L=INSTR("ACP",CHOICE$)
140 IF L=0 THEN 120
```

If desired, the code can be made even shorter by acting directly on the result of the function rather than assigning it to a variable.

Example:

```
120 INPUT "CHOICE";CHOICE$
130 IF INSTR("ACP",CHOICE$)=0 THEN 120
```

The code can be made more structured by using a WHILE . . . WEND loop similar to the one used for a simple two-choice response. However, instead of using an IF . . . THEN statement, the INSTR function is used inside the loop. Note that the variable is set to an invalid character before entering the loop. In this case, if the variable were allowed to start out as its default null (nothing), the INSTR function would think it had found a valid character.

Example:

```
210 CHOICE$="X"
220 WHILE INSTR("ACP",CHOICE$)=0
230     INPUT "CHOICE";CHOICE$
240 WEND
```

Getting Data Without Pressing ENTER/RETURN

For user responses that consist of only one character, such as "Y" or "N", it is frequently desirable to input the character data without pressing the ENTER/RETURN key. While this method gets a character and assigns it to a variable, it cannot be used to print a prompt message before getting the character. Prompts must be handled by separate PRINT statements. Also, this method does not print the character that is entered from the keyboard. A separate PRINT statement must be used to print the character entered. Once a single character has been input from the keyboard using this method, it may be examined for validity using any of the methods described earlier.

In deciding whether to get input without requiring the user to press the ENTER/RETURN key, you should be consistent—that is, all one-character responses should require the use of ENTER/RETURN, or all one-character responses should not require the use of ENTER/RETURN. Programs should not be written so that pressing the ENTER/RETURN key is required in some instances and is not in others. Writing programs in this fashion is confusing to users of the programs and makes their operation more difficult.

The **INKEY$** function may be used to get one character from the keyboard and assign it to a character variable.

General Form: *line number character variable*=INKEY$

Example: `140 C$=INKEY$`

When the keyword INKEY$ is executed, the keyboard is quickly scanned to see if a key is pressed. If a key is pressed, its character is placed in the variable. The program continues regardless of whether a key is pressed. Therefore, INKEY$ is almost always placed inside a tight loop.

Example:

```
80 PRINT "STRIKE ANY KEY TO CONTINUE"
90 C$=INKEY$:IF C$="" THEN 90
```

Only character variables may be used with INKEY$; any digit (number) key entered is stored as character data.

The **INPUT$** function (not available on the TRS-80 Model III) is a more sophisticated method of getting data from the keyboard without pressing the ENTER/RETURN key.

General Form:
line number character variable=INPUT$(*# characters*)

Example: `140 C$=INPUT$(1)`

When a program line containing INPUT$ is executed, the computer waits until a key is pressed. The character keyed from the keyboard is then placed in the variable. The feature that makes INPUT$ more useful than the INKEY$ statement, however, is the ability to wait for more than one character. The number inside the parentheses indicates the number of characters to be inputted. For example, if a 3 is placed inside the parentheses, the computer will wait until three characters have been keyed and will place all three of them in the variable. Note that the exact number of characters indicated in the INPUT$ function must be entered. Program execution will not continue until the required number of characters has been entered, while any extra characters will not be placed in the variable. This function is especially useful when fixed-length words (such as passwords) need to be entered on the keyboard without appearing on the screen.

Handling Lower-Case Letters

In response to a choice-type question, the user might enter either an upper-case or a lower-case letter. To keep from having to validate for both upper case and lower case, a range check can be done to see if the letter is lower case. If so, it can be converted to upper case before checking. One way to do this is to use the

ASCII code of a letter. As listed in Appendix C, each character is represented internally by the computer as an ASCII number. An upper-case A, for example, is number 65, while a lower-case a is 97. This same relationship—32 numbers apart—holds true for the entire alphabet. Therefore, if you check the ASCII code of a number and find it to be greater than 96 and less than 123, you know you have a lower-case letter. By subtracting 32 and restoring the value, you can convert it to an upper-case letter. Two new functions are necessary to accomplish this.

The **ASC** function (short for ASCII) is used to determine the ASCII code of data. If the data consists of more than one character, the code of the first character is returned. The code can be compared immediately or assigned to a numeric variable (as shown in the following example) for later comparison.

General Form: ASC(*character data*)

Example: `330 Z=ASC(CLASS$)` ⟵ If CLASS$ contains "a", the numeric variable Z will be 97

The **CHR$** function (short for character string) is used to convert an ASCII number back into a character. The resulting character may be used immediately, such as by printing, or it can be assigned to a character variable (as shown in the following example) for later use.

General Form: CHR$(*numeric value*)

Example: `360 CLASS$=CHR$(Z)` ← If Z contains 65, the character variable CLASS$ will be "A"

Here is an example of converting to verify a "Y" or "N" response.

Example:

```
210 INPUT "CONTINUE (Y/N)";CHOICE$
220 A=ASC(CHOICE$)
230 IF A>96 AND A<123 THEN CHOICE$=CHR$(A-32)
240 IF CHOICE$<>"Y" AND CHOICE$<>"N" THEN 210
```

In line 210, the INPUT statement stores the keyboard response in the variable CHOICE$. In line 220, the ASCII code number of the response is derived by the ASC function and placed in variable A. Line 230 first determines whether the character entered was a lower-case letter (codes 97 through 122 are lower-case "a" through "z"). If the character was lower case, 32 is subtracted from its ASCII number, and the resulting number is turned into an upper-case letter by using the CHR$ function. This works correctly since all lower-case letters have a code that is 32 greater than the corresponding upper-case letter.

ENSURING THAT THE PROGRAM WILL ACCEPT ALL DESIRED CHARACTERS

A disadvantage of using the INPUT statement is that a comma character cannot be entered as a part of the data unless the data is enclosed in quotation marks. For example, you would have to use quotation marks when entering a last name and a first name separated by a comma (e.g., "Lyle, Martha"). Since the quotation marks are used to enclose other data, the quotation marks cannot be entered as part of the data. Although this limits the kind of data that can be entered and stored, this disadvantage can be overcome by using the keyword **LINE INPUT**.

Except for the following differences, LINE INPUT is used in the same way as INPUT. LINE INPUT is used to input any characters from the keyboard and place them into a character or string variable. This means that even commas and quotation marks may be keyed and stored in a string variable. Remember that the regular INPUT statement uses commas to separate values that go into different variables. Since everything except the ENTER/RETURN key is considered to be data, there can be only one variable in the LINE INPUT statement. That variable must be a character or string variable as indicated by a dollar sign ($) at the end of its name. The LINE INPUT statement does not automatically print a prompt of any kind (such as the INPUT statement's question mark); therefore, you will probably want to always include one. The LINE INPUT statement's general form is as follows:

General Form:
line number LINE INPUT *"prompt";string variable*

Example:

```
310 LINE INPUT "LAST NAME, COMMA, FIRST NAME: ";NAM$
```

ENSURING THAT CHARACTER DATA IS A VALID LENGTH

A simple program design for checking the length of character data is as follows:

1. Get the data from the keyboard.
2. If its length is less than one or greater than the maximum desired, go back to step 1 for reentry.

Implementation of this program design requires that the LEN function be used. The **LEN** function determines the number of characters in a string value. The result of the LEN function may be either assigned to a variable (see the general form that follows) or used immediately. Examples of both uses are shown.

General Form:
line number numeric variable=LEN (*character data*)

Example: `95 LGTH=LEN(NAM$)`

Assuming that variable NAM$ contains the word "VIGOROUS", the variable LGTH will have an 8 placed in it, which represents the number of characters in "VIGOROUS".

For an example that implements the program design, assume that the maximum number of characters (length) you want entered for the variable NAM$ is 25.

Example:

```
910 PRINT "USING NO MORE THAN 25 CHARACTERS, ENTER"
920 INPUT "A NAME: ";NAM$
930 IF LEN(NAM$)<1 OR LEN(NAM$)>25 THEN 910
```

If you are using a computer with WHILE . . . WEND, this same task may be accomplished as follows:

1. Set name variable to null.
2. While length of name is less than one or greater than the maximum desired, get a name from the keyboard.

Example:

```
910 NAM$=""
920 WHILE LEN(NAM$)<1 OR LEN(NAM$)>25
930     PRINT "USING NO MORE THAN 25 CHARACTERS, ENTER"
940     INPUT "A NAME: ";NAM$
950 WEND
```

CHECKING TO DETERMINE WHETHER DATA IS NUMERIC

If a program is to perform computations using data input from the keyboard, it is extremely important that only numeric data be entered in numeric variables. If a numeric variable is specified in the INPUT statement, BASIC will print an error message if any nonnumeric character is keyed. However, these error messages are usually very brief and may not be understood by the occasional operator of the computer. Therefore, you may find it useful for the program itself to error trap incorrect data types and print the necessary messages to the operator. However, before you can code a program in such a manner, you must learn some new keywords.

The **VAL** (short for "value") function is used to convert string data into its numeric value. It can be used as part of a PRINT statement, a LET statement, or a logical statement, and the string data may be in the form of a literal, a variable, or an expression.

General Form: VAL(*string data*)

Example 1: `80 PRINT VAL(STUFF$)`

Example 2: `80 NUMBER=VAL(STUFF$)`

Example 3: `80 IF VAL(STUFF$)>100 THEN GOSUB 2000`

Assume in these three examples that STUFF$ contains "315.49". Since this is stored in a string variable, no arithmetic can be done with it. The VAL function, however, modifies the ASCII coding used to store the data in the computer's memory. In Example 1, the numeric value (315.49) is simply printed. In Example 2, it is placed in the numeric variable called NUMBER. Arithmetic can be done with the value stored in NUMBER, which is 315.49 in numeric form. In Example 3, the numeric value of the string STUFF$ is compared to 100. If it is greater than 100 it will execute a subroutine at line 2000.

One word of caution is in order regarding the VAL function. Some versions of BASIC on the Tandy Model III give error messages if the string data contains certain characters (e.g., a colon or percent sign). If you are using one of these versions of BASIC, you must check the input string data for the presence of these troublesome characters before using the VAL function. If one of the characters is present, the VAL function must not be used. To check for the invalid characters, you may use the INSTR function already discussed.

The **STR$** (short for "string") function is the opposite of the VAL function. The STR$ function takes a numeric value and recodes it internally to a string. As with the VAL function, STR$ can be used as part of a PRINT statement, a LET statement, or a logical statement. The numeric value may be in the form of a constant, a variable, or an expression.

General Form:
line number string variable=STR$(*numeric value*)

Example: `210 AMT$=STR$(AMT)`

In the example, suppose that the numeric variable AMT contains 4.16. The STR$ function recodes the value into string form and stores it in the string variable called AMT$ as " 4.16 ". Note that the variables AMT and AMT$ are different variables, even though their names are the same except for the dollar sign.

As you use the STR$ function, you need to be aware of the fact that one or two blanks are produced along with the value of the result. The string produced always begins with a minus sign for negative numbers or a blank space for positive numbers and always ends with a blank space. In following the numeric verification routine discussed in this chapter, any blank spaces must be "stripped off" before using the resulting value. The method for doing this is shown later in this chapter in example programs C7E1A and C7E1B.

The **RIGHT$** function is used to examine characters at the right end of string data. It functions very similarly to the LEFT$ function discussed earlier. For example, the function could be used to examine the last six characters of a string, as shown in the following example.

General Form: RIGHT$(*string data,number of characters*)

Example: `310 PRINT RIGHT$("CATERPILLAR",6)`

Output: `PILLAR`

The **MID$** (short for "mid string") function is used to examine any sequence of consecutive characters within string data. In the example below, the function is used to print starting at the sixth character and continuing for four characters.

General Form:
MID$(*string data,start position,number of characters*)

Example: `440 PRINT MID$("CATERPILLAR",6,4)`

Output: `PILL`

If the number of characters is not specified, the function examines all characters from the start position to the end of the string data.

Now that you have examined several functions, let's see how to code a program that verifies that inputted data is numeric. To accomplish this, a character variable is used to store all inputted data (even numeric data). Then the program converts the character data into numeric form as the checking process is completed. Although there are several possible methods that may be used to check for valid numeric type data, we will examine only one of them. The following program design may be used:

1. Input the data from the keyboard into a string (character) variable. If possible, use LINE INPUT.
2. Convert the string data to numeric data and store it in a numeric variable.
3. Convert the stored numeric data back to string data and store the data in a different string variable.
4. Strip off any leading or trailing blanks in the string variable.
5. Compare the original string variable with the string variable created in step 3. If they are the same, the data contains only numeric characters. If they are different, there was at least one nonnumeric character in the data entered from the keyboard.

Two versions of code developed from this program design are given. The first version works with all the computers covered in this text. However, unless you are using a TRS-80 Model III whose VAL function gives error messages with some characters, lines 70 and 80 may be omitted; these lines force reentry of the input if it contains a colon or a percent sign.

Example:

```
10 ' C7E1A
20 ' STUDENT NAME, CHAPTER 7, EXAMPLE 1A
30 ' VERIFIES THAT DATA IS NUMERIC
40 '
50 ' ***** BEGINNING OF DATA ENTRY LOOP
60 LINE INPUT "ENTER A NUMBER";NUMBER$ ←——— 1
70 IF INSTR(NUMBER$,":")>0 THEN PRINT "REENTER":GOTO 50
80 IF INSTR(NUMBER$,"%")>0 THEN PRINT "REENTER":GOTO 50
90 NUMBER=VAL(NUMBER$) ←——— 2
100 NNUMBER$=STR$(NUMBER) ←——— 3
110 IF LEFT$(NNUMBER$,1)=" " THEN NNUMBER$=MID$(NNUMBER$,2) ←——— 4
```

```
120 IF RIGHT$(NNUMBER$,1)=" " THEN NNUMBER$=LEFT$(NNUMBER$,
    LEN(NNUMBER$)-1) <------------------------------------------ 4
140 IF NUMBER$<>NNUMBER$ THEN PRINT "REENTER":GOTO 50 <-------- 5
150 ' ***** END OF DATA ENTRY LOOP
160 PRINT "THE NUMBER IS ";NUMBER
170 END
```

The second version uses the WHILE . . . WEND control structure and works for computers other than the TRS-80 Model III. This second method is the preferred one for computers with which it can be used. Step numbers from the program design are indicated to help you see how the program design was coded in BASIC.

Example:

```
10 ' C7E1B
20 ' STUDENT NAME, CHAPTER 7, EXAMPLE 1B
30 ' VERIFIES THAT DATA IS NUMERIC
40 '
50 NNUMBER$="INVALID"
60 WHILE NNUMBER$<>NUMBER$ <--------------------------------------- 5
70    INPUT "ENTER A NUMBER";NUMBER$ <----------------------------- 1
80    NUMBER=VAL(NUMBER$) <---------------------------------------- 2
90    NNUMBER$=STR$(NUMBER) <-------------------------------------- 3
100      IF LEFT$(NNUMBER$,1)=" " THEN NNUMBER$=MID$(NNUMBER$,2) <-- 4
110      IF RIGHT$(NNUMBER$,1)=" " THEN NNUMBER$=LEFT$(NNUMBER$,
         LEN(NNUMBER$)-1) <---------------------------------------- 4
130 WEND
140 PRINT "THE NUMBER IS ";NUMBER
150 END
```

Note that the comparison from step 5 of the program design was performed by the WHILE statement in line 60, which keeps the loop repeating until the values are the same.

ENSURING APPROPRIATENESS OF DATA

Ensuring the appropriateness of data means checking two input data items against each other to see if they make sense as data that should go together. For example, let's code a program that handles ticket sales for two concerts. The High Hope concert is on March 7, while the Down Under concert is March 16. Once the data is input, the program must simply make comparisons. Study the following example to see how it is done.

Example:

```
40 INPUT "WHICH CONCERT (HIGH OR DOWN) ";CCERT$
50 IF CCERT$<>"HIGH" AND CCERT$<>"DOWN" THEN 40
60 INPUT "WHICH DAY OF THE MONTH ";DAY
70 IF CCERT$="HIGH" AND DAY<>7 THEN PRINT "INVALID":GOTO 40
80 IF CCERT$="DOWN" AND DAY<>16 THEN PRINT "INVALID":GOTO 40
90 PRINT
100 PRINT "TICKET FOR ";CCERT$;" ON DATE: ";DAY
```

ENSURING THAT DATA IS ON A LIST OF POSSIBLE VALUES

In previous sections, you have learned how to check for validity of choice-type data when the number of choices was small. When the number of valid choices is larger, the use of READ and DATA statements may make the checking easier. To do this, the data is input, and a loop is entered. The loop reads data items in succession, until the entered item is found or until the data is used up. If the item is found, the likelihood that the data is valid is higher. If the entered item is not found, the data is not valid. Suppose that a hotel has five meeting rooms. Each day the computer is used to enter the names of the rooms, the names of the groups meeting there, and the times of the meetings. A sign is then printed to post on the doors of the rooms. To make sure no invalid rooms are entered and to ensure that no rooms are misspelled, a lookup is used. The program design is as follows:

1. Get the name of the room from the keyboard.
2. Enter a loop to begin checking the name against each valid name. If it is found, exit the loop and continue. If it is not found, go back to step 1 for reentry of the name.
3. Get the name of the group from the keyboard.
4. Get the meeting time from the keyboard.
5. Print the sign.

The program design may be converted into BASIC code as follows:

Example:

```
10 ' C7E2
20 ' STUDENT NAME, CHAPTER 7, EXAMPLE 2
30 ' MAKES HOTEL MEETING ROOM SIGNS
40 ' ***** BEGINNING OF LOOP
50 INPUT "WHICH ROOM ";ROOM$
60 RESTORE
70 FOR N=1 TO 5
80     READ NAM$
90     IF NAM$=ROOM$ THEN 130 ' EXIT LOOP
100 NEXT N
110 PRINT "INVALID ROOM" ' GETS HERE ONLY IF NOT FOUND
120 GOTO 40 ' **** REPEAT LOOP
130 INPUT "NAME OF GROUP: ";WHO$
140 INPUT "HOUR OF MEETING: ";HOUR$
150 LPRINT "ROOM:    ";ROOM$
160 LPRINT "GROUP:   ";WHO$
170 LPRINT "TIME:    ";HOUR$
180 END
200 DATA PINE,OAK,PECAN,SWEETGUM,PERSIMMON
```

REVIEW QUESTIONS

1. For what kinds of data validation techniques are IF . . . THEN or WHILE . . . WEND statements appropriately used? (Obj. 4)
2. What statement is used to allow the input of commas into a character variable? (Obj. 4)
3. How is the length of input data checked? (Obj. 4)
4. What kind of data validation technique can be implemented by using VAL and STR$, among other functions? (Obj. 4)
5. Explain how the LEFT$, RIGHT$, and MID$ functions work. (Obj. 4)
6. What kind of data validation may be performed by using READ and DATA? (Obj. 4)

VOCABULARY WORDS

The following vocabulary words were introduced in this chapter:

data validation   error trap

KEYWORDS

The following keywords were introduced in this chapter:

ASC	INSTR	MID$
CHR$	LEFT$	RIGHT$
INKEY$	LEN	STR$
INPUT$	LINE INPUT	VAL

PROGRAMS TO WRITE

In this chapter, you will plan programs and code their data input and calculation routines. Keep your work because in the next chapter you will code the printout routines for these same programs. All programs should be planned in modular form, with a main module, one module for data input, one for computation (if needed), and one for output. For purposes of this chapter, each output module should consist of statements that print the contents of all variables used in your program, using no particular format. This will allow you to thoroughly test your programs and make sure that the input and calculation modules are working properly. Complete the appropriate documentation for each program before doing the coding for this chapter's modules. Remember to use appropriate data validation routines in all programs. Even though it is not stated in the assignment, be sure to accept either upper-case or lower-case letters in response to choice-type questions.

Program 1

You want to use the computer to print name tags for participants in a business meeting. Due to the size of the tags, no name longer than 25 characters and spaces per line may be printed. Therefore, the program should check the length of each name entered to be sure it is no longer than this. For testing purposes, use the names Frederick P. McGillicuddy, Susan Henry, and William Randolph Buschmann. The first two names should be accepted, while the last should be rejected and require reentry in abbreviated form.

Program 2

Farmers in a particular area sell their grain to the Ochlochnee Area Farmers' Cooperative. The trucks bringing grain to the market are weighed twice, once while they are still full of grain and again after the grain is emptied. The difference is the weight of the load of grain, for which the farmer will be paid. Your program should ask for the weight of the full truck and the weight of the empty truck. There are two sets of scales, one for small trucks and one for larger trucks. For purposes of the program, you will work with small trucks only. Validate that the empty truck weighs at least 2,800 pounds but not more than 4,000. Also, if the load is more than the weight of the truck, the entry is considered invalid and both data items should be reentered.

Program 3

You want a program that will either add, subtract, multiply, or divide two numbers entered from the keyboard. The program should also ask for the entry of the first letter of A(dd), S(ubtract), M(ultiply), or D(ivide) to indicate the arithmetic operation to take place. Write the program so it will check that the choice entered is a valid one.

Program 4

In a particular state, the penalty for speeding is $10.79 for each mile per hour over the speed limit. Since the county courts in the state are all equipped with computers, computers will perform the computation. Input to the program consists of the name of the offender, the speed limit, and the clocked speed of the offender. The program should continue operating for as many offenders as desired. To test your program, use the following data: George Samuels, 35 miles per hour in a 25-mile-per-hour zone; Jane Elfman, 71 miles per hour in a 55-mile-per-hour zone; and Robert Abels, 58 miles per hour in a 45-mile-per-hour zone. After computation of each fine, the program should ask the user whether to continue. Check the validity of this input before acting on it.

Program 5

A convention center assigns groups to meeting rooms. Write a program that will ask for the name of the room to which a group is being assigned, along with the number of people in the group. The program should then check for a match between the room and the size of the group to verify that the room is large enough for the group. The rooms and their capacities are: North, 50; South, 24; East, 12; and West, 75. To test your program, use three group sizes for each room: (1) one person less than the capacity, (2) exact capacity, and (3) one person over capacity. Enter the data in different sequences to make sure the program can handle all conditions. Set up the program to operate as long as the operator wants to continue. The program should check the validity of the user's choice to continue or stop.

Program 6

A county is divided into three different districts, numbered 1 through 3, for property tax collection purposes. The rate, which varies with the district, is $12.56, $10.95, and $15.41, respectively, per $1,000 of valuation of real estate property. The program should compute the tax bill for individuals and ask for the tax district and the tax rate. It also should check them against each other to help ensure that no error was made in data entry (requiring entry of two related values that can be checked against each other for appropriateness is one way of confirming that no error in data entry was made). If there are no errors, the amount of tax should be computed. Set up the program for continuous operation.

Program 7

A frog falls into a well. Since the sides of the well are slippery, he slides back down one foot for each two feet he jumps up. The program should calculate how many times the frog must jump to get out of the well. The user enters the depth of the well and how many feet the frog jumps each time. If the depth of the well is less than or equal to the size of the jump, the program should simply say that the frog can jump out in one leap. Otherwise, it should calculate the number of jumps. To test the program, use a depth of 2 feet with a jump size of 2 feet, a depth of 24 feet with a jump size of 3 feet, and a depth of 3 feet with a jump size of 3 feet.

Program 8

Modify Program 4 to improve the data entry routines. This time, the program should ensure that only numbers are entered for the speeds. No nonnumeric characters will be allowed. Along with valid entries, enter speeds of 55-, 5Y, $70, and 5:55. All these attempts should be rejected.

Program 9

Your corporation maintains a list of all persons who are willing to speak before civic clubs, school groups, and so on. When a club calls and requests a particular person to speak, the computer checks to see that the person is available as a speaker. The person's name is entered (last name, comma, space, first name), and a list of the speakers is checked. If the person is on the list, the caller is informed by letter. To complete your program, store the names of speakers as "Adams, Robin", "Clifton, Byron", "Fletcher, Marcie", "March, Glynda", "Talbott, Ryan", and "Wyatt, Le". To test the program, enter the names Robin Adams, Mike Marion, Le Wyatt, and Byron Clifton. All of these names should be found except for Mike Marion, whose name should not have been stored in the program.

Program 10

Modify Program 7 to verify that only numbers are entered for the depth and jump size. Also, input the kind of well casing in use—dirt, terra cotta, or pipe. Dirt wells have a slide back of three-fourths of the jump distance. Terra cotta wells and pipe wells have a slide back of one-half the jump distance. Include error validation routines to check these new data items. Also, modify old data validation routines if required.

8

Improved Report Formats

> **OBJECTIVES**
>
> After studying this chapter, you will be able to
>
> 1. Describe how a report is planned.
> 2. Describe how to format numeric output with BASIC.
> 3. Code programs to print output as planned on the spacing chart.

Neatly arranged output is easy to read and understand. This is true whether the printout is to appear on a CRT or on a printer. This chapter presents methods that may be used to make reports attractive and easy to read.

TOPIC 8.1 PLANNING THE REPORT

Generating a useful and neatly organized report requires care and planning. The content must be determined and the format (column or row organization), the headings, the output device to be used, the editing, and the separation of data must be considered. These items are discussed in the following sections.

ITEMS TO CONSIDER IN PLANNING A REPORT

Content of the Report

The content of a report is more useful if only necessary information is included. For example, consider a report of customers who bought merchandise from a store on credit—that is, they agreed to pay for it at a later date. The management of the store uses the report to determine which customers have not paid by the due date.

The information in the report is printed on detail lines. A **detail line** represents a line of output for each data item processed. One way of preparing the report is to print a detail line for each customer, showing the amount each owes. A much better method, however, is to print detail lines just for those customers who have not paid as agreed. Such a report includes only the information management needs; it is not cluttered with unnecessary details.

Headings

All reports should have headings. While the format of the headings is determined by the person designing the report, four types of headings are usually considered. The **report heading**, which is the title of the report, should identify what the report contains. It may also contain a company name, an identification number of the report, and any other desired data. The report heading is printed once on the first page of the report. It may contain one or more lines. A **page heading** contains data that is to be printed on each page of the report. Typical examples of page headings include a brief version of the report name, the date it was prepared, and the page number. If there are columns or rows in a report, each column or row should also have a heading identifying its contents. A heading over a column is known as a **column heading**. A heading next to data on a printed line is known as a **row heading**.

The report in Figure 8-1 shows the number of overtime hours worked by employees in three departments of a business. It includes a report heading, subheading, six column headings, and three detail lines.

Output Device to Be Used

The output device to be used in printing a report should be determined by the nature of the report. Short reports that change

```
          OVERTIME HOURS REPORT  <----------------  Report heading
                JULY 1-5, 19--  <-----------------  Subheading
Department       Mon  Tue  Wed  Thu  Fri  <-----  Column headings
Accounting         0    0    0   10    0  <--+
Assembly          25   10   15   20   12  <--+---  Detail lines
Shipping           0    0    6    8    0  <--+
```

Figure 8-1 Parts of a Report

frequently may be more useful if they are displayed on the screen whenever needed by the user. Permanent reports, or those that require more in-depth study, should be printed as hard copy on a printer. An example of a report that changes frequently is one that shows the number of seats still available on a particular airline flight. An example of a more permanent report is the annual income statement of a business, which shows the amount of profit or loss.

Editing

Once the content and general arrangement of a report have been decided upon, you must decide how to edit the data. **Editing** is the spacing and punctuating of individual data items. Some editing techniques, such as lining up numbers at the decimal point, are commonly used, while others are left to the user's discretion. For example, how many decimal places should each number contain? Should dollar signs be used? Should amounts contain commas? In making these decisions, emphasis should be placed on making the report as easy to read as possible.

Separation of Data

Good separation or spacing of data can make a report much easier to read. For instance, a report should usually start on a clear (erased) display screen or on a new sheet of paper. Generally, white space and rulings are used to arrange data within the report for easier reading. **White space** refers to blank space between the rows (lines) and columns of a report. **Rulings** are lines made from hyphens, underlines, or other characters. Rulings are used to separate the parts of a report, such as separating the headings from the detail lines. Figure 8-2 shows how rulings improve the appearance of a report.

```
        OVERTIME HOURS REPORT
            JULY 1-5, 19--
======================================
Department     Mon  Tue  Wed  Thu  Fri
--------------------------------------

Accounting       0    0    0   10    0
Assembly        25   10   15   20   12
Shipping         0    0    6    8    0
```

Rulings

Figure 8-2 Report with Rulings

USE OF A SPACING CHART

As decisions are made about the items discussed previously, a spacing chart is completed. If a display screen is being used for output, the number of characters available on the screen is as follows:

IBM & compatibles—25 rows, 40 or 80 columns

TRS-80 Model 4—24 rows, 40 or 80 columns (16 rows, 64 columns on Model III)

If a printer is being used, there are usually 66 lines on a page. Not all the lines are shown on the spacing chart. The number of columns for a printer might be any number from 40 to 132 or more. Note that the rows and columns of the spacing chart are numbered for easy reference (see Figure 8-3).

The use of a spacing chart allows the programmer to see and plan the exact placement of headings, rulings, and detail lines. The completed chart then serves as a guide during programming. When writing a spacing chart, use a pencil so items may be erased and rewritten in different locations if necessary.

Figure 8-4 shows a completed spacing chart. Observe that literals such as headings are written on the spacing chart exactly as they should appear on the report to be printed by the computer. Fields containing variable values are filled with an image representing data (see rows 8 and 9 of Figure 8-4 for examples). The backslashes and the space between them (\   \) mark the areas in which a word (string/character data) is to be printed. The number signs (###) mark areas in which numbers are to be printed. Detailed instructions for writing those images are given in Topic 8.2.

Note that the spacing chart does not contain a detail line for each row of data that may be printed. It contains just two detail lines to show the format of the data and the fact that there may be multiple detail lines.

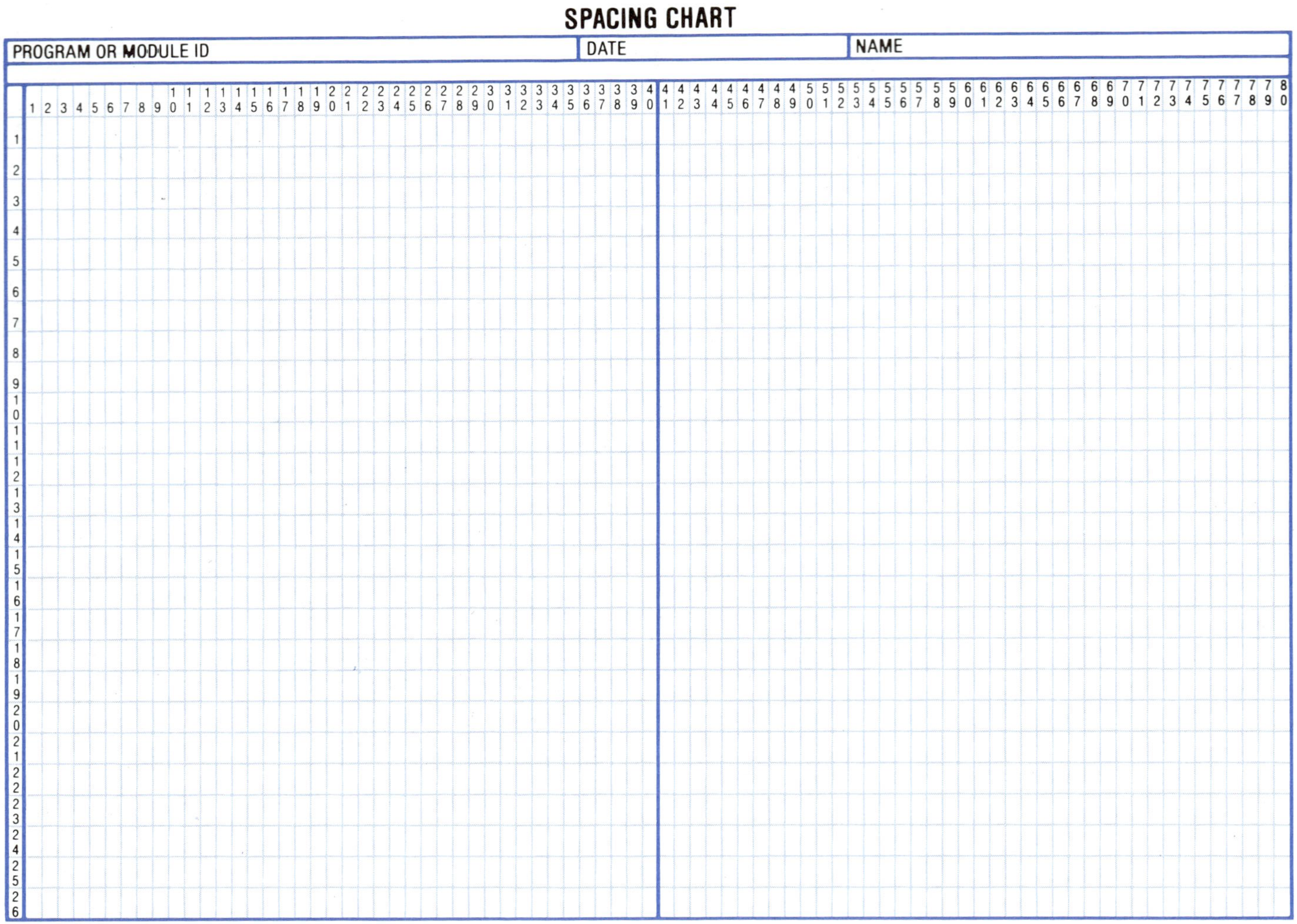

Figure 8-3 Spacing Chart

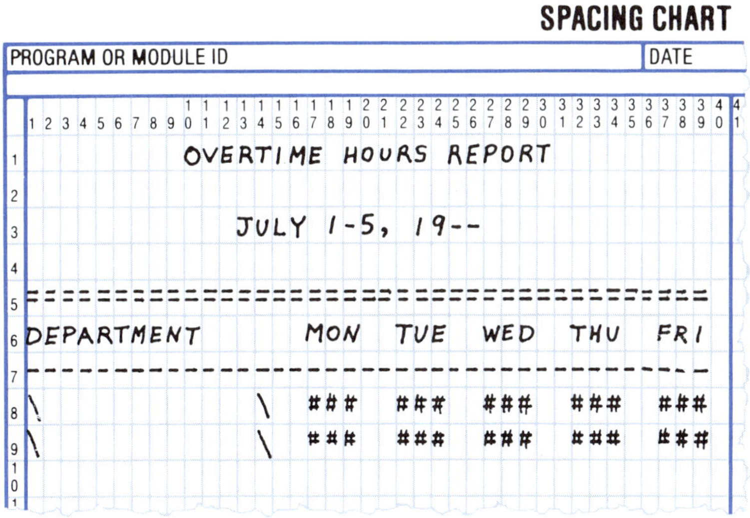

Figure 8-4 Completed Spacing Chart

REVIEW QUESTIONS

1. What is a detail line? (Obj. 1)
2. Sometimes it is preferable not to print a detail line for each data item processed. Explain. (Obj. 1)
3. List two factors that should be considered when deciding whether to display a report on a CRT or to print it on paper. (Obj. 1)
4. Name and describe four kinds of headings that may be used in a report. (Obj. 1)
5. List five items to be considered when planning a report. (Obj. 1)
6. Describe what is meant by the use of white space and rulings. (Obj. 1)
7. Review the items contained on a spacing chart. (Obj. 1)
8. Why should a pencil be used when writing a spacing chart? (Obj. 1)

TOPIC 8.2 USING BASIC TO FORMAT A REPORT

Topic 8.1 discussed some of the factors to be considered when setting up attractive, easy-to-read reports. This topic describes some of the techniques that may be used to format such reports using the BASIC language.

CLEARING THE SCREEN

One of the most frequently used techniques for improving the appearance of printed output on a CRT is to erase or clear the screen. Recall that in Chapter 2 you learned how to use the CLS statement to accomplish this.

CENTERING A HEADING

A heading may be centered by calculating the amount of "left-over" blank space on the line. Then, by leaving half of this left-over space at the beginning of the line, the heading will appear centered. Study the labeling of the following illustration:

|——blank space——THE HEADING——blank space——|

The logic or program design that can be used is as follows:

1. Find the length of the heading to be centered.
2. Subtract the heading length from the total width of the report, giving the total amount of leftover space on the line.
3. Leave half of the leftover space at the beginning of the line and print the heading.

The program design is converted into BASIC code in the following program. Note that the heading is placed in a variable by the program and that the line length is the 80 characters of a standard screen width.

Example:

```
10 ' C8E1A
20 ' STUDENT NAME, CHAPTER 8, EXAMPLE 1A
30 ' CENTERS HEADING
40 '
50 HEAD$="THE MOST FUN OF ALL"
60 LGTH=LEN(HEAD$)
70 BLANK=80-LGTH ' FOR 40-COLUMN SCREEN, CHANGE 80 TO 40
80 PRINT TAB(BLANK/2);HEAD$
```

To reduce the number of statements, the LENgth function and division by two can be combined in one argument for TAB. Note that the heading is still placed in a variable, although it could just as easily be a literal.

Example:

```
10 ' C8E1B
20 ' STUDENT NAME, CHAPTER 8, EXAMPLE 1B
30 ' CENTERS HEADING
40 '
50 HEAD$="THE MOST FUN OF ALL"
60 PRINT TAB((80-LEN(HEAD$))/2);HEAD$
```

CONTROLLING THE HORIZONTAL PLACEMENT OF DATA

In earlier chapters you learned that horizontal spacing of data can be controlled by use of the comma or semicolon—that is, items separated with a comma in the PRINT statement are printed in columns and those separated with a semicolon are printed next to each other. You also learned how to use the TAB function to control horizontal spacing. While these methods work well in appropriate situations, there are also other ways of controlling horizontal spacing.

The SPC Function

As described in Chapter 2, SPC is an abbreviation of space. The SPC function (which is not available on TRS-80 Model III) is similar to the TAB function and must be used as part of a PRINT statement. However, instead of causing the cursor to move to a particular column, as the TAB function does, the SPC function causes the cursor to move the specified number of blank spaces. Like the TAB function, the SPC function should be separated from other items in the PRINT statement by semicolons. It also may be used repeatedly in the same PRINT statement.

General Form:
line number PRINT SPC (*# of spaces*);*item to print*

Example: `40 PRINT SPC(20);"HI!"`

Some sample BASIC statements using the SPC function follow.

Example 1:

```
40 T=20
50 PRINT SPC(T);"GOOD MORNING!"
```

Output:

```
                    GOOD MORNING!
```

Example 2:

```
40 PRINT "WORD 1";SPC(10);"WORD 2"
```

Output:

```
WORD 1          WORD 2
```

The SPACE$ Function

The **SPACE$** function, like SPC, produces a string of spaces. Instead of having to be included with a PRINT statement, however, SPACE$ may also be used to assign spaces to a character variable. (The SPACE$ function is not available on TRS-80 Model III.)

General Form:
line number PRINT SPACE$(*# of spaces*);*item to print*

Example: `40 PRINT SPACE$(20);"HI!"`

General Form:
line number variable$*=SPACE$(# of spaces*)

Example: `40 L$=SPACE$(20)`

The STRING$ Function

Another function that may be used similarly to SPACE$ is known as **STRING$**. While SPACE$ produces a string of spaces or blanks, STRING$ produces a string of any desired character. The string of characters may be printed immediately, as shown in the first example. Alternately, it may be assigned to a character variable for printing at a later time, as shown in the second example.

General Form:
line number PRINT STRING$(*length, character*)

Example:
```
40 PRINT STRING$(20,"*")
```

or

General Form:
*line number variable$*=STRING$(*length, character*)

Example:
```
40 L$=STRING$(30,"-")
```

The length of the string may be represented as a constant, a numeric variable, or a numeric expression. The character may be represented as a literal in quotes as shown here, as a character variable, or as a numeric variable or expression. If a numeric variable or expression is used, it must represent the ASCII code of the desired character. For example, the ASCII value of the hyphen is 45. Therefore, the second example could have been written as:

Example:
```
40 L$=STRING$(30,45)
```

As before, the first expression inside the parentheses (30) represents the length of the string. The second expression, regardless of whether it is a literal or an ASCII code (45 in this case), identifies the character from which the string is to be made.

The STRING$ function is particularly useful for separating columns with **leaders** (a string of periods) or for printing rulings between the parts of a report. The following example program shows both of these uses.

Example:

```
40 PRINT
50 L$=STRING$(10,".")
60 PRINT "ITEM";SPC(15);"PRICE"
70 PRINT STRING$(24,"=")
80 PRINT "HAMBURGER";L$;" 1.97"
90 PRINT "FRIES    ";L$;"  .90"
```

Output:

```
ITEM               PRICE
========================
HAMBURGER.......... 1.97
FRIES    ..........  .90
```

Line 50 of the program uses the STRING$ function to create a string of ten leaders and assign them to variable L$. Line 60 prints the column headings. Line 70 prints the ruling separating the headings from the detail lines. In lines 80 and 90, the variable L$ is printed between the name of the item and the price to produce the leaders. Note the extra spaces after FRIES and inside the quotation marks on line 90. This causes blanks to be printed after the word FRIES so the leaders start in the same column as they did for HAMBURGER. The numbers in this example are written as literals to make sure they line up at the decimal point.

Rather than using the STRING$ function, a string of characters can also be printed by using a loop. In the following example, a string of 30 hyphens will be printed:

Example:

```
40 FOR X=1 TO 30
50     PRINT "-";
60 NEXT X
70 PRINT
```

The FOR . . . NEXT loop from lines 40 to 60 does the printing. The semicolon at the end of line 50 keeps the output from moving to a new line after each hyphen is printed. Once the line of hyphens is complete, line 70 (which prints nothing) produces a return to a new line since it is not followed by a semicolon.

In similar fashion, a variable containing a string of characters can be created for later printing by using the process of catenation, which you were briefly introduced to in Chapter 7. **Catenation** means connecting data items together. The operator used in this process is the plus sign (+), the same symbol used for arithmetic addition.

General Form:
line number string variable = string value + string value

Example: `200 C$=C$+"A"`

Assuming that variable C$ had an "A" stored in it already, the variable will contain "AA" after this instruction has been executed.

Example:

```
200 NAM$=FIRST$+" "+LAST$
```

Assuming that FIRST$ contains "MARILYN" and LAST$ contains "GEORGE", the variable NAM$ will contain "MARILYN GEORGE" after the statement has been executed.

By using the catenation operator inside a loop, a character can be repeatedly catenated onto a growing string of characters as follows:

Example:

```
40 L$="" ' MAKE SURE THERE IS NOTHING IN THE VARIABLE WHEN WE START
50 FOR X=1 TO 30
60 L$=L$+"-" ' ADD ONE MORE HYPHEN TO THE GROWING STRING EACH TIME
   THROUGH THE LOOP
70 NEXT X
80 PRINT L$ ' PRINT THE COMPLETED STRING
```

EDITING DATA

The editing of data refers to such procedures as lining up numbers at the decimal point, inserting commas in numbers, and placing dollar signs at the beginning of amounts of money. BASIC has a built-in statement for editing data for printing and/or displaying.

PRINT USING

PRINT USING is the built-in data editing statement. Among its capabilities are:

1. Alignment of decimal points
2. Rounding to any desired number of decimal places
3. Placement of commas in longer numbers
4. Printing of dollar signs at the beginning of amounts
5. Exact horizontal placement of data

The PRINT USING statement is so named because it PRINTs while USING a string of characters as its guide. The character string provides an image of how the data should look. It shows how the data is to be edited and serves as a model to be followed during printing. The character string for the image may be included as a literal in the PRINT USING line itself, or it may be contained in a character variable.

General Form:
line number PRINT USING "*character string*";*items to print*

Example: `40 PRINT USING "###.##";397.5`

or

General Form:
line number PRINT USING *variable$*;*items to print*

Example: `50 PRINT USING P$;23983.23`

Examination of some example programs will help clarify the use of this statement.

Example 1:

```
40 PRINT USING "###.##";397.5
```

Output:

```
397.50
```

In Example 1, the three number signs (###), decimal point (.), and two more number signs (##) serve as the image—that is, the printed result is to have three places to the left of the decimal and two places to the right of the decimal point. Since there is only one digit to the right of the decimal in 397.5, a zero is added by the computer to fill the required two places.

Example 2:

```
40 P$="##,###.##"
50 PRINT USING P$;23983.23
60 PRINT USING P$;74.345
70 PRINT USING P$;3982.3
80 END
```

Output:

```
23,983.23
    74.35
 3,982.30
```

In Example 2, note that the image placed into variable P$ is long enough to represent the longest number to be printed. Even though the three values printed vary greatly in length, they all line up at the decimal point. Note that the second value (74.345) is rounded off to 74.35, while the last value (3982.3) has a zero added to the end. Also, observe that commas are correctly placed in the longer numbers.

Example 3:

```
40 L$="TOTAL $$##,###.##"
50 A=32.39
60 R=12983
70 PRINT USING L$;A
80 PRINT USING L$;R
90 END
```

Output:

```
TOTAL        $32.39
TOTAL   $12,983.00
```

Example 3 illustrates two concepts. First, the image (contained in L$) contains a literal ("TOTAL") as well as the area to be filled with numeric value. Second, the use of two dollar signs at the beginning of the numeric area causes a floating dollar sign to be placed in front of the numbers. A **floating dollar sign** moves to the right as far as necessary to appear immediately before the amount. Even though two dollar signs are used in the image, only one is actually printed.

Example 4:

```
40 X$="\        \ ####"
50 PRINT USING X$;"FRED",27
60 PRINT USING X$;"SUSAN",291
```

Output:

```
FRED         27
SUSAN       291
```

The first part of the image (\   \) in Example 4 specifies an area to be occupied by character data. Since there are two backslashes, with eight blanks between them, ten spaces are reserved for the character data (the two backslashes and the eight spaces). The number signs (####) specify an area to be occupied by numeric data. (Note: The TRS-80 Model III indicates character data with percent signs (%) rather than backslashes.)

Example 5:

```
40 P$="###.##      ###.##"
50 A=456.344
60 B=344.176
70 PRINT USING P$;A,B
80 END
```

Output:

```
456.34      344.18
```

The image created in line 40 of Example 5 shows how the horizontal spacing of numbers may be controlled with the PRINT USING statement. Changing the number of blank spaces between the two sets of number signs will change the horizontal spacing.

Remember that all characters in the image string will be printed as they appear, except for the formatting characters such as number signs and backslashes. The more common editing or formatting characters that may be used on the IBM and compatible computers including the TRS-80 models are given in Table 8-1. Refer to the reference manual for your version of BASIC to determine other characters that may be used.

EXAMPLES	EXPLANATION OF PRINTOUT
######	This image is used for numeric output. Each number sign represents the print position for one digit. Blanks are filled in at the beginning of the image if necessary. The length of the image may be varied as required by the numbers being used.
###,###	A comma inserted anywhere in the image will cause commas to be printed every three positions.
###,###.##	A decimal point may be placed in the image at any desired point and will print in that location. Zeros are added to the end of the number if necessary to set the required number of places to the right of the decimal.
###,###.##-	This image is the same as the previous example, except that negative numbers will be printed with a minus sign at the end rather than the beginning.

Table 8-1 Common PRINT USING Images

EXAMPLES	EXPLANATION OF PRINTOUT
$$##,###.##	This image specifies that a dollar sign should be printed immediately to the left of the first digit. Even though two dollar signs appear in the image, only one will be printed. A digit may appear in the other position.
$###,###.##	A dollar sign will be placed at the left side of the space reserved for the number. If the number is shorter than the image used, spaces will be printed between the dollar sign and the number.
\ \ or % %	This image represents space in which character data should be printed. If the data is shorter than the image, blanks will be added to the right. If the data is longer than the image, the right end will be **truncated** (cut off). (Use percent signs with the TRS-80 Model III; use backslashes with the TRS-80 Model IV and with the IBM and compatibles. On the TRS-80 a backslash is keyed by pressing the CLEAR key and the ? key.)
!	An exclamation mark specifies that a one-character alphabetic field will be used.

Table 8-1 (continued)

REVIEW QUESTIONS

1. Name two BASIC functions that may be used for spacing. (Obj. 2)
2. How are the two functions referred to in question 1 alike? How are they different? (Obj. 2)

3. Which BASIC function can create a string of any desired character, for immediate printing or storage for later use? (Obj. 2)
4. Describe the capabilities of the PRINT USING statement. (Obj. 2)
5. What controls the type of editing done by the PRINT USING statement? (Obj. 2)
6. What is the purpose of the catenation operator? (Obj. 2)
7. In English, describe the steps that must be carried out when using the PRINT USING statement in order to align numbers at the decimal point. (Obj. 2)

VOCABULARY WORDS

The following vocabulary words were introduced in this chapter:

catenation	floating dollar sign	row heading
column heading	leader	ruling
detail line	page heading	truncated
editing	report heading	white space

KEYWORDS

The following keywords were introduced in this chapter:

PRINT USING	SPACE$	STRING$

PROGRAMS TO WRITE

You will plan and code the printout routines for the programs you wrote in Chapter 7. The original instructions from Chapter 7 are repeated here for your easy reference in planning the printout. Note that additional instructions for the format of the output are included. Be sure to prepare a spacing chart for each program before beginning the coding.

Program 1

You want to use the computer to print name tags for participants in a business meeting. Due to the size of the tags, no name longer than 25 characters and spaces per line may be printed. Therefore, the program should check the length of each name entered to be sure it is no longer than this. For testing purposes, use the names Frederick P. McGillicuddy, Susan Henry, and William Randolph Buschmann. The first two names should be accepted, while the last should be rejected and require reentry in abbreviated form. In planning the output, use appropriate blank lines (white space) to make the names appear centered vertically on the name tags. Center the name horizontally on the tag. The program should calculate the centering based on the length of each name. If your printer can handle it, you may want to use enlarged print for the names. Check with your instructor or the printer's manual for such instructions.

Program 2

Farmers in a particular area sell their grain to the Ochlochnee Area Farmers' Cooperative. The trucks bringing grain to the market are weighed twice, once while they are still full of grain and again after the grain is emptied. The difference is the weight of the load of grain, for which the farmer will be paid. Your program should ask for the weight of the full truck and the weight of the empty truck. There are two sets of scales, one for small trucks and one for larger trucks. For purposes of the program, you are working with small trucks only. Validate that the empty truck weighs at least 2,800 pounds but not more than 4,000. Also, if the load is more than the weight of the truck, the entry is considered invalid and both data items should be reentered. Make sure all numbers on the printout are aligned at the decimal point.

Program 3

You want a program that will either add, subtract, multiply, or divide two numbers entered from the keyboard. The program should also ask for the entry of the first letter of A(dd), S(ubtract), M(ultiply), or D(ivide) to indicate the arithmetic operation to take place. Write the program so it will check that the choice entered is a valid one. Make sure the output is arranged in an easy-to-read format with the operation, the input numbers, and the computed result easily identifiable.

Program 4

In a particular state, the penalty for speeding is $10.79 for each mile per hour over the speed limit. Since the county courts in the state are all equipped with computers, the computers will perform the computations. Input to the program consists of the name of the offender, the speed limit, and the clocked speed of the offender. The program should continue operating for as many offenders as desired. To test your program, use the following data: George Samuels, 35 miles per hour in a 25-mile-per-hour zone; Jane Elfman, 71 miles per hour in a 55-mile-per-hour zone; and Robert Abels, 58 miles per hour in a 45-mile-per-hour zone. After computation of each fine, the program should ask the user whether to continue. Check the validity of this input before acting on it. The name and fine amount should be printed, with the fine amount rounded to two decimal places. Do not print the speed limit and clocked speed on the output.

Program 5

A convention center assigns groups to meeting rooms. Write a program that will ask for the name of the room to which a group is being assigned, along with the number of people in the group. The program should then check for a match between the room and the size of the group to verify that the room is large enough for the group. The rooms and their capacities are: North, 50; South, 24; East, 12; and West, 75. To test your program, use three group sizes for each room: (1) one person less than capacity, (2) exact capacity, and (3) one person over capacity. Enter the data in different sequences to make sure the program can handle all conditions. Set up the program to operate as long as the operator wants to continue. The program should check the validity of the user's choice to continue or stop. For this chapter, add to the program so that the capacity and rental rate for the room will be printed on the screen along with whether the room is large enough. The rates should be stored in the program along with the rooms' names and capacities. The North room rents for $205.75 per day, the South room for $97.50, the East room for $48.50, and the West room for $357.94. All capacities should be output as whole numbers. The rental amounts should be lined up at the decimal point with two places after the decimal.

Program 6

A county is divided into three different districts, numbered 1 through 3, for property tax collection purposes. The rate, which varies with the district, is $12.56, $10.95, and $15.41, respectively, per $1,000 of valuation of real estate property. The program should compute the tax bill for individuals and ask for the tax district and the tax rate. It also should check them against each other to help ensure that no error was made in data entry (requiring entry of two related values that can be checked against each other for appropriateness is one way of confirming that no error in data entry was made). If there are no errors, the amount of tax should be computed. Set up the program for continuous operation. All numbers on the printout should be aligned at the decimal point. The printout should include the tax district, tax rate, valuation of the property, and tax amount. Monetary amounts should include two decimal places.

Program 7

A frog falls into a well. Since the sides of the well are slippery, he slides back down one foot for each two feet he jumps up. The program should calculate how many times the frog must jump to get out of the well. The user enters the depth of the well and how many feet the frog jumps each time. If the depth of the well is less than or equal to the size of the jump, the program should simply say that the frog can jump out in one leap. Otherwise, it should calculate the number of jumps. To test the program, use a depth of 2 feet with a jump size of 2 feet, a depth of 24 feet with a jump size of 3 feet, and a depth of 3 feet with a jump size of 3 feet. The printout should include all relevant figures, including well depth, jump distance, slide back distance, and number of jumps required to get out. The numbers should align at the decimal point, with a provision for one digit to the right of the decimal.

Program 8

Modify Program 4 to improve the data entry routines. This time, the program should ensure that nothing but numbers are entered for the speeds. No nonnumeric characters will be allowed. Along with valid entries, enter speeds of 55-, 5Y, $70, and 5:55. All these attempts should be rejected. Change the printout so that the speed limit and clocked speed are printed, as well as the amount of fine. Check that related numbers are aligned at the decimal.

Program 9

Your corporation maintains a list of all persons who are willing to speak before civic clubs, school groups, and so on. When a club calls and requests a particular person to speak, the computer checks to see that the person is available as a speaker. The person's name is entered (last name, comma, space, first name), and a list of the speakers is checked. If the person is on the list, the caller is informed by letter. To complete your program, store the names of speakers as "Adams, Robin", "Clifton, Byron", "Fletcher, Marcie", "March, Glynda", "Talbott, Ryan", and "Wyatt, Le". To test the program, enter the names Robin Adams, Mike Marion, Le Wyatt, and Byron Clifton. All of these names should be found except Mike Marion, whose name should not have been stored in the program. The output module should prepare a neatly arranged letter announcing the availability. Also included in a columnar printout within the letter should be the speaker's rates, including figures per hour, per half day, and per day. These figures should be read from DATA statements by the program. The rates, which you need to add to the program, are as follows for the various speakers: Robin Adams, 50, 175, 300; Byron Clifton, 60, 200, 390; Marcie Fletcher, 100, 300, 570; Glynda Marsh, 30, 100, 175; Ryan Talbott, 50, 200, 400; and Le Wyatt, 40, 150, 300.

Program 10

Modify Program 7 to verify that only numbers are entered for the depth and jump size. Also, input the type of well casing in use—dirt, terra cotta, or pipe. Dirt wells have a slide back of three-quarters of the jump distance. Terra cotta wells and pipe wells have a slide back of one-half the jump distance. Include error validation routines to check these new data items. Also, modify old data validation routines if required. This time, have the program print the results of each jump as a row in a table of all the jumps, taking care to keep the numbers aligned at the decimal. Columns should be printed for depth before jump, height of jump, amount of slide back, and depth after slide back. On all columns, provide for two digits after the decimal.

PROJECT 3

You are probably familiar with computer-driven systems used by the cashiers in fast-food restaurants. In this project, you will plan and write a program to make the computer serve as such a point-of-sale device. Here is how it will work.

When a customer orders, the cashier presses a key for each item ordered. If more than one of the same item is ordered, the key is pressed the appropriate number of times. As each key is pressed, the name of the item and its price are displayed on the next available line on the screen. Typically, a customer will order a sandwich, then fries or onion rings, and finally a drink and/or a dessert.

After the customer finishes ordering, a key is pressed indicating that the order is finished. The computer at this point displays a total. The customer gives the cashier money, the cashier enters the amount tendered on the keyboard and presses the ENTER/RETURN key and the computer displays the amount tendered. Finally, the computer calculates and displays the amount of change that should be returned to the customer. If the amount tendered is insufficient to cover the total, the program should alert the cashier to the fact and ask for reentry of the tendered amount. Once a valid amount tendered is entered and the amount of change displayed, the operator should press the ENTER/RETURN key again to proceed to the next customer. All amounts on the display should be aligned at the decimal point. For purposes of this program, assume that there is no sales tax on food.

In planning the program, use the keyboard layout in Figure 8-5 to represent the items on the menu. If your teacher agrees, prepare small labels for the keys or make a paper template to indicate the key that represents each food. In examining the layout, note that the sandwiches are grouped at the left, the fries and onion rings are next, then desserts and drinks. Since this restaurant hands customers a cup of ice and the customers fill the cups themselves, it doesn't matter what kind of soft drink is ordered. Therefore, just the sizes are indicated. Following the left-to-right progression for operating the keyboard, the apostrophe (single quote) key is used to tell the computer to total the order. The ENTER/RETURN

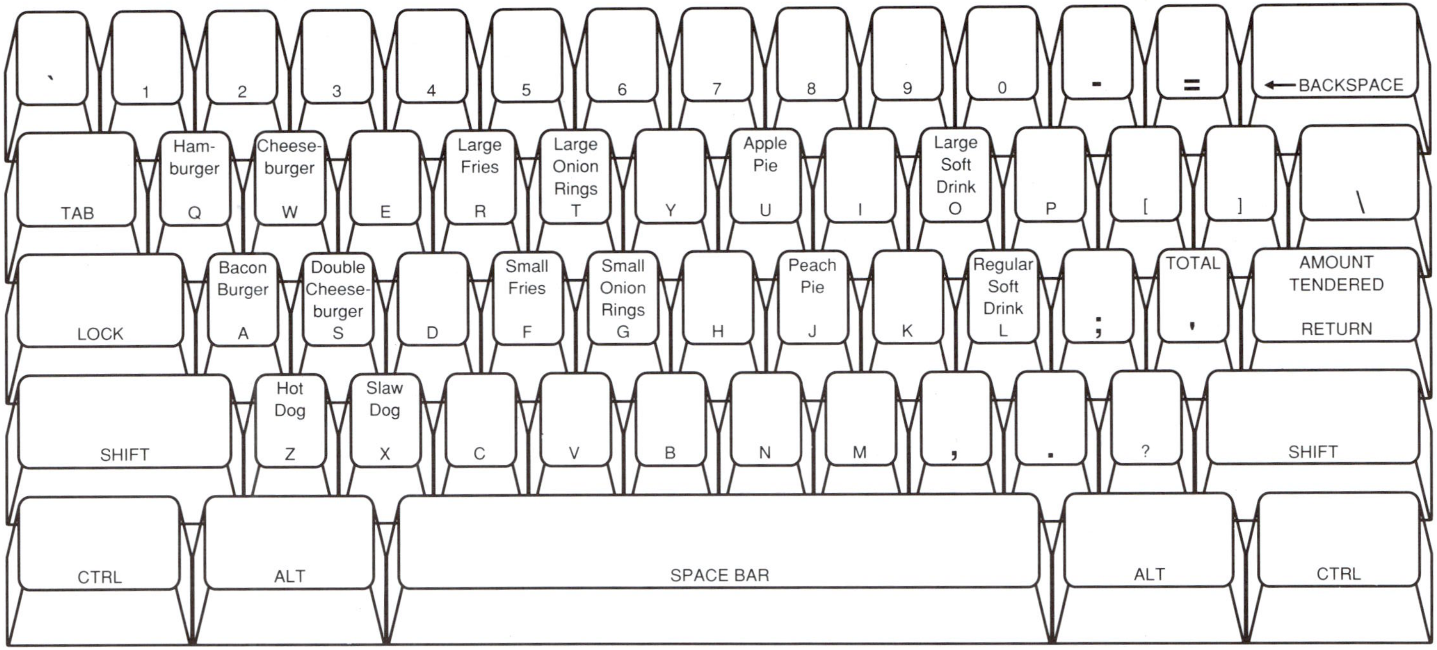

Figure 8-5 Keyboard Layout for Project 3

key is then used to enter the amount of money tendered by the customer.

The names and prices of the different menu items should be stored in the program on DATA lines. Here is the entire menu with prices. It is given in alphabetical order, which may not be the sequence you use in the program. For your reference, the key used to enter the item is given before the item.

U	Apple Pie	1.25
A	Bacon Burger	3.40
W	Cheeseburger	2.95
S	Double Cheeseburger	3.50
Q	Hamburger	2.45
Z	Hotdog	1.90
R	Large Fries	1.90
T	Large Onion Rings	2.50
O	Large Soft Drink	1.50
J	Peach Pie	1.25
L	Regular Soft Drink	1.20
X	Slawdog	2.25
F	Small Fries	1.00
G	Small Onion Rings	1.50

As always, prepare the documentation before beginning to code the program. You should complete a spacing chart, a hierarchy chart, and program designs.

PART FOUR
WORKING WITH QUANTITIES OF DATA

9

Data Tables

OBJECTIVES

After studying this chapter, you will be able to

1. Describe a table and tell the advantage of its use in data processing.
2. Describe the method of referencing data stored in a table.
3. List the steps in searching a table for given data.
4. Explain how tables are created with BASIC.
5. Explain how data is entered into a table and printed from a table.
6. Write programs using tables to store data.

TOPIC 9.1 USING TABLES TO STORE DATA

In previous chapters, a separate variable has been used for each data item, which has made writing programs dealing with large quantities of data cumbersome. The use of tables makes the planning and coding of such programs much easier.

WHAT IS A TABLE?

A **table** is a variable that can store more than one piece of data at a time. A regular variable can hold only one piece of data at a time.

The organization of tables is shown in Figure 9-1. Observe that the tables are just lists of data items. Each item is stored in one row of the list. The rows are numbered starting with 0. Individual data items stored in a table are referred to as **elements**.

	Table B
Row 0	319
Row 1	126
Row 2	293

	Table X$
Row 0	ATLANTA
Row 1	CHICAGO
Row 2	DALLAS
Row 3	SAN FRANCISCO

Figure 9-1 Organization of Tables

The use of tables makes many programming assignments easier. For example, consider a program to store and print out names. Without tables, each name would have to be stored in a separate variable. If there were 25 names, you would have to use 25 variables, which would require at least 25 program statements to get the names into the variables. With tables, all names can be stored in the same variable name, thus greatly reducing the amount of coding required.

REFERENCING DATA IN A TABLE

Refer to Figure 9-1 as you study this paragraph. Remember that each individual location in a table is called a row, while each value stored in each row is an element. If you refer to row 0 in table B, you find element 0, which is the number 319. Element 1, which is found in row 1, is 126. Element 2 is 293 and is stored in row 2. The number of the row or element being referred to is known as the **subscript**. In BASIC, subscripts are written inside parentheses. Therefore, a reference to row 0 of table B is written as B(0), row 1 is B(1), and row 2 is B(2). B(0) has a value of 319, B(1) has a value of 126, and B(2) has a value of 293. In table X$, X$(0) contains

ATLANTA, X$(1) contains CHICAGO, X$(2) contains DALLAS, and X$(3) contains SAN FRANCISCO.

A table can also be referred to as an **array** or **matrix**. In mathematics, there are differences in the meanings of the words. In programming, however, the terms may be used interchangeably.

SEARCHING A TABLE

Many computer applications require the **searching** of a table. Searching a table means looking up a desired value. For example, a state police department may have stored (in a computer) a table of license numbers of stolen automobiles. When an officer stops a suspicious car, the officer can instruct the computer to search the table to see if the car is listed as stolen.

Many table searches are done sequentially—that is, the computer examines the first element of the table and if it is not the desired one, the next element is examined. This process continues until the desired value is found or the end of the table is reached. If a match has not been made when the computer searches to the end of the table, the desired value is not in the table. When the value is not found, the program should print an appropriate message or take appropriate action.

TWO-DIMENSIONAL TABLES

The tables you have examined so far consist of several rows, but just one column; therefore, they can be thought of as **one-dimensional tables**. However, a table may have several columns. Tables that have more than one row and more than one column are known as **two-dimensional tables**—that is, they have rows and more than one column.

As with one-dimensional tables, items in a two-dimensional table are referred to with subscripts. Now, however, there will be two subscripts rather than one. The first subscript will refer to the row, the second to the column. Examine the two-dimensional table of names and phone numbers in Figure 9-2 for an example. KATHY can be located at PEOPLE$(0,0), while her phone number is located at PEOPLE$(0,1). GREG's name is located at PEOPLE$(1,0), while his phone number is located at PEOPLE$(1,1). Element PEOPLE$(2,0) is the name LEA, while element PEOPLE$(2,1) is the phone number 689-3572.

Table PEOPLE$

	Column 0	Column 1
Row 0	KATHY	987-3987
Row 1	GREG	431-9873
Row 2	LEA	689-3572

Figure 9-2 Two-Dimensional Table

REVIEW QUESTIONS

1. Describe how a one-dimensional table is organized. Describe how a two-dimensional table is organized. (Obj. 1)
2. Why does the use of tables make programming easier? (Obj. 1)
3. What is a subscript? (Obj. 2)
4. What is an element? (Obj. 2)
5. How are subscripts written when using a one-dimensional table? A two-dimensional table? (Obj. 2)
6. Explain how a computer sequentially searches a one-dimensional table. (Obj. 3)

TOPIC 9.2 WRITING PROGRAMS USING TABLES

When programming in BASIC, tables may be used with any keywords with which regular variables may be used—that is, keywords such as LET, READ, INPUT, and PRINT may refer to tables. The only difference is that the table name must include a subscript in parentheses. This tells the computer which element to READ or PRINT for instance.

CREATING A TABLE

Before data can be placed in a table by a BASIC program, the table must be created. Creation of a table sets aside computer memory for storing the data in the table. Tables used by BASIC may be created to hold numeric data or character data. Numeric tables must contain only numbers. Character tables may hold what is sometimes known as alphanumeric data. **Alphanumeric data** consists of any letters, numbers, or symbols that can be entered into the computer. The same table may not be used to hold both numeric and character data. Tables are given names based on the same rules used when naming regular variables. As with regular variables, the table name is followed by a dollar sign ($) if the table is to hold character and/or alphanumeric data.

A program may use a regular variable and a table with the same name. Although a program will not confuse them, it is a good idea to keep these names different.

Creation of a table is also known as **dimensioning** the table. It is done with the keyword **DIM**, which is short for dimension.

General Form: *line number* DIM *table name* (*size or sizes*)

Example: `100 DIM NAM$(10)`

The number in parentheses tells the computer the largest subscript that may be used when referring to data in the table. In the example, the 10 in parentheses means that the largest possible subscript is 10. Since the smallest subscript is 0, a total of 11 elements may be stored in the table that has been dimensioned. Since only one number was contained in the parentheses, a one-dimensional table has been defined. For a two-dimensional table, two numbers would appear in parentheses:

Example:

```
100 DIM NAM$(10,1)
```

In this example, the 10 indicates that the maximum row subscript is 10, while the 1 means the maximum column subscript is 1. Therefore, the table can hold a maximum of 11 rows (subscripts 0 through 11) and two columns (subscripts 0 and 1).

When dimensioning a table, the number or numbers in parentheses may be expressed as a constant, as was done in the examples. Alternately, they may be expressed as numeric variables or numeric expressions. When a numeric table is dimensioned, it is automatically filled with zeros. When a character table is dimensioned, it is automatically filled with **nulls** ("nothings").

The DIM statement may be placed anywhere in the program before the table is used the first time. A good practice, however, is to place the DIM statement near the beginning of the program.

If desired, more than one table may be created with the same DIM statement.

Example:

```
50 DIM NAM$(25,1),IDNUM(25)
```

This example creates two tables, a two-dimensional character table named NAM$ and a one-dimensional numeric table named IDNUM. Table NAM$ is a character table whose last row is 25. Its row subscripts are 0 through 25, for a total of 26 rows. It has column subscripts of 0 and 1, for a total of two columns. One of its columns might be designated to hold last names, while the other could hold first names. Table IDNUM is a numeric table whose last element is also 25, for a total of 26 elements (0 through 25). Even though multiple tables dimensioned on the same line frequently contain the same number of elements, this is not a requirement. For example, one table could have a maximum subscript of 10, while another could have a maximum subscript of 50.

GETTING INDIVIDUAL ELEMENTS INTO A TABLE

Once a table has been created, data may be stored in it with any of the keywords used with regular variables. LET, READ, and INPUT, for example, may all be used normally. Simply place a subscript after the name of the table variable to tell the computer the number of the row and/or column in which the element should be placed. You may use constants, numeric variables, or numeric expressions when stating the row and/or column subscripts.

As an example, the number 328 could be stored in row 6 of table A with any of the following lines:

Examples:

```
60 A(6)=328 ←———— Direct assignment with LET statement.
```

```
60 READ A(6) ←———— Read the value from a DATA line.
70 DATA 328
```

```
60 INPUT A(6) ←—— Get the number from the keyboard with INPUT.
```

For examples using a two-dimensional table, examine the following lines. They will all place the name "KIM" in row 12, column 1 of table NAM$:

Examples:

```
60 NAM$(12,1)="KIM"  ←—— Direct assignment with LET statement.
```

```
60 READ NAM$(12,1)  ←—— Read the data from a DATA line.
70 DATA KIM
```

```
60 INPUT NAM$(12,1)  ←— Get the data from the keyboard with INPUT.
```

PRINTING INDIVIDUAL ELEMENTS FROM A TABLE

All the keywords and functions used for printing regular variables may also be used with tables. As with storing data in a table, include subscripts in parentheses to indicate the element to print. For a one-dimensional table, there will be one subscript value. For a two-dimensional table, there will be two subscript values. The following examples show two methods for printing the number stored in row 6 of table A.

Examples:

```
80 PRINT A(6)  ←—— Prints at left margin.
```

```
80 PRINT TAB(20);A(6)  ←—— Moves over to column 20 to print.
```

An example of printing the value from the twelfth row and first column of table NAM$ follows:

Example:

```
80 PRINT NAM$(12,1)
```

While these examples have all used constants as the subscript values, numeric variables are frequently used.

PERFORMING CALCULATIONS WITH TABLES

Any element in a numeric table may be used as part of an arithmetic calculation. Again, simply write the subscript value(s) after the table name to indicate which element to use.

Examples:

```
100 X=A(3)+A(7)  ←——  Adds the third and seventh elements of
                      table A and places the sum in variable X.
```

```
100 A(9)=A(2)*3  ←——  Multiplies the second element of table
                      A times the constant 3 and places the
                      product in row 9 of the table.
```

```
100 PRINT A(2,3)^2  ←——  Prints the square of the number stored
                         in row 2, column 3 of table A.
```

USING LOOPS TO PROCESS ENTIRE TABLES

One of the primary advantages of using tables is that the entire table may be processed with very little coding. This is accomplished by using loops. Consider the following program that creates tables and fills them with names and ages from DATA lines:

Example:

```
40 DIM NAM$(5),AGE(5)  ←——  Dimensions two tables with
                            rows 0 through 5.
50 FOR ROW=0 TO 5  ←——  Starts FOR . . . NEXT loop with
                        ROW counter going from 0 to 5.
60    READ NAM$(ROW),AGE(ROW)  ←——  Reads a name and age from a
                                    DATA line into the row of the
                                    tables.
70 NEXT ROW  ←——  Increments variable ROW and
                  runs the loop again if ROW has
                  not exceeded its ending value
                  of 5.
200 DATA ALVAREX,15  ←——  Provides DATA lines from
210 DATA ARGO,14          which names and ages are read
220 DATA MORRIS,17        into the tables.
```

```
230 DATA OKANO,16
240 DATA ROGERS,13
250 DATA VANDERSLICE,15
```

If desired, an INPUT statement could have been used on line 60 and the DATA lines omitted. This would allow entry of the names and ages from the keyboard.

To print the contents of a table, a loop may also be used. The following lines, when added to the previous program, will print the names and ages after the tables are filled.

Example:

```
80 FOR R=0 TO 5
90     PRINT NAM$(R),AGE(R)
100 NEXT R
```

Note that it was not necessary to use the same counter variable when printing as was used when filling the table. However, the same variable could have been used if desired.

SEARCHING A TABLE

Once data has been placed into a table, the table may be searched to locate particular information. This is done by means of an IF . . . THEN statement inside a loop. Examine a program that fills a table with numbers from DATA lines. It allows the person running the program to guess whether certain numbers are in the table.

Example:

```
40 DIM N(10) <------------------ Dimensions table N.
50 FOR R=0 TO 10 <-------------- Fills the table with numbers from DATA line.
60     READ N(R)
70 NEXT R
80 INPUT "WHAT NUMBER DO YOU GUESS";GUESS <------ Gets user's guess.
90 FOR R=0 TO 10 <------------------------------ Starts search loop.
100    IF N(R)=GUESS THEN MESSAGE$="YOU <--- Puts congratulatory message in
       GOT ONE!":GOTO 130                     variable and exits loop if
                                              number is found.
```

```
110 NEXT R ←—————— Repeats loop.
120 MESSAGE$="SORRY!" ←—— If the loop runs all the way from 0 through 10 and
                          the guessed number is not found, control will "fall
                          through" to this line, where the "not found"
                          message is placed in a variable.
130 PRINT MESSAGE$ ←—— Prints the message variable to tell user
                       whether a number was guessed correctly.
140 GOTO 80 ←—————— Repeats for another guess.
200 DATA 4,27,51,49,96,67,73,89,32,48,13 ←—— DATA line.
```

As an example of using a two-dimensional table, consider a character or string table containing two columns. The first column will contain a word, while the second column contains a definition. When a word is entered by the operator, it will be looked up in column 1 and its definition from column 2 will be printed.

Example:

```
40 DIM WORD$(10,1) ←—————— Dimensions table.
50 FOR R=0 TO 10
60     READ WORD$(R,0),WORD$(R,1) ←—— Fills both columns from DATA lines.
70 NEXT R
80 INPUT "ENTER THE WORD TO LOOK UP:   ";LOOK$ ←—— Gets word from user.
90 FOR R=0 TO 10 ←—————— Starts loop.
100    IF WORD$(R,0)=LOOK$ THEN
       PRINT WORD$(R,1):GOTO 130 ←—— Checks word and prints definition.
110 NEXT R
120 PRINT "NOT FOUND" ←—————— Executes this line if not found.
130 PRINT
140 GOTO 80 ←—————— Repeats loop for next word.
150 END
200 DATA CENTNER, GERMAN UNIT OF WEIGHT
210 DATA DILL, A PLANT OF THE CARROT FAMILY
220 DATA DRUMSTICK, PART OF A CHICKEN LEG
230 DATA GOWNSMAN, AN ACADEMIC
240 DATA LEVOROTATORY, ROTATING COUNTERCLOCKWISE
250 DATA NOVITIATE, A NOVICE
260 DATA QUESTIONARY, A GROUP OF QUESTIONS
270 DATA RODENTIATE, USE A MOUSE
280 DATA SCEPTER, A ROYAL STAFF
290 DATA SPIROGYRA, A GREEN ALGAE
300 DATA ZINKENITE, A GRAY MINERAL
```

EXAMPLE PROGRAM

Assume you are to operate a summer employment clearing house for students in your school. Students with skills in yard work, maintenance, babysitting, and pet grooming have signed up. When a person in the community calls the clearing house and requests someone to do one of these jobs, you look up the names of persons specializing in that job and give a name and phone number to the caller.

You decide to use the computer to keep your list current. The computer program must be able to (1) read the student worker information into tables, (2) print out a master list of all student workers, and (3) look up potential employees when employers call for workers. A student will be recommended to only one prospective employer per day. These three functions can be translated into a hierarchy chart for your program as shown in Figure 9-3.

You decide to keep three items of information for each student worker: (1) name, (2) work specialty, and (3) phone number. For each of these items a table will be used. Figure 9-4 gives an example of what the first four rows of the tables might contain. Notice that the specialties are abbreviated to the first letter of the job. Whenever a student is recommended for employment, the specialty code will be removed from the table. This will prevent recommendation of persons already working.

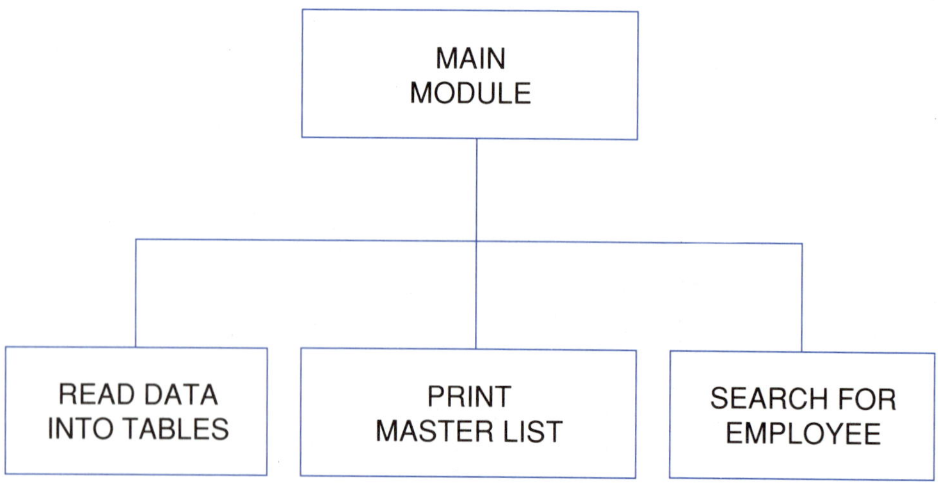

Figure 9-3 Hierarchy Chart

Table NAM$	Table SPEC$	Table TELE$
SAM ALLEN	B	983-2383
KATHY BRYAN	M	378-3243
MARY SPEIR	Y	298-3478
KENT KIMES	P	762-9873

Note: Table SPEC$ indicates the kind of work a student wishes to do: B = babysitting, M = maintenance, P = pet grooming, and Y = yard work.

Figure 9-4 Sample Table Contents

Next, you must complete the program documentation sheet (see Figure 9-5) and the spacing chart (see Figure 9-6). TRS-80 Model III users should use percent signs rather than backslashes when setting up PRINT USING images.

PROGRAM DOCUMENTATION SHEET		
Program: C9E1	Programmer: STUDENT NAME	Date: 3-19-xx
Purpose: This program keeps records for a summer job clearing house. It stores information on workers and looks up the name and phone number of persons qualified for various work.		
Input: Worker data from DATA lines; type of worker desired from INPUT statement.	Output: Master list and individual referrals on CRT.	
Data Terminator: EOD		

Figure 9-5 Program Documentation Sheet

Variables Used:

NAM$() = Table of worker names
SPEC$() = Table of worker specialties
B = Babysitting
M = Maintenance
P = Pet grooming
Y = Yard work
TELE$() = Table of phone numbers

NAM$, SPEC$, TELE$ are "Work" variables used for counting the number of persons on the list of work desired by a customer.

ROW = Counter variable for FOR . . . NEXT loops
N = Number of persons in tables
CHOICE = Number of choice chosen from main menu
Z = Number of persons recommended for work
Z$ = "Work" variable used with pause input

Figure 9-5 (continued)

Following completion of the program documentation sheets and the spacing chart, module documentation sheets are prepared. These are shown in Figures 9-7 through 9-10, along with the BASIC code written from them.

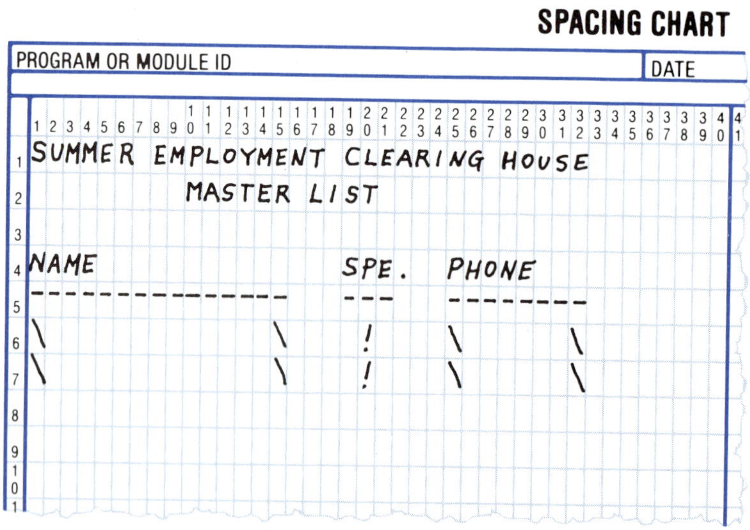

Figure 9-6 Spacing Chart

MODULE DOCUMENTATION SHEET	
Program: C9E1	Module: MAIN Lines: 10-999

Module Description: This is the main module.

Module Function (Program Design):

1. Clear memory space for character data. (TRS-80 Model III)
2. Perform "Read Data Into Tables" module.
3. Print list of program options (print master list, search for employee, stop) on screen.
4. Get user's choice of option.
5. Depending on user's choice, perform either "Print Master List" module, "Search for Employee" module, or stop.
6. Go to step 3 to get next choice of option.

```
10 'C9E1
20 'STUDENT NAME, CHAPTER 9, EXAMPLE 1
30 'THIS PROGRAM HANDLES SUMMER EMPLOYMENT REFERRALS
40 '*************************
50 '* MAIN MODULE           *
60 '*************************
70 'ON TRS-80 MOD III USE 70 CLEAR 1000
80 GOSUB 1000 'READ DATA INTO TABLES
90 CLS
100 PRINT "SUMMER EMPLOYMENT CLEARING HOUSE"
110 PRINT "    MAIN MENU"
120 PRINT
130 PRINT "1 - PRINT MASTER LIST"
140 PRINT "2 - SEARCH FOR EMPLOYEE"
150 PRINT "3 - STOP"
160 PRINT
170 INPUT "CHOICE";CHOICE
180 CLS
190 ON CHOICE GOSUB 2000,3000,999
200 GOTO 90
999 END
```

Figure 9-7 Documentation Sheet and Code for Main Module

Lines 1030 through 1050 read through all the data to count the number of rows needed in tables; then the DATA lines are restored in line 1060. The tables are dimensioned to the needed sizes in line 1070, and data is read into them in lines 1080

MODULE DOCUMENTATION SHEET

Program: C9E1	Module: READ DATA INTO TABLES Lines: 1000-1999

Module Description: Counts the number of data items, dimension tables, and reads data into tables.

Module Function (Program Design):

1. Count the number of persons on DATA lines.
2. Restore the data pointer.
3. Dimension tables NAM$, SPEC$, and TELE$ to hold the number of persons who were counted on the DATA lines.
4. Read the data items into the tables.

```
1000 ' ************************
1010 ' * READ DATA MODULE     *
1020 ' ************************
1030 N=0
1040 READ NAM$,SPEC$,TELE$
1050 IF NAM$<>"EOD" THEN N=N+1:GOTO 1040
1060 RESTORE
1070 DIM NAM$(N),SPEC$(N),TELE$(N)
1080 FOR ROW=1 TO N
1090     READ NAM$(ROW),SPEC$(ROW),TELE$(ROW)
1100 NEXT ROW
1999 RETURN
```

Figure 9-8 Documentation Sheet and Code for Read Data Module

through 1100. If you desire, you can dimension the tables using a constant value, such as 100. If you do, be sure to use a size large enough to handle all the data you plan to enter on DATA lines.

MODULE DOCUMENTATION SHEET	
Program: C9E1	Module: PRINT MASTER LIST Lines: 2000-2999
Module Description: Prints master list of all workers.	
Module Function (Program Design): 1. Print heading on report. 2. Loop through tables printing detail lines on report.	

```
2000 ' ************************
2010 ' * PRINT MASTER LIST     *
2020 ' ************************
2030 PRINT "SUMMER EMPLOYMENT CLEARING HOUSE"
2040 PRINT "   MASTER LIST"
2050 PRINT
2060 PRINT "NAME";TAB(20);"SPE.";TAB(25);"PHONE"
2070 PRINT "----";TAB(20);"----";TAB(25);"-----"
2080 FOR ROW=1 TO N
2090    PRINT NAM$(ROW);TAB(20);SPEC$(ROW);TAB(25);TELE$(ROW)
2100 NEXT ROW
2110 PRINT
2120 INPUT "...PRESS RETURN TO CONTINUE";Z$
2999 RETURN
```

Figure 9-9 Documentation Sheet and Code for Print Master List Module

MODULE DOCUMENTATION SHEET	
Program: C9E1	Module: SEARCH FOR EMPLOYEE Lines: 3000-3999
Module Description: Searches for and prints the name and phone number of a worker who has the skill desired by a caller.	
Module Function (Program Design): 1. Get code of skill needed by caller. 2. If code is "EOD", then return. 3. Search the specialty table looking for the code. When it is found, print student's row number, name, and phone. Continue through entire table so all students with the requested code will be printed. 4. Get the row number of the student who is being recommended. Remove the specialty code from his or her row in the table.	

```
3000 ' ***************************
3010 ' * SEARCH FOR EMPLOYEE      *
3020 ' ***************************
3030 PRINT "ENTER CODE OF SPECIALTY DESIRED:"
3040 PRINT "B = BABYSITTING"
3050 PRINT "M = MAINTENANCE"
3060 PRINT "P = PET GROOMING"
3070 PRINT "Y = YARD WORK"
3080 PRINT
3090 INPUT "CODE (EOD TO END) ";CHOICE$
3100 IF CHOICE$="EOD" THEN 3999
3110 PRINT
3120 IF CHOICE$<>"B" AND CHOICE$<>"M" AND CHOICE$<>"P"
AND CHOICE$<>"Y" THEN 3090
3130 FOR ROW=1 TO N
3140     IF SPEC$(ROW)=CHOICE$ THEN PRINT
ROW;TAB(5);NAM$(ROW);TAB(20);TELE$(ROW)
3150 NEXT ROW
3160 PRINT
```

Figure 9-10 Documentation Sheet and Code for Search for Employee Module

```
3170 INPUT "NUMBER OF PERSON RECOMMENDED (OR 0) ";Z
3180 SPEC$(Z)=""
3999 RETURN
```

Figure 9-10 (continued)

Here is the entire program as planned and coded, including sample DATA lines beginning at line 4000. Because the DATA lines are at the end of the program and the tables are dimensioned as large as needed for all the data, the program can handle as many student workers as desired.

Example:

```
10 ' C9E1
20 ' STUDENT NAME, CHAPTER 9, EXAMPLE 1
30 ' THIS PROGRAM HANDLES SUMMER EMPLOYMENT REFERRALS
40 ' **********************
50 ' * MAIN MODULE        *
60 ' **********************
70 ' ON TRS-80 MOD III USE 70 CLEAR 1000
80 GOSUB 1000   ' READ DATA INTO TABLES
90 CLS
100 PRINT "SUMMER EMPLOYMENT CLEARING HOUSE"
110 PRINT "    MAIN MENU"
120 PRINT
130 PRINT "1 - PRINT MASTER LIST"
140 PRINT "2 - SEARCH FOR EMPLOYEE"
150 PRINT "3 - STOP"
160 PRINT
170 INPUT "CHOICE";CHOICE
180 CLS
190 ON CHOICE GOSUB 2000,3000,999
200 GOTO 90
999 END
1000 ' ***********************
1010 ' * READ DATA MODULE     *
1020 ' ***********************
1030 N=0
1040 READ NAM$,SPEC$,TELE$
1050 IF NAM$<>"EOD" THEN N=N+1:GOTO 1040
1060 RESTORE
1070 DIM NAM$(N),SPEC$(N),TELE$(N)
1080 FOR ROW=1 TO N
```

```
1090    READ NAM$(ROW),SPEC$(ROW),TELE$(ROW)
1100 NEXT ROW
1999 RETURN
2000 ' ************************
2010 ' * PRINT MASTER LIST     *
2020 ' ************************
2030 PRINT "SUMMER EMPLOYMENT CLEARING HOUSE"
2040 PRINT "    MASTER LIST"
2050 PRINT
2060 PRINT "NAME";TAB(20);"SPE.";TAB(25);"PHONE"
2070 PRINT "----";TAB(20);"----";TAB(25);"-----"
2080 FOR ROW=1 TO N
2090    PRINT NAM$(ROW);TAB(20);SPEC$(ROW);TAB(25);TELE$(ROW)
2100 NEXT ROW
2110 PRINT
2120 INPUT "...PRESS RETURN TO CONTINUE";Z$
2999 RETURN
3000 ' *************************
3010 ' * SEARCH FOR EMPLOYEE    *
3020 ' *************************
3030 PRINT "ENTER CODE OF SPECIALTY DESIRED:"
3040 PRINT "B = BABYSITTING"
3050 PRINT "M = MAINTENANCE"
3060 PRINT "P = PET GROOMING"
3070 PRINT "Y = YARD WORK"
3080 PRINT
3090 INPUT "CODE (EOD TO END) ";CHOICE$
3100 IF CHOICE$="EOD" THEN 3999
3110 PRINT
3120 IF CHOICE$<>"B" AND CHOICE$<>"M" AND CHOICE$<>"P" AND
     CHOICE$<>"Y" THEN 3090
3130 FOR ROW=1 TO N
3140    IF SPEC$(ROW)=CHOICE$ THEN PRINT ROW;TAB(5);NAM$(ROW);
     TAB(20);TELE$(ROW)
3150 NEXT ROW
3160 PRINT
3170 INPUT "NUMBER OF PERSON RECOMMENDED (OR 0) ";Z
3180 SPEC$(Z)=""
3999 RETURN
4000 DATA SAM ALLEN,B,983-2383
4010 DATA KATHY BRYAN,M,378-3243
4020 DATA MARY SPEIR,Y,298-3478
4030 DATA KENT KIMES,P,762-9873
```

```
4040 DATA SANCHEZ VANN,Y,322-3389
4050 DATA KEN CSINISEK,M,231-4983
4999 DATA EOD,EOD,EOD
```

This program used separate tables for each of the different kinds of data. However, the three character tables could be combined into a single two-dimensional table of three columns. The only difference in the processing, then, would be that each reference to the table would use both row and column subscript values, with the column value indicating the type of data (name, specialty, telephone). Study the following listing of the program using a two-dimensional table. Statements that have been changed from the previous version are in bold to make them easy to identify.

Example:

```
10 ' C9E2
20 ' STUDENT NAME, CHAPTER 9, EXAMPLE 2
30 ' THIS PROGRAM HANDLES SUMMER EMPLOYMENT REFERRALS
40 ' **********************
50 ' * MAIN MODULE        *
60 ' **********************
70 ' ON TRS-80 MOD III USE 70 CLEAR 1000
80 GOSUB 1000   ' READ DATA INTO TABLES
90 CLS
100 PRINT "SUMMER EMPLOYMENT CLEARING HOUSE"
110 PRINT "    MAIN MENU"
120 PRINT
130 PRINT "1 - PRINT MASTER LIST"
140 PRINT "2 - SEARCH FOR EMPLOYEE"
150 PRINT "3 - STOP"
160 PRINT
170 INPUT "CHOICE";CHOICE
180 CLS
190 ON CHOICE GOSUB 2000,3000,999
200 GOTO 90
999 END
1000 ' ***********************
1010 ' * READ DATA MODULE     *
1020 ' ***********************
1030 N=0
```

```
1040 READ NAM$,SPEC$,TELE$
1050 IF NAM$<>"EOD" THEN N=N+1:GOTO 1040
1060 RESTORE
1070 DIM NAM$(N,2)          ←—— Dimensions table with three columns.
1080 FOR ROW=1 TO N
1090    READ NAM$(ROW,0),NAM$(ROW,1),NAM$(ROW,2)   ←—— Reads data into
1100 NEXT ROW                                            three columns
1999 RETURN                                              of same table.
2000 ' ************************
2010 ' * PRINT MASTER LIST     *
2020 ' ************************
2030 PRINT "SUMMER EMPLOYMENT CLEARING HOUSE"
2040 PRINT "   MASTER LIST"
2050 PRINT
2060 PRINT "NAME";TAB(20);"SPE.";TAB(25);"PHONE"
2070 PRINT "----";TAB(20);"----";TAB(25);"-----"
2080 FOR ROW=1 TO N
2090    PRINT NAM$(ROW,0);TAB(20);NAM$(ROW,1);TAB(25);NAM$(ROW,2)
2100 NEXT ROW
2110 PRINT
2120 INPUT "...PRESS RETURN TO CONTINUE";Z$
2999 RETURN
3000 ' *************************
3010 ' * SEARCH FOR EMPLOYEE    *
3020 ' *************************
3030 PRINT "ENTER CODE OF SPECIALTY DESIRED:"
3040 PRINT "B = BABYSITTING"
3050 PRINT "M = MAINTENANCE"
3060 PRINT "P = PET GROOMING"
3070 PRINT "Y = YARD WORK"
3080 PRINT
3090 INPUT "CODE (EOD TO END) ";CHOICE$
3100 IF CHOICE$="EOD" THEN 3999
3110 PRINT
3120 IF CHOICE$<>"B" AND CHOICE$<>"M" AND CHOICE$<>"P" AND
     CHOICE$<>"Y" THEN 3090
3130 FOR ROW=1 TO N
3140    IF NAM$(ROW,1)=CHOICE$ THEN PRINT ROW;TAB(5);NAM$(ROW,0);
     TAB(20);NAM$(ROW,2)
3150 NEXT ROW
3160 PRINT
3170 INPUT "NUMBER OF PERSON RECOMMENDED (OR 0) ";Z
3180 NAM$(Z,1)=""
3999 RETURN
```

```
4000 DATA SAM ALLEN,B,983-2383
4010 DATA KATHY BRYAN,M,378-3243
4020 DATA MARY SPEIR,Y,298-3478
4030 DATA KENT KIMES,P,762-9873
4040 DATA SANCHEZ VANN,Y,322-3389
4050 DATA KEN CSINISEK,M,231-4983
4999 DATA EOD,EOD,EOD
```

REVIEW QUESTIONS

1. Describe how a dimension statement is written. What differences are there between one-dimensional and two-dimensional arrays? (Obj. 4)
2. With what numbers are numeric tables automatically filled when dimensioned? (Obj. 4)
3. With what characters are character tables automatically filled when dimensioned? (Obj. 4)
4. List two kinds of statements that may be used for getting data into tables. (Obj. 5)
5. Why are subscripts placed after the names of tables? (Obj. 5)
6. Explain how a loop may be used to fill an entire table with data or to print the contents of an entire file. (Obj. 5)

VOCABULARY WORDS

The following terms were introduced in this chapter:

array	nulls	subscript
dimensioning	one-dimensional tables	table
elements	searching	two-dimensional tables
matrix		

KEYWORD

The following keyword was introduced in this chapter:

DIM

PROGRAMS TO WRITE

For each of the following programs, prepare the necessary documentation prior to writing the BASIC code. Although it is possible to write some of the programs without using tables, you should use one or more tables in each program.

Program 1

A concert is being sponsored by your organization. Ticket prices are based on the section of the arena in which the seats are located. Prices are $18.00 in section 1, $15.00 in section 2, $12.00 in section 3, and $8.00 in section 4. Write a program that will be used when selling tickets to the concert. Read the prices into rows 1 through 4 of a table (ignore row 0). Have the user input the section number desired and the number of tickets needed. The computer should use the price from the table to calculate the total amount for the tickets and display it. The program should continue running for one customer after the next. To test the program use four customers. The first customer requests 2 tickets in section 1, the second requests 5 tickets in section 4, the third requests 6 tickets in section 3, and the fourth requests 4 tickets in section 2.

Program 2

A local delivery company bases its charges on delivery zones. The city has been divided into four districts based on distance. For each district, there is a different charge per pound. Write a program that asks for the district number (1 through 4) and the weight of the shipment. The program then looks in a table to find the base rate for the district and multiplies this base rate times the weight (rounded to the nearest pound) to get the delivery charge, which should be displayed on the screen. Base rates for districts 1 through 4 are $5.00, $7.00, $10.00, and $12.00, respectively. Consider modifying Program 1 to complete this assignment. Use the following data: zone 4, 2.6 pounds; zone 1, 3.1 pounds; zone 3, 7 pounds; and zone 2, .9 pounds.

Program 3

A miniature golf emporium is conducting a tournament. As each player completes a round, his or her name and city are placed in a two-dimensional character table, while the score is placed in a one-dimensional numeric table. At the end of the tournament, the names and scores of all players are printed. There may be up to 20 players in a tournament. For testing purposes, use the following player data: Myra Locks, San Antonio, 36; Larry Byron, Euliss, 41; Mack Morris, Gary, 27; and Mary White, Alexandria, 34.

Program 4

Different parts of a metropolitan area are served by different cable television companies. Each company uses different channels to transmit programs. For example, broadcast channel 8 comes in on channel 5 on some cable systems, channel 2 on others, and channel 27 on still others. In addition, there are cable channels that are not broadcast locally. Because of this wide variety, the daily newspaper prints only the original channel number (6 in this example) or name of the cable channel in its television listings. Write a program that will allow a viewer to enter the original channel number or cable channel name from the television listing and receive a display of the cable channel to which he or she should tune the set. The call letters or name of the channel should also be printed. The numbers or abbreviations as published in the listing, the channel to tune to, and the name are as follows:

PUBLISHED	TUNE TO	NAME
8	23	WKEA
3	11	KXC
7	28	KBLR
21	17	WQRX
OEN	5	Original Entertainment Network
THC	9	TV Hit Classics Network

Since some of the published channels are numbers and some are letters, store this data in a character table; the names can be stored in a second column of this same table. The "tune to" numbers can be stored in a numeric table or in the third column of the same table. To test your program, enter the published channels in reverse order, verifying that the correct "tune to" and name data is printed.

Program 5

Many states impose a sales tax. Usually the tax is stated as a percentage of the selling price of merchandise. Sometimes, however, the cents portion of sales cannot be accurately calculated by a simple multiplication. For example, the tax brackets in one state might be 1 cent on sales up through 11 cents, 3 cents on sales of 12 through 35 cents, 4 cents on sales of 36 through 65 cents, and 5 cents on sales of 66 through 99 cents. The tax on whole dollars would be 5 percent. Write a program that will store the fractional dollar tax brackets in a two-dimensional table. Then, when the salesperson enters the total amount of a sale, the program will compute the tax. The whole dollar amount will be multiplied by 5 percent, while the cents portion will be looked up in the table. These two amounts are added to determine the total amount of tax. In writing the program, use the tax brackets described earlier in this program. To test the program, enter sales of $7.11, $98.66, $132.12, $3.65, and $9.36.

Program 6

A common responsibility of receptionists in offices is to answer the phone and connect calls with the desired person. However, there are occasions when persons are out of their offices, involved in conferences, or for some other reason cannot answer the phone. The receptionist should know about such circumstances so that the situation can be explained to callers.

Write a program that will read all employees' names into the first column of a two-dimensional table. It should then use the second column to record from the keyboard whenever an employee is out or unavailable. When a caller asks for a person, the receptionist keys the first few letters of the person's name into the computer. The computer finds the name, checks the matching column, and prints the person's status. An "in" message will indicate that the person is available, while any other message will indicate unavailability. Employees White, Jones, Brogdon, Smithfield, Murphy, and Bryan have "in" status when the program run is started. Use the following actions in the order presented to test your program:

1. A call comes in for Brogdon.
2. Smithfield says he will be in conference.
3. Brogdon leaves for a meeting.
4. A call comes in for Smithfield.
5. A call comes in for Brogdon.
6. A call comes in for Smithfield.
7. Smithfield says he is out of conference.
8. A call comes in for Murphy.
9. A call comes in for Smithfield.

Program 7

Write a program that will code and decode secret messages. Here's how a message will be coded. The message that is input from the keyboard will be converted letter by letter to ASCII code. Then the code will be transformed by reference to a corresponding code in another coded table and that code will be converted into a printable character. The decoding process will be the reverse of this. As an example, let's examine the coding of the letter C. First, the letter C is converted to its ASCII code, which is 67 (see Figure 9-11). Then the corresponding arbitrary code number is read from the table. In this case, that code is 82. Assume that this arbitrary code number is an ASCII code and convert it into a printable character. Although the arbitrary codes can be any numbers that produce printable characters (be sure to use each number only once), use the codes from Figure 9-11 to test your program. By using different codes in the table, messages will be encoded differently.

CHARACTER	ASCII	CORRESPONDING CODE
space	32	56
A	65	70
B	66	36
C	67	82
D	68	73
E	69	86
F	70	38
G	71	84
H	72	71
I	73	79
J	74	74
K	75	85
L	76	47
M	77	83
N	78	72
O	79	80
P	80	42
Q	81	76
R	82	88
S	83	66
T	84	67
U	85	43
V	86	87
W	87	89
X	88	68
Y	89	77
Z	90	75

Figure 9-11 Code Conversion Table

The program should be written so that the user indicates via a menu choice whether to code or decode. Then the original or encoded form of the message is entered with the output being produced. To test your program, first encode, then decode, the message "THIS IS MY SECRET CODE".

Program 8

Write a program that the state police can use to check for stolen automobiles. Read the license numbers of stolen cars into a table from DATA lines. Into a matching table (or a second column of the same table), read the descriptions of the cars. When a license number is entered from the keyboard, the program should search the table for it. If it is found, print the description of the car. If it is not found, print a "NOT REPORTED STOLEN" message. The program should continue running for one inquiry after another. Additionally, there should be the capability to display a list of all stolen cars whenever desired. Read the following data into the table(s):

GNP615, 1986 Camaro, Blue

I2SEE, 1981 Eldorado, Yellow

XR4CP, 1989 Fiero, Red

BMP832,1989 Ciera, Blue

DE3983, 1985 Rabbit, Orange

HIYO, 1988 Bronco II, Silver

To test the program, enter license plate numbers of BMP832, WYS312, BMM382, and HIYO.

Program 9

An automobile dealer wants to use the computer to calculate the price of new cars for customers. To do this, the computer must have stored the base price of each model as well as the price of each option. The salesperson enters into the computer the code for the model desired and the codes for the options desired. After the entry of each code, an updated price printout should be displayed in a format similar to the following:

Code	*Item*	*Price*
GXS	GX SPORTS SEDAN	16,483.41
AC	AIR CONDITIONING	948.53
PSS	EXTENDED SOUND SYSTEM	650.32
	TOTAL PRICE	18,082.26

The program should be written so that the salesperson can change the vehicle model and add or delete options as frequently as desired, receiving an updated display after each change.

The following data should be included in tables:

	GX 4-DOOR SEDAN (CODE GX4)	GX SPORTS SEDAN (CODE GXS)	GX CONVERTIBLE (CODE GXC)
Base Price	11,431.21	13,987.39	16,483.41
Air Conditioning (AC)	948.53	948.53	948.53
Premium Sound System (PSS)	1,210.27	847.12	650.32
Automatic Transmission (AT)	427.50	427.50	0.00
Ultra Wheels (UL)	600.00	400.00	200.00
Aerodynamics Package (AP)	1,987.53	1,432.32	1,593.32

As you work on this program, remember that there must be some way for the computer to keep up with the model and options selected. There must also be a way to drop certain options and select new ones. To test the program, assume you have a customer who wants a convertible with all the options. Upon seeing the total price, the customer decides to leave off the ultra wheels and change the model to the sports sedan. After changing to the sports sedan, the customer decides to delete the aerodynamics package and include the ultra wheels.

Program 10

Write a program that will convert English to metric. Allow the user to choose from a menu the conversion possibility desired: inches to centimeters, pounds to kilograms, or quarts to liters.

1 inch = 2.54 centimeters

1 pound = .4536 kilogram

1 quart = .946 liter

Once the user selects from the menu, the program should ask for the number of units to be converted. It should then do the conversion, printing the output in a form similar to the following:

xxx *unit name* = xxx *unit name*

The program should use tables to store the names of the "from" units of measurement, the names of the "to" units of measurement, and the conversion factors to change from one unit to the other. The unit names in the menu and result displays should come from the tables—not from lines that print literals.

10

Sort Routines

OBJECTIVES

After studying this chapter, you will be able to

1. Define sorting.
2. Name several applications that require sorting.
3. Describe a typical sort algorithm.
4. Write programs containing sort routines.

TOPIC 10.1 ARRANGING DATA

In many computer applications data must be arranged in numeric order or in alphabetic order. For example, a telephone directory needs to be in alphabetic order. An airline timetable needs to be arranged by city and time. A printout of credit card holders referred to by number needs to be in numeric order. The process of arranging data in either an ascending or descending sequence is known as **sorting**. An **ascending sequence** is an arrangement from the smallest element to the largest. A **descending sequence** is an arrangement from the largest element to the smallest.

SORTING A SINGLE TABLE OF NUMBERS

To illustrate the logic in a sort routine, a list of five numbers will be used. The numbers will be placed in a table (array) named NUM, as shown in Figure 10-1.

NUM(1)	10
NUM(2)	5
NUM(3)	8
NUM(4)	3
NUM(5)	7

Figure 10-1 Original Order of Table NUM

The data is placed in the table in unsorted order as shown. It is to be sorted within the table so that it is arranged in ascending order (3, 5, 7, 8, 10). While any one of several sort algorithms may be used, the one to be presented here is based on the method you would probably employ in mentally sorting the numbers. If you were to sort this list of numbers mentally, you would scan the table from top to bottom looking for the smallest number. Upon finding the smallest number, you would place it at the top of the table. Then you would scan again to find the second smallest, which you would place in the second position in the table. You would continue this process until the table was in the designated sequence.

The computer can scan the list in a similar manner. However, it must be given detailed instructions. It must repeatedly examine pairs of numbers to determine which comes first. While there are many different algorithms that may be used in asking the computer to examine the numbers for proper order, let's examine one that is closest to the mental process just described. We will start with table NUM in Figure 10-1 and will show how it is changed during the sorting process. The procedure is as follows:

1. Look through the table for the smallest number. It is the 3 found in row 4. Swap the number in row 1 (10) for the smallest number that was found in row 4 (3). This swap is illustrated in Figure 10-2.

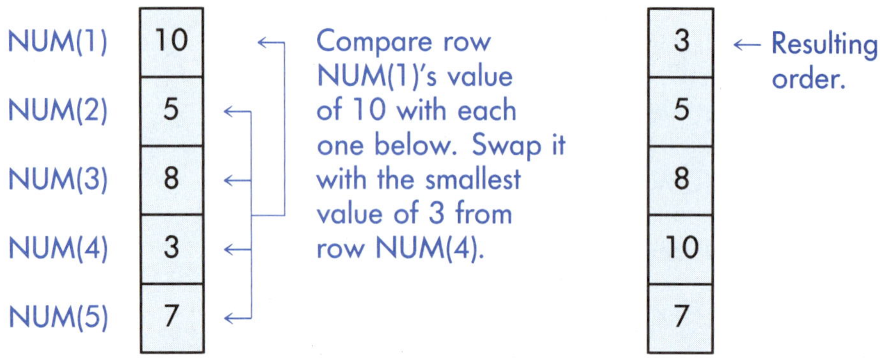

Figure 10-2 First Step in Sorting Table NUM

2. Now that the smallest number has been found and placed in row 1, row 1 is correct and we no longer need to examine it. Therefore, as shown in Figure 10-3, look for the smallest number from rows 2 through 5 and place it in row 2. Since the smallest number is the 5 and it is already in row 2, it is not necessary to swap numbers. To keep from building complications into our computer program, however, we can let the swap happen since it has no effect on the outcome.

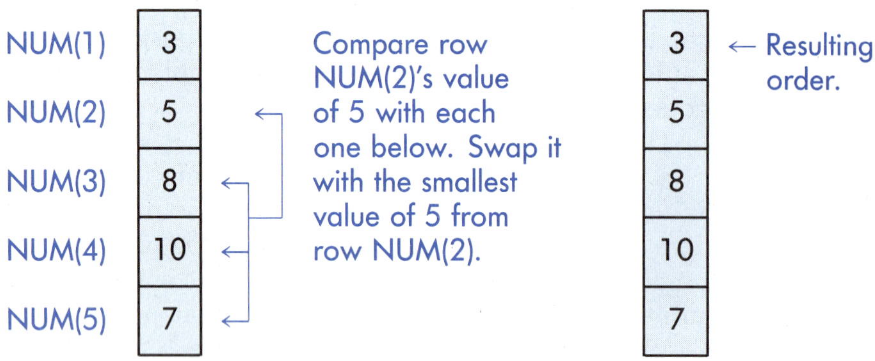

Figure 10-3 Second Step in Sorting Table NUM

3. With the second smallest number now in row 2, it is no longer necessary to consider that row. Examine rows 3 through 5 and find the smallest number. It is the 7 found in row 5. Therefore, swap the number presently in row 3 with the 7 from row 5. The effect of this swap is shown in Figure 10-4.

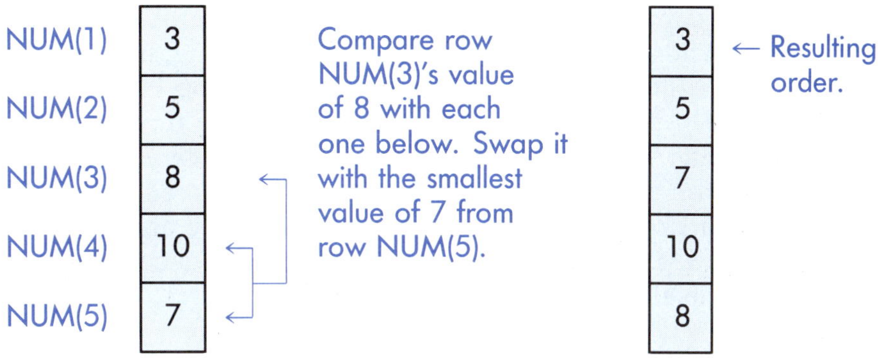

Figure 10-4 Third Step in Sorting Table NUM

4. The smallest number in rows 4 and 5 is the 8. Therefore, swap the 10 in row 4 for the 8 in row 5 as shown in Figure 10-5.

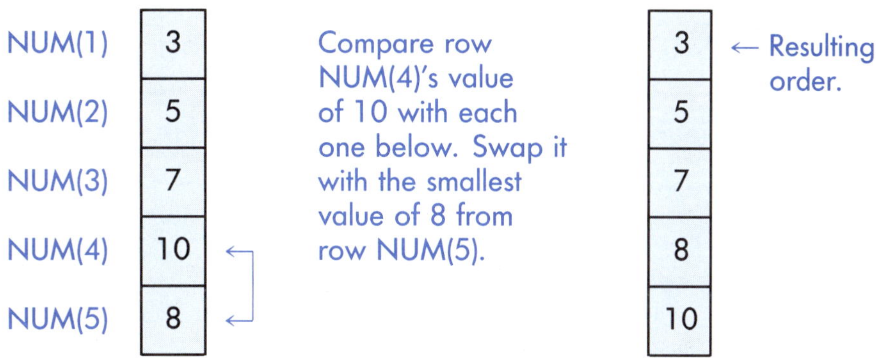

Figure 10-5 Fourth Step in Sorting Table NUM

The sort is now finished, and the numbers in the table are in ascending sequence. Sorting in descending sequence uses essentially the same algorithm. The only difference is that you search for the largest number at each step rather than the smallest number.

SORTING ALPHABETIC DATA

Alphabetic sorting is identical to numeric sorting except the table containing the data is a character table rather than a numeric table. To the computer, values closer to the beginning of the alphabet are "less than" values closer to the end of the alphabet. For example, CAT is "less than" DOG, and SAM is "less than" SUE. When entering data for alphabetic sorting, however, be consistent in the use of upper-case and lower-case letters. This is because all upper-case letters are considered by the computer to be "less than" all lower-case letters. Therefore, everything entered in upper case would appear before anything entered in lower case. Study Figures 10-6 through 10-9, which show alphabetic data in table NAM$ being sorted in ascending sequence. Follow the steps of the algorithm as you study the figures.

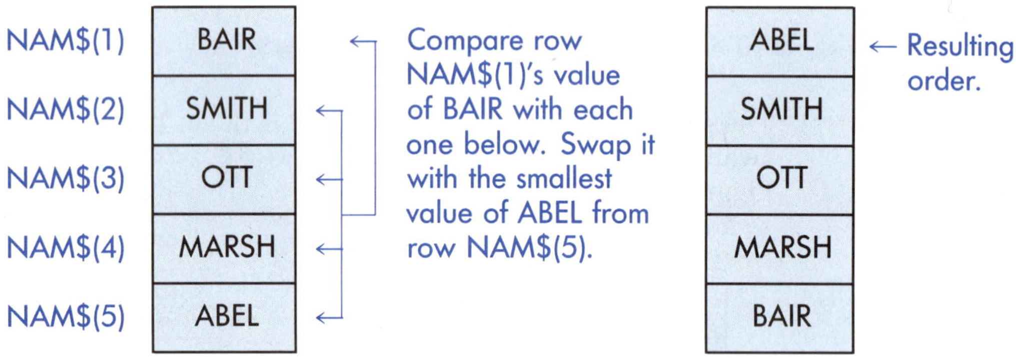

Figure 10-6 First Step in Sorting Table NAM$

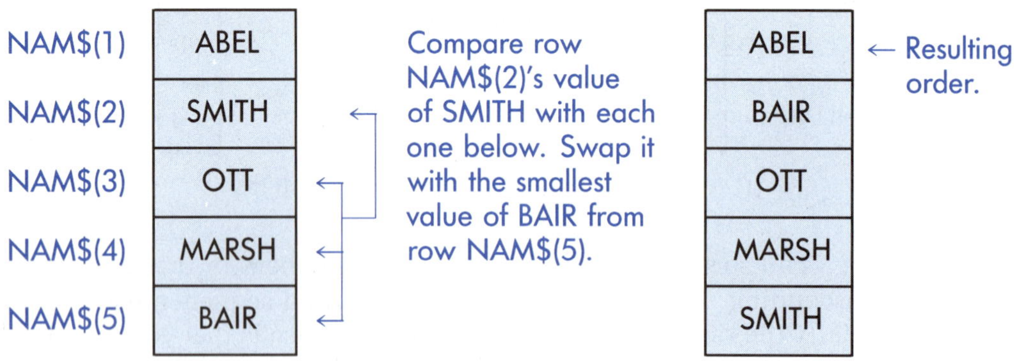

Figure 10-7 Second Step in Sorting Table NAM$

Note in Figure 10-9 that no swap was actually made. The table was already in order before that step. However, the computer would have no way of knowing that the table was in order without performing the step.

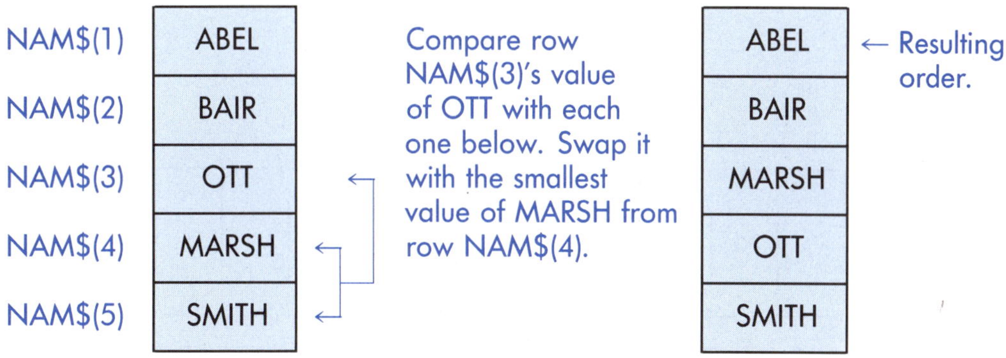

Figure 10-8 Third Step in Sorting Table NAM$

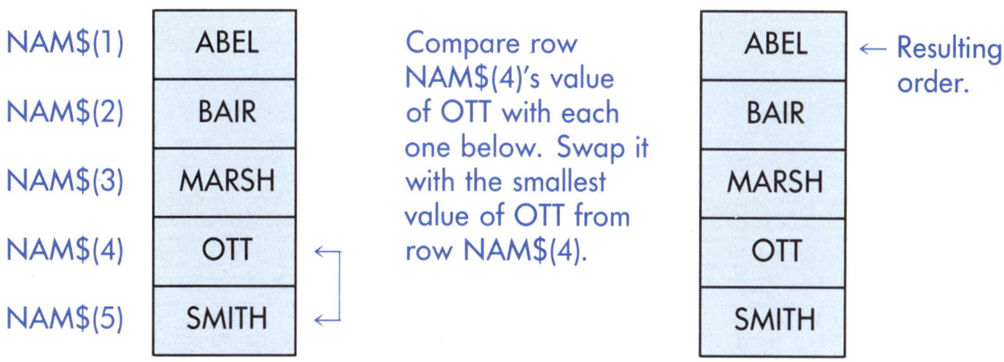

Figure 10-9 Fourth Step in Sorting Table NAM$

SORTING MULTIPLE COLUMNS OR TABLES OF DATA

In both examples given so far, a table of one column of data was sorted. Frequently, however, the column being sorted may contain more than one column of data or there may be two or more tables to be sorted. For example, the names of racers may be in a character table, while the order of their finish is indicated in a matching numeric table. To produce a printout of the racers in order of their finish involves rearranging both tables based on a sort of the values in the numeric table. In other words, the numeric table is sorted, and all the rows in the character table "tag along" into the same sequence in the racer's table. Study Figures 10-10 through 10-13 to see how it is done. The racers' names are in table NAM$, while their finish order is in table SEQ, which is short for sequence.

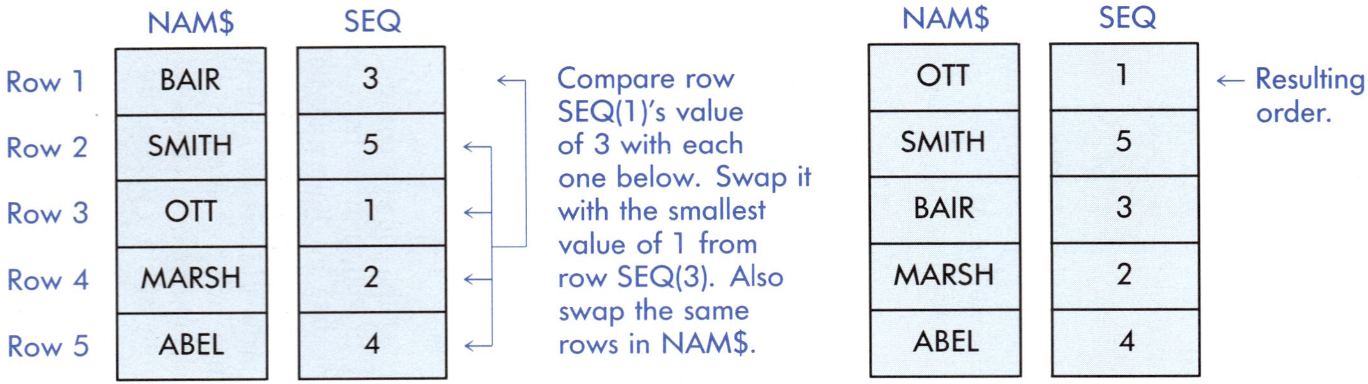

Figure 10-10 First Step in Sorting Two Tables

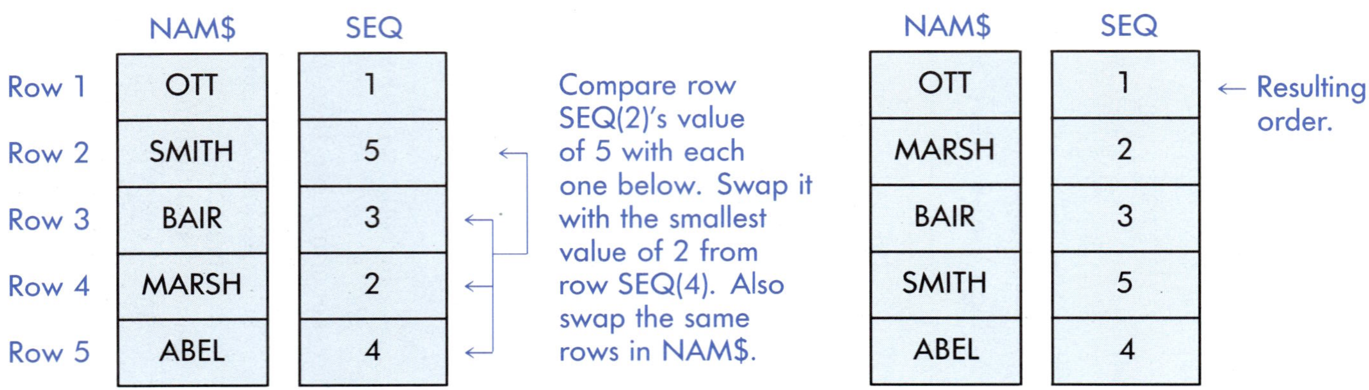

Figure 10-11 Second Step in Sorting Two Tables

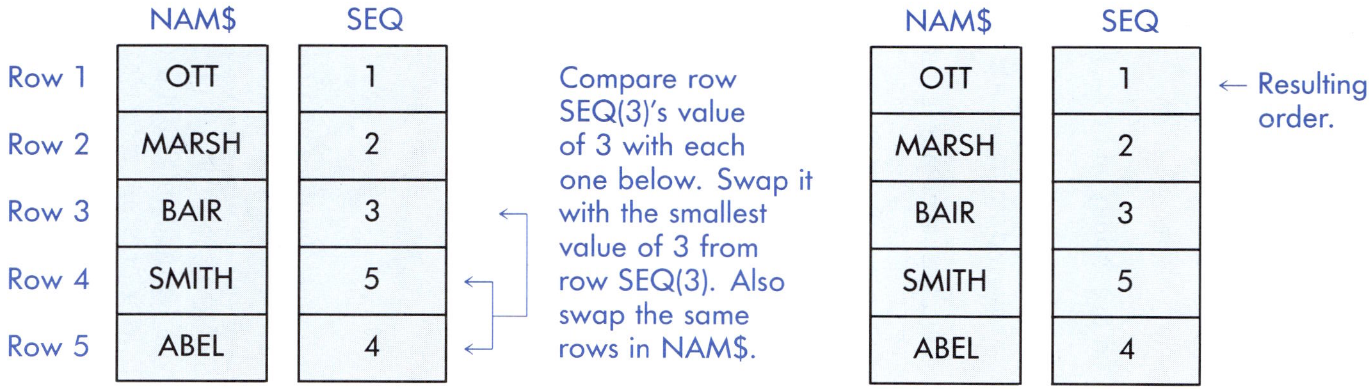

Figure 10-12 Third Step in Sorting Two Tables

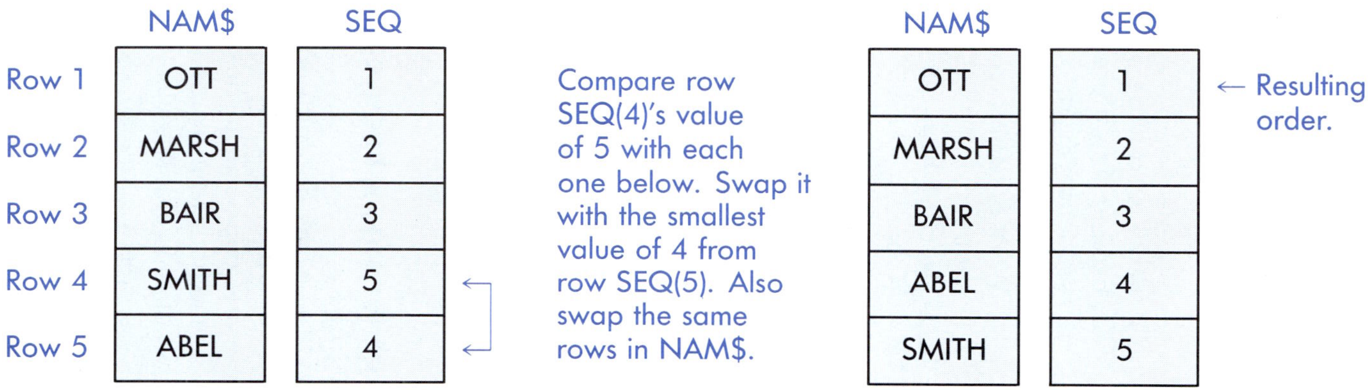

Figure 10-13 Fourth Step in Sorting Two Tables

Note that the values in the third rows of Figure 10-12 were swapped with themselves, resulting in no change. This happened because the item was already in its proper position.

REVIEW QUESTIONS

1. What is sorting? (Obj. 1)
2. Explain the difference between an ascending and a descending sequence. (Obj. 1)
3. Why are sort routines used? (Obj. 1)
4. What are some applications that require data to be in a specific sequence? (Obj. 2)
5. Describe how a human might manually sort numbers into order. (Obj. 3)
6. How can the human algorithm from question 5 be adapted for use by the computer? (Obj. 3)
7. What is the difference between sorting numeric items and alphabetic items? (Obj. 3)
8. What is the process for sorting several tables based on the values in one of the tables? (Obj. 3)

TOPIC 10.2 PROGRAMMING A SORT ALGORITHM

This topic explains how to convert the sort algorithm from Topic 10.1 into BASIC code. Several programs of varying complexity will be covered, but the same fundamental algorithm is used for all of them.

SORTING WITHIN A PROGRAM

Many sorting programs contain a main module and three submodules—one to create and load a table, one to do the sorting, and one to print the results. The table can be loaded by any of the methods you learned in Chapter 9 (READ, INPUT, LET). Printing of the values is also the same as you learned in Chapter 9. Since a create and load module, as well as a printing module, will be used with the sort module that is introduced, review these steps in the following program code. Note that the create and load module reads data from DATA lines. The first item on the first DATA line indicates the number of data items to be read from the DATA lines. The print module simply steps through the table one row at a time, printing the value stored on each row.

Example:

```
10 ' C10E1
20 ' STUDENT NAME, CHAPTER 10, EXAMPLE 1
30 ' SORT DEMONSTRATION PROGRAM
40 '
50 ' ******************************
60 ' * MAIN MODULE                *
70 ' ******************************
75 ' ←——————————————————————
80 GOSUB 1000 ' CREATE   LOAD TABLE
90 GOSUB 2000 ' SORT DATA
100 GOSUB 3000 ' PRINT SORTED DATA
999 END
1000 ' ******************************
1010 ' * CREATE   LOAD TABLE        *
1020 ' ******************************
1030 READ N ' FIRST DATA ITEM SPECIFIES NUMBER OF ITEMS
1040 DIM NUM(N) ' DIMENSION THE TABLE TO MATCH THE NUMBER OF ITEMS
1050 FOR ROW=1 TO N
1060    READ NUM(ROW)
1070 NEXT ROW
1999 RETURN
```

On TRS-80 Model III, use 75 CLEAR 1000.

(Sort module will be inserted here later.)

```
3000 ' ******************************
3010 ' * PRINT SORTED DATA          *
3020 ' ******************************
3025 CLS
3030 FOR ROW=1 TO N
3040    PRINT NUM(ROW)
3050 NEXT ROW
3999 RETURN
5000 ' ******************************
5010 ' * DATA                       *
5020 ' ******************************
5030 DATA 5 ' THIS IS THE NUMBER OF VALUES TO BE READ INTO THE TABLE
5040 DATA 10,5,8,3,7
```

THE SORT ALGORITHM

In Topic 10.1, the description of the sort algorithm was in the form of sequential steps, with essentially the same instructions being repeated at each step. For the algorithm to work with large quantities of data on the computer, it is necessary to describe the algorithm in steps that can be repeated for the different data items as shown in the following code. The line numbers begin with line 2000 so they will fit into the preceding program modules, which place the data values in a table and print them out after the sort. Study the program code and compare it with the steps of the algorithm, which immediately follow the code. The step numbers from the algorithm are indicated with arrows.

Example:

```
2000 ' *****************************
2010 ' * SORT (ASCENDING)           *
2020 ' *****************************
2030 PRINT "BEGINNING SORT..."
2040 PRINT
2050 FOR START=1 TO N-1 <-------------------------------- 1
2060     SMALL=START <----------------------------------- 2
2070     FOR LOOK=START+1 TO N <------------------------- 3
2080         IF NUM(SMALL)>NUM(LOOK) THEN SMALL=LOOK <--- 4
2090     NEXT LOOK <------------------------------------- 5
2100     TEMP=NUM(START) <------------------------------- 6
2110     NUM(START)=NUM(SMALL) <------------------------- 6
2120     NUM(SMALL)=TEMP <------------------------------- 6
2130 NEXT START <---------------------------------------- 7
2999 RETURN
```

The preceding code was developed from the following steps, which will put the data in ascending order—from smallest to largest.

1. Begin a loop that counts from the *first row of the table* to the *next to the last row.* This loop will control the starting point for each cycle and will be called the STARTING POINT loop. In the example being used, this loop counts from 1 to 4.

2. Store the starting row number of the loop in a *location of smallest value* variable. The reasoning is that before you have looked at any other values, the number in the starting row is the smallest one. If a smaller number is found in another row, the location of that row will be placed in this variable.
3. Set up a nested loop that counts from the *starting point plus one* to the *end of the table*. This loop will control the numbers being looked at in the search for smaller values and will be called the LOOK AT loop.
4. Make a comparison of two numbers in the table. The first of these is pointed out by the *location of smallest value* variable. The other is pointed out by the count in the *looked at* loop. If the *looked at* number is smaller than the *smallest value*, place the row number of the *looked at* value in the *location of smallest value* variable.
5. Increment the counter variable for the LOOK AT loop and repeat the loop if it has not reached its exit point.
6. Swap the smallest number found with the number in the starting row. The smallest number found will be the one indicated by the *location of smallest value* variable. The starting row will be indicated by the count of the STARTING POINT loop.
7. Increment the counter variable for the STARTING POINT loop and repeat the loop if it has not reached its exit point.

When the sort module is added to the other program modules listed earlier, and the program is run, the output is as follows:

```
3
5
7
8
10
```

Note that in lines 2100 through 2120 the two data items are swapped. This is accomplished by placing the “start” item in a temporary variable (TEMP) on line 2100. The “small” value is then copied into the “start” row of the table. Finally, the value is copied from the temporary variable to the "small" row. However, you can use the keyword **SWAP** to accomplish the swap in one statement.

> **General Form:**
> *line number* SWAP *first variable, second variable*
>
> **Example:** `2100 SWAP NUM(START),NUM(SMALL)`

The example shows how lines 2100, 2110, and 2120 of the program may be replaced by a single line. In addition to being easier to code, the use of the keyword SWAP also speeds up operation of the program. The following program shows how the entire module looks when the keyword SWAP is used. (SWAP is not available on the TRS-80 Model III.)

Example:

```
2000 ' ******************************
2010 ' * SORT (ASCENDING)           *
2020 ' ******************************
2030 PRINT "BEGINNING SORT..."
2040 PRINT
2050 FOR START=1 TO N-1  <------------------------ 1
2060    SMALL=START  <---------------------------- 2
2070    FOR LOOK=START+1 TO N  <------------------ 3
2080       IF NUM(SMALL)>NUM(LOOK) THEN SMALL=LOOK  <-- 4
2090    NEXT LOOK  <------------------------------ 5
2100    SWAP NUM(START),NUM(SMALL)  <------------- 6
2130 NEXT START  <-------------------------------- 7
2999 RETURN
```

SORTING IN DESCENDING ORDER

To sort in descending order requires only a minor change in the algorithm. Instead of looking for the smallest value during each loop, the program looks for the largest value. Study the code for the sort module as it has been modified to sort in descending order.

The changes, which are in lines 2060, 2080, 2110, and 2120, are shown in bold.

Example:

```
2000 ' ******************************
2010 ' * SORT (DESCENDING)          *
2020 ' ******************************
2030 PRINT "BEGINNING SORT..."
2040 PRINT
2050 FOR START=1 TO N-1
2060 LARGE=START
2070     FOR LOOK=START+1 TO N
2080         IF NUM(LARGE)<NUM(LOOK) THEN LARGE=LOOK
2090     NEXT LOOK
2100     TEMP=NUM(START)
2110     NUM(START)=NUM(LARGE)
2120     NUM(LARGE)=TEMP
2130 NEXT START
2999 RETURN
```

The output will be:

```
10
8
7
5
3
```

SORTING A VARIABLE NUMBER OF ITEMS

In the previous example, we knew in advance that five numbers would be sorted, so we included the 5 as the first data item (see line 5030) and used it to dimension the table. Many times, however, the number of elements to be sorted is not known before the program is run. A program to alphabetize names, for example, might be used with 15 names on one run and 25 names on another. For such programs, you must dimension the table large enough to handle the maximum number of data items that might be entered. This method is required when there will be keyboard entry of the data, and it may also be used when the data is stored in DATA lines. It does not matter if the table is larger than the number of elements actually used.

Regardless of the source of the data, a program loop is used to store the data into the table. The loop continues storing data into the table until a data terminator is found. You will note in the following example that the data terminator is actually placed in the table before the loop exits, but it should not be processed as a data item. To keep it from being processed, one is subtracted from the number in the counter variable to determine the actual number of data items.

The following example program sorts alphabetic items (in ascending sequence) that are entered from the keyboard. The table is dimensioned at 50. Rows 1 through 50 are used for storing data, which is terminated by entering EOD. In addition to showing the use of a terminator, the program also illustrates the sorting of alphabetic data. Remember, however, that there is no difference in the algorithm for sorting alphabetic and numeric data.

Example:

```
10 ' C10E2
20 ' STUDENT NAME, CHAPTER 10, EXAMPLE 2
30 ' SORT PROGRAM--VARIABLE NUMBER OF ALPHABETIC ITEMS
40 '
50 ' ******************************
60 ' * MAIN MODULE                *
70 ' ******************************
75 ' ON TRS-80 MOD III USE 75 CLEAR 1000
80 GOSUB 1000 ' CREATE & LOAD TABLE
90 GOSUB 2000 ' SORT DATA
100 GOSUB 3000 ' PRINT SORTED DATA
999 END
1000 ' ****************************
1010 ' * CREATE & LOAD TABLE      *
1020 ' ****************************
1030 DIM ITEM$(50)
1040 CLS
1050 PRINT "THIS PROGRAM SORTS UP TO 50 ITEMS."
1060 FOR ROW=1 TO 50
1070     INPUT "ENTER AN ITEM (OR EOD):  ";ITEM$(ROW)
1080     IF ITEM$(ROW)="EOD" THEN 1100
1090 NEXT ROW
1100 N=ROW-1 ' 1 IS SUBTRACTED FROM COUNT OF DATA SO
1999 RETURN '        TERMINATOR WILL NOT BE PROCESSED
```

```
2000 ' ******************************
2010 ' * SORT                       *
2020 ' ******************************
2030 PRINT "BEGINNING SORT..."
2040 PRINT
2050 FOR START=1 TO N-1
2060 SMALL=START
2070    FOR LOOK=START+1 TO N
2080       IF ITEM$(SMALL)>ITEM$(LOOK) THEN SMALL=LOOK
2090    NEXT LOOK
2100    TEMP$=ITEM$(START)
2110    ITEM$(START)=ITEM$(SMALL)
2120    ITEM$(SMALL)=TEMP$
2130 NEXT START
2999 RETURN
3000 ' ******************************
3010 ' * PRINT SORTED DATA          *
3020 ' ******************************
3030 FOR ROW=1 TO N
3040    PRINT ITEM$(ROW)
3050 NEXT ROW
3999 RETURN
```

Assume that the operator inputs the following words in this order: ELEPHANT, DOG, CAT, MONKEY, HORSE, ARMADILLO, EOD. The output after sorting will be:

```
ARMADILLO
CAT
DOG
ELEPHANT
HORSE
MONKEY
```

SORTING WITH MULTIPLE COLUMNS

The sorting examples thus far have involved the use of one table containing only one column or one field to be sorted. As indicated in Topic 10.1, however, sorting more than one table on different columns may be needed. To illustrate this concept, we will examine a program used by a civic club to prepare sales reports from a fund-raising project. Reports are needed to list the salespersons, the number of items sold, and the value of those sales. Sometimes the report needs to be printed in alphabetic order by salesperson, and sometimes the report needs to be ranked by number of items sold from high salesperson to low. This program is an interactive one that allows the user to specify the current date, the price of the item sold, the name of each salesperson, and the number of items sold. The user then may select the type of report to be printed.

The two output reports of the program are shown here. Note that the report in sales order sequence illustrates sorting in descending order.

```
SALES REPORT--ALPHABETIZED      12/27/--
----------------------------------------
SALESPERSON               QTY SOLD  AMOUNT
----------------------------------------
ADAMS HARRY                   3      12.75
CONNOR BRAD                  19      80.75
HUNTER BARBARA                5      21.25
LEE GREG                      5      21.25
MERRILL SUE                  25     106.25
MIMMS HARRY                  15      63.75
SHINODA OKI                   7      29.75
VALDEZ MARY                   8      34.00

SALES REPORT--BY SALES AMOUNT   12/27/--
----------------------------------------
SALESPERSON               QTY SOLD  AMOUNT
----------------------------------------
MERRILL SUE                  25     106.25
CONNOR BRAD                  19      80.75
MIMMS HARRY                  15      63.75
VALDEZ MARY                   8      34.00
SHINODA OKI                   7      29.75
HUNTER BARBARA                5      21.25
LEE GREG                      5      21.25
ADAMS HARRY                   3      12.75
```

The program can be divided into four functions: (1) module to get data, (2) module to sort tables in alphabetic sequence by name, (3) module to sort tables in numeric sequence by number of items sold, and (4) module to print out the report. These modules are represented in the hierarchy chart shown in Figure 10-14.

The program documentation sheet is shown in Figure 10-15. Figure 10-16 is the spacing chart for the output.

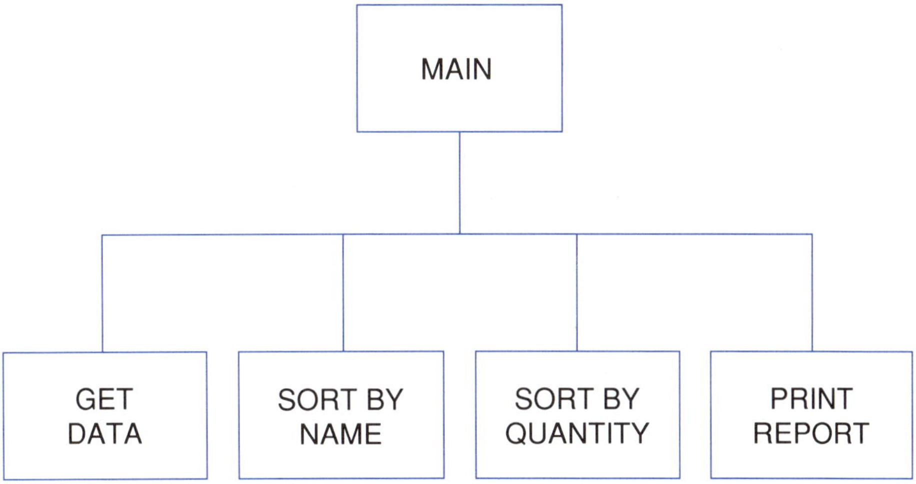

Figure 10-14 Hierarchy Chart

PROGRAM DOCUMENTATION SHEET

Program: C10E3	Programmer: STUDENT NAME	Date: 12-1-xx

Purpose: The program prepares sales reports. Names and the quantities sold are input into tables. The tables may be sorted and printed in alphabetical order or ranked by quantity sold. The dollar value of the items sold is calculated and printed.

Input: Keyed in by the operator.	Output: Report printed on the screen.

Data Terminator: EOD

Variables Used:

D$ = Date
SELL = Price of the item being sold
NAM$ = Table for names of sellers
QTY = Table for quantity of items sold
ROW = Counter variable in loading and printing loops
START = Counter for outside sorting loop
LOOK = Counter for inside sorting loop
SMALL = Row of smallest item
LARGE = Row of largest item
IMAG$ = Print using image

Figure 10-15 Program Documentation Sheet

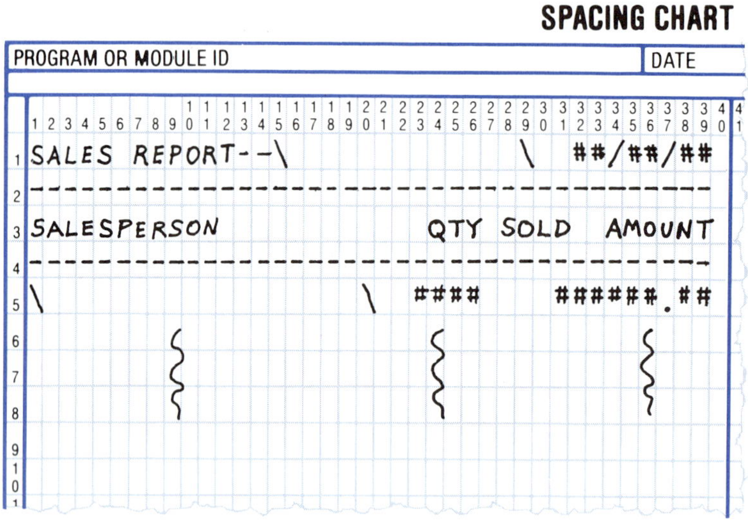

Note: Use % rather than \ on TRS-80 Model III.

Figure 10-16 Spacing Chart

Figures 10-17 through 10-21 show the module documentation sheets for each of the modules of the program. Following the

MODULE DOCUMENTATION SHEET

Program: C10E3	Module: MAIN Lines: 10-999

Module Description: Main module.

Module Function (Program Design):

1. Clear space for character data (TRS-80 Model III).
2. Perform the Get Data module.
3. Print menu and get user's choice of report desired.
4. On user's choice, perform Sort by Name, Sort by Quantity, or terminate program.
5. Perform Print Report module.
6. Go back to step 3 for user's next choice.

Figure 10-17 Documentation Sheet for Main Module

MODULE DOCUMENTATION SHEET	
Program: C10E3	Module: GET DATA Lines: 1000-1999
Module Description: Gets data from user.	
Module Function (Program Design): 1. Print instructions to user. 2. Get date. 3. Get price of item that was sold. 4. Dimension tables for names and quantities sold. 5. Get names and quantities until user enters EOD for a name.	

Figure 10-18 Documentation Sheet for Get Data Module

documentation sheets is the BASIC code for the entire program. Compare the code to the documentation sheet for each module to be sure you understand how each module works.

MODULE DOCUMENTATION SHEET	
Program: C10E3	Module: SORT BY NAME Lines: 2000-2999
Module Description: Sorts the tables in alphabetic order by name of salesperson.	
Module Function (Program Design): 1. Sort the two tables using the sort algorithm described in this chapter.	

Figure 10-19 Documentation Sheet for Sort by Name Module

<table>
<tr><th colspan="2">MODULE DOCUMENTATION SHEET</th></tr>
<tr><td>Program: C10E3</td><td>Module: SORT BY QUANTITY
Lines: 3000-3999</td></tr>
<tr><td colspan="2">Module Description: Sorts the tables in descending order by quantity sold.</td></tr>
<tr><td colspan="2">Module Function (Program Design):
1. Sort the two tables using the sort algorithm described in this chapter.</td></tr>
</table>

Figure 10-20 Documentation Sheet for Sort by Quantity Module

<table>
<tr><th colspan="2">MODULE DOCUMENTATION SHEET</th></tr>
<tr><td>Program: C10E3</td><td>Module: PRINT REPORT
Lines: 4000-4999</td></tr>
<tr><td colspan="2">Module Description: Prints report of sales.</td></tr>
<tr><td colspan="2">Module Function (Program Design):
1. Print headings.
2. Print detail lines until all items in the tables have been processed.</td></tr>
</table>

Figure 10-21 Documentation Sheet for Print Report Module

The BASIC code of the entire program is as follows. The program will produce either of two reports upon demand—the first lists salespeople in alphabetic order and the second lists salespeople by quantity of sales in descending order. The program for IBM and TRS computers is the same except for the few cases where differences are noted in the listing for the TRS-80 Model III.

Example:

```
10 ' C10E3
20 ' STUDENT NAME, CHAPTER 10, EXAMPLE 3
30 ' PREPARES CLUB SALES REPORT
40 '
50 ' ******************************
60 ' * MAIN MODULE                *
70 ' ******************************
80 ' ON TRS MOD III - 80 CLEAR 1000
90 GOSUB 1000 ' GET DATA
100 ' ***** BEGIN LOOP
110    CLS
120    PRINT "WHAT IS YOUR CHOICE?"
130    PRINT
140    PRINT "<1> ALPHABETIZED REPORT"
150    PRINT "<2> REPORT RANKED BY SALES"
160    PRINT "<3> TERMINATION OF PROGRAM"
170    PRINT
180    INPUT "SELECTION:  ";CHOICE
190    IF CHOICE>3 OR CHOICE<1 THEN PRINT "INVALID ENTRY":GOTO 180
200    ON CHOICE GOSUB 2000,3000,999
210    GOSUB 4000 ' PRINT REPORT
220 GOTO 100 ' REPEAT LOOP
999 END
1000 ' ******************************
1010 ' * GET DATA                   *
1020 ' ******************************
1030 CLS
1040 PRINT "THIS PROGRAM PREPARES REPORTS OF THE"
1050 PRINT "SALES OF A PRODUCT BY A CIVIC CLUB."
1060 PRINT "PLEASE INPUT THE REQUESTED DATA."
1070 PRINT
1080 INPUT "DATE (MM/DD/YY):  ";D$
1090 INPUT "PRICE OF ITEM BEING SOLD:  ";SELL
1100 PRINT
1110 PRINT "ONE AT A TIME, ENTER THE NAME OF EACH"
1120 PRINT "SELLER, THEN THE NUMBER OF ITEMS SOLD"
1130 PRINT "BY THAT PERSON.  AFTER ALL THE DATA"
1140 PRINT "HAS BEEN ENTERED, INPUT 'EOD'"
1150 PRINT "WHEN ASKED FOR THE NEXT SELLER'S NAME."
1160 PRINT
1170 DIM NAM$(100),QTY(100)
```

```
1180     FOR ROW=1 TO 100
1190     INPUT "SALESPERSON (OR EOD): ";NAM$(ROW)
1200     IF NAM$(ROW)="EOD" THEN 1240
1210     INPUT "NUMBER OF ITEMS SOLD:  ";QTY(ROW)
1220     PRINT
1230 NEXT ROW
1240 N=ROW-1
1999 RETURN
2000 ' ******************************
2010 ' * SORT BY NAME               *
2020 ' ******************************
2030 PRINT "BEGINNING SORT..."
2040 PRINT
2050 FOR START=1 TO N-1
2060 SMALL=START
2070 FOR LOOK=START+1 TO N
2080     IF NAM$(SMALL)>NAM$(LOOK) THEN SMALL=LOOK
2090 NEXT LOOK
2100 SWAP NAM$(START),NAM$(SMALL)
2110 SWAP QTY(START),QTY(SMALL)
```

TRS-80 Model III must use temp. area.

```
2120 NEXT START
2999 RETURN
3000 ' ******************************
3010 ' * SORT BY QUANTITY           *
3020 ' ******************************
3030 PRINT "BEGINNING SORT..."
3040 PRINT
3050 FOR START=1 TO N-1
3060     LARGE=START
3070     FOR LOOK=START+1 TO N
3080        IF QTY(LARGE)<QTY(LOOK) THEN LARGE=LOOK
3090     NEXT LOOK
3100     SWAP QTY(START),QTY(LARGE)
3110     SWAP NAM$(START),NAM$(LARGE)
```

TRS-80 Model III must use temp. area.

```
3120 NEXT START
3999 RETURN
4000 ' ******************************
4010 ' * PRINT REPORT               *
4020 ' ******************************
4030 IF CHOICE=1 THEN HEAD$="--ALPHABETIZED"
4040 IF CHOICE=2 THEN HEAD$="--BY SALES AMOUNT"
4050 CLS
4060 PRINT "SALES REPORT";HEAD$;TAB(32);D$
```

```
4070 PRINT STRING$(39,"-")
4080 PRINT "SALESPERSON QTY SOLD AMOUNT"
4090 IMAG$="\              \ #### ######.##"
4095 ' ON TRS MOD III REPLACE 4090'S BACKSLASHES WITH PERCENTS (%)
4100 PRINT STRING$(39,"-")
4110 FOR ROW=1 TO N
4120    PRINT USING IMAG$;NAM$(ROW);QTY(ROW);QTY(ROW)*SELL
4130 NEXT ROW
4140 INPUT "HIT RETURN TO CONTINUE...";Z$
4999 RETURN
```

REVIEW QUESTIONS

1. Name and describe the functions of the three modules into which most sorting programs can be written. (Obj. 4)
2. How many loops are used in coding the sorting algorithm used in this chapter? What is the purpose of each? (Obj. 4)
3. What is the difference in coding a BASIC sort routine as an ascending sort and a descending sort? (Obj. 4)
4. What is the purpose of the keyword SWAP? When the keyword is not used, how is its function carried out? (Obj. 4)

VOCABULARY WORDS

The following terms were introduced in this chapter:

ascending sequence
descending sequence
sorting

KEYWORD

The following keyword was introduced in this chapter:

SWAP

PROGRAMS TO WRITE

For each of the programs, prepare the necessary documentation prior to writing the BASIC code. Write all the programs in modular form.

Program 1

Write a program to read the following ten numbers from a DATA line and sort them in ascending order: 38, 6, 12, 29, 14, 9, 86, 97, 32, 54. The program should then print the list of sorted numbers.

Program 2

Modify Program 1 so that the numbers are sorted and printed in descending order.

Program 3

Write a program to sort a maximum of 30 positive numbers entered from the keyboard. Entry of a negative number should be used as the data terminator to indicate that all numbers have been input. Sort and print the numbers in ascending order. Use the following numbers, entered in the order shown, to test your program: 34, 98, 12, 987, 532, 875, 343, 222, 901, 914, 328, 257.

Program 4

Write a program to sort a maximum of 30 pairs of alphabetic data items entered from the keyboard into a table with two columns. The sort should be in ascending sequence based on the contents of the first column. The terminator of EOD (entered in the first column) will indicate that all items have been input. Print the sorted data. Use the following data items, entered in the order given, to test your program: SMITH HOUSE, 321 FIRST STREET; CONCERT HALL, 1983 HIGH ROAD; HARDY CASTLE, RT. 6; ABC CENTER, 987 PLAZA COURT; CITY HALL, 32 FIRST STREET; COUNTY JAIL, 98 ALE WAY; KISSING ROCK, 389 MARCH RD.

Program 5

A local retailer wishes to produce a report showing the performance of its salespersons during each month, listed in descending order by sales. The salespersons and their sales figures are to be entered from the keyboard. Since the number of salespersons varies from one month to another, the program should be capable of handling a maximum of 50 persons. Use the following data, entered in the order shown, to test your program: JONES SAM, $32321; ADAMS SUSAN, $42893; MARCO PAUL, $93212; MILLER LEE, $52343; AYRES SALLY, $47321; and BRYERS HELEN, $61234.

Program 6

During a special one-day promotion, a store offers to send its next major catalog free to all customers who request it in person at the store. The request process is to be handled by having customers enter their own names and addresses into a computer. At the end of the day, mailing labels are to be produced for the catalog. Since the catalogs must be grouped by zip code before mailing, the names and addresses should be sorted by zip code before the labels are printed. The program should use separate columns of a table for customer name, street, city, state, and zip. To test your program, enter the following customers in the order shown:

Mable White, 983 Eight Avenue, New Town, NH 98732

Samuel Jonathon, Route 6, Beaumont, VT 98234

Marabel Adams, 578 Release Drive, Early, CN 49843

Maxwell Lyre, 404 First Street, Hamilton, CN 49832

Leticia Smith, 331 Highland Avenue, Byrd, VT 98231

Program 7

A civic club is launching a membership campaign, with each member assigned to bring in as many new persons as possible from March 1 to 7. To get the campaign off to a fast start, prizes are being offered to the members who sign up six new persons, with the most valuable prizes going to those who sign up new members first. To keep track of this information, each membership form contains space for the name of the recruiter and for the day and time the new member was signed. The day and time are character data in one column. For example, a form completed on March 3 at 2:05 P.M. would be coded as 3-14:05. Note that the time is entered in 24-hour format, making sure to use a leading zero for one-digit hours or minutes. For example, instead of 9:15 A.M. you enter 09:15.

When the forms come in, the data is entered in the computer, which sorts the data in ascending order by the date and time on the cards. The output should include the date and time, the name of recruiter, and name of the new member. Use the following data to test your program. The order of input is the random order in which the membership cards were turned in; this is the order in which the data should be entered:

RECRUITER	NEW MEMBER	DAY AND TIME
MELANIE MARS	SAM BURK	3-15:15
JOHN SAMUELS	MARY MARSHALL	2-07:33
MEGAN BRUCE	CONNIE STRUTHERS	1-09:15
JULIAN SALAS	TOM THOMAS	2-12:10
JOE JERSEY	HANNAH MISCALLY	1-10:20
WILL BRYAN	JACK JONES	2-15:06
BRAD EGLESTONE	BURMA ABRAMS	4-09:50
CLARICE JOHNS	LILLI SPEAR	3-15:50

Program 8

Write a program that will allow a teacher to key in up to 35 student names and two test scores—one for language skills and one for math. The program should sort the same data three ways—in ascending alphabetic sequence by student name, in descending sequence on language score (first test score), and in descending sequence on math score (second test score). Printouts should be provided for all three sequences. Sample data to test your program (to be entered in the order given) includes the following: Barbara Davenport, 85, 94; Gloria Valdez, 82, 97; Earl Hunter, 54, 76; Mary Garcia, 78, 61; Oki Shinoda, 78, 78; Kevin Smith, 69, 73; Bill Hoover, 73, 61; and Greg Lee, 84, 75.

Program 9

For this assignment, you will modify Program 5. To stimulate sales, the store has decided to hold a contest each month among its salespersons, with bonuses going to sellers based on their sales. The person with the most sales gets a bonus of 1 percent of his or her sales, the second-place finisher gets .9 percent, the third-place finisher receives .8 percent, and so on until zero percent is reached. The printout of the program should have a column added showing the amount of bonus money to be awarded to each salesperson.

Program 10

Write a program to load the following course information into tables from DATA lines. The user should then be able to choose whether a list is to be printed in alphabetic order by courses within departments or in numeric order by course number. Alphabetic within departments means, for example, that all courses in the business administration department are grouped alphabetically before courses in the mathematics department. As you work on this program, remember that the contents of two different character variables may be catenated and worked on as one variable. Use the following data:

COURSE NUMBER	DEPARTMENT	TITLE
1219	SOC SCI	AMERICAN HISTORY I
1532	SCIENCE	BIOLOGY I
1298	JOURNALISM	COMPOSITION I
3419	BUSINESS	INTRO TO MARKETING
3516	BUSINESS	INSURANCE PRINCIPLES
3199	SCIENCE	BOTANY I
1347	SOC SCI	EUROPEAN HISTORY
1543	SCIENCE	BOTANY II
1392	JOURNALISM	TV REPORTING
1319	SOC SCI	PREHISTORIC HISTORY
1231	BUSINESS	INTRO TO COMPUTERS

11

Summarizing Data

OBJECTIVES

After studying this chapter, you will be able to

1. Explain the importance of summaries.
2. Define totaling, counting, and subtotaling as methods of summarizing data.
3. Describe the difference between unconditional and conditional summarizing.
4. Distinguish between detail and group printing.
5. Write programs to summarize data.

TOPIC 11.1 WHAT IS SUMMARIZING?

A **summary** shows information in a condensed form that makes the "big picture" easier to see. For example, a report of the number of credits earned by a student is a summary of progress toward graduation. Likewise, a statement of the number of parts produced by several factories in a day is a summary. The process of producing a summary is known as **summarizing**. This section discusses methods used in summarizing data.

TOTALS AND COUNTS

Totaling, counting, and subtotaling are commonly used methods of summarizing data. Although you have used some of these methods in earlier programs, the following sections will help ensure a thorough understanding of summaries. Variations of the same report will be used to illustrate the various methods of summarizing.

Totaling

A **total** is the sum of two or more numbers. For example, if you must find the number of items produced by several factories in a week's time, you add the quantities produced by the different factories (see Figure 11-1). This total is important because it is the

PRODUCTION REPORT
WEEK ENDING JULY 5, 19--

PLANT	DAY	QTY
ATHENS	MON	50
BOSTON	MON	49
ROME	MON	37
ATHENS	TUE	45
BOSTON	TUE	52
ROME	TUE	41
ATHENS	WED	52
BOSTON	WED	49
ROME	WED	49
ATHENS	THU	49
BOSTON	THU	48
ROME	THU	43
ATHENS	FRI	51
BOSTON	FRI	50
ROME	FRI	44
ATHENS	SAT	0
BOSTON	SAT	0
ROME	SAT	0
ATHENS	SUN	0
BOSTON	SUN	0
ROME	SUN	20
TOTAL		729

Figure 11-1 Report with Total

record of progress toward the production goal that has been established, and because it provides information for planning future production. Without the ability to derive this total, it would be impossible to make sound management decisions for operating the company. This information allows company managers to better plan for future production.

There are many other examples of totals. In working toward graduation, students need to know the total credits they have earned in courses. In making a bank deposit, the coins, currency, and checks are totaled to find the amount of the deposit. The phone bill shows the total amount due for all the calls made during the month. The items on a sales slip are totaled to determine the amount of money to be paid.

Counting

While a total is a sum of data items, a **count** shows how many data items have been processed. Counts are used in many computer applications. For example, to compute grade averages, the number of grades must be known. When ordering meals, an airline needs to know how many passengers need each kind of meal (e.g., 84 regular meals, 2 no-salt meals, and 3 sugar-free meals). When entering data for the computer to process, it may be necessary to ensure that the correct number of items have been entered. To illustrate this, the report in Figure 11-1 always requires 21 records of data, since there are three plants and seven days in a week. If less than 21 records are processed, it can be assumed that some of the data is missing; the missing data must be added and the report reprinted. Examine Figure 11-2 to see how this report looks with a count of the items added.

When a sum of all data items is computed as in Figure 11-1, it is called an **unconditional total**. When all data items are counted as in Figure 11-2, it called an **unconditional count**. However, there are times when totals or counts need to be updated only under particular circumstances—that is, when a specified variable contains specified data. A **conditional total** is a total that is updated only if a certain condition is true, while a **conditional count** is a count that is updated only if a certain condition is true. For example, totals and counts for each of the three plants in Figure 11-1 could be given (see

PRODUCTION REPORT
WEEK ENDING JULY 5, 19--

PLANT	DAY	QTY
ATHENS	MON	50
BOSTON	MON	49
ROME	MON	37
ATHENS	TUE	45
BOSTON	TUE	52
ROME	TUE	41
ATHENS	WED	52
BOSTON	WED	49
ROME	WED	49
ATHENS	THU	49
BOSTON	THU	48
ROME	THU	43
ATHENS	FRI	51
BOSTON	FRI	50
ROME	FRI	44
ATHENS	SAT	0
BOSTON	SAT	0
ROME	SAT	0
ATHENS	SUN	0
BOSTON	SUN	0
ROME	SUN	20
TOTAL		729

21 RECORDS PROCESSED

Figure 11-2 Report with Total and Count

Figure 11-3 for the results). To accomplish this report, three totaling variables and three counting variables would be used, with one set of variables devoted to each plant.

Subtotaling

In Figures 11-1, 11-2, and 11-3, totals were printed only after all data items were processed. At times, however, it is desirable for totals to be printed at intermediate points during the processing. These intermediate totals are referred to as **subtotals** or **minor**

```
PRODUCTION REPORT
WEEK ENDING JULY 5, 19--

PLANT      DAY   QTY

ATHENS     MON    50
BOSTON     MON    49
ROME       MON    37
ATHENS     TUE    45
BOSTON     TUE    52
ROME       TUE    41
ATHENS     WED    52
BOSTON     WED    49
ROME       WED    49
ATHENS     THU    49
BOSTON     THU    48
ROME       THU    43
ATHENS     FRI    51
BOSTON     FRI    50
ROME       FRI    44
ATHENS     SAT     0
BOSTON     SAT     0
ROME       SAT     0
ATHENS     SUN     0
BOSTON     SUN     0
ROME       SUN    20

ATHENS TOTAL     247
( 7 RECORDS)

BOSTON TOTAL     248
( 7 RECORDS)

ROME TOTAL       234
( 7 RECORDS)

GRAND TOTAL      729

 21 RECORDS PROCESSED
```

Figure 11-3 Report with Conditional Totals and Counts

totals. Figure 11-4 shows the weekly report from the previous examples printed with the use of subtotals.

To print subtotals as shown in Figure 11-4, the data must be in groups—that is, all items for the same plant must be together. The plant name is the **control variable**, so named because it is the item whose change will control when a subtotal and count are printed. The data may be entered in the correct order, or it may be placed in order by the program. A common method of grouping data is to load items into tables and then sort them in order from smallest to largest (ascending) or largest to smallest (descending) according to the value of the control variable item.

To produce the report in Figure 11-4, data items are processed one after another. Whenever the plant name differs from the previous name, the control variable has changed and a subtotal should be printed. A change in the value of the control variable is known as a **control break**.

To determine when the control variable has changed, another variable known as a **compare variable** is used. Once a plant name and quantity have been read or examined and processed, the plant name is placed into the compare variable. Thus, when the next plant name is read, the old name will still be available for comparison.

When printing both subtotals and a final total in a report, two different variables are used to accumulate the totals—one to accumulate the subtotal and one to accumulate the final total. After each subtotal is printed, a 0 is placed in the subtotal accumulator. This clears the previous subtotal so the accumulator starts over for the next group of data. In the same manner, two different variables are used for the counts—one for the individual plant count and one for the count of all items.

Study the following steps to see how subtotals are computed. The data used in these steps is from Figure 11-4.

Set up variables for compare, qty. subtotal, qty. total, subcount, and count.

COMPARE	QTY SUBTOTAL	QTY TOTAL	SUBCOUNT	COUNT

PRODUCTION REPORT
WEEK ENDING JULY 5, 19--

PLANT	DAY	QTY	
ATHENS	MON	50	
ATHENS	TUE	45	
ATHENS	WED	52	
ATHENS	THU	49	
ATHENS	FRI	51	
ATHENS	SAT	0	
ATHENS	SUN	0	
	TOTAL		247
	COUNT		7
BOSTON	WED	49	
BOSTON	MON	49	
BOSTON	THU	48	
BOSTON	TUE	52	
BOSTON	FRI	50	
BOSTON	SAT	0	
BOSTON	SUN	0	
	TOTAL		248
	COUNT		7
ROME	FRI	44	
ROME	TUE	41	
ROME	WED	49	
ROME	SAT	0	
ROME	MON	37	
ROME	THU	43	
ROME	SUN	20	
	TOTAL		234
	COUNT		7
	GRAND TOTAL		729
	NO. RECORDS		21

Figure 11-4 Report with Subtotals

Get first data item. Put the plant name into compare. Add quantity (50) to qty. total and qty. subtotal. Increment the subcount and count totals. Print a detail line for the report with Athens, Mon, and 50.

COMPARE	QTY SUBTOTAL	QTY TOTAL	SUBCOUNT	COUNT
ATHENS	50	50	1	1

Get next data items (Athens, Tue, and 45). Compare with the value in the compare variable. Since it is not different, add the quantity (45) to the qty. subtotal and qty. total variables. Increment the subcount and count variables. Put the newly processed plant name in the compare variable in place of the one already there.

COMPARE	QTY SUBTOTAL	QTY TOTAL	SUBCOUNT	COUNT
ATHENS	95	95	2	2

Continue processing the items one by one in this same manner. When the seventh data item is processed, Athens will again be placed in the compare variable, and the subtotal and total accumulators will have grown to 247. Now, continue processing the eighth item.

COMPARE	QTY SUBTOTAL	QTY TOTAL	SUBCOUNT	COUNT
ATHENS	247	247	7	7

The eighth item is Boston, Wed, 49. Boston is compared with the compare variable, which contains Athens. Since the values are different, it is control break time. Therefore, a subtotal line is printed on the report, and the qty. subtotal and subcount variables are set back to 0.

COMPARE	QTY SUBTOTAL	QTY TOTAL	SUBCOUNT	COUNT
ATHENS	0	247	0	7

Note that the total variable is not set back to 0, and neither is the count. Once the resetting of the subtotal and subcount variables is accomplished, continue to process the current data item by printing a detail line, adding the quantity (49) to the qty. subtotal and qty. total variables, incrementing the subcount and count variables, and placing Boston in the compare variable.

COMPARE	QTY SUBTOTAL	QTY TOTAL	SUBCOUNT	COUNT
BOSTON	49	296	1	8

Continue processing data items in this manner until all items are finished, at which time the last qty. subtotal, subcount, qty. total, and count are printed.

GROUP PRINTING

Most of the programs presented previously have printed a detail line for each data item processed. This is known as **detail printing**. In Figure 11-4, each plant and quantity was printed. When there was a control break, a subtotal was printed.

Many times only subtotals are needed. Having all the records printed in such detail is not only a waste of paper and time, but it also makes the desired information more difficult to locate. When only the subtotals are needed, a report may be group printed. **Group printing** simply omits the printing of detail lines. A subtotal is still printed each time there is a control break. The print format may be changed, if desired, to make it easier to read. If group printed, the report from Figure 11-4 might appear as shown in Figure 11-5.

PRODUCTION REPORT
WEEK ENDING JULY 5, 19--

PLANT	QTY	NO. DAYS
ATHENS	247	7
BOSTON	248	7
ROME	234	7
GRAND TOTAL	729	21

Figure 11-5 Report with Group Printing

REVIEW QUESTIONS

1. Why are summaries important? (Obj. 1)
2. Define totaling. (Obj. 2)
3. Define counting. (Obj. 2)
4. Describe two applications that require totaling of data. (Obj. 1)
5. Describe two applications that require counting of data. (Obj. 1)
6. What is conditional totaling? (Obj. 3)
7. What is conditional counting? (Obj. 3)
8. What is a subtotal? (Obj. 2)
9. What is a control variable? (Obj. 5)
10. When does a control break occur? (Obj. 5)
11. Why are data items grouped before printing a report with subtotals? (Obj. 5)
12. What is detail printing? (Obj. 4)
13. What is group printing? (Obj. 4)
14. Why is group printing sometimes preferred over detailed printing? (Obj. 4)

TOPIC 11.2 SUMMARIZING WITH BASIC

This section illustrates some of the techniques that may be used for summarizing with the BASIC language. Each of the examples from Figures 11-1 through 11-5 will be coded. For the first three programs, data will come from data lines in the program. The last program will use data entered from the keyboard and stored in a table. For each program, study the program documentation, the program design, and the program code.

UNCONDITIONAL TOTALING AND COUNTING

Figure 11-6 shows the program documentation for the example of unconditional totaling. Since this program performs only one function, it will not be written in modular format.

<table>
<tr><th colspan="3">PROGRAM DOCUMENTATION SHEET</th></tr>
<tr><td>Program: C11E1</td><td>Programmer: STUDENT NAME</td><td>Date: 4-16-xx</td></tr>
<tr><td colspan="3">Purpose: This program produces a report showing the production figures for three plants for a week. A total for the entire production is printed at the end.</td></tr>
<tr><td colspan="2">Input: Report date, plant names, day names, and production figures from data lines.</td><td>Output: Report displayed on CRT.</td></tr>
<tr><td colspan="3">Data Terminator: EOD as plant name.</td></tr>
<tr><td colspan="3">Variables Used:
DT$ = Date
TQTY = Total production for all plants (accumulator variable)
PLANT$ = Name of factory
DAY$ = Day of week
QTY = Production of one plant for one day</td></tr>
</table>

Figure 11-6 Program Documentation for Unconditional Totaling

The program design for unconditional totaling is as follows:

1. Clear screen. (Clear memory space on TRS-80 Model III.)
2. Read date for report from DATA line.

3. Print report headings.
4. Initialize total variable (accumulator).
5. Set up loop that runs until the end of data; when inside the loop, these steps should be followed:
   a. Read plant name, day, and quantity from DATA line.
   b. Add quantity produced to total quantity accumulator variable.
   c. Print detail line on report.
   d. Repeat loop.
6. Print total line on report.

The code for the program is as follows. Steps from the program design are indicated by arrows.

Example:

```
10 ' C11E1
20 ' STUDENT NAME, CHAPTER 11, EXAMPLE 1
30 ' DOES UNCONDITIONAL PRODUCTION COUNT
40 '
45 ' CLEAR 1000 ON TRS-80 MODEL III  <----------------  1
50 CLS  <-------------------------------------------  1
60 READ DT$  <--------------------------------------  2
70 PRINT "PRODUCTION REPORT"     ┐
80 PRINT "WEEK ENDING ";DT$      │
90 PRINT                         │  <--------------  3
100 IMAGE$="\      \ \ \  ###"   │
110 PRINT  "PLANT   DAY  QTY"    │
120 PRINT                        ┘
130 TQTY=0  <---------------------------------------  4
150 ' ***** BEGIN LOOP  <---------------------------  5
160   READ PLANT$,DAY$,QTY  <-----------------------  5a
170   IF PLANT$-"EOD" THEN 220
180   TQTY=TQTY+QTY  <------------------------------  5b
200   PRINT USING IMAGE$;PLANT$,DAY$,QTY  <---------  5c
210   GOTO 150 ' REPEAT LOOP FOR NEXT DATA ITEM  <--  5d
220 PRINT
230 PRINT USING IMAGE$;"TOTAL"," ",TQTY  <----------  6
260 END
1000 ' DATA LINES
1010 DATA "JULY 5, 19--"
1020 DATA ATHENS,MON,50
1030 DATA BOSTON,MON,49
1040 DATA ROME,MON,37
1050 DATA ATHENS,TUE,45
```

```
1060 DATA BOSTON,TUE,52
1070 DATA ROME,TUE,41
1080 DATA ATHENS,WED,52
1090 DATA BOSTON,WED,49
1100 DATA ROME,WED,49
1110 DATA ATHENS,THU,49
1120 DATA BOSTON,THU,48
1130 DATA ROME,THU,43
1140 DATA ATHENS,FRI,51
1150 DATA BOSTON,FRI,50
1160 DATA ROME,FRI,44
1170 DATA ATHENS,SAT,0
1180 DATA BOSTON,SAT,0
1190 DATA ROME,SAT,0
1200 DATA ATHENS,SUN,0
1210 DATA BOSTON,SUN,0
1220 DATA ROME,SUN,20
1230 DATA EOD,EOD,0
```

When the program is executed, the output will be as follows:

Output:

```
PRODUCTION REPORT
WEEK ENDING JULY 5, 19--

PLANT    DAY   QTY

ATHENS   MON    50
BOSTON   MON    49
ROME     MON    37
ATHENS   TUE    45
BOSTON   TUE    52
ROME     TUE    41
ATHENS   WED    52
BOSTON   WED    49
ROME     WED    49
ATHENS   THU    49
BOSTON   THU    48
ROME     THU    43
ATHENS   FRI    51
BOSTON   FRI    50
ROME     FRI    44
ATHENS   SAT     0
```

```
BOSTON  SAT    0
ROME    SAT    0
ATHENS  SUN    0
BOSTON  SUN    0
ROME    SUN   20

TOTAL        729
```

Figure 11-7 shows the program documentation for the same program as the previous example except that counting has been added to the process. The additions are in bold for easy recognition.

PROGRAM DOCUMENTATION SHEET		
Program: C11E2	Programmer: STUDENT NAME	Date: 4-16-xx
Purpose: This program produces a report showing the production figures for three plants for a week. A total for the entire production is printed at the end; **a count of the items processed is also printed at the end of the report.**		
Input: Report date, plant names, day names, and production figures from data lines.	Output: Report displayed on CRT.	
Data Terminator: EOD as plant name.		
Variables Used: DT$ = Date TQTY = Total production for all plants (accumulator variable) PLANT$ = Name of factory DAY$ = Day of week QTY = Production of one plant for one day **COUNT = Count of the items processed**		

Figure 11-7 Program Documentation for Unconditional Totaling and Counting

The program design for unconditional totaling and counting is as follows:

1. Clear screen. (Clear memory space on TRS-80 Model III.)
2. Read date for report from DATA line.
3. Print report headings.
4. Initialize total variable (accumulator) **and counter variable**.
5. Set up loop that runs until the end of data; when inside the loop, these steps should be followed:
   a. Read plant name, day, and quantity from DATA line.
   b. Add quantity produced to total quantity accumulator variable.
   c. Add 1 to counter variable.
   d. Print detail line on report.
   e. Repeat loop.
6. Print total line on report.
7. **Print count on report.**

The code for the program is as follows. Steps from the program design are indicated by the arrows.

Example:

```
10 ' C11E2
20 ' STUDENT NAME, CHAPTER 11, EXAMPLE 2
30 ' DOES UNCONDITIONAL PRODUCTION TOTAL AND COUNT
40 '
45 ' CLEAR 1000 ON TRS-80 MODEL III  <---------------- 1
50 CLS  <------------------------------------------- 1
60 READ DT$  <-------------------------------------- 2
70 PRINT "PRODUCTION REPORT"          ┐
80 PRINT "WEEK ENDING ";DT$           │
90 PRINT                              │ <------------ 3
100 IMAGE$="\    \ \ \  ###"          │
110 PRINT  "PLANT   DAY  QTY"         │
120 PRINT                             ┘
130 TQTY=0  <--------------------------------------- 4
140 COUNT=0  <-------------------------------------- 4
150 ' ***** BEGIN LOOP  <--------------------------- 5
160   READ PLANT$,DAY$,QTY  <---------------------- 5a
170   IF PLANT$="EOD" THEN 220
180   TQTY=TQTY+QTY  <----------------------------- 5b
190   COUNT=COUNT+1  <----------------------------- 5c
200   PRINT USING IMAGE$;PLANT$,DAY$,QTY  <-------- 5d
```

```
210   GOTO 150 ' REPEAT LOOP FOR NEXT DATA ITEM  ←——— 5e
220 PRINT
230 PRINT USING IMAGE$;"TOTAL"," ",TQTY  ←——— 6
240 PRINT
250 PRINT COUNT;"RECORDS PROCESSED"  ←——— 7
260 END
1000 ' DATA LINES
1010 DATA "JULY 5, 19--"
1020 DATA ATHENS,MON,50
1030 DATA BOSTON,MON,49
1040 DATA ROME,MON,37
1050 DATA ATHENS,TUE,45
1060 DATA BOSTON,TUE,52
1070 DATA ROME,TUE,41
1080 DATA ATHENS,WED,52
1090 DATA BOSTON,WED,49
1100 DATA ROME,WED,49
1110 DATA ATHENS,THU,49
1120 DATA BOSTON,THU,48
1130 DATA ROME,THU,43
1140 DATA ATHENS,FRI,51
1150 DATA BOSTON,FRI,50
1160 DATA ROME,FRI,44
1170 DATA ATHENS,SAT,0
1180 DATA BOSTON,SAT,0
1190 DATA ROME,SAT,0
1200 DATA ATHENS,SUN,0
1210 DATA BOSTON,SUN,0
1220 DATA ROME,SUN,20
1230 DATA EOD,EOD,0
```

When the program is executed, the output will be as follows:

Output:

```
PRODUCTION REPORT
WEEK ENDING JULY 5, 19--

PLANT   DAY  QTY

ATHENS  MON   50
BOSTON  MON   49
ROME    MON   37
ATHENS  TUE   45
BOSTON  TUE   52
```

```
ROME     TUE   41
ATHENS   WED   52
BOSTON   WED   49
ROME     WED   49
ATHENS   THU   49
BOSTON   THU   48
ROME     THU   43
ATHENS   FRI   51
BOSTON   FRI   50
ROME     FRI   44
ATHENS   SAT    0
BOSTON   SAT    0
ROME     SAT    0
ATHENS   SUN    0
BOSTON   SUN    0
ROME     SUN   20

TOTAL         729

 21 RECORDS PROCESSED
```

CONDITIONAL TOTALING AND COUNTING

Review Figure 11-3 and note that the report is the same as that produced by the previous example program, except that totals and counts are printed at the bottom of the report for each of the three factories. Study the program documentation in Figure 11-8, which produces a report with conditional totals and counts. Differences from the previous program, which produced the report shown in Figure 11-7, are shown in bold.

The program design for conditional totals and counts is as follows:

1. Clear screen. (Clear character space on TRS-80 Model III.)
2. Read date for report from DATA line.
3. Print report headings.
4. Initialize **all** total variables (accumulators) and counter variables.
5. Set up loop that runs until the end of data; when inside the loop, these steps should be followed:
   a. Read plant name, day, and quantity from DATA line.
   b. Add quantity produced to total factory quantity accumulator variable.
   c. Add 1 to counter variable.

PROGRAM DOCUMENTATION SHEET		
Program: C11E3	Programmer: STUDENT NAME	Date: 4-16-xx

Purpose: This program produces a report showing the production figures for three plants for a week. **At the end of the report, a total and count is printed for each of the three plants.** A total of the entire production quantity and a count of the items processed are the final two items of the report.

Input: Report date, plant names, day names, and production figures from data lines.	Output: Report displayed on CRT.

Data Terminator: EOD as plant name.

Variables Used:

DT$ = Date
TQTY = Total production for all plants (accumulator variable)
AQTY = Total production for Athens plant (accumulator)
BQTY = Total production for Boston plant (accumulator)
RQTY = Total production for Rome plant (accumulator)
PLANT$ = Name of factory
DAY$ = Day of week
QTY = Production of one plant for one day
COUNT = Count of the items processed
ACOUNT = Count of the items processed by the Athens plant
BCOUNT = Count of the items processed by the Boston plant
RCOUNT = Count of the items processed by the Rome plant

Figure 11-8 Program Documentation for Conditional Totals and Counts

d. **Update appropriate factory accumulator and counter.**
e. Print detail line on report.
f. Repeat loop.

6. **Print production quantity totals and counts for each plant.**
7. Print grand total production quantity line on report.
8. Print total count on report.

The code for the program is as follows. Steps from the program design are indicated by the arrows.

Example:

```
10 ' C11E3
20 ' STUDENT NAME, CHAPTER 11, EXAMPLE 3
30 ' DOES CONDITIONAL TOTALING AND COUNTING
40 '
45 ' CLEAR 1000 ON TRS-80 MODEL III
50 CLS  <---------------------------------------------- 1
60 READ DT$  <------------------------------------------ 2
70 PRINT "PRODUCTION REPORT"          ]
80 PRINT "WEEK ENDING ";DT$           ]
90 PRINT                              ]  <-------------- 3
100 IMAGE$="\      \  \ \  ###"       ]
110 PRINT  "PLANT   DAY  QTY"         ]
120 PRINT                             ]
130 TQTY=0:AQTY=0:BQTY=0:RQTY=0             ]  <-------- 4
140 COUNT=0:ACOUNT=0:BCOUNT=0:RCOUNT=0      ]
150 ' ***** BEGIN LOOP  <------------------------------- 5
160    READ PLANT$,DAY$,QTY  <-------------------------- 5a
170    IF PLANT$="EOD" THEN 220
175    TQTY=TQTY+QTY:COUNT=COUNT+1  <------------ 5b and 5c
180    IF PLANT$="ATHENS" THEN AQTY=AQTY+QTY:ACOUNT=ACOUNT+1 ]
185    IF PLANT$="BOSTON" THEN BQTY=BQTY+QTY:BCOUNT=BCOUNT+1 ] <-- 5d
190    IF PLANT$="ROME" THEN RQTY=RQTY+QTY:RCOUNT=RCOUNT+1   ]
200    PRINT USING IMAGE$;PLANT$,DAY$,QTY  <------------ 5e
210    GOTO 150 ' REPEAT LOOP FOR NEXT DATA ITEM  <----- 5f
220 PRINT
230 PRINT USING "ATHENS TOTAL ###";AQTY    ]
232 PRINT "(";ACOUNT;"RECORDS)"            ]
233 PRINT                                  ]
234 PRINT USING "BOSTON TOTAL ###";BQTY    ]  <--------- 6
236 PRINT "(";BCOUNT;"RECORDS)"            ]
237 PRINT                                  ]
238 PRINT USING "ROME TOTAL   ###";RQTY    ]
240 PRINT "(";RCOUNT;"RECORDS)"            ]
```

```
242 PRINT
244 PRINT USING "GRAND TOTAL  ###";TQTY  <————————— 7
246 PRINT
250 PRINT COUNT;"RECORDS PROCESSED"  <————————— 8
260 END
1000 ' DATA LINES
1010 DATA "JULY 5, 19--"
1020 DATA ATHENS,MON,50
1030 DATA BOSTON,MON,49
1040 DATA ROME,MON,37
1050 DATA ATHENS,TUE,45
1060 DATA BOSTON,TUE,52
1070 DATA ROME,TUE,41
1080 DATA ATHENS,WED,52
1090 DATA BOSTON,WED,49
1100 DATA ROME,WED,49
1110 DATA ATHENS,THU,49
1120 DATA BOSTON,THU,48
1130 DATA ROME,THU,43
1140 DATA ATHENS,FRI,51
1150 DATA BOSTON,FRI,50
1160 DATA ROME,FRI,44
1170 DATA ATHENS,SAT,0
1180 DATA BOSTON,SAT,0
1190 DATA ROME,SAT,0
1200 DATA ATHENS,SUN,0
1210 DATA BOSTON,SUN,0
1220 DATA ROME,SUN,20
1230 DATA EOD,EOD,0
```

When executed, the output of the program will be as follows:

Output:

```
PRODUCTION REPORT
WEEK ENDING JULY 5, 19--

PLANT   DAY  QTY

ATHENS  MON   50
BOSTON  MON   49
ROME    MON   37
ATHENS  TUE   45
```

```
BOSTON  TUE    52
ROME    TUE    41
ATHENS  WED    52
BOSTON  WED    49
ROME    WED    49
ATHENS  THU    49
BOSTON  THU    48
ROME    THU    43
ATHENS  FRI    51
BOSTON  FRI    50
ROME    FRI    44
ATHENS  SAT     0
BOSTON  SAT     0
ROME    SAT     0
ATHENS  SUN     0
BOSTON  SUN     0
ROME    SUN    20

ATHENS TOTAL 247
( 7 RECORDS)

BOSTON TOTAL 248
( 7 RECORDS)

ROME TOTAL   234
( 7 RECORDS)

GRAND TOTAL  729

 21 RECORDS PROCESSED
```

CODING FOR SUBTOTALS

The following example illustrates the program to print the report shown in Figure 11-4. Remember that this report does detail printing with subtotals for each shift. The spacing chart for this program is shown in Figure 11-9.

The program design will help explain the logic of the program. First, study the hierarchy chart in Figure 11-10. Next, study the program documentation sheet in Figure 11-11 and the module documentation sheets and corresponding codes in Figures 11-12 through 11-15.

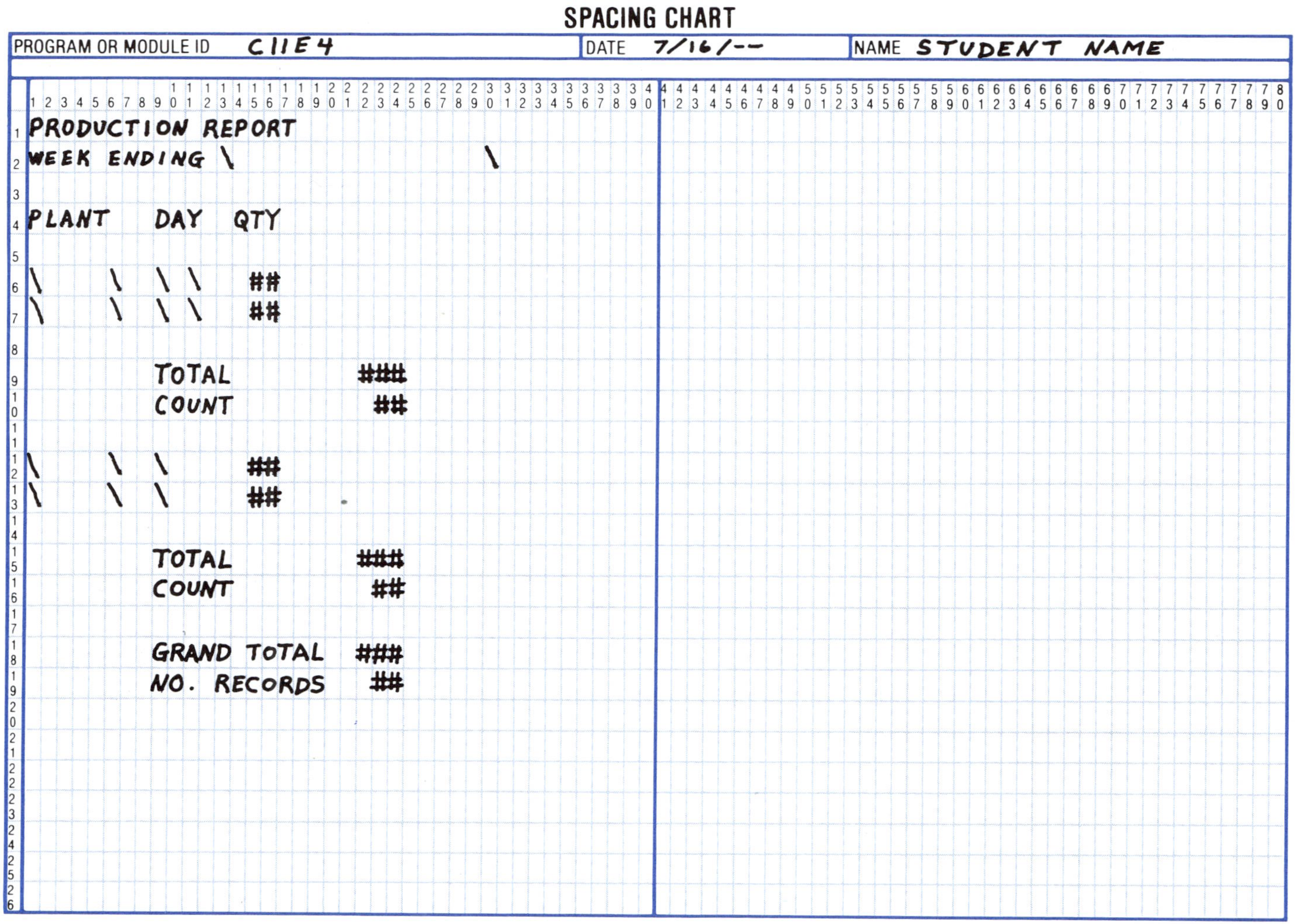

Figure 11-9 Spacing Chart for Detail Report

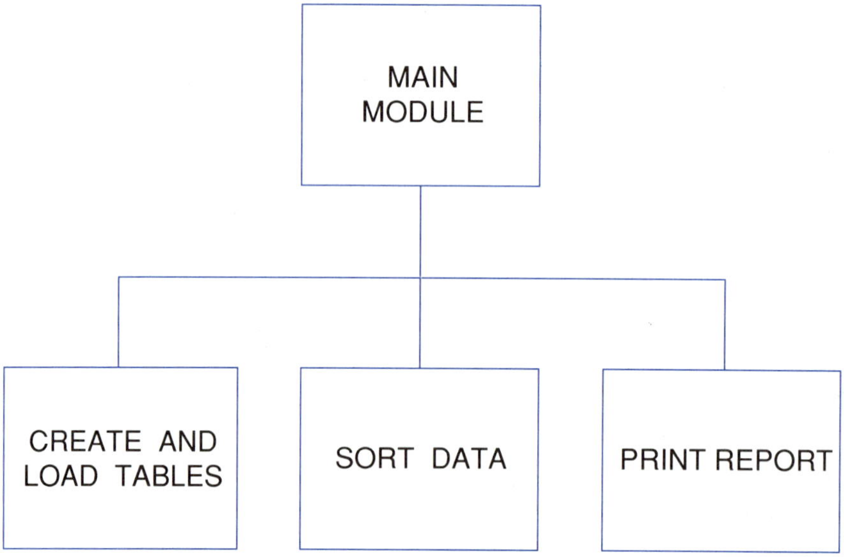

Figure 11-10 Hierarchy Chart for Detail Subtotal Printing

The output of the program is as follows:

Output:

```
PRODUCTION REPORT
WEEK ENDING JULY 5, 19--

PLANT    DAY  QTY

ATHENS   MON   50
ATHENS   TUE   45
ATHENS   WED   52
ATHENS   THU   49
ATHENS   FRI   51
ATHENS   SAT    0
ATHENS   SUN    0

         TOTAL         247
         COUNT           7

BOSTON   WED   49
BOSTON   MON   49
BOSTON   THU   48
BOSTON   TUE   52
BOSTON   FRI   50
BOSTON   SAT    0
BOSTON   SUN    0

         TOTAL         248
         COUNT           7

ROME     FRI   44
```

```
ROME    TUE   41
ROME    WED   49
ROME    SAT    0
ROME    MON   37
ROME    THU   43
ROME    SUN   20

        TOTAL          234
        COUNT            7

        GRAND TOTAL    729
        NO. RECORDS     21
```

PROGRAM DOCUMENTATION SHEET		
Program: C11E4	Programmer: STUDENT NAME	Date: 4-30-xx
Purpose: This program prints a detailed production report by plant.		
Input: Data is input from the keyboard and stored in tables.	Output: Report printed on stock paper.	
Data Terminator: EOD as plant name.		
Variables Used: DA$ = Day of week DT$ = Date for which report is prepared D = Loop variable PLANT$() = Table with columns 0 (plant name) and 1 (day name) PL$ = Letter of plant name entered from keyboard PROD() = Table with column for production N = Number of data items (records) to be processed SUBTOTAL = Subtotal TOTAL = Total SUBCOUNT = Group count COUNT = Count of all items		

Figure 11-11 Program Documentation Sheet for Detail Subtotal Printing

MODULE DOCUMENTATION SHEET	
Program: C11E4	Module: MAIN Lines: 10-999

Module Description: This is the main (control) module.

Module Function (Program Design):

1. Clear memory space for character data (TRS-80 Model III).
2. Clear the screen.
3. Get the date from the user.
4. Perform the Create and Load Tables Module.
5. Perform the Sort Module.
6. Perform the Print Module.

```
10 ' C11E4
20 ' STUDENT NAME, CHAPTER 11, EXAMPLE 4
30 ' PRODUCES DETAILED PRODUCTION REPORT
40 '
50 ' ************************
60 ' * MAIN MODULE          *
70 ' ************************
80 ' CLEAR 1000 GOES HERE FOR TRS-80 MODEL III  <-------- 1
90 CLS  <------------------------------------------------ 2
100 PRINT "THIS PROGRAM PRODUCES A DETAILED"
110 PRINT "WEEKLY PRODUCTION REPORT.  PLEASE"
120 PRINT "ENTER THE DATE ON WHICH THE WEEK"
130 LINE INPUT "ENDS:  ";DT$  <-------------------------- 3
140 GOSUB 1000 ' CREATE AND LOAD TABLES  <--------------- 4
150 GOSUB 2000 ' SORT DATA  <---------------------------- 5
160 GOSUB 3000 ' PRINT REPORT  <------------------------- 6
999 END
```

Figure 11-12 Documentation Sheet and Code for Main Module

MODULE DOCUMENTATION SHEET

Program: C11E4	Module: CREATE AND LOAD TABLES Lines: 1000-1999

Module Description: This is the main module that creates and fills tables with data.

Module Function (Program Design):

1. Dimension tables for plant name, day of week, and quantity.
2. Clear the screen.
3. Run a loop for as long as the user wants to continue, getting data from the keyboard and storing it in the tables. The data consists of plant name, day of the week, and quantity produced.
4. Store the number of records in the number of records variable.

```
1000 ' ********************************
1010 ' * CREATE AND LOAD TABLES MODULE *
1020 ' ********************************
1030 DIM PLANT$(50,1),PROD(50) <------------------------- 1
1040 CLS <----------------------------------------------- 2
1050 PRINT "ENTER THE PRODUCTION FIGURES FOR"
1060 PRINT "EACH PLANT FOR EACH DAY.  WHEN"
1070 PRINT "FINISHED, ENTER EOD FOR PLANT."
1080 PRINT
1090 FOR N=0 TO 50                                         ┐
1100   INPUT "LETTER OF PLANT NAME (OR EOD):  ";PL$        │
1110   IF PL$="EOD" THEN 1240 ' EXIT WHEN DONE             │
1120   IF PL$<>"A" AND PL$<>"B" AND PL$<>"R" THEN 1100     │
1130   IF PL$="A" THEN PLANT$(N,0)="ATHENS"                │ <- 3
1140   IF PL$="B" THEN PLANT$(N,0)="BOSTON"                │
1150   IF PL$="R" THEN PLANT$(N,0)="ROME"                  │
1160   INPUT "ENTER DAY OF WEEK (3 LETTERS):  ";DA$        │
1170   FOR D=0 TO 6                                        │
1180     IF MID$("MONTUEWEDTHUFRISATSUN",D*3+1,3)=DA$ THEN 1210┘
```

Figure 11-13 Documentation Sheet and Code for the Create and Load Tables Module

```
1190    NEXT D
1200    GOTO 1160 ' REENTER IF INVALID DAY OF WEEK
1210    PLANT$(N,1)=DA$                                    ← 3
1220    INPUT "QUANTITY PRODUCED:  ";PROD(N)
1230 NEXT N
1240 N=N-1 ←                                               4
1999 RETURN
```

Figure 11-13 (continued)

MODULE DOCUMENTATION SHEET

Program: C11E4	Module: SORT Lines: 2000-2999

Module Description: This is the module that sorts the data that has been entered into the tables.

Module Function (Program Design):

1. Use the sort algorithm of choice to arrange data in the two tables in ascending order according to the plant location. Note that PLANT$ has two columns—0 and 1—while PROD has one column. The sort algorithm makes its comparisons on the basis of the plant location, which is column 0. Whenever the sort algorithm calls for a swap of data to be made, however, you must swap not only column 0 of table PLANT$, but also column 1 of table PLANT$ and the single column of table PROD. These multiple swaps keep all the associated data together as the sort progresses.

```
2000 ' *****************************
2010 ' * SORT (ASCENDING)          *
2020 ' *****************************
2030 PRINT "BEGINNING SORT..."
2040 PRINT
```

Figure 11-14 Documentation for Create and Load Tables Module

```
2050 FOR START=0 TO N-1
2060 SMALL=START
2070   FOR LOOK=START+1 TO N
2080      IF PLANT$(SMALL,0)>PLANT$(LOOK,0) THEN SMALL=LOOK
2090   NEXT LOOK
2100   ATEMP$=PLANT$(START,0):BTEMP$=PLANT$(START,1):TEMP=PROD(START)
2110   PLANT$(START,0)=PLANT$(SMALL,0):PLANT$(START,1)=PLANT$(SMALL,
       1) :PROD(START)=PROD(SMALL)
2120   PLANT$(SMALL,0)=ATEMP$:PLANT$(SMALL,1)=BTEMP$:PROD(SMALL)=TEMP
2130 NEXT START
2999 RETURN
```

Figure 11-14 (continued)

MODULE DOCUMENTATION SHEET

Program: C11E4	Module: PRINT REPORT Lines: 3000-3999

Module Description: This is the module that prints the production report from sorted data in the tables.

Module Function (Program Design):

1. Print report headings.
2. Initialize compare, subtotal, total, subcount, and count variables.
3. Print detail line for first record data item.
4. Set up loop to run through remainder of rows of data in table; when inside the loop, these steps should be followed:
   a. If plant is not equal to (<>) the compare variable, process a subtotal/subcount line.
   b. Print detail line for the data being processed.
   c. Update compare and accumulator variables.
   d. Repeat loop.
5. Print final subtotal, subcount, grand total, and count.

Figure 11-15 Documentation Sheet and Code for the Print Report Module

```
3000 ' ********************************
3010 ' * PRINT REPORT MODULE          *
3020 ' ********************************
3030 CLS
3040 PRINT "PRODUCTION REPORT"
3050 PRINT "WEEK ENDING ";DT$                              ← 1
3060 PRINT
3070 PRINT "PLANT    DAY  QTY"
3080 PRINT
3090 COMPARE$=PLANT$(0,0):SUBTOTAL=PROD(0):TOTAL=PROD(0)  ← 2
3095 SUBCOUNT=1:COUNT=1                                    ← 2
3100 PRINT USING "\    \ \ \  ###";PLANT$(0,0),PLANT$(0,1),
     PROD(0)                                               ← 3
3110 FOR R=1 TO N                                          ← 4
3120   IF PLANT$(R,0)<>COMPARE$ THEN GOSUB 3200 ' PROCESS
       SUBTOTAL                                            ← 4a
3130   PRINT USING "\    \ \ \  ###";PLANT$(R,0),PLANT$(R,1),
       PROD(R)                                             ← 4b
3140   COMPARE$=PLANT$(R,0):SUBTOTAL=SUBTOTAL+PROD(R):
       TOTAL=TOTAL+PROD(R)                                 ← 4c
3145 SUBCOUNT=SUBCOUNT+1:COUNT=COUNT+1
3150 NEXT R                                                ← 4d
3160 GOSUB 3200 ' PROCESS FINAL SUBTOTAL
3170 PRINT
3180 PRINT USING "          GRAND TOTAL     ###";TOTAL     ← 5
3190 PRINT USING "          NO. RECORDS      ##";COUNT
3199 RETURN
3200 ' ********************************
3210 ' * PROCESS SUBTOTALS            *
3220 ' ********************************
3230 PRINT
3240 PRINT USING "          TOTAL           ###";SUBTOTAL
3245 PRINT USING "          COUNT            ##";SUBCOUNT
3250 SUBTOTAL=0:SUBCOUNT=0
3260 PRINT
3999 RETURN
```

Figure 11-15 (continued)

GROUP PRINTING

Group printing is done the same way as subtotaling, except that detail lines are omitted. To get the names of the cities on the subtotal lines as shown in Figure 11-5, the contents of the compare variable are printed on the subtotal line instead of the word TOTAL. These changes are shown in the print report module code that follows.

Example:

```
3000 ' *********************************
3010 ' * PRINT REPORT MODULE           *
3020 ' *********************************
3030 CLS
3040 PRINT "PRODUCTION REPORT"
3050 PRINT "WEEK ENDING ";DT$
3060 PRINT
3070 PRINT "PLANT           QTY  NO. DAYS"
3080 PRINT
3090 COMPARE$=PLANT$(0,0):SUBTOTAL=PROD(0):TOTAL=PROD(0)
3095 SUBCOUNT=1:COUNT=1
3110 FOR R=1 TO N
3120    IF PLANT$(R,0)<>COMPARE$ THEN GOSUB 3200 ' PROCESS SUBTOTAL
3140    COMPARE$=PLANT$(R,0):SUBTOTAL=SUBTOTAL+PROD(R):TOTAL=TOTAL+
        PROD(R)
3145    SUBCOUNT=SUBCOUNT+1:COUNT=COUNT+1
3150 NEXT R
3160 GOSUB 3200 ' PROCESS FINAL SUBTOTAL
3170 PRINT
3180 PRINT USING "GRAND TOTAL    ###    ###";TOTAL,COUNT
3199 RETURN
3200 ' *********************************
3210 ' * PROCESS SUBTOTALS             *
3220 ' *********************************
3240 PRINT USING "\          \    ###    ###";COMPARE$,SUBTOTAL,
     SUBCOUNT
3250 SUBTOTAL=0:SUBCOUNT=0
3999 RETURN
```

The following output will be produced when the program is executed:

Output:

```
PRODUCTION REPORT
WEEK ENDING JULY 5, 19--

PLANT          QTY  NO. DAYS

ATHENS         247      7
```

```
BOSTON         248     7
ROME           234     7

GRAND TOTAL    729    21
```

REVIEW QUESTIONS

1. Describe how to do unconditional totaling and counting with BASIC. (Obj. 5)
2. Describe how to do conditional totaling and counting with BASIC. (Obj. 5)
3. Explain the roles of control variables and compare variables in handling control breaks. (Obj. 5)
4. How must data be arranged before printing a report with subtotals? Why? (Obj. 5)

VOCABULARY WORDS

The following terms were introduced in this chapter:

compare variable	count	summarizing
conditional count	detail printing	summary
conditional total	group printing	total
control break	minor total	unconditional count
control variable	subtotal	unconditional total

PROGRAMS TO WRITE

For each of the programs, prepare the necessary documentation prior to writing the BASIC code. When a program is to perform more than one primary function, write the program in modular form.

Program 1

A frozen yogurt store wishes to know the total number of waffle cones sold during the month. They have maintained sales quantities on a daily basis, and the program needs to read those figures from DATA lines and produce a total. To test the program, use daily sales quantities of 60, 54, 75, 81, 76, 53, 68, 80, 73, 79, 76, 59, 67, 83, 79, 81, 68, 69, 73, 67, 54, 67, 83, 67, 71, 70, 76, 68, 69, 75, and 66. In addition to computing and printing the total quantity sold for the month, the program should compute and print the total number of data items processed. This count will be used by the store to verify that the proper number of figures have been entered. For example, the test data is for a 31-day month; therefore, a count of 31 should be produced and printed by the program.

Program 2

An automobile dealer wants to use the computer to print a report of unit sales of new and used cars for each salesperson, with the data being read from DATA lines in the program. The report should resemble the following format (use the data from the sample report in testing your program):

```
REPORT OF UNIT SALES

SALESPERSON    TYPE          QTY

BROCKWAY       N              12
JACKSON        N              14
MILLER         N              21
BROCKWAY       U              13
JACKSON        U              11
MILLER         U              19

TOTAL                         90
 6 RECORDS PROCESSED
```

Program 3

One of the statistics maintained by the weather bureau is that of rainfall amount by month, which is measured in inches. Write a program that will store the amount of each rain during the month on a DATA line. The program should print a report showing the individual rain amounts and the total amount of rain for the month. It should also print the number of days on which rain fell. To test your program, use rainfall amounts of 1.23, .13, .87, .39, and .63 during a month.

Program 4

The names of courses taken by a student, along with the grade points earned for each course, should be stored on DATA lines in a program. The program should print a report that lists each of the courses and its grade points. At the end of the listing, the report should include the grade point average, which is computed by dividing the total number of grade points by the number of courses taken. To test your program, use the following data:

COURSE	GRADE POINTS
English 101	4
Biology 101	3
Humanities 102	4
English 102	3
Biology 102	2
Humanities 103	3
English 103	4
Biology 103	2
Humanities 104	4

Program 5

The Rickley family operates Syd and Ralph's Old Family Candy Factory. Candy is produced in even-sized batches during the day, and formed by hand into various shapes. Since the candy is hand formed, the number of pieces per batch varies. In order to know how consistently production is being done, Syd and Ralph put the number of pieces made per batch into their computer at the end of the day, and the computer produces a total of the pieces made for the day. It also produces a count of the number of batches less than 20 pieces, equal to 20 pieces (which is the desired yield), and greater than 20 pieces. As a check that all batches were entered, it also tells them how many batches were entered. Write the program to accomplish this, with the data to be entered from the keyboard. For test data, enter batches that have piece counts of 21, 20, 17, 23, 19, 22, 22, 20, 18, and 21.

Program 6

Modify Program 2 of this chapter so that the program prints the total number of new cars sold and the total number of used cars sold at the end of the report.

Program 7

For this program, you may either modify your solution to Program 3 of this chapter or you may write a solution from scratch. The program should allow a weather bureau person to enter (from the keyboard at the end of the month) all the precipitation received during the month, with the data being stored in one or more tables.

The date, amount of precipitation, and its type (either R for rain or S for snow) are entered. The report printed by the program should display all the precipitation amounts, distinguishing between rain and snow. At the end of the report, the total amount of rain and total amount of snow should be printed, as well as a count of the number of days each fell. Use the following test data:

12/04/--	.75 inches of rain
12/07/--	.63 inches of rain
12/09/--	1.20 inches of snow
12/11/--	.87 inches of rain
12/14/--	.05 inches of rain
12/17/--	4.80 inches of snow
12/21/--	.83 inches of rain
12/29/--	4.80 inches of snow

Program 8

The text of the Program 8 assignment from Chapter 10 is given here in italics. Make the modifications indicated in regular print at the end of the italics. *Write a program that will allow a teacher to key in up to 35 student names and two test scores—one for language skills and one for math. The program should sort the same data three ways—in alphabetic sequence by names, in descending sequence on language score (first test score), and in descending sequence on math score (second test score). Printouts should be provided for all three sequences. Sample data to test your program (to be entered in the order given) includes the following: Barbara Davenport, 85, 94; Gloria Valdez, 82, 97; Earl Hunter, 54, 76; Mary Garcia, 78, 61; Oki Shinoda, 78, 78; Kevin Smith, 69, 73; Bill Hoover, 73, 61; and Greg Lee, 84, 75.* When a printout is sorted by language arts score, the average language arts score and the number of persons passing and failing the language arts test should also be printed. When a printout is sorted by math scores, the average math score and the number of persons passing and failing the math test should be printed. All scores of 70 and above are passing.

Program 9

A business has employees in several departments. To help provide information to management, it wants a report of all salaries, arranged by department. At the end of each department's listing, a subtotal for that department's salaries, along with a count of the number of employees in the department, should be printed. A total for all the employees of the company should appear at the end of the report, along with a count of all employees. To test your program, enter the following data from the keyboard:

EMPLOYEE	DEPARTMENT	SALARY
MARTIN	ATG	44000
SMITH	MKG	32000
RYDELL	ATG	21480
JOHNSON	ATG	38470
ADAMS	MKG	34298
BROCKWAY	MFG	22849
MANGUM	MFG	31983
RIDGEWAY	MFG	21983
REGISTER	MGT	62982

Program 10

Rewrite or modify Program 4 of this chapter so that data is entered from the keyboard and there is a control break after each subject (i.e., after Biology, English, and Humanities). Calculate and print a grade point average for each subject. The overall grade point average should still be printed at the end of the report. The program should arrange the courses in subject order before beginning the report. To test your program, enter the data in the order in which it was given in Program 4.

PROJECT 4

During a special week each year called "Money on the Set," a public television station regularly interrupts its programming with pledge breaks. During these breaks, viewers are urged to call in and pledge to send a contribution. When a viewer calls in, a phone operator enters the caller's name, address, and amount of pledge into a computer.

At the end of the evening's pledge breaks, the computer prints out notices to each person thanking them for the pledge, reminding them of its amount, and giving the address to which their contribution should be mailed. These notices are printed in order by zip code to qualify for the lowest postage rates. In addition to the notices, the computer prints a list of the callers' names, addresses, and pledge amounts. The list should be grouped first by zip code area, then alphabetically. The number of pledges, average pledge amount, and total amount from each zip code area should be printed at the end of the list of callers from the area. At the end of the entire list, the count of the total number of callers is printed, along with the average amount of all pledges and the grand total of the pledges from all the areas.

Write a program to perform these functions for the television station. Design the formats of the notices and pledge list so that they are attractive and contain all the needed information. As always, prepare the appropriate documentation before beginning to code the program. Use the following data to test the program:

Marilyn Alison, 987 Eighth Avenue, Thomasville, GA 31792, $75.00

Frank & Myrtle Hicks, Route 1, Boston, GA 31626, $50.00

Lars Maeckler, 9 President Way, Thomasville, GA 31792, $100.00

Clark Mimms, Route 1, Boston, GA 31626, $200.00

Celia Drum, 987 A Street, Thomasville, GA 31792, $25.00

Felton & Thelma Scarbrough, 212 Way Road, Thomasville, GA 31792, $200.00

PART FIVE
DISK FILES

12

Storage of Data Using Sequential Files

> **OBJECTIVES**
>
> After studying this chapter, you will be able to
>
> 1. Explain the purpose of data files.
> 2. Describe the operation of sequential data files.
> 3. Write programs using sequential data files.

TOPIC 12.1 CONCEPTS OF SEQUENTIAL DATA FILES

Many of the programs you have written to this point would be more useful if the data could be entered from the keyboard and saved on a disk (also commonly referred to as a diskette) for later use. For example, names and addresses stored in tables could be stored on disk between program runs. As the quantity of data used by a program becomes larger, it becomes even more important that data be stored on disk for later reference. Some examples include accounting programs, airline and hotel reservations programs, and student records programs. For these applications, the computer must be able to store on disk data that is entered from the keyboard. It must then be able to read the data from the disk or tape when necessary. Groups of data stored on disk are known as **files**.

WHAT IS A FILE?

You are probably familiar with file drawers typically found in offices and schools. Each of these file drawers usually contains related information. For example, one file drawer may contain copies of student schedules. Another file drawer may contain names, addresses, and phone numbers of students. Perhaps you have your own phone list containing the names and phone numbers of your friends.

In all these examples, records are maintained. Each student schedule is a record. All the data about each person on your phone list (the combination of each name, address, and phone number) is a record. From these examples, you can see that a **record** is all the related information maintained about one thing—about one student, for example. Each item in a record is known as a **field**. In your phone list, for example, the name is one field, while the phone number is another field.

Let's review the terms by thinking about your phone list again. The smallest piece of information on the list is a single name or phone number. These items are known as fields. All of the fields about one person are known as a record—that is, one person's name and phone number together make up a record about that person. All of the records together make up a file. Therefore, the entire phone list may be thought of as a file. This is shown in Figure 12-1, which represents a person's phone list. The list is known as a file. In the file are three records, one for each person. In each record there are two fields, one each for name and phone number. Note that a group of one or more related fields is known

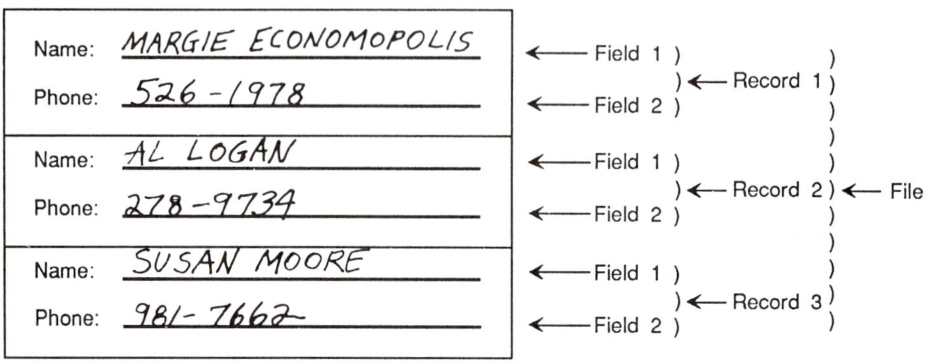

Figure 12-1 Parts of a File

as a record, while a group of one or more related records is known as a file.

If a file (e.g., the phone list) is to be stored by the microcomputer, each name and phone number is recorded—most likely magnetically—on a disk. The disk is divided into recording circles known as tracks. The names and numbers are recorded one after another on the tracks of the disk. Figure 12-2 shows how the three names and phone numbers from the address book might appear on a disk if they could be seen. Note that carriage returns (CR) are recorded on the disks to separate the data. Recording data on the disk is somewhat similar to printing on paper, except that characters are recorded magnetically in code rather than being printed with ink.

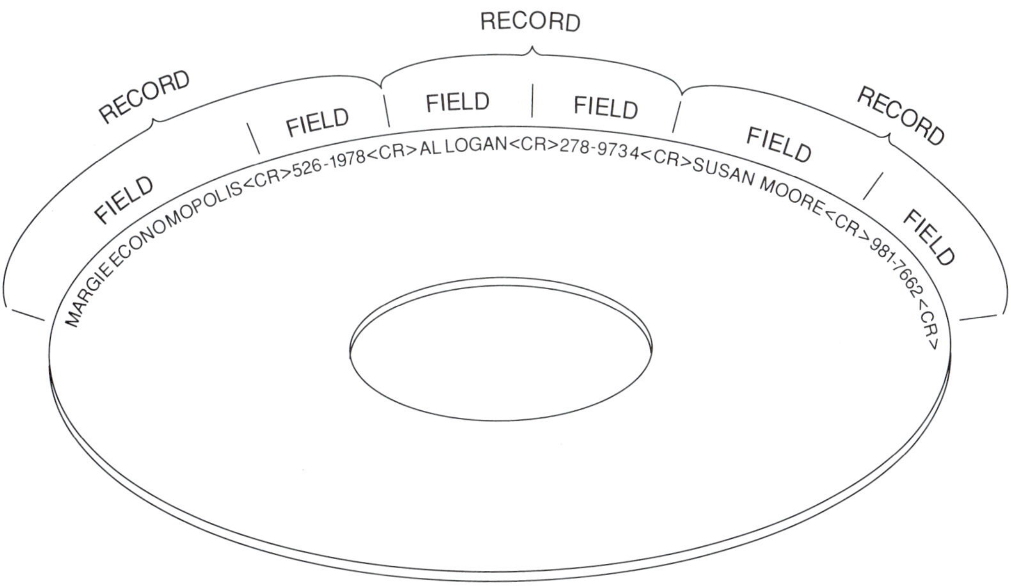

Figure 12-2 File of Names, Addresses, and Phone Numbers on Disk

In Figure 12-2 each name and number takes only the amount of space required by its length—that is, short names do not use as much space as long names. Each field starts immediately at the end of the previous field, with only a carriage return character separating them. A file of this type is known as a sequential file.

Sequential means that the items are recorded one after another. In the same way, when the items are to be read from the disk, they are read one after another. The reading must occur in the same order in which the recording took place.

CREATING AND WRITING TO SEQUENTIAL DATA FILES

If you are going to place a paper in a file cabinet, you must take three steps: (1) open the drawer, (2) place the paper in the drawer, and (3) close the drawer. The same three steps are necessary when recording data to a file on disk.

Opening the Data File

Opening a data file on the computer is analogous to opening the drawer of a file cabinet. The opening operation tells the computer the name of the file to which the computer is to output the data. The name of the file is used by the computer to set up a location on the disk in which the data is to be placed. The names of data files are created by the programmer. The same rules are followed as when naming programs on the disk. A file may be opened in such a manner that new data replaces any already existing data, or it may be opened so that new data is added to the end of already existing data.

Writing the Data

Once a data file is opened, data is written to the disk. The effect is the same as printing to the screen or printer except that the information is written on the disk rather than appearing on the CRT or printer. A special statement is used to tell the computer to write the data on the disk. Individual data items may be written or the contents of tables may be written. Writing to the diskette may also be referred to as recording or printing.

Closing the File

When all data has been written on the diskette, the file must be closed. The closing operation is similar to closing the drawer of a file cabinet after everything has been placed in it. The computer is told that the use of the file is finished for the present time. Once the data is on the disk and the file is closed, the computer may be turned off and the data will remain on the disk for later use.

READING FROM SEQUENTIAL DATA FILES

Bringing data from a file on disk back into the computer is similar to writing the data to the file. Like writing, reading uses a three-step process: (1) opening the file, (2) reading the data from the file, and (3) closing the file.

Opening the Data File for Input

Opening a data file to read data back into the computer from the disk is almost identical to opening the file for output. The name of the file is given to tell the computer where to go to retrieve the data.

Reading Data from the Disk

Once the file is open for input, data is read from the disk and placed in variables. If a data item is numeric, it must be placed in a numeric variable when it is read. If an item is character data, it must be placed in a character variable. The data is always read from a sequential file in the same order in which it was written, starting with the first data item and continuing as far as desired or to the end of the file. Therefore, if the data is written to the file in the order of AUDREY PLANT, NORMA CAMPBELL, the first data item to be read from the file will be AUDREY PLANT, while the second item will be NORMA CAMPBELL. When read from the disk, data may be placed in regular variables or tables. (Reading from the disk may also be referred to as inputting). Note that data is read from the file, it is not removed or erased from the disk. This means that, unless the data is intentionally erased, it remains on the disk and can be read repeatedly.

Closing the File

Closing the file after input is identical to closing it after output.

MODIFYING SEQUENTIAL FILES

Since sequential files can only be written in order from start to finish and can only be read in order from start to finish, the possibilities for modifying them are somewhat limited. As you are already aware, you may add new data at the end of existing data. However, the only way to modify data that is already in the file is to read from one file and write to another, making whatever change is desired. For example, to drop a record from a sequential file, you would read records from one file and write them to another, omitting from the writing process the record that you want to drop.

If you want the modified file to have the same name as the original file once the process is complete, you can do one of two things. One approach is to copy the original file to a temporary file before beginning the modification and then write back to the original file, thereby overwriting data that was previously there. The other approach is to erase the original file, once the updating process is complete, and rename the newly created one using the same name as the original file.

REVIEW QUESTIONS

1. What is a file? (Obj. 1)
2. Why are data files needed? (Obj. 1)
3. List three applications in which data files are used. (Obj. 1)
4. What is the relationship among files, records, and fields? (Obj. 2)
5. What is a track? (Obj. 2)
6. What characteristic makes a file sequential? (Obj. 2)
7. Describe the three steps necessary for writing data to a file on a disk. (Obj. 2)
8. Describe the three steps necessary for reading data from a file on disk. (Obj. 2)
9. How can the contents of a sequential file be modified? (Obj. 2)

TOPIC 12.2 IMPLEMENTING SEQUENTIAL DATA FILES

As an example of using sequential data files, let's examine a simple program. It will illustrate the concepts of using a sequential file.

Documentation of Simple Example Program

The program will have a main module and two submodules. One submodule will request that the user enter company names and phone numbers from the keyboard. As they are entered, they are written to the disk in a file named INCS. The other submodule will read back from disk all company names and numbers that have been placed there and display them on the screen. The hierarchy chart for the program is shown in Figure 12-3.

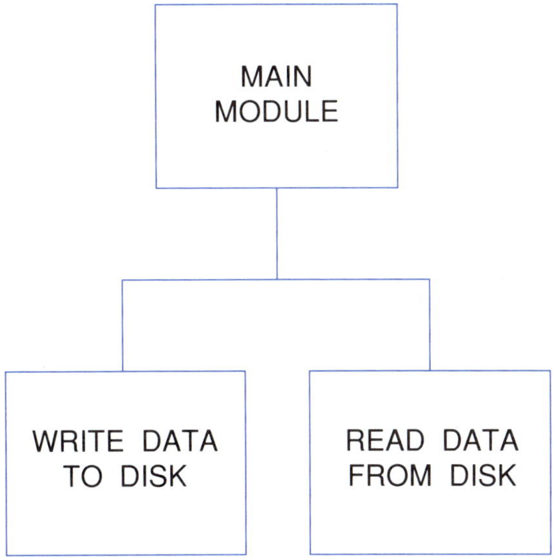

Figure 12-3 Hierarchy Chart for Using a Sequential File

The main module for the program is shown in Figure 12-4.

When chosen, the write data to disk module performs the three steps discussed in the first topic of this chapter for outputting data to a file. They are documented in Figure 12-5.

MODULE DOCUMENTATION SHEET	
Program: C12E1	Module: MAIN Lines: 10-999

Module Description: This is the main module, which performs the menu function.

Module Function (Program Design):

1. Clear the screen.
2. Put menu choices on screen and get user's choice.
3. Perform function chosen by user.
4. If user wants to continue, repeat all steps.

Figure 12-4 Documentation Sheet for the Main Module

<table>
<tr><th colspan="2">MODULE DOCUMENTATION SHEET</th></tr>
<tr><td>Program: C12E1</td><td>Module: WRITE DATA TO DISK
Lines: 1000-1999</td></tr>
<tr><td colspan="2">Module Description: This module gets company names and phone numbers from the keyboard and stores them in a file on disk.</td></tr>
<tr><td colspan="2">Module Function (Program Design):
1. Open data file on disk for output.
2. As long as user wants to continue:
a. Get company name and phone number from keyboard.
b. Write name and phone number to disk.
3. Close the data file.</td></tr>
</table>

Figure 12-5 Documentation Sheet for the Write Data to Disk Module

When it is chosen, the read data from disk module follows these steps: (1) opens the data file, (2) reads the data and prints it on the screen, and (3) closes the data file. Figure 12-6 documents these steps.

KEYWORDS NEEDED FOR THE PROGRAM

Now that you have studied the documentation for the program, let's examine several new BASIC keywords that are necessary in order to write the program. Recall that the first step in each of the submodules is to open the data file (once for the output module, and once for input). That is accomplished with the keyword **OPEN**.

Opening a Sequential File

Sequential files may be opened for either output, input, or append operations. The OPEN statement is used for all three. The general form for the OPEN statement is as follows:

MODULE DOCUMENTATION SHEET	
Program: C12E1	Module: READ DATA FROM DISK Lines: 2000-2999
Module Description: This module reads company names and phone numbers from a data file on the disk and prints them on the screen.	
Module Function (Program Design): 1. Open data file on disk for input. 2. Until the end of data is reached: a. Read name and phone number from disk. b. Print name and phone number on screen. 3. Close the data file.	

Figure 12-6 Documentation Sheet for the Read Data from Disk Module

General Form:
line number OPEN "*file name*" FOR *mode* AS #*file number*

Example 1: `1030 OPEN "INCS" FOR OUTPUT AS #1`

Example 2:
`1030 OPEN FNAM$ FOR OUTPUT AS #1 ...where FNAM$="INCS"`

Example 3: `2030 OPEN "INCS" FOR INPUT AS #1`

The mode specifies how the file is to be opened. It may be either OUTPUT, APPEND, or INPUT. Opening a file for output erases anything that may have previously been in the file. Opening a file for **APPEND** adds new data written to the file to the end of any previously existing data. The number is used for referring to the file in PRINT and INPUT statements later in the program. Usually, the number is #1 unless more than one file is opened at once. In that case, the first file would be #1, the second #2, and so forth. The number has nothing to do with where the data is stored on the disk. The file name is the name of the location on disk that is to be used for storing the information. This name is used by the computer to locate the data. The name of the file must be created according to the same rules used for naming programs. The file name may be enclosed within quotes in the OPEN statement or it may be stored in a character variable, whose name is used in the OPEN statement.

An alternate form for opening sequential files may also be used. This alternate form must be used with the TRS-80 Model III.

General Form:
line number OPEN "*mode*",*file number*,"*file name*"

Example: `1030 OPEN "O",1,"INCS"`

The mode should be entered as an O for output, I for input, or E (extend) for append. The number before the file name is the number by which the file will be referred in later PRINT and INPUT statements.

Writing to a File

Once a file has been opened for output, the **PRINT#** statement is used for writing to the file. This is a keyword used in the second step of the write data to disk module.

General Form:
line number PRINT#*number,items(s) to print*

Example: `1090 PRINT#1,NAM$`

The number following the keyword PRINT is the number under which the file was opened—that is, if the file was opened as #1, #1 will follow the keyword PRINT. This tells the computer the file to which the data should be printed. If you have several variables to print to disk, you should use separate PRINT# statements for each of them rather than putting all the variables after one PRINT statement. This will ensure that each value is followed by a return character to separate it from the next item. Either numeric or character variables may be used after PRINT#. As long as the file remains open, you can continue to add data with repeated PRINT# statements.

Reading from a File

When a file has been opened for input, the **INPUT#** statement is used to read information from the disk into variables. As with PRINT, the file number is written after the statement. The number tells the computer to get the data from the referenced file on disk rather than from the keyboard. When using the INPUT# statement to get data from the disk, no prompt can be used.

General Form:
line number INPUT#*number,variable name(s)*

Example: `2090 INPUT#1,NAM$`

The **LINE INPUT#** statement may also be used to input data from the disk if desired. It is used exactly the same way. Remember that when using LINE INPUT, you can use only one variable in the statement.

Finding the End of a File Being Read

If the number of data items in a file is known, the exact number may be read. Frequently, however, there is no way of knowing in advance how many items are in the file. In these cases, the program must be written to detect when the end of the file is reached. This is done with the **EOF** function and an IF . . . THEN statement.

General Form:
line number IF EOF*(file number)* THEN *action*

Example: `2080 IF EOF(1) THEN GOTO 2120`

EOF stands for end of file. It is a special function to determine if the end of file has been reached. The number in parentheses tells which file is being referenced. The IF . . . THEN statement checks to see if the end of the file has been reached. The EOF function must be checked immediately before each input from a file.

Closing the File

As soon as a program is finished using a file, the file should be closed. This is done with the **CLOSE** statement.

General Form: *line number* CLOSE#*number*

Example: `2150 CLOSE#1`

Remember that the file must be opened with OUTPUT or APPEND if you intend to write data to the disk. It must be opened with INPUT if you intend to read data from the disk. You cannot do writing and reading using the same file opening. Therefore, if you want to write data to the disk and then read it back, you must close the file after the writing is done and open it again to do the reading.

CODING THE PROGRAM

Now that you know the keywords necessary to use a sequential file, study how they are implemented in the example program that follows. As you study them, refer to the module documentation sheets. Step numbers from the sheets are given with the program code to help you follow the flow of the program. Note that in using the program, you must choose option 1 first on the initial run of the program in order to create your file. After the initial run, you may pick options in either order since the data file will exist. If you want to continue adding names to ones entered in previous data entry sessions, change OUTPUT to APPEND in line 1030 or O to E on line 1035 for the TRS-80 Model III.

Example:

```
10 ' C12E1
20 ' STUDENT NAME, CHAPTER 12, EXAMPLE 1
30 ' PRINTS TO DISK AND READS BACK
40 '
50 CLS  ←————— 1
60 PRINT "PHONE DIRECTORY PROGRAM"
70 PRINT
80 PRINT "1 - WRITE NAMES & NUMBERS TO DISK"
90 PRINT "2 - PRINT NAMES & NUMBERS FROM DISK"  ←— 2
100 PRINT "3 - QUIT"
110 PRINT
120 INPUT "CHOICE ";CH
130 ON CH GOSUB 1000,2000  ←————— 3
140 IF CH<>3 THEN 50  ←————— 4
999 END
1000 ' ******************************
1010 ' * WRITE DATA TO DISK          *
1020 ' ******************************
1030 OPEN "INCS" FOR OUTPUT AS #1  ←————— 1
1035 ' OPEN "O",1,"INCS" ON TRS-80 MODEL III
1040 ' ***** BEGIN LOOP
1050    CLS
1060    LINE INPUT "NAME OF COMPANY:   ";NAM$  ←— 2a
1070    LINE INPUT "PHONE NUMBER:      ";PHO$
1080    PRINT
1090    PRINT#1,NAM$  ←— 2b
1100    PRINT#1,PHO$  ←— 2b
1110    PRINT "DATA HAS BEEN WRITTEN TO DISK"
1120    PRINT
1130    PRINT "ENTER ANOTHER NAME & PHONE (Y/N)?";
1140    CH$=INKEY$:IF CH$="" THEN 1140  ←— 2
1150    IF ASC(CH$)>96 THEN CH$=CHR$(ASC(CH$)-32)
1160    IF CH$<>"Y" AND CH$<>"N" THEN 1140
1170    IF CH$="Y" THEN 1040   ' REPEAT LOOP
```

```
1180 CLOSE#1  ←—————————————————————— 3
1999 RETURN
2000 ' *****************************
2010 ' * READ DATA FROM DISK        *
2020 ' *****************************
2030 OPEN "INCS" FOR INPUT AS #1  ←—————————— 1
2035 ' OPEN "I",1,"INCS" ON TRS-80 MODEL III
2040 CLS
2050 PRINT "NAME","PHONE"  ←———————— Print heading
2060 PRINT
2070 ' ***** BEGIN LOOP
2080   IF EOF(1) THEN 2130  ←———————— Quit if out of data
2090   LINE INPUT#1,NAM$  ←————————————— 2a
2100   LINE INPUT#1,PHO$  ←————————————— 2a
2110   PRINT NAM$,PHO$  ←——————————————— 2b
2120   GOTO 2070   ' REPEAT LOOP
2130 CLOSE  ←——————————————————————— 3
2140 PRINT
2150 PRINT "PRESS ANY KEY TO CONTINUE"
2160 CH$=INKEY$:IF CH$="" THEN 2160
2999 RETURN
```

Assume that you run the program and input the following data using menu choice 1: Xymore Co., 732-9832; Smith Inc., 213-9821; Adams Assoc., 399-3449; and Miller Bros., 343-9875. The output of the program upon choosing menu choice 2 will be

```
NAME            PHONE


XYMORE CO.      732-9832
SMITH INC.      213-9821
ADAMS ASSOC.    399-3449
MILLER BROS.    343-9875
```

If you want to erase a file, use the keyword KILL. **KILL** erases any file named in the command, regardless of whether it contains data or a program. The keyword is generally used in immediate mode as a command, although it can be placed inside a program as a statement.

General Form: KILL "*file name*"

Example: `KILL "INCS"`

DEVELOPING A MORE COMPLEX PROGRAM

By using a table along with the storage of data on disk, additional processing can be performed. For example, by using a table, data put on the disk by the previous example program in this chapter can be read from the disk, sorted into alphabetic sequence, and printed. The design of such a program can be broken into three modules as shown in the hierarchy chart (see Figure 12-7).

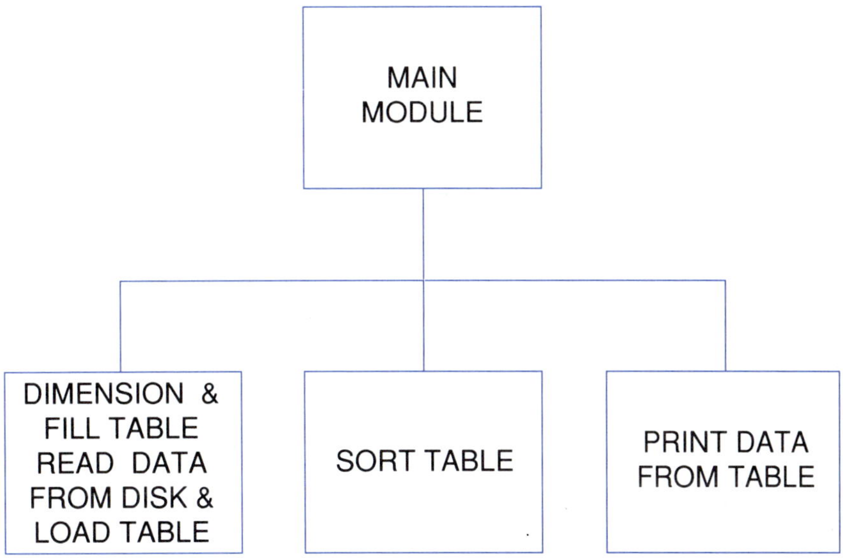

Figure 12-7 Hierarchy Chart for a More Complex Program

The coding of this program calls for no new keywords or algorithms. Therefore, study the module documentation sheets in Figures 12-8 through 12-11 for their program designs. The program code that follows shows how these program designs were converted into BASIC.

The code for this program follows. Steps from the module documentation sheets are indicated.

MODULE DOCUMENTATION SHEET	
Program: C12E2	Module: MAIN Lines: 10-999
Module Description: Main module.	
Module Function (Program Design): 1. Perform the dimension, read data from disk, and load table module. 2. Perform sort module. 3. Perform print module. 4. End.	

Figure 12-8 Documentation Sheet for the Main Module

MODULE DOCUMENTATION SHEET	
Program: C12E2	Module: DIMENSION, READ DATA FROM DISK, AND LOAD TABLE Lines: 1000-1999
Module Description: Dimensions table, reads data from disk, and loads table with data.	
Module Function (Program Design): 1. Dimension a table large enough to hold the greatest expected amount of data. 2. Open the disk file for input. 3. Load the table with data read from disk. 4. Close the disk file.	

Figure 12-9 Documentation Sheet for the Dimension, Read Data From Disk, and Load Table Module

MODULE DOCUMENTATION SHEET

Program: C12E2	Module: SORT Lines: 2000-2999

Module Description: This module sorts the table of data into alphabetic sequence.

Module Function (Program Design):

1. Sort table by any desired algorithm.

Figure 12-10 Documentation Sheet for the Sort Module

MODULE DOCUMENTATION SHEET

Program: C12E2	Module: PRINT DATA Lines: 3000-3999

Module Description: Prints sorted data from table.

Module Function (Program Design):

1. Set up a loop that runs from the first of the table to the numbers of data items.
2. On each iteration of the loop, print the elements in the corresponding row of the table.

Figure 12-11 Documentation Sheet for the Print Module

Example:

```
10 ' C12E2
20 ' STUDENT NAME, CHAPTER 12, EXAMPLE 2
30 ' SORTS & PRINTS DATA STORED ON DISK
50 CLS
60 PRINT "THIS PROGRAM SORTS DATA FROM DISK"
70 PRINT "AND THEN PRINTS IT ON SCREEN."
80 PRINT "PLEASE WAIT . . ."
90 GOSUB 1000 ' DIMENSION & LOAD TABLE  <---------- 1
100 GOSUB 2000 ' SORT DATA  <---------- 2
110 GOSUB 3000 ' PRINT DATA  <---------- 3
999 END  <---------- 4
1000 ' ******************************************
1010 ' * DIMENSION, READ DATA, & LOAD TABLE      *
1020 ' ******************************************
1025 ' CLEAR 1000 GOES HERE ON TRS-80 MOD III
1030 DIM NAM$(100,1)  <---------- 1
1040 OPEN "INCS" FOR INPUT AS #1  <---------- 2
1045 ' 1040 OPEN "I",1,"INCS" ON TRS-80 MOD III
1050 FOR ROW=0 TO 100                 ]  <---------- Set up loop
1060   IF EOF(1) THEN 1100            ]  <---------- Check for file end
1070   LINE INPUT#1,NAM$(ROW,0)       ]  <---------- 3
1080   LINE INPUT#1,NAM$(ROW,1)       ]
1090 NEXT ROW                         ]
1100 CLOSE#1  <---------- 4
1110 N=ROW-1
1999 RETURN
2000 ' ******************************
2010 ' * SORT DATA                  *
2020 ' ******************************
2030 PRINT "BEGINNING SORT..."
2040 PRINT
2050 FOR START=0 TO N-1
2060 SMALL=START
2070   FOR LOOK=START+1 TO N
2080      IF NAM$(SMALL,0)>NAM$(LOOK,0) THEN SMALL=LOOK
2090   NEXT LOOK                                          <-- 1
2100   SWAP NAM$(START,0),NAM$(SMALL,0)
2110   SWAP NAM$(START,1),NAM$(SMALL,1)
2115 ' USE TEMPORARY VARIABLE INSTEAD OF SWAP ON TRS-80 MOD III
2120 NEXT START
2999 RETURN
```

```
3000 ' ******************************
3010 ' * PRINT DATA                 *
3020 ' ******************************
3030 CLS
3040 PRINT "NAME","PHONE"
3050 PRINT
3060 FOR ROW=0 TO N ←—————————————————— 1
3070   PRINT NAM$(ROW,0),NAM$(ROW,1) ←——— 2
3080 NEXT ROW
3999 RETURN
```

Assuming that you entered the sample data for program C12E1 and then ran this program, the output would be sorted and printed to appear as follows:

```
NAME            PHONE

ADAMS ASSOC.    399-3449
MILLER BROS.    343-9875
SMITH INC.      213-9821
XYMORE CO.      732-9832
```

REVIEW QUESTIONS

1. What are some uses of data files? (Obj. 1)
2. What is the difference between opening a file for output and for append? (Obj. 2)
3. Describe the syntax of the keyword used to open a data disk file. (Obj. 2)
4. What keywords are used to read data from a disk file? How do they differ from the same keywords used in non–disk file settings? (Obj. 2)
5. How can a program determine when all data has been read from a disk file? (Obj. 2)
6. How is a data disk file closed? (Obj. 2)

VOCABULARY WORDS

The following terms were introduced in this chapter:

field	record	sequential
file		

KEYWORDS

The following keywords were introduced in this chapter:

APPEND	INPUT#	OPEN
CLOSE	KILL	PRINT#
EOF		

PROGRAMS TO WRITE

For each of the programs, prepare the necessary documentation prior to writing the BASIC code. When a program is to perform more than one primary function, write the program in modular form.

Program 1

Write a program to get city, state, and zip code data from the keyboard and write it to a disk file. Use character variables for all the data, including the zip code. Use the following data to test your program:

Corvallis, OR, 97333

Modesto, CA, 95354

Tallahassee, FL, 32312

Portland, OR, 97210

Macon, GA, 31201

Albany, NY, 12202

Nashville, TN, 37202

Program 2

Write a program to read the data stored by Program 1 from disk and print it in columns on the screen.

Program 3

Write a program to store a customer list in a sequential file on disk; the data should be input from the keyboard. Open the data file for output as opposed to append. The data to be stored should include last name, first name, street address, and zip code. A second option from the program's menu should read back the data stored on disk and print it in columns on the screen. For test data, use the following customers, entered in the order given:

Smith, Marcie	987 Fifth Street	97333
Abrams, Brian	Route 1	32301
Miller, Marie	38 April Lane	95350
Cason, Lea	674 Washington	31213
Barge, Roger	378 Sunset Trail	37202
Smiley, George	956 First Avenue	12201
Cason, Margie	43 Brewer Avenue	97208

Program 4

A biologist is studying how far certain animals travel from their "home base." A male animal and a female animal are tagged with radio transmitters that send signals periodically indicating their location; from these signals, distance can be derived. The data collected at each interval includes the number of the transmitter (which identifies male or female), the time, and the distance from "home" for the animal. Write a program that will get all this data from the keyboard during one run of the program and store it in a sequential file on disk. A second option from the program's menu will read the data back from disk and display it in columns on the screen. Use the following sample data:

ANIMAL	TIME	DISTANCE
M	06	3
F	06	4
M	12	2.5
F	12	3.7
M	18	1.5
F	18	5.8
M	24	.3
F	24	1

Program 5

Modify Program 3 so that the menu item to add people to disk is replaced with one that will display on the screen data for all persons whose last name matches that entered by the user. Do this by adding a module that will load the data from disk into one or more tables, from which data will be displayed. Write the program so that the master listing of all names and addresses is done by printing from the table(s) as well. To test the program, have it display a master list of all the data for all persons, verifying that all names are printed. Request the program to print the data for all persons named Johnson; next request data for all those named Cason.

Program 6

Add a module to Program 5 to allow the printing of mailing labels in the following format:

FIRSTNAME LASTNAME
STREET ADDRESS
ZIP

The names and addresses should be sorted into ascending order by zip code before being printed. Since you do not have city and state fields to print, just print the zip as shown. To test your program, print labels for all persons in the file.

Program 7

Write a program that uses the data previously stored on disk by Program 4. The program should print a report showing the average distance from home reported by each transmitter. In addition, it should also print the time at which each transmitter was closest to home and farthest from home. The format of the report should be as follows:

```
TRAVELS OF A MALE AND FEMALE ANIMAL

MALE'S AVERAGE DISTANCE:        #.##
FEMALE'S AVERAGE DISTANCE:      #.##

WHEN MALE IS CLOSEST:           ##
WHEN FEMALE IS CLOSEST:         ##

WHEN MALE IS FARTHEST:          ##
WHEN FEMALE IS FARTHEST:        ##
```

Program 8

Rewrite your solution to Program 6 (but use the same data file) so that the user can add, modify, or delete persons. Modification to data should be done by working on data in the table(s). Write the data from the table(s) to the disk, overwriting the previous data. Test the program by removing the existing data for Miller. Add the following data: John Johnson, 898 Riddle St., 98732. Change Lea Cason's street address to 58 Wall Road. Print a new master list and verify its accuracy. Run the program again from the beginning, printing another master list; this will confirm that updates were properly made to the disk.

Program 9

Modify Program 8 so that the printing mailing label module prints the name of the city and state on the line with the zip code. This should be done by creating a zip code table that includes the zip code, city name, and state name, and loading this table with data from the file created by Program 1. During the printing process for each label, the zip code from the file of persons should be searched for in the zip code table, and the corresponding city and state should be printed. Test your program by printing labels for all persons in the file.

Program 10

Write a program that has three menu choices. The first choice should enable you to enter data for a household goods inventory. The second choice should print a master list of the items in the file. The third choice should allow you to edit previously made entries. The edit module should copy all data from the current file to a temporary file. From the temporary file, each record should be read in, displayed on the screen, and corrected by the user if desired. The data as corrected should then be written back to disk under the original file name, overwriting data that was previously there. Test the program by entering the following items:

ROOM	DESCRIPTION	VALUE
LR	Sofa	$500
LR	Chair	$210
DR	Table	$450
DR	Chairs (4)	$400
MBR	Queen-sized Bed	$600
MBR	Dresser w/Mirror	$800
MBR	Wall Mirror	$100

After the items are entered, print a master list. Then use the edit option to change the number of dining room chairs to 6 and to remove the mirror from the dresser. Print another master list, observing that the changes have been made correctly on disk.

13

Storage of Data Using Random Files

> **OBJECTIVES**
>
> After studying this chapter, you will be able to
>
> 1. Describe the difference between sequential data files and random data files.
> 2. Describe the operation of random data files.
> 3. Write programs using random data files.

TOPIC 13.1 PRINCIPLES OF RANDOM DATA FILES

In Chapter 12 you learned about sequential data files. In a sequential file, data must be read from the disk in the same order in which it was written—that is, the first data item that was written to the file on disk must be the first one read back. If the data item a program needs is not the first one in the file, all the items in front of it must be read to get to it. A sequential file is similar to a scroll or roll of paper with words written on it; the scroll must be unwound in order to read it.

A **random data file**, on the other hand, is more like a book that can be opened immediately to any desired page—that is, a random file can be written and read in any order. If desired, a program can go to record 521 of the file and write data. Similarly, it can go to record 18, for example, and read back the data. The similarities and differences between sequential files and random files are examined in the following sections.

COMPARISON OF SEQUENTIAL AND RANDOM FILES

With both sequential and random files, data may be stored on disk for later use. Records in sequential files must be written to disk consecutively, beginning with record 1, followed by record 2, and so on. When read from the disk, they must be read in the same order, beginning with record 1. Records in random files, on the other hand, may be written and read in any order desired. For example, suppose that Van Hughes's name and address are in record 15 of a random file. If the address changes, the record may be read without reading records 1 through 14 first. The new address may be entered and the record written back to the same location in the file.

HOW RANDOM FILES ARE CONSTRUCTED

To use random files, all records must be the same length. Review the structure of a sequential file as shown in Figure 13-1, and examine the structure of a random file in Figure 13-2. The records must all be the same length in the random file so that the computer can find them without reading all preceding records. Note that the name fields in the sequential file vary in length (i.e., 19 for Margie Economopolis, 8 for Al Logan, and 11 for Susan Moore). The name fields in the random file are all 20 characters in length; the extra space is unused at the end of the name.

When the actual data length varies greatly from one record to another, random files tend to require more disk space. Since all records are the same length, short items have blank characters placed after them. For many applications, however, this is a minor problem compared to the advantages gained.

Consider the best way to create a mailing list file. The easiest way is to set up tables in the computer's memory to hold all names and addresses. Then the entire contents of the tables may be printed out to a sequential file at the end of a data entry session. When a printout is needed, the names and addresses may all be read back into tables from the sequential file. However,

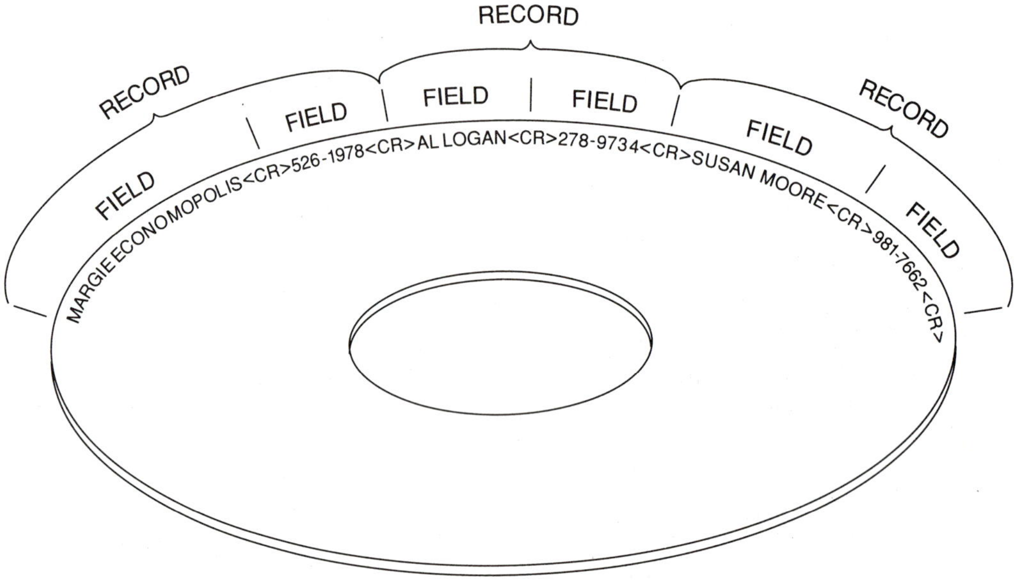

Figure 13-1 Sequential File

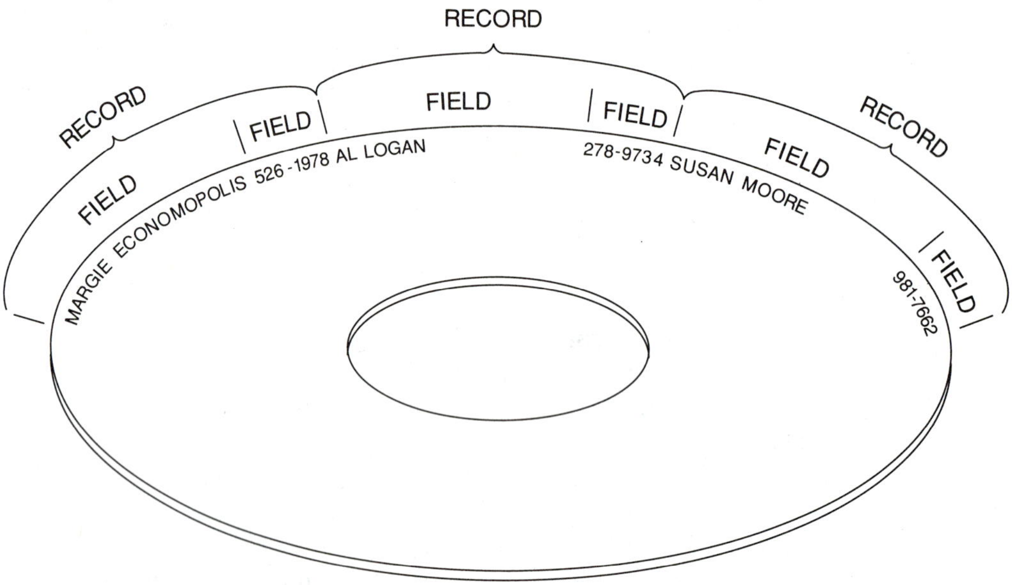

Figure 13-2 Random File

placing all names and addresses of a mailing list in tables in memory becomes unusable when there is not enough memory in the computer to hold all the entries. When a list is expected to grow this large, use of a random file becomes necessary. Most of the information can remain on the disk until needed. Writing and reading of random files may also be performed faster than sequential operations.

CREATING AND USING RANDOM FILES

The general steps in the use of random files are discussed in the following paragraphs.

Opening and Closing

As with sequential files, random files must be opened before use and closed after use. They may be written to and read from at any time they are open. This is in contrast to sequential files, which may be either written or read while open, but not both.

Using a Buffer

When a random file is opened, a special area of memory called a **buffer** is automatically set aside for use in writing and reading data. Before writing data to the disk, the data must be placed into the buffer memory by the program. Once in the buffer, an entire record is written to disk at once. For example, you would not write a stock number to disk, then a description, and then a price. Instead, you would place all three pieces of data in the buffer, and then write them all to disk at once. Likewise, when a record is read from the disk, the data from the entire record (all three fields in the example) is placed in the buffer at once; from there it may be accessed by the program.

Think of the buffer as a money drawer at the bank's drive-in window. If you are depositing money, you place the money in the drawer. Once all the money is in, the drawer transports it into the bank for safekeeping. If you're withdrawing the money, the teller places currency in the drawer. The drawer then transports the money out of the bank to you. You remove the money from the drawer and use it. Remember when dealing with data files, however, that withdrawals (reads) don't physically remove the data from the disk. They simply copy data or play data back.

Updating a Record in a Random File

To update one or more fields in a record that already exists in a random file, the following three steps are necessary.

1. Get the record from the disk, which places the entire record in the buffer.
2. Put the changed data into the buffer; only the fields that change need to be placed since other fields will retain their original contents in the buffer.
3. Write the buffer contents back to the same record number on the disk.

Dealing with Record Numbers

Typically, new data to be added to a file is simply added in the next available record number. **Record numbers** begin with 1 for the first record, 2 for the second record, and continue as large as necessary. It is easy to write data to the next available record number or read all records from a file in record number order. However, when working with the data in random order, additional program code to handle this processing is required.

The simplest way to retrieve data from random files is for the user to supply the number of the record to be used for writing or reading. For example, if the user wants to read the data stored in record 15, the record number is entered from the keyboard and the record is retrieved. As you can imagine, this method has many problems. It is highly unlikely that the user will remember the appropriate record number(s) to use for retrieving desired data.

Another method is to treat the entire random file on disk as if it were a table of data. When data is needed, simply start at the beginning record in the file, reading and examining records until the desired one is found. For example, if you have employee data on disk and need to retrieve the data for the person with employee number 252-98-3892, you might read the first record to see if it is the desired number. If it is not, you would continue reading record after record until the correct one is found, which is similar to sequential file access. The biggest drawback to this approach is its slow speed. Reading and examining the records from disk generally is not nearly as fast as searching data in memory.

Using an Index

The disadvantages of the user supplying a record number or having the program search an entire file can be overcome by using an index. The concept is very similar to that of an index in a book. To find the data about a particular person or thing, an index is consulted. The index tells which record to retrieve to obtain the data. The field that goes in the index is known as the key. As an example, consider a file of stock numbers and descriptions of the merchandise carried by a store. On disk in a random file, it might resemble Figure 13-3.

	STOCK NO. (KEY)	DESCRIPTION	PRICE
Record 1	BX3898	GARDEN HOSE—50 FT	19.76
Record 2	BX3899	GARDEN HOSE—75 FT	29.87
Record 3	3G98731	AERATOR—PULL BEHIND	189.49
Record 4	X4T68JM2	MOWER—RIDING 10 HP	999.99
Record 5	X4T68JM1	MOWER—RIDING 8 HP	899.99
Record 6	X4T68M32	MOWER—22" PROPELLED	359.49
Record 7	N6D32	SPRAYER—THOMAS #129	49.95
Record 8	N63S13	SPRAYER—JARMAN	59.49

Figure 13-3 Data in a Random File of Merchandise Carried

When a program that will use this data is run, the program should read through all the records one time, storing the key (stock number) into a table in memory and discarding the other data (note that it is still on the disk; it is just not stored into memory). The rows into which the numbers are loaded match the record numbers in the file (see Figure 13-4).

Since only the stock numbers are loaded into memory, the bulk of the data remains on the disk. This makes it possible to handle very large data files without running out of memory. When the program needs to find data, it looks in the index and then refers to the disk. For example, to find the data for stock number N6D32,

Table STOCKNO

INDEX	KEY
Row 0	
Row 1	BX3898
Row 2	BX3899
Row 3	3G98731
Row 4	X4T68JM2
Row 5	X4T68JM1
Row 6	X4T68M32
Row 7	N6D32
Row 8	N63S13

Figure 13-4 Index Table for a Random File

the program searches the table until it finds the desired number in row 7. Then it goes to the disk and retrieves record 7, which contains all the data needed. This method is very fast since the table lookup is done in memory, with only one access to the disk to obtain the desired data.

If a new record is added to the file while using an index, the key is added to the table at the same time the record is added to the file. If a record is moved or deleted while using an index, the key in the index is moved or deleted in the same manner. When an index is constructed at the beginning of a program run as shown in this example, it is not necessary to store the index to a file at the end of the program run.

There are many variations in using random files that are beyond the scope of this text. However, the basic knowledge of how random files function detailed in this chapter will enable you to write very useful programs.

REVIEW QUESTIONS

1. What is the difference between sequential and random processing? (Obj. 1)
2. For which file type must all records in a file be the same length? What advantages are derived from making all of them the same length? (Obj. 1)
3. Once a random file is opened, what kinds of operations can be done with the records? (Obj. 2)
4. How is a buffer used with random files? (Obj. 2)
5. Describe the procedure used to update a record in a random file. (Obj. 2)
6. What is the purpose of an index when using random files? (Obj. 2)
7. Describe how an index is used with a random file. (Obj. 2)

TOPIC 13.2 IMPLEMENTING RANDOM FILES IN BASIC

Random files can be used in three different ways. Even though you are free to both read and write in any order once a file is open, there are applications for which only writing is desired, as well as applications for which only reading is desired. For example, for initially setting up the file of data shown in Figure 13-3, only writing is necessary. For printing a copy of the data for reference purposes, only reading is necessary. At other times while using the data, both writing and reading might be necessary.

To introduce you to coding random files, we will first write a program that will create the data file shown in Figure 13-3. Then we will write a program to read the data back and display it. Finally, we will write a program that uses an index and changes a record.

Users of the TRS-80 Model III will be asked to specify the number of files when bringing up BASIC. When the computer asks, "How many files?" enter 3 or just hit RETURN.

WRITING DATA TO A RANDOM FILE

Figure 13-5 shows the program documentation sheet for writing to a random file.

PROGRAM DOCUMENTATION SHEET		
Program: C13E1	Programmer: STUDENT NAME	Date: 4-16-xx
Purpose: This program writes to a random file of stock numbers, descriptions and prices to demonstrate the writing of data to a random file.		
Input: Data from keyboard.	Output: Write records to disk.	
Data Terminator: None		
Variables Used: NUM$ = Stock number entered from keyboard BNUM$ = Stock number in buffer DESC$ = Description entered from keyboard BDESC$ = Description in buffer PRICE = Price entered from keyboard BPRICE$ = Price in buffer RECNO = Record number in file		

Figure 13-5 Program Documentation Sheet for Writing to a Random File

The program design for writing data to a random file is as follows:

1. Open a random file.
2. Field the buffer.
3. Find the last record number.
4. Find out whether the user wants to enter a record or quit.
5. If the user wants to quit, close file and end program.
6. If the user wants to enter a record:
   a. Get data from keyboard and store in variables.
   b. Increment the record number variable.

c. Copy data from variables to the file buffer.
d. Write the contents of the file buffer to disk, using the record number indicated by the record number variable.
e. Go back to step 4 for user's option.

Based on the documentation you have just reviewed, the following sections introduce the necessary BASIC keywords and show how they are used in coding the example program. When using random files, any characters for which there is no space are simply discarded by the computer, with no warning to the user—that is, the record or field length specified in the program cannot be exceeded. The program will check to make sure lengths have not exceeded that for which storage space is available.

Opening a Random File

Opening a random file is similar to opening a sequential file. Here is the syntax:

General Form:
line number OPEN "*file name*" AS #*file number* LEN=*record length*

Example: `80 OPEN "MERCH" AS #1 LEN=33`

On the TRS-80 Model III (and as an alternate method on IBM), the following syntax is used, with a mode of "R" for random:

General Form:
line number OPEN "R", *file number*, "*file name*", L*record length*

Example: `80 OPEN "R",1,"MERCH",L33`

The only thing new in the OPEN statements is the record length. Remember from Topic 13-1 that each record requires the same amount of disk space, whether something is stored in all the positions or not. This fixed amount of space is what is designated with the record length parameter of the OPEN statement.

To decide on the length of the record to use, you must know how data is stored—that is, there is no separator character at the end of each field or record. Here is how the length of 33 was determined in the example, based on the table of stock numbers in Figure 13-3. The maximum space allowable for a stock number is 9 characters; 20 characters is the maximum allowed for an item description. The price will require 4 memory locations (bytes) when it is compressed into character form in the buffer. The total of 9, 20, and 4 is 33, the length to be specified in the OPEN statement.

Locating the End of File

Once you have opened a random file, you can start recording data with record 1, or you may determine the last record used and add new data to the end of existing data. When you worked with sequential files, you used the end of file (EOF) function to determine when you had run out of data being read in; the EOF function works because a special "end-of-file" character is written at the end of a sequential file. Since no special character is written at the end of a random file, the EOF function cannot be used. Instead, a function called **LOF** for "last of file" is used. The LOF function is used to tell how many records are in the random file. That way, you can increment the number by 1 and add data to that which already exists.

General Form:
line number variable name = LOF(*file number*)/*record length*

Example: `100 RECNO=LOF(1)/33`

The LOF function gives the number of bytes (characters) in the file and must have its result divided by the record length as shown in the general form and example to give the actual record number last used. Note: On the TRS-80 Model III, the LOF function gives the actual record number, so you omit the "divided by record length" at the end of the statement. (LOF will not work for this

purpose if you are using version 1.1 or less of BASIC on the IBM and compatible machines.)

Fielding the Buffer

Your program must tell the computer the name(s) you are going to use when putting data into the buffer or copying data from the buffer. Then you must use the buffer for writes and reads. **Fielding** the buffer is dividing the buffer space into data fields. Use of the keyword **FIELD** can accomplish this.

General Form:
line number FIELD#*file number,length* AS *field name,length* AS *field name,length* AS *field name*, etc.

Example: `90 FIELD#1,9 AS BNUM$,20 AS BDESC$,4 AS BPRICE$`

In the preceding example, which is based on the stock data from Figure 13-3, the #1 indicates that the file that was opened as number 1 is being fielded. The first 9 characters in the buffer will be known as BNUM$ and will hold the stock number. The next 20 characters will be known as BDESC$ and will hold the description. The last 4 characters will be known as BPRICE$, and they will hold the money amount or price. Notice that all field names used in the FIELD statement have string variable names even though BPRICE$ represents a number. Remember that the OPEN statement specified the length of the buffer—33 characters in the example. The FIELD statement has the effect of dividing the buffer in the following manner for the preceding example:

9 characters	20 characters	4 characters
BNUM$	BDESC$	BPRICE$

Remember that the field names used in fielding the buffer are not variables and *must not* be used elsewhere in the program with INPUT, LINE INPUT, or on the left side of the equal sign in a LET statement. Your program must not attempt to change their values by any method other than placing data into them in the buffer.

Placing Data in the Buffer

Once a random file has been opened and fielded, the program may fill the buffer space with the data to be written to the disk. The keyword **LSET** is used to place data into the buffer.

General Form:
line number LSET *buffer field name*=*data*

Example:
```
280 LSET BNUM$=NUM$
290 LSET BDESC$=DESC$
```

LSET places characters into the buffer field starting at the left, with blanks at the right if the item is shorter than the field. For example, if a stock number input from the keyboard into variable NUM$ is only seven characters long and is LSET into BNUM$, which was fielded as nine characters, there will be two blanks at the right of the stock number. (If you want the data at the right of the field with blanks at the left, **RSET** can be used instead of LSET.)

Remember, we mentioned earlier that numbers are compressed to make them fit into less disk space. The keyword **MKS$** is used to perform the compression. MKS$ stands for MaKe a Single precision string of characters from a number. The following general form shows how it is used directly with LSET:

General Form:
line number LSET *buffer field name*=MKS$(*numeric variable*)

Example:
```
300 LSET BPRICE$=MKS$(PRICE)
```

MKS$ compresses numbers into four characters for storage on the diskette. The LSET then places the compressed number into the buffer field.

Writing the Buffer to the Disk

After all data for a record has been placed in the buffer with LSET, the entire record is written to disk with the **PUT** statement.

PROGRAM DOCUMENTATION SHEET		
Program: C13E2	Programmer: STUDENT NAME	Date: 4-16-xx
Purpose: This program reads from a random file and displays the contents.		
Input: Data from the random MERCH file on disk.	Output: Display to screen.	
Data Terminator: None		
Variables Used: BNUM$ = Stock number in buffer BDESC$ = Description in buffer BPRICE$ = Price in buffer PRICE = Price as converted back to numeric format		

Figure 13-6 Program Documentation Sheet for Reading a Random File

Getting Data from a Random File

Reading a random file is just the reverse of writing it. First, the data is read from diskette with the keyword **GET**.

General Form:
line number GET#*file number,record number*

Example: `110 GET#1,RECNO`

When the GET statement is executed, the data from the indicated record number on the disk is automatically placed in the file buffer fields. Once there, character data may be used directly—that

is, you may use the file buffer field name in a PRINT statement or on the right side of a LET statement.

Converting Compressed Numeric Data

Since numeric data is stored on diskette as character string data, it must be converted back to numeric data before it can be used. The keyword **CVS**, which stands for ConVert Single, is used.

> **General Form:**
> *line number numeric variable*=CVS(*buffer field name*)
>
> **Example:** `120 PRICE=CVS(BPRICE$)`

When a number is converted, it is usually assigned to a variable. However, it may be printed directly or used in a computation if desired.

The example program may be coded as follows. The steps from the program design are provided to help you understand the program.

Example:

```
10 ' C13E2
20 ' STUDENT NAME, CHAPTER 13, EXAMPLE 2
30 ' READS RANDOM FILE FROM DISK AND DISPLAYS IT
40 '
50 CLS
60 PRINT "CONTENTS OF FILE 'MERCH'"
70 PRINT
80 OPEN "MERCH" AS #1 LEN=33 <------------------------------ 1
85 ' ON TRS-80 MOD III USE 80 OPEN "R",1,"MERCH",L33
90 FIELD#1,9 AS BNUM$,20 AS BDESC$,4 AS BPRICE$ <------------ 2
100 FOR RECNO=1 TO LOF(1)/33  ' LEAVE OFF /33 ON TRS-80 MOD III <-- 3
110   GET#1,RECNO <------------------------------------------- 3a
120   PRICE=CVS(BPRICE$) <------------------------------------ 3b
130   PRINT USING "\        \ \                 \ ###.##";
      BNUM$,BDESC$,PRICE <------------------------------------ 3c
135 ' ON TRS-80 MOD III USE % IN PLACE OF \ IN LINE 130
140 NEXT RECNO
150 CLOSE#1 <------------------------------------------------- 4
160 END
```

When the program is executed, the following output is produced:

Output:

```
CONTENTS OF FILE 'MERCH'

BX3898     GARDEN HOSE--5Ø FT      19.76
BX3899     GARDEN HOSE--75 FT      29.87
3G98731    AERATOR--PULL BEHIND  189.49
X4T68JM2   MOWER--RIDING 1Ø HP   999.99
X4T68JM1   MOWER--RIDING 8 HP    899.99
X4T68M32   MOWER--22" PROPELLED  359.49
N6D32      SPRAYER--THOMAS #129   49.95
N63S13     SPRAYER--JARMAN        59.49
```

USING AN INDEX AND CHANGING A RECORD

As the third example of using random files, examine a program that uses an index, retrieves a specific record, writes a new record, deletes an old record, and changes a price. We will use the same data file that we used for C13E1 and C13E2. The hierarchy chart for the program is shown in Figure 13-7.

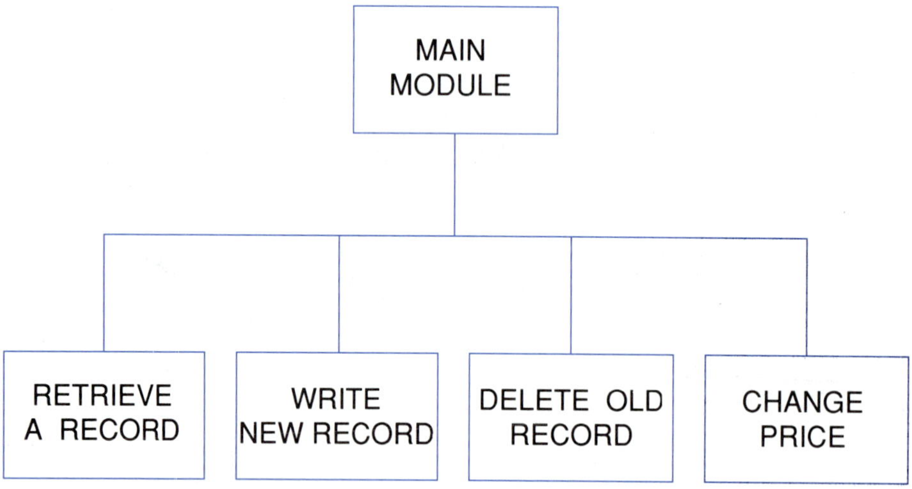

Figure 13-7 Hierarchy Chart for Working with an Indexed File

Figure 13-8 shows the program documentation sheet for working with an index file, while Figures 13-9 through 13-13 show the module documentation sheets and the code for each module.

PROGRAM DOCUMENTATION SHEET		
Program: C13E3	Programmer: STUDENT NAME	Date: 4-16-xx
Purpose: This program allows the user to retrieve a merchandise record, write a new record to the file, delete an existing record, or change a price.		
Input: User input is from the keyboard.	Output: Write record to disk or display data on screen depending on chosen function.	
Data Terminator: None.		
Variables Used: CHOICE = User's menu choice INDEX$ = Table for stock number index NUM$ = Stock number entered from keyboard BNUM$ = Stock number in buffer DESC$ = Description entered from keyboard BDESC$ = Description in buffer PRICE = Price entered from keyboard BPRICE$ = Price in buffer RECNO = Record number in file ROW = Loop counter variable with FOR . . . NEXT		

Figure 13-8 Program Documentation Sheet

MODULE DOCUMENTATION SHEET	
Program: C13E3	Module: MAIN Lines: 10-999

Module Description: This module opens a random file for merchandise stock data. It creates an index of stock numbers in memory for use in locating items in the file. It prints a menu on the CRT and gets the user's choice for retrieving, writing, deleting a record, or for changing a price. When the user has made a choice, the module calls the required subroutine. Process continues until the user chooses to stop, at which time the file is closed.

Module Function (Program Design):

1. Open the random file.
2. Field the random file.
3. Determine the last record number in file.
4. Dimension an index table large enough to hold the largest expected number of index keys.
5. Load the index table with stock numbers from disk, stripping the trailing blanks as the data is put in the table; if the blanks are not stripped, searches will not be successful unless the user types in blanks as part of the stock number to be found.
6. Print the menu on screen and get the user's choice.
7. Call the needed subroutine based on the user's choice.
8. Go back to step 6 unless the user chooses to quit.
9. Close file if the user is done.

Figure 13-9 Documentation and Code for the Main Module

```
10 ' C13E3
20 ' STUDENT NAME, CHAPTER 13, EXAMPLE 3
30 ' MAINTAINS RANDOM FILE
40 ' CLEAR 1000 ON TRS-80 MOD III
50 OPEN "MERCH" AS #1 LEN=33 <---- 1
55 ' TRS-80 MOD III USE 50 OPEN "R",1,"MERCH",L33
60 FIELD#1,9 AS BNUM$,20 AS BDESC$,4 AS BPRICE$ <---- 2
70 RECNO=LOF(1)/33 ' OMIT /33 ON TRS-80 MOD III <---- 3
80 DIM INDEX$(50)'DIMENSION TO HOLD LARGEST POSSIBLE
   NUMBER OF RECORDS <---- 4
90 FOR ROW=1 TO RECNO
100    GET#1,ROW
110    INDEX$(ROW)=BNUM$ <---- 5
115    BLK=INSTR(INDEX$(ROW)," ")
120    IF BLK>0 THEN INDEX$(ROW)=LEFT$(INDEX$(ROW),BLK-1)
130 NEXT ROW
140 CLS
150 PRINT "**********************************"
160 PRINT "* MENU                           *"
170 PRINT "**********************************"
180 PRINT "1 - RETRIEVE RECORD"
190 PRINT "2 - WRITE NEW RECORD"
200 PRINT "3 - DELETE OLD RECORD" <---- 6
205 PRINT "4 - CHANGE PRICE IN EXISTING RECORD"
210 PRINT "5 - QUIT"
220 PRINT
230 INPUT "CHOICE:  ";CHOICE
240 IF CHOICE<1 OR CHOICE>5 THEN 230
250 ON CHOICE GOSUB 1000,2000,3000,4000 <---- 7
260 PRINT
270 PRINT "HIT ANY KEY TO PROCEED . . ."
280 Z$=INPUT$(1)
290 IF CHOICE<>5 THEN 140 <---- 8
300 CLOSE#1 <---- 9
999 END
```

Figure 13-9 (continued)

MODULE DOCUMENTATION SHEET

Program: C13E3	Module: RETRIEVE A RECORD Lines: 1000-1999

Module Description: This module gets a stock number from the user, retrieves the matching record, and displays the data on the screen.

Module Function (Program Design):

1. Get desired stock number from user.
2. Look up the stock number in index table in memory.
3. If the number is not found, print a "not found" message and exit.
4. If the number is found, get the data from the matching record number on disk and display it on the screen.

```
1000 ' ******************************
1010 ' * RETRIEVE RECORD            *
1020 ' ******************************
1030 CLS
1040 PRINT "ENTER THE STOCK NUMBER OF THE"
1050 INPUT "ITEM TO BE LOCATED:  ";NUM$ ←——— 1
1060 FOR ROW=1 TO RECNO                          ]
1070    IF INDEX$(ROW)=NUM$ THEN 1110 ' EXIT ON FIND ] ←——— 2
1080 NEXT ROW                                    ]
1090 PRINT "NOT FOUND" ←——— 3
1100 GOTO 1999 ' EXIT LOOP ←——— 3
1110 GET#1,ROW ' GET DATA FROM DISK ←——— 4
1120 PRINT
1130 PRINT USING "\       \ \                    \ ###.##";BNUM$,
     BDESC$,CVS(BPRICE$) ←——— 4
1140 ' ON TRS-80 MOD III USE % IN PLACE OF \ IN LINE 1130
1999 RETURN
```

Figure 13-10 Documentation and Code for the Retrieve a Record Module

MODULE DOCUMENTATION SHEET

Program: C13E3	Module: WRITE NEW RECORD Lines: 2000-2999

Module Description: This module gets a stock number, description, and price from the user and writes it to the next available record in the random file. The next available record may be a space where previous data has been deleted (indicated by "NULL" stored in the index and record) or at the end of all existing records.

Module Function (Program Design):

1. Input the new item from the keyboard.
2. Search the index table, looking for "NULL" as stock number (new data will go in that record if one is found).
3. Put the new data into the file buffer.
4. Write the record to disk, using a "NULL" row if one was found; otherwise, use a new record at the end of the file.
5. If data was added to the end of the file, update the value of the last record variable.
6. Place the new key in its proper row in the index table.

```
2000 ' ********************************
2010 ' * WRITE NEW RECORD             *
2020 ' ********************************
2030 CLS
2040 PRINT "ENTER DATA FOR NEW RECORD"
2050 PRINT
2060 INPUT "STOCK NUMBER:  ";NUM$
2070 IF LEN(NUM$)>9 THEN PRINT "TOO LONG; REENTER":GOTO 2060     ←1
2080 PRINT
2090 INPUT "DESCRIPTION:  ";DESC$
2100 IF LEN(DESC$)>20 THEN PRINT "TOO LONG; REENTER":GOTO 2090
```

Figure 13-11 Documentation and Code for the Write New Record Module

```
2110 PRINT
2120 INPUT "PRICE:  ";PRICE                              <- 1
2130 PRINT
2140 FOR ROW=1 TO RECNO
2150     IF INDEX$(ROW)="NULL" THEN 2170 ' EXIT UPON FINDING
         BLANK ROW                                       <- 2
2160 NEXT ROW
2170 LSET BNUM$=NUM$
2180 LSET BDESC$=DESC$                                   <- 3
2190 LSET BPRICE$=MKS$(PRICE)
2200 PUT#1,ROW                                           <- 4
2210 IF ROW>RECNO THEN RECNO=ROW                         <- 5
2220 INDEX$(ROW)=NUM$                                    <- 6
2230 PRINT
2240 PRINT "RECORD HAS BEEN WRITTEN"
2999 RETURN
```

Figure 13-11 (continued)

MODULE DOCUMENTATION SHEET

Program: C13E3	Module: DELETE OLD RECORD Lines: 3000-3999

Module Description: This module deletes an existing record by recording "NULL" as the stock number, nothing as the description, and 0 as the price. "NULL" is also placed in the index table for the deleted item.

Module Function (Program Design):

1. Input the stock number to delete.
2. Search the index table looking for the stock number.
3. If the number is not found, print "not found" message and exit.
4. If the number is found, put "NULL" in buffer as stock number, "" in buffer as description, and 0 in buffer as price.
5. Put the data from buffer to disk in the record number to be deleted.
6. Put "NULL" in the index table row that matches the deleted record.

Figure 13-12 Documentation and Code for the Delete Old Record Module

```
3000 ' ******************************
3010 ' * DELETE OLD RECORD          *
3020 ' ******************************
3030 CLS
3040 PRINT "ENTER THE STOCK NUMBER OF THE"
3050 INPUT "ITEM TO BE DELETED:  ";NUM$          ← 1
3060 FOR ROW=1 TO RECNO                          ┐
3070    IF NUM$=INDEX$(ROW) THEN 3110 ' EXIT ON MATCH  ← 2
3080 NEXT ROW                                    ┘
3090 PRINT "NOT FOUND"                           ← 3
3100 GOTO 3999 ' EXIT IF NOT FOUND               ← 3
3110 LSET BNUM$="NULL"                           ┐
3120 LSET BDESC$=""                              ← 4
3130 LSET BPRICE$=MKS$(0)                        ┘
3140 PUT#1,ROW                                   ← 5
3150 INDEX$(ROW)="NULL"                          ← 6
3160 PRINT
3170 PRINT NUM$;" HAS BEEN DELETED"
3999 RETURN
```

Figure 13-12 (continued)

MODULE DOCUMENTATION SHEET	
Program: C13E3	Module: CHANGE PRICE Lines: 4000-4999
Module Description: This module first inputs (from the keyboard) the stock number of the item whose price is to be changed. Then it gets the matching record and displays its data on the screen. After inputting the new price from the keyboard, the updated data is written on disk, overwriting the original data.	

Figure 13-13 Documentation and Code for the Change Price Module

Module Function (Program Design):

1. Input the stock number from the user.
2. Look up the stock number in the index table in memory.
3. If the number is not found, print a "not found" message and exit.
4. If the number is found, get the data from the matching record number on disk and display it on the screen.
5. Input the new price.
6. Put the new price in the buffer and write the buffer to disk.

```
4000 ' *******************************
4010 ' * CHANGE PRICE                *
4020 ' *******************************
4030 CLS
4040 PRINT "ENTER THE STOCK NUMBER OF THE"
4050 INPUT "ITEM TO BE CHANGED  ";NUM$ ←—————— 1
4060 FOR ROW=1 TO RECNO
4070    IF INDEX$(ROW)=NUM$ THEN 4110 ' EXIT ON FIND ]
4080 NEXT ROW                                        ] ←—— 2
4090 PRINT "NOT FOUND"     ]
4100 GOTO 4999 ' EXIT LOOP ] ←—————— 3
4110 GET#1,ROW ' GET DATA FROM DISK                  ]
4120 PRINT                                           ]
4130 PRINT USING "\        \ \                \ ###.##";BNUM$, ] ← 4
     BDESC$,CVS(BPRICE$)                             ]
4135 ' ON TRS-80 MOD III USE % IN PLACE OF \ IN LINE 4130
4140 PRINT
4150 INPUT "ENTER NEW PRICE:  ";PRICE ←—————— 5
4160 LSET BPRICE$=MKS$(PRICE) ]
4170 PUT#1,ROW                ] ←—————— 6
4180 PRINT "PRICE HAS BEEN UPDATED"
4999 RETURN
```

Figure 13-13 (continued)

The program code is repeated in full here to make it easier to study the interaction between the different subroutines.

Example:

```
10 ' C13E3
20 ' STUDENT NAME, CHAPTER 13, EXAMPLE 3
30 ' MAINTAINS RANDOM FILE
40 ' CLEAR 1000 ON TRS-80 MOD III
50 OPEN "MERCH" AS #1 LEN=33
55 ' ON TRS-80 MOD III USE 50 OPEN "R",1,"MERCH",L33
60 FIELD#1,9 AS BNUM$,20 AS BDESC$,4 AS BPRICE$
70 RECNO=LOF(1)/33 ' OMIT /33 ON TRS-80 MOD III
80 DIM INDEX$(50)'DIMENSION TO HOLD LARGEST POSSIBLE NUMBER OF RECORDS
90 FOR ROW=1 TO RECNO
100   GET#1,ROW
110   INDEX$(ROW)=BNUM$
115   BLK=INSTR(INDEX$(ROW)," ")
120   IF BLK>0 THEN INDEX$(ROW)=LEFT$(INDEX$(ROW),BLK-1)
130 NEXT ROW
140 CLS
150 PRINT "**********************************"
160 PRINT "* MENU                           *"
170 PRINT "**********************************"
180 PRINT "1 - RETRIEVE RECORD"
190 PRINT "2 - WRITE NEW RECORD"
200 PRINT "3 - DELETE OLD RECORD"
205 PRINT "4 - CHANGE PRICE IN EXISTING RECORD"
210 PRINT "5 - QUIT"
220 PRINT
230 INPUT "CHOICE:  ";CHOICE
240 IF CHOICE<1 OR CHOICE>5 THEN 230
250 ON CHOICE GOSUB 1000,2000,3000,4000
260 PRINT
270 PRINT "HIT ANY KEY TO PROCEED . . ."
280 Z$=INPUT$(1)
290 IF CHOICE<>5 THEN 140
300 CLOSE#1
999 END
1000 ' ******************************
1010 ' * RETRIEVE RECORD            *
1020 ' ******************************
1030 CLS
1040 PRINT "ENTER THE STOCK NUMBER OF THE"
1050 INPUT "ITEM TO BE LOCATED:  ";NUM$
```

```
1060 FOR ROW=1 TO RECNO
1070    IF INDEX$(ROW)=NUM$ THEN 1110 ' EXIT ON FIND
1080 NEXT ROW
1090 PRINT "NOT FOUND"
1100 GOTO 1999 ' EXIT LOOP
1110 GET#1,ROW ' GET DATA FROM DISK
1120 PRINT
1130 PRINT USING "\       \ \                  \ ###.##";BNUM$,
     BDESC$,CVS(BPRICE$)
1140 ' ON TRS-80 MOD III USE % IN PLACE OF \ IN LINE 1130
1999 RETURN
2000 ' ******************************
2010 ' * WRITE NEW RECORD           *
2020 ' ******************************
2030 CLS
2040 PRINT "ENTER DATA FOR NEW RECORD"
2050 PRINT
2060 INPUT "STOCK NUMBER:  ";NUM$
2070 IF LEN(NUM$)>9 THEN PRINT "TOO LONG; REENTER":GOTO 2060
2080 PRINT
2090 INPUT "DESCRIPTION:  ";DESC$
2100 IF LEN(DESC$)>20 THEN PRINT "TOO LONG; REENTER":GOTO 2090
2110 PRINT
2120 INPUT "PRICE:  ";PRICE
2130 PRINT
2140 FOR ROW=1 TO RECNO
2150    IF INDEX$(ROW)="NULL" THEN 2170 ' EXIT UPON FINDING BLANK ROW
2160 NEXT ROW
2170 LSET BNUM$=NUM$
2180 LSET BDESC$=DESC$
2190 LSET BPRICE$=MKS$(PRICE)
2200 PUT#1,ROW
2210 IF ROW>RECNO THEN RECNO=ROW
2220 INDEX$(ROW)=NUM$
2230 PRINT
2240 PRINT "RECORD HAS BEEN WRITTEN"
2999 RETURN
3000 ' ******************************
3010 ' * DELETE OLD RECORD          *
3020 ' ******************************
3030 CLS
3040 PRINT "ENTER THE STOCK NUMBER OF THE"
```

```
3050 INPUT "ITEM TO BE DELETED:  ";NUM$
3060 FOR ROW=1 TO RECNO
3070   IF NUM$=INDEX$(ROW) THEN 3110 ' EXIT ON MATCH
3080 NEXT ROW
3090 PRINT "NOT FOUND"
3100 GOTO 3999 ' EXIT IF NOT FOUND
3110 LSET BNUM$="NULL"
3120 LSET BDESC$=""
3130 LSET BPRICE$=MKS$(0)
3140 PUT#1,ROW
3150 INDEX$(ROW)="NULL"
3160 PRINT
3170 PRINT NUM$;" HAS BEEN DELETED"
3999 RETURN
4000 ' ******************************
4010 ' * CHANGE PRICE               *
4020 ' ******************************
4030 CLS
4040 PRINT "ENTER THE STOCK NUMBER OF THE"
4050 INPUT "ITEM TO BE CHANGED  ";NUM$
4060 FOR ROW=1 TO RECNO
4070    IF INDEX$(ROW)=NUM$ THEN 4110 ' EXIT ON FIND
4080 NEXT ROW
4090 PRINT "NOT FOUND"
4100 GOTO 4999 ' EXIT LOOP
4110 GET#1,ROW ' GET DATA FROM DISK
4120 PRINT
4130 PRINT USING "\       \ \                  \ ###.##";BNUM$,
     BDESC$,CVS(BPRICE$)
4135 ' ON TRS-80 MOD III USE % IN PLACE OF \ IN LINE 4130
4140 PRINT
4150 INPUT "ENTER NEW PRICE:  ";PRICE
4160 LSET BPRICE$=MKS$(PRICE)
4170 PUT#1,ROW
4180 PRINT "PRICE HAS BEEN UPDATED"
4999 RETURN
```

NOTES FOR ADVANCED PROGRAMMERS

When you simply use a numeric variable as you have throughout the text to this point, the variable is set up as a **single precision variable**. When large numbers need to be used by programs, sin-

gle precision variables have round-off problems, meaning that the number you get back when you print or use a numeric variable is just a little bit different than the number you stored. To overcome this problem, you can use a **double precision variable**. There are two ways to obtain double precision variables. The first is to add a number sign to the end of the variable name. Therefore, PRICE is a single precision variable, and PRICE# is a double precision variable. The second way is to use the keyword **DEFDBL**.

General Form: *line number* DEFDBL *first letter range*

Example 1: `50 DEFDBL P`

Example 2: `50 DEFDBL P-R`

In the first example, DEFDBL P denotes that all numeric variables beginning with the letter P are double precision. In the second example, DEFDBL P-R denotes that all variables beginning with P, Q, and R are double precision. The DEFDBL statement must appear in the program before you attempt to use any variables beginning with the designated letter.

Arithmetic is done more slowly with double precision variables, and the variables consume more storage space. When working with random files, you must use a field length of eight for double precision compared with the four you used for single precision. Also, you must use the **MKD$** function rather than the MKS$ function to place numbers in the file buffer. To convert compressed numeric values back to numeric form, you must use **CVD** rather than CVS.

In addition to single precision and double precision variables, there are also integer variables, designated by either a % at the end of the name or a **DEFINT** statement.

General Form: *line number* DEFINT *first letter range*

Example 1: `60 DEFINT I`

Example 2: `60 DEFINT I-N`

In Example 1, all variables beginning with I are defined to be integer variables. In Example 2, all variables with first letters I through N are defined as integers. As their name implies, integer variables can have no decimal portion, and their maximum size is somewhat limited. However, programs using integer variables run faster (e.g., integer variables on FOR . . . NEXT loops that repeat many times can make a noticeable speed improvement). If you want to use integer variables with a random file, field them at a length of two characters, and use the keywords **MKI$** and **CVI** to place numbers in the buffer and later convert them back to numeric data.

REVIEW QUESTIONS

1. Describe the difference in the OPEN statement for sequential files and random files. (Obj. 2)
2. Describe the role of the buffer in random file operation. (Obj. 2)
3. When all the field names in the buffer must be set up as character fields, how can numeric data be stored? (Obj. 2)
4. What are the five steps that must take place in order for data to be written to a random file? Name the keywords used to accomplish each of them. (Obj. 2)
5. What are the steps that must take place in order for data to be read from a random file? Name the keywords used to accomplish each of them. (Obj. 2)
6. Explain how record length is determined. (Obj. 2)

VOCABULARY WORDS

The following terms were introduced in this chapter.

buffer	fielding	record number
double precision variable	key	single precision variable
	random data file	

KEYWORDS

The following keywords were introduced in this chapter:

CVD	FIELD	MKI$
CVI	GET	MKS$

CVS	LOF	PUT
DEFDBL	LSET	RSET
DEFINT	MKD$	

PROGRAMS TO WRITE

For each of the programs, prepare the necessary documentation before writing the BASIC code. For modularly designed programs, be sure to do a module documentation sheet for each module.

Program 1

Good Deal Motors is an automobile dealer that maintains a fleet of eight cars to be rented to customers while their cars are in the shop. The dealer was able to arrange with the state for prestige license plates for the cars, so all the plates read GDEAL followed by a single digit. The dealer wants to store the following data about the cars in a random file:

LICENSE PLATE	MODEL	RENTAL RATE	RENTER'S NAME
GDEAL1	Camaro	$39.95	None
GDEAL2	Escort	$19.95	None
GDEAL3	Caravan	$34.95	None
GDEAL4	Sentra	$19.95	None
GDEAL5	Cressida	$49.95	None
GDEAL6	Mark	$49.95	None
GDEAL7	Celebrity	$29.95	None
GDEAL8	Taurus	$29.95	None

Write a program to allow a user to enter the data from the keyboard and have it written to a random file. Allow a length of 20 for the renter's name, even though you will enter "NONE" for each car when you try to program.

Program 2

Write a program to read the data stored by Program 1 and display it on the screen.

Program 3

A college operates a desktop publishing laboratory for use by various employees and students, and the rooms are available on a first-come, first-served basis. These rooms are numbered from 101 through 105. Write a program to get the following data about the rooms from the keyboard and store it in a random file.

ROOM NUMBER	SOFTWARE	HARDWARE	USER'S NAME
101	Ventura	IBM	None
102	Ventura	IBM	None
103	PageMaker	Macintosh	None
104	PageMaker	Macintosh	None
105	PageMaker	IBM	None

Write the program so that the field for the user's name is 25 character's long, even though you will be entering "NONE" when testing the program.

Program 4

Write a program to read the data stored by Program 3 and display it on the screen.

Program 5

Write a program that uses the functions of Programs 1 and 2 as two of its menu choices. Add a choice that allows rental of the car (a person's name goes into the "renter's name" field) and one that allows return of a car (the person's name is replaced with "NONE"). The digit from the license plate number should be entered by the user and used by the program as the record number in order to locate a record. To test your program, make the following data entries and display the data after each one to make sure the file is correct:

Rent car 2 to Susan Ware

Rent car 4 to William Barnhardt

Rent car 5 to Lillian Marsh

Check out Richard Kimes from room 102 on 8/13/--

Rent room 102 to Sally Roper on 8/13/--

Attempt to rent room 203 to Harry Frederick (should not be allowed)

Check out Sally Wright from room 103 on 8/14/--

Rent room 103 to Brad Simons on 8/14/--

Check out Amy Michigan from room 203 on 8/15/--

Program 10

A charity organization raises money by setting up teams representing different segments of the community. These teams then solicit contributions from their part of the community. For example, business teams go to corporations looking for support, while education teams go to schools looking for donations. During the fund drive each year, leaders of the teams call in reports on how much has been raised by their teams. At various times during the campaign, it is desired to know how much money has been pledged. Write a program to help the charity keep up with the total pledges. It should have the following menu functions available: (1) add a new team, (2) enter current pledge total for a team, and (3) print a pledge report. The pledge report should list all teams, the amount of their pledges, and the total pledges for all teams. Use an indexed file, with the team names being the key. To test the program, enter the following transactions:

Add teams for LARGE BUS, SMALL BUS, STATE GOV, LOCAL GOV, and HIGHER ED.

Enter pledge total of $5,038 for large business, $3,982 for state government, $9,832 for higher education, and $1,343 for local government.

Print a pledge report.

Add a team for PUBLIC ED.

Enter pledge totals of $6,793 for public education, $3,432 for small business, $2,789 for local government, and $7,893 for large business.

Print a pledge report.

PROJECT 5

The program you write for this project is one that can be very useful to you, even after you finish the course. The program should be a combination mailing list and telephone directory program, written using both sequential and random files.

The last names, first names, and phone numbers of persons should be stored in a sequential file and loaded into one or more tables in memory each time the program is executed. This will make looking up phone numbers easy and fast. The remainder of the data about each person (street address, city, state, zip, and a user-defined code) should be stored in a random file for access when needed.

The functions the program should perform are (1) add person, (2) delete person, (3) edit data about person, (4) look up phone number, and (5) print address labels for persons whose code matches that entered from the keyboard.

To test your program, take the following actions in sequence:

1. Add Mary Weatherford, 983-9873, Rt. 1, Willie, NH 03343, code 2.
2. Add Fred Samson, 323-2198, 342 First Rd., Martin, CA 95322, code 1.
3. Add Ying Wang, 120-3897, 1 Akers Pl., Pensacola, FL 32503, code 2.
4. Print address labels to all persons with code 2.
5. End execution of the program.
6. Run the program again, changing Samson's phone number to 232-2198.
7. Look up Ying Wang's phone number.
8. Add Mary Smith, 332-9811, 83 First Ave., Keene, NH 03431, code 1.
9. Add Larry Milam, 899-9987, Rt. 2, Mayberry, FL 32343, code 1.
10. Print address labels for everyone with code 1.
11. Delete Fred Samson.
12. Change Mary Smith's street number to 65.
13. Attempt to look up Samson's phone number.
14. Print address labels to everyone with code 1.
15. End execution of the program.
16. Rerun the program, printing labels for everyone with code 1.

PART SIX
SIMPLE GRAPHICS

14

Simple Graphics

> **OBJECTIVES**
>
> After studying this chapter, you will be able to
>
> 1. Explain what is meant by graphics.
> 2. Identify applications that use graphics.
> 3. Describe the differences between character graphics and pixel graphics.
> 4. Write programs to produce graphics.

TOPIC 14.1 INTRODUCTION TO GRAPHICS

USES OF GRAPHICS

Graphics refers to any pictorial representation. Graphics are important in many computer applications and may be used to enhance many types of programs. From something as simple as drawing attractive boxes around program menus, to creating entertaining games, to programming educational software, graphics are used in many varied applications. In the business world, graphics may be used to represent data in a form that is easily comprehended. By using graphs, volumes of data may be presented in a visual format that makes the relationships between different data items easy to see. Commonly used types of graphs include bar graphs, line graphs, and pie charts. These are illustrated in Figure 14-1.

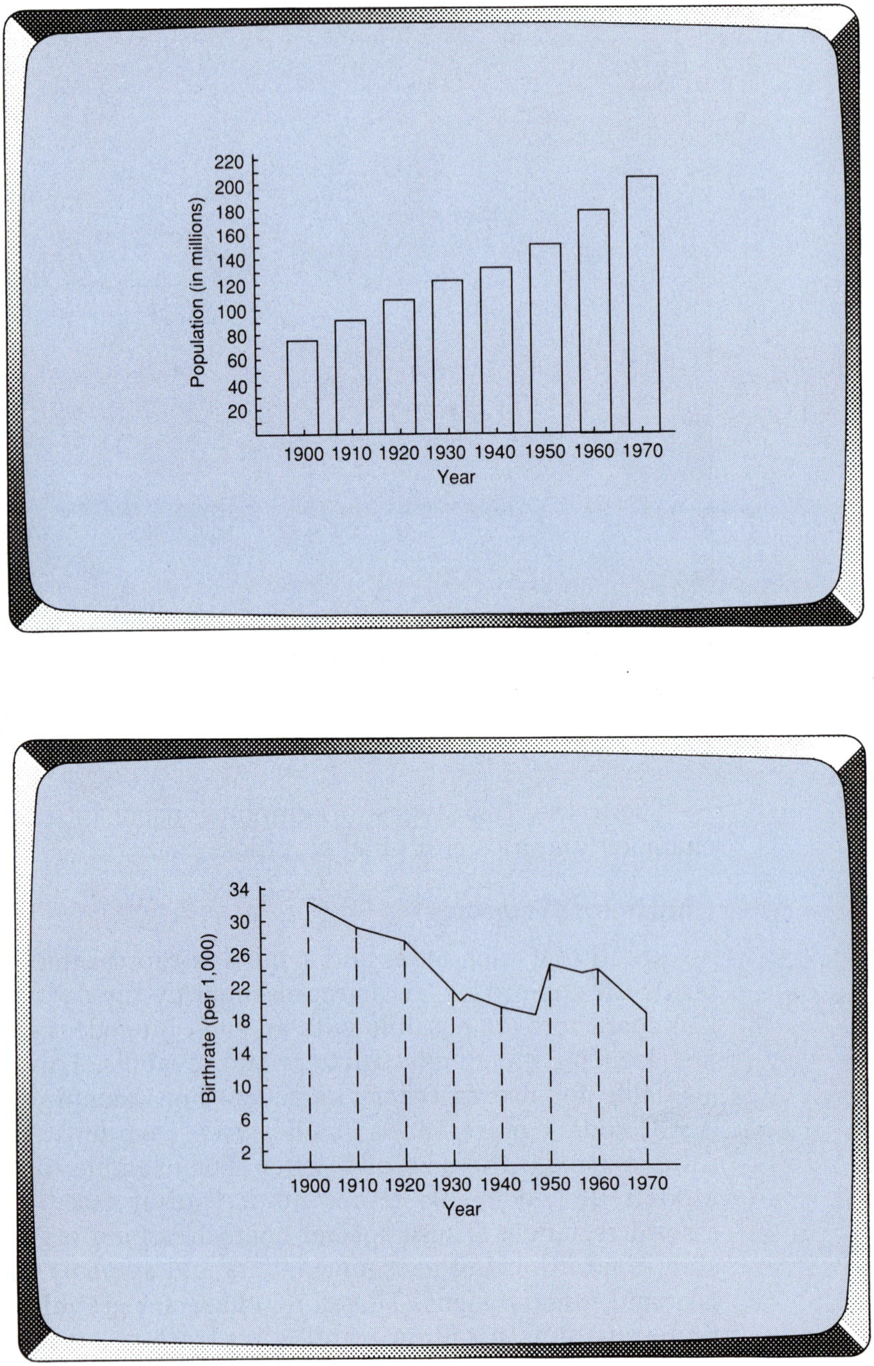

Figure 14-1 Various Types of Graphs

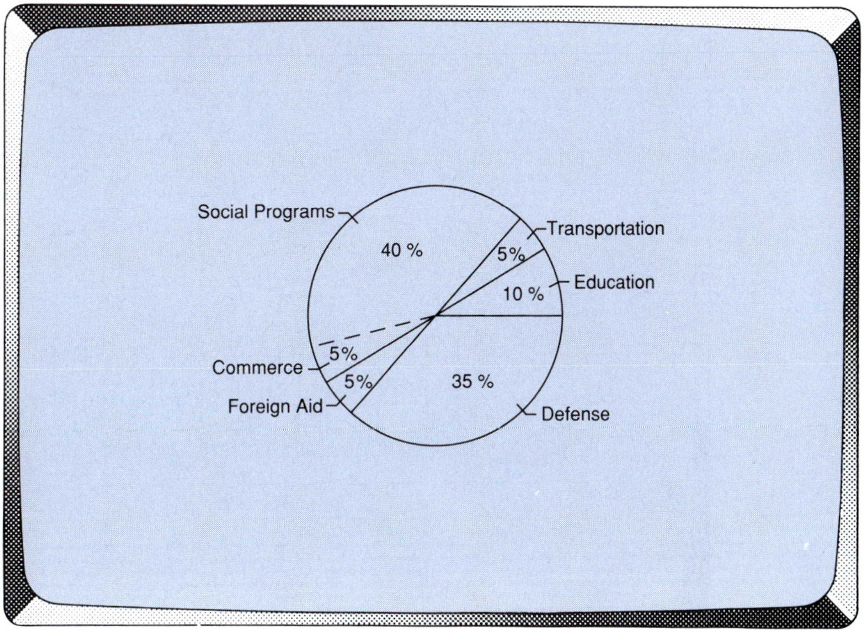

Figure 14-1 (continued)

TYPES OF GRAPHICS

There are two types of graphics used in programming—character graphics and pixel graphics.

Character Graphics

Recall that each letter and symbol is represented by a particular ASCII code (e.g., "A" is represented by the code of 65). Since 256 characters are possible with an eight-bit code, many codes are not used for the standard letters and symbols. This makes them available for use as other characters. For example, on the IBM, ASCII code 1 represents a "smiley face," while 219 represents a solid rectangle the size of a letter. For example, on the TRS-80 Models III and 4, 196 represents a "smiley face," while 191 is a solid rectangle. These special characters (and others) are available in addition to the regular letters and symbols such as asterisks and number signs. Therefore, **character graphics** are graphic representations made by printing characters—made up of ASCII codes—on the screen.

To produce graphics by using characters, the characters are printed onto the screen at the desired locations. For example, a

shaded area can be drawn on the screen by printing the character that represents a half-tone (see Figure 14-2). Generally the use of such a character results in what appears to be a solid block rather than individual characters. In the illustration, dotted lines are used to show you where the individual characters are joined to make up the block.

Figure 14-2 Shaded Area Made with Graphics Characters

In similar fashion, a box may be printed. Using the character that represents a solid rectangle, the box will appear as shown in Figure 14-3.

By combining the two examples you have just seen, plus adding a line of text, a framed box of text can be produced as shown in Figure 14-4.

By their nature, there are certain advantages and disadvantages to character graphics. Since each shape is predefined in the computer and is printed on the screen as if it were a letter, the graphics may be displayed very quickly. This same feature, however, results in the biggest disadvantages—you are limited to using the predefined characters and shapes, and you cannot work with an area of the screen smaller or larger than that occupied by each character.

Figure 14-3 Box Made of Graphics Characters

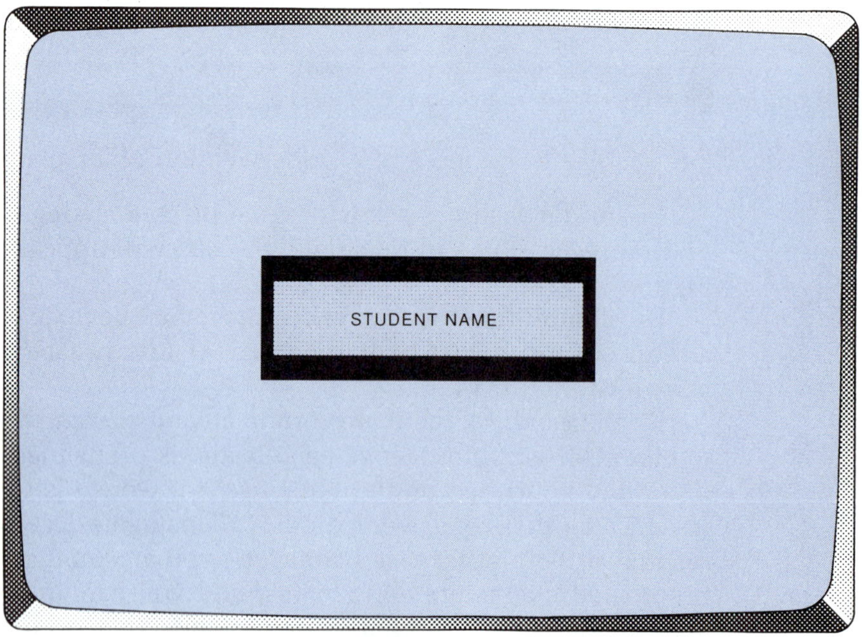

Figure 14-4 Framed Box Made with Graphics Characters

Pixel Graphics

Whereas character graphics print predefined graphics characters, the use of pixel graphics allows total creativity on the part of the programmer. The word **pixel** is derived from *picture element* and represents the smallest dot that can be displayed on the screen. Therefore, **pixel graphics** is the use of individual picture elements on the screen to accomplish the desired graphic effect (see Figure 14-5 for an example of output made through the use of pixel graphics).

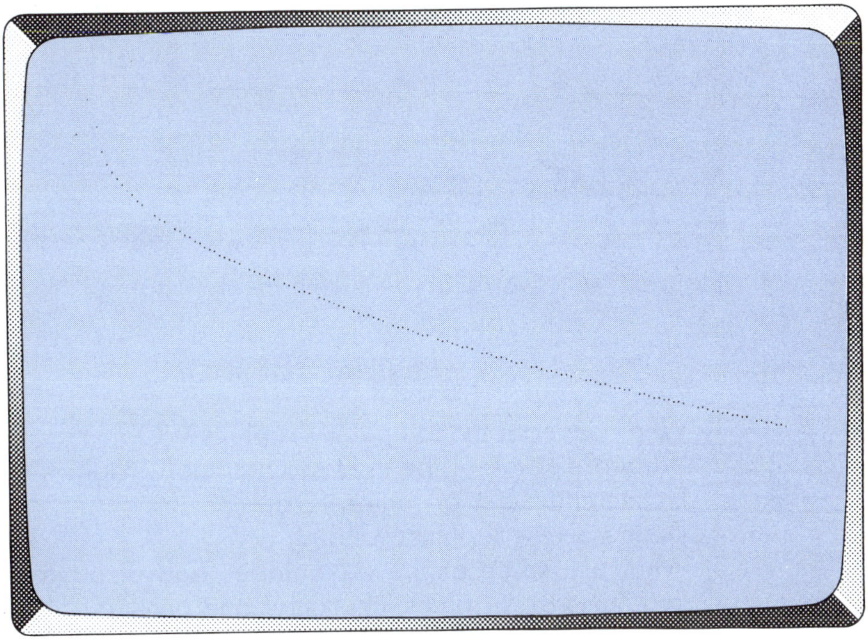

Figure 14-5 Line Drawn with Pixel Graphics

Complex graphics screens, such as those used in computer games, are usually done with pixel graphics (see Figure 14-6). Complex screens are usually done with pixel graphics because the ability to manipulate each and every dot on the screen (as opposed to working with character-sized rectangles) gives the programmer great flexibility. However, since each dot must be handled separately, the speed with which the computer can draw the graphics is slower. Also, programming with pixel graphics can become very complex.

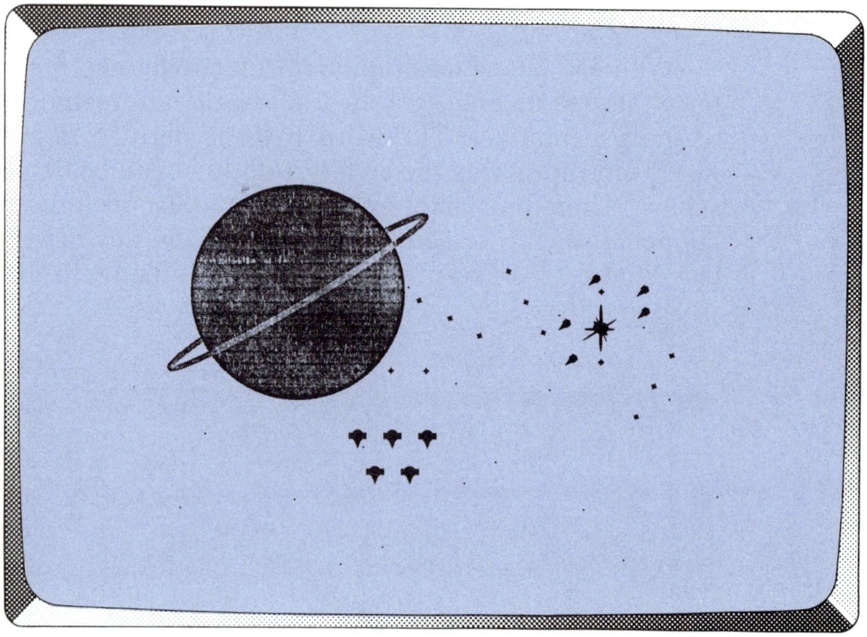

Figure 14-6 Game Screens Use Pixel Graphics

REVIEW QUESTIONS

1. What is meant by computer graphics? (Obj. 1)
2. What are some of the uses of computer graphics? (Obj. 2)
3. Define character graphics. (Obj. 3)
4. Define pixel graphics. (Obj. 3)
5. What are some of the advantages and disadvantages of the two types of graphics (character and pixel)? (Obj. 3)

TOPIC 14.2 PROGRAMMING GRAPHICS WITH BASIC

The complexity with which graphics may be done is such that entire volumes have been written on the subject. The IBM and compatible personal computers are capable of far more complex graphics than described in this text. This topic is intended as a brief introduction to what may be done using graphics.

While IBM personal computers and the TRS-80 Models III and 4 are all capable of doing character graphics, the character sets and the methods of handling them are different. The TRS-80 Models III and 4 are not capable of pixel graphics. Therefore, refer to the following section that applies to the computer you are using.

IBM AND COMPATIBLES

When planning to use graphics with the IBM, it is recommended that you always load BASICA instead of BASIC. While character graphics can be done with BASIC, pixel graphics require the use of BASICA.

Character Graphics

When you start up BASICA (or BASIC) on the IBM, you can immediately begin doing character graphics. No preliminary steps are necessary to prepare your computer.

Printing Character Graphics. Since graphics characters can be printed anywhere on the screen, the first step is to position the printing point to the desired location. A convenient way to do this is through the use of the **LOCATE** statement.

General Form:
line number LOCATE *row number,column number*

Example: `70 LOCATE 8,26`

The example statement will position the printing point to row 8, column 26. The next thing printed will appear beginning in that position.

Once the printing point has been established, the keyword PRINT is used to put the graphics characters on the screen. If only one character is to be displayed, the PRINT statement will use the CHR$ function, such as PRINT CHR$(1). Since 1 is the code of the "smiley face" character, that is what would be printed.

If several of the same characters are to be placed in a row, such as printing 26 half-tone blocks (code of 176), the STRING$ function is frequently used in the PRINT statement, such as PRINT STRING$(26,176). Recall that the STRING$ function prints the number of characters designated by the first number in parentheses. The value after the comma gives the character to print, either in the form of its ASCII code or in quotes. The codes for all of the characters that can be printed are given in Appendix C.

The general program design for implementing character graphics is as follows:

1. Until the desired graphic has been finished, repeat the following:
   a. Position the printing point with LOCATE.
   b. Print the desired character(s).

Obviously, the steps of producing a particular graphic can be outlined before beginning. For example, to plan the program for printing the graphic illustrated in Figure 14-4, you can plan step 3 in at least two different ways. One way would be to print the graphic a line at a time—all of line 1, then all of line 2, all of line 3, and so on. Another way would be to print all the outer ring, then all the interior shading, and then the wording. Characters to be printed can be included directly in the PRINT statement, or the codes may be read from DATA lines. The output shown in Figure 14-4 can be obtained by any one of the following three programs; they simply use different methods to do the same thing.

Example:

```
10 ' C14E1
20 ' STUDENT NAME, CHAPTER 14, EXAMPLE 1
30 ' MAKES FRAMED CHARACTER GRAPHIC BOX
40 ' AND PUTS WORDING IN BOX
50 CLS
60 LOCATE 8,26                                        ] <- Print line 1
70 PRINT STRING$(28,219)                              ]
80 LOCATE 9,26                                        ] <- Print line 2
90 PRINT CHR$(219);STRING$(26,176);CHR$(219)          ]
100 LOCATE 10,26                                      ] <- Print line 3
110 PRINT CHR$(219);STRING$(7,176);"STUDENT NAME";    ]
    STRING$(7,176);CHR$(219)
120 LOCATE 11,26                                      ] <- Print line 4
130 PRINT CHR$(219);STRING$(26,176);CHR$(219)         ]
140 LOCATE 12,26                                      ] <- Print line 5
150 PRINT STRING$(28,219)                             ]
160 END
```

Example:

```
10 ' C14E2
20 ' STUDENT NAME, CHAPTER 14, EXAMPLE 2
30 ' MAKES FRAMED CHARACTER GRAPHIC BOX
40 ' AND PUTS WORDING IN BOX
50 CLS
60 LOCATE 8,26
70 PRINT STRING$(28,219)
80 FOR ROW=9 TO 11
90     LOCATE ROW,26
100    PRINT CHR$(219)          ← Print outer ring
110    LOCATE ROW,53
120    PRINT CHR$(219)
130 NEXT ROW
140 LOCATE 12,26
150 PRINT STRING$(28,219)
160 FOR ROW=9 TO 11
170    LOCATE ROW,27
180    PRINT STRING$(26,176)    ← Print inner shading
190 NEXT ROW
200 LOCATE 10,34
210 PRINT "STUDENT NAME"        ← Print student name
220 END
```

Example:

```
10 ' C14E3
20 ' STUDENT NAME, CHAPTER 14, EXAMPLE 3
30 ' MAKES FRAMED CHARACTER GRAPHIC BOX
40 ' AND PUTS WORDING IN BOX
50 CLS
60 FOR ROW=8 TO 12              ← One line at a time:
70    LOCATE ROW,26             ← Locate the printing point
80    FOR CHAR=1 TO 28          ← Loop across the line length
90       READ CODE              ← Read code from DATA line
100      PRINT CHR$(CODE);      ← Print code's character
110   NEXT CHAR
120   PRINT
130 NEXT ROW
140 LOCATE 10,34
150 PRINT "STUDENT NAME"        ← Print the student name
```

```
160 END
200 DATA 219,219,219,219,219,219,219,219,219,219,219,219,219,219
210 DATA 219,219,219,219,219,219,219,219,219,219,219,219,219,219
220 DATA 219,176,176,176,176,176,176,176,176,176,176,176,176,176
230 DATA 176,176,176,176,176,176,176,176,176,176,176,176,176,219
240 DATA 219,176,176,176,176,176,176,176,176,176,176,176,176,176
250 DATA 176,176,176,176,176,176,176,176,176,176,176,176,176,219
260 DATA 219,176,176,176,176,176,176,176,176,176,176,176,176,176
270 DATA 176,176,176,176,176,176,176,176,176,176,176,176,176,219
280 DATA 219,219,219,219,219,219,219,219,219,219,219,219,219,219
290 DATA 219,219,219,219,219,219,219,219,219,219,219,219,219,219
```

Setting Colors. If your computer has color capability, you may use the keyword **COLOR** to set the colors that appear on the screen. You can set the color for the foreground (the characters), for the background (the color against which the characters are displayed), and for a border around the edge of the screen. As an example, you could set a screen to use white letters (the foreground) on a blue background, with a cyan border. All colors that you set will apply to both regular text and character graphics that are displayed. The syntax of the COLOR statement is as follows:

General Form:
line number COLOR *foreground, background, border*

Example: `60 COLOR 7,1,3`

The example will set the foreground to white, the background to blue, and the border around the edge of the screen to cyan. However, you do not have to use all three numbers after the keyword COLOR to change colors. For example, if you want to change just the foreground color, you may have just one number (i.e., COLOR 3). If you want to change just the background color, put a comma in front of the number to indicate that the foreground number is omitted (i.e., COLOR ,4). The colors that may be used for the foreground and the border are listed here with their corresponding numbers. Notice that colors 8 through 15 are "brighter" versions of colors 0 through 7:

0	Black	8	Gray
1	Blue	9	Light Blue
2	Green	10	Light Green
3	Cyan	11	Light Cyan
4	Red	12	Light Red
5	Magenta	13	Light Magenta
6	Brown	14	Yellow
7	White	15	High-intensity White

Monitors vary in their ability to depict particular colors. Therefore, colors may not look exactly as you would expect them to. You can make foreground characters blink by adding 16 to the color number you want to use.

For the background, you may use only colors 0 through 7. Remember that if you make the foreground and background the same color, anything printed on the screen will be invisible since the letters and the background upon which they are placed will be the same color. The display will again become visible if you change one of the colors. If your program does not contain a COLOR statement, all characters you print will appear in the default colors of white on black.

To see how the COLOR statement is used, examine the following code for program C14E4 below. It prints the same graphics box as the previous example program, but allows you to specify the colors to be used.

Example:

```
10 ' C14E4
20 ' STUDENT NAME, CHAPTER 14, EXAMPLE 4
30 ' MAKES FRAMED CHARACTER GRAPHIC BOX
40 ' AND PUTS WORDING IN BOX
50 CLS
51 PRINT "YOU CAN CHOOSE THE COLORS TO BE USED."
52 INPUT "NUMBER OF FOREGROUND COLOR:  ";FORE
53 IF FORE<0 OR FORE>15 THEN PRINT "INVALID NUMBER"
   :GOTO 52
54 INPUT "NUMBER OF BACKGROUND COLOR:  ";BACK
55 IF BACK<0 OR BACK>7 THEN PRINT "INVALID NUMBER"
   :GOTO 54
56 INPUT "BORDER COLOR:  ";BORDER
57 IF BORDER<0 OR BORDER>15 THEN PRINT "INVALID
   NUMBER":GOTO 56
```

← Get user's choice of colors (lines 50–57)

```
58 COLOR FORE,BACK,BORDER  ←——— Set the colors
59 CLS
60 LOCATE 8,26
70 PRINT STRING$(28,219)
80 FOR ROW=9 TO 11
90     LOCATE ROW,26
100    PRINT CHR$(219)
110    LOCATE ROW,53
120    PRINT CHR$(219)
130 NEXT ROW
140 LOCATE 12,26
150 PRINT STRING$(28,219)
160 FOR ROW=9 TO 11
170     LOCATE ROW,27
180     PRINT STRING$(26,176)
190 NEXT ROW
200 LOCATE 10,34
210 PRINT "STUDENT NAME"
220 END
```

Screen Types

If you want to do more complex graphics applications, you need to understand the various screen types that are available as well as the colors that may be used. Screen type does not refer to the physical CRT upon which graphics are displayed, but to the way in which BASIC handles the screen. (The CRT you are using must be capable of displaying the degree of resolution called for by the screen type, but there is no physical or electrical connection between the screen types and the actual CRT.) If your program does not contain a SCREEN command, the computer defaults to text or character mode as used in the previous examples in this chapter. Alternately, if your program contains a SCREEN 0 command, the computer will be in text or character mode.

IBM PCs equipped with the monochrome display adapter have no pixel graphics or color ability. Therefore, the program examples in the following paragraphs, which require graphic screen types and color settings, will not run on this configuration.

IBM PCs with a color graphics adapter or similar video card, IBM PCjrs, IBM PS2 models, and many compatible computers do have pixel graphics capability. On these machines, you may use the keyword **SCREEN** to set the type of display (text or graphics), the degree of resolution, and the number of colors that may be used for graphics.

General Form: *line number* SCREEN *mode*

Example 1: `50 SCREEN 0`

Example 2: `50 SCREEN 1`

When the mode is 0, as given in Example 1, the computer is in text mode and only character graphics may be used. This is the default setting if the SCREEN statement is not used in the program. A screen mode of 1, as shown in the Example 2, sets the computer to medium resolution graphics. Medium resolution is defined as 320 pixels or dots across the screen, 200 pixels down the screen, and a maximum of 4 colors. When in SCREEN 1, your program can still print text on the screen intermixed with the graphics, but the text will be larger, with a maximum of 40 characters per line.

Depending on the computer hardware and version of BASIC you are using, there may be additional screen modes of still higher resolution and more colors. Refer to your BASIC reference manual and your computer's configuration to determine what else may be available on your machine. Also, there are other parameters that may be added to the end of the SCREEN statement for other purposes, but they are beyond the scope of this chapter.

Note, when execution of a program is finished, the computer stays in the screen mode it was placed in by the program. Therefore, after running a program that sets the screen to mode 1, for example, the computer will still be in that mode, giving you a 40-character screen. If, after executing a pixel graphics program, you want to go back to an 80-column text screen, you can enter (at the keyboard) SCREEN 0 (return) followed by **WIDTH** 80 (return). You can also put these statements at the end of the pixel graphics program if you desire. If you do, however, the screen will be cleared when they are executed, removing any output your program produced.

Pixel Graphics

Once a graphics screen has been chosen with the SCREEN 1 or similar command, you are ready to do pixel graphics. Typically, a program will set colors and then put graphic output on the screen.

Setting Colors. The syntax of the COLOR command in graphics mode is as follows:

> **General Form:** *line number* COLOR *background,palette*
>
> **Example:** `60 COLOR 1,0`

When in a graphics screen mode, the background color number is chosen from the 0 to 15 range shown earlier. Either of two palettes may be selected. Palette 0 contains the colors green, red, and brown. Palette 1 contains the colors cyan, magenta, and white. Therefore, the example COLOR statement above sets the background to blue (color 1) and selects palette 0, which gives access to colors green, red, and brown on the blue background. The exact color used is chosen at the time of displaying a pixel with one of the graphics statements discussed in the following sections.

While it is beyond the scope of this text to discuss all the statements that may be used for manipulating pixel graphics, we will discuss a few of the simpler ones. Before using any of these statements, a program must switch to graphics mode (we assume SCREEN 1 in all examples). The COLOR statement may be used if desired to set colors; otherwise, default colors will be used.

Using PSET. PSET is short for point set. It is the simplest pixel graphics command and simply lights up a designated pixel on the screen. The syntax is as follows.

> **General Form:** *line number* PSET*(x,y),color*
>
> **Example:** `80 PSET(40,20),1`

The example line will light up pixel 40 on row 20 of pixels, using color 1. The color (which IBM calls an attribute) may be omitted if desired; if it is left out, a default color is used.

The PSET statement may be used within loops that control the placement of the pixel. For example, the following program will draw a line on the screen.

Example:

```
10 ' C14E5
20 ' STUDENT NAME, CHAPTER 14, EXAMPLE 5
30 ' DRAWS LINE ON SCREEN USING PSET
40 '
50 SCREEN 1 ←—— Switch to graphics screen
60 COLOR 1,0 ←—— Set background color blue, palette 0
70 CLS ←—— Clear screen
80 FOR X=0 TO 319 ←—— Have X coordinate go from 0 to 319
90 Y=SQR(X)*10 ←—— Compute Y coordinate based on X
100 PSET(X,Y) ←—— Turn on designated X,Y pixel
110 NEXT X ←—— Repeat loop
120 END
```

The output of the program is as follows:

Output:

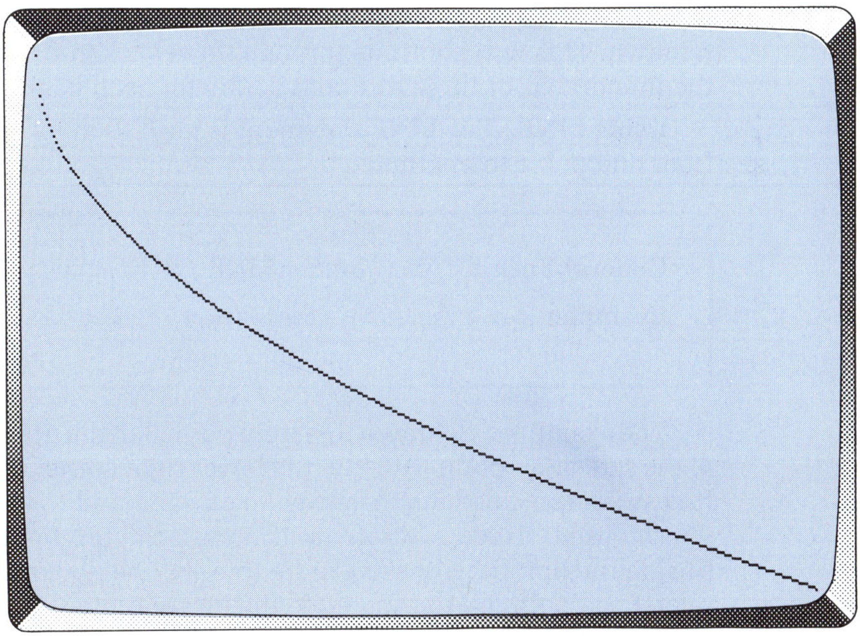

Using additional statements, the line can be drawn repeatedly, using different background and pixel colors.

Example:

```
10 ' C14E6
20 ' STUDENT NAME, CHAPTER 14, EXAMPLE 6
30 ' DRAWS LINE ON SCREEN USING PSET
40 ' AND VARYING SCREEN COLORS
50 SCREEN 1                  ← Switch to graphics screen
60 FOR BACK=0 TO 2           ← Run loop cycling through 3 background colors
70    COLOR BACK,1           ← Set background color based on loop value
80    CLS
90    FOR COL=1 TO 3         ← Loop through three colors of palette
100       FOR X=0 TO 319     ┐
110          Y=SQR(X)*10     │ ← Draw line on screen using
120          PSET(X,Y),COL   │   palette color from loop
130       NEXT X             ┘
140   NEXT COL
150 NEXT BACK
160 END
```

Note that when you run this version of the program, the screen background color will be set and the line will be drawn. Then the screen will be switched to the next color and the line will be redrawn. This will continue through three background colors, with the line drawn in three different colors for each background color.

Using LINE. The **LINE** statement is used to draw a straight line from one point to another.

General Form: *line number* LINE *(x1,y1)–(x2,y2),color*

Example: `80 LINE(0,0)-(319,199),1`

The example will draw a line from point 0,0 (the upper left corner of the screen) to point 319,199 (the lower right corner of the screen). If desired, the color number may be omitted and the default color will be used. If you desire, you can omit the origination X and Y (inside the first parenthesis) and a line will be drawn from the last referenced point on the screen to the destination X,Y coordinates.

Example:

```
90 LINE -(100,50),1
```

The LINE statement can be used inside a loop to draw multiple lines. For example, the following program draws a series of diagonal lines.

Example:

```
10 ' C14E7
20 ' STUDENT NAME, CHAPTER 14, EXAMPLE 7
30 ' USES LINE STATEMENT
40 '
50 SCREEN 1 ←—— Set screen to graphics
60 COLOR 1,1 ←—— Set background color to blue, palette 1
70 CLS
80 FOR X=0 TO 300 STEP 10 ←—— Loop X coordinate from 0 to 300 by tens
90     LINE(X,0)-(X+20,100) ←—— Draw diagonal line
100 NEXT X ←—— Repeat loop
110 END
```

In the preceding example, line 80 sets up a loop to draw lines. Since the loop repeats 30 times and a line is drawn each time the loop executes, there will be 30 lines on the screen. Inside the loop (on line 90) the ending point of each line is defined as being 20 pixels ahead of the beginning point. Therefore, the lines will be diagonal. The output of the program is as follows:

Output:

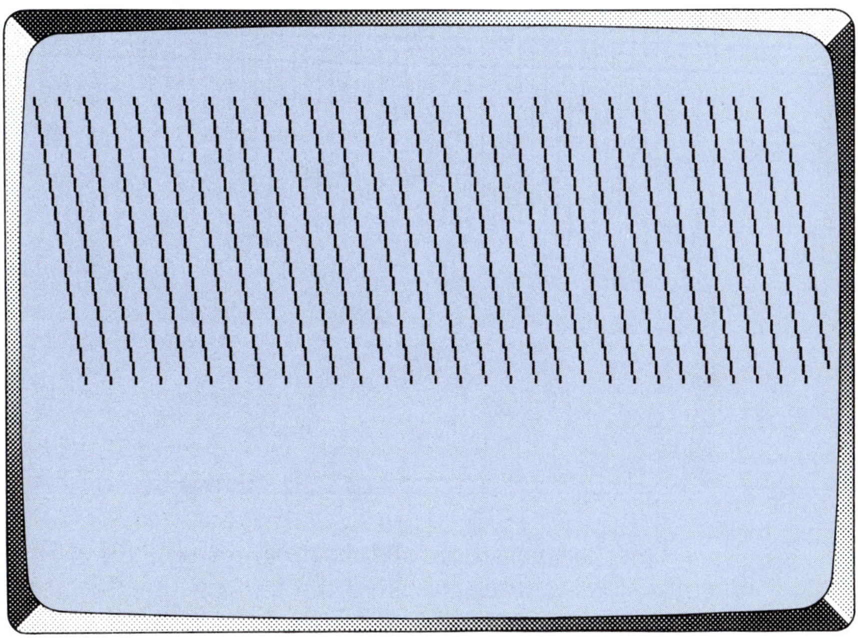

By using the letter B at the end of the LINE statement, the X and Y coordinates represent the corners of boxes rather than a diagonal line.

Example:

```
10 ' C14E8
20 ' STUDENT NAME, CHAPTER 14, EXAMPLE 8
30 ' USES LINE STATEMENT
40 ' TO MAKE BOXES
50 SCREEN 1
60 COLOR 1,1
70 CLS
80 FOR X=0 TO 300 STEP 10 ←
90     LINE(X,0)-(X+5,100),2,B ←
100 NEXT X
110 END
```

Loop X coordinate from 0 to 300 by 10s

B makes LINE draw a box; the +5 in the second X coordinate determines the width of the box

The output of the program is as follows:

Output:

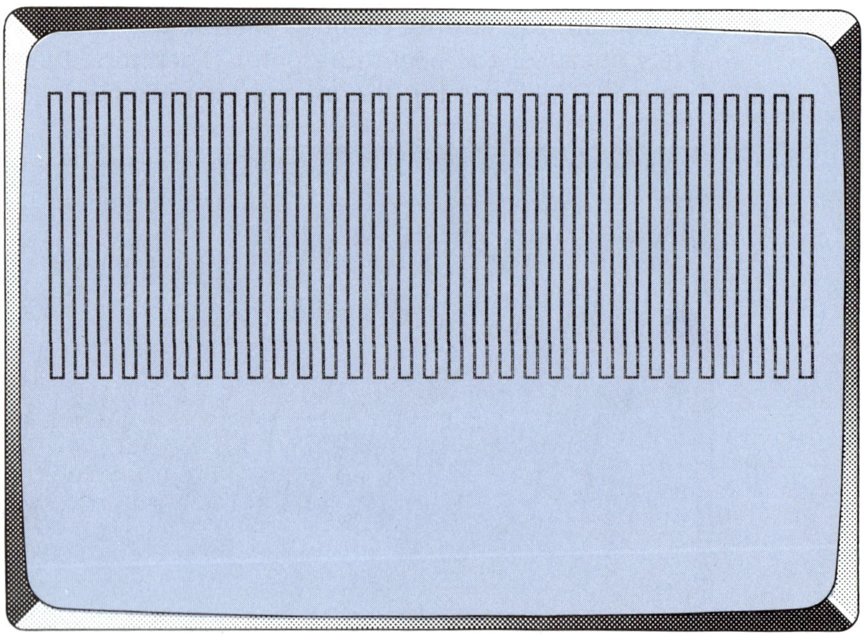

One last variation of this program will fill in the boxes with color. This is done by using the letter F (for fill) at the end of the LINE statement. Study the program as follows:

Example:

```
10 ' C14E9
20 ' STUDENT NAME, CHAPTER 14, EXAMPLE 9
30 ' USES LINE STATEMENT
40 ' TO MAKE BOXES
50 SCREEN 1
60 COLOR 1,1
70 CLS
80 FOR X=0 TO 300 STEP 10
90    LINE(X,0)-(X+5,100),2,BF  <---------- F fills in the box
100 NEXT X
110 END
```

The output of the program is as follows:

Output:

While there are many other pixel graphics commands that may be used with the IBM personal computer and compatible machines, these two will enable you to produce many interesting screens. Refer to your BASIC reference manual to study the other graphics statements that can be used.

Using Random Values. You can make many interesting graphics patterns by randomly generating the values to be used for colors, pixel locations, line beginning and ending points, and so on. The **RND** function is used to generate random numbers.

General Form: *line number numeric variable*=RND

Example: `400 X=RND`

The random function produces a random number between 0 and 1. Therefore, your program must multiply it by a factor to get the size number desired. For example, if you want the number to be in the range of 0 to 319, your program should multiply the generated number times 320 (i.e., 400 X=RND*320). To ensure that you have a different sequence of random numbers each time you run a program, you should put the keywords **RANDOMIZE TIMER** in the program before the first random number is generated (i.e., 40 RANDOMIZE TIMER). If you have an older version of BASICA and this does not work, just leave off TIMER and enter a number when RANDOMIZE asks you to do so upon executing the program.

The following example shows how to plot points on the screen in random positions using the PSET statement. Note that this example uses the random numbers directly (see line 80) rather than placing them in variables first.

Example:

```
10 ' C14E10
20 ' STUDENT NAME, CHAPTER 14, EXAMPLE 10
30 ' PLOTS RANDOM POINTS
40 SCREEN 1
50 CLS
60 RANDOMIZE TIMER
70 FOR P=1 TO 1000
80     PSET(RND*320,RND*200)
90 NEXT P
100 END
```

Sample output of the program follows. Note that it will be slightly different each time it is run.

Output:

TRS-80 MODELS III AND 4

When you program in BASIC on the TRS-80 Model III or 4, you can use the PRINT statement to display character graphics on the screen. (See Appendix C for all the characters that can be used, along with their codes.) Any character with a code from 32 to 191 can be printed by simply printing the character. If you need to use any character with a code of 192 to 255, you must place a PRINT CHR$(21) statement in your program before beginning to print graphics. Use of characters with codes of 0 to 31 requires a method that is beyond the scope of this chapter.

Since graphics characters can be printed anywhere desired on the screen, a variation of the PRINT statement, which uses the keyword **PRINT@**, is used to position the printing point to the desired location. For any special character, the CHR$ function is used to convert the ASCII code number into the desired character.

General Form (Model III):
line number PRINT@*position,item(s) to print*

Example: `70 PRINT@93,CHR$(191)`

Output:

The print positions on the Model III screen begin with 0 and continue through 1023. Positions 0 through 63 are on the first line of the screen, positions 64 through 127 are on the second line, and so on.

The PRINT@ keyword is also used for Model 4.

General Form (Model 4):
line number PRINT@*(row,column),item(s) to print*

Example: `70 PRINT@(1,30),CHR$(191)`

Output:

The Model 4 has 24 rows of 80 columns. The rows are numbered 0 to 23, and the columns are numbered 0 to 79. (If desired, you can use the Model III PRINT@ format on the Model 4, but referring to rows and columns is much easier.) If only one character is to be printed, the PRINT@ statement will use the CHR$ function, such as CHR$(191) as shown in the previous examples. Since 191 is the code of the solid rectangle, that is what would be printed. If several of the same characters are to be placed in a row, such as printing 26 small blocks (code of 132), the STRING$ function is frequently used in the PRINT@ statement, such as STRING$(26,132). Recall that the STRING$ prints the number of characters indicated by the first number in parentheses, while the value after the comma (either an ASCII code or a character in quotes) gives the character to be printed.

The general program design is to simply place and print characters until the graphic is finished. Obviously, the steps of producing a particular graphic can be outlined before beginning. For example, to plan the program for printing the graphic illustrated in Figure 14-4, you can use at least two different methods. One way would be to print the graphic a line at a time—all of line 1, then all of line 2, all of line 3, and so on. Another method would be to print all the outer ring, then all the interior shading, and then the wording. Characters to be printed can be included directly in the PRINT statement, or the codes may be read from DATA lines. The output shown in Figure 14-4 can be obtained by any one of the following three programs; the first two indicate the characters to print directly in the PRINT statements. The third one illustrates reading the values from DATA lines. Versions of each program are given for both the TRS-80 Model III and Model 4. Study the one that is appropriate for your computer.

Example:

```
10 ' C14E11
20 ' FOR TRS-80 MODEL III
30 ' STUDENT NAME, CHAPTER 14, EXAMPLE 11
40 ' MAKES FRAMED CHARACTER GRAPHIC BOX
50 ' AND PUTS WORDING IN BOX
60 CLS
70 PRINT@274,STRING$(28,191) ←—————— Print line 1
80 PRINT@338,CHR$(191);STRING$(26,132);CHR$(191) ←—— Print line 2
90 PRINT@402,CHR$(191);STRING$(7,132);"STUDENT NAME";
   STRING$(7,132);CHR$(191) ←—————— Print line 3
100 PRINT@466,CHR$(191);STRING$(26,132);CHR$(191) ←—— Print line 4
110 PRINT@530,STRING$(28,191) ←—————— Print line 5
120 END
```

Example:

```
10 ' C14E11
20 ' FOR TRS-80 MODEL 4
30 ' STUDENT NAME, CHAPTER 14, EXAMPLE 11
40 ' MAKES FRAMED CHARACTER GRAPHIC BOX
50 ' AND PUTS WORDING IN BOX
60 CLS
70 PRINT@(8,26),STRING$(28,191) ←—————— Print line 1
80 PRINT@(9,26),CHR$(191);STRING$(26,132);CHR$(191) ←—— Print line 2
90 PRINT@(10,26),CHR$(191);STRING$(7,132);"STUDENT
   NAME";STRING$(7,132);CHR$(191) ←—————— Print line 3
100 PRINT@(11,26),CHR$(191);STRING$(26,132);CHR$(191) ←—— Print line 4
110 PRINT@(12,26),STRING$(28,191) ←—————— Print line 5
120 END
```

The output of the program:

Output:

In the code for program C14E12, note that semicolons are placed at the ends of the lines. This is done because this program does not go a line at a time; instead, it does the outer ring, and then the inner ring. If the cursor were allowed to drop to the next line, as it would do with no semicolon, characters already on the screen would be destroyed.

Example:

```
10 ' C14E12
20 ' FOR TRS-80 MODEL III
30 ' STUDENT NAME, CHAPTER 14, EXAMPLE 12
40 ' MAKES FRAMED CHARACTER GRAPHIC BOX
50 ' AND PUTS WORDING IN BOX
60 CLS
70 PRINT@274,STRING$(28,191)
80 FOR ROW=338 TO 466 STEP 64
90    PRINT@ROW,CHR$(191);
100   PRINT@ROW+27,CHR$(191);
110 NEXT ROW
120 PRINT@530,STRING$(28,191);
130 FOR ROW=339 TO 467 STEP 64
140   PRINT@ROW,STRING$(26,132);
150 NEXT ROW
```

Lines 70–120: ← Print outer ring

Lines 130–150: ← Print inner shading

```
160 PRINT@410,"STUDENT NAME"; <-------- Print student name
170 PRINT@800, <----------------------- Move print point off
180 END                                 graphic so okay at end of
                                        program run won't ruin it
```

Example:

```
10 ' C14E12
20 ' FOR TRS-80 MODEL 4
30 ' STUDENT NAME, CHAPTER 14, EXAMPLE 12
40 ' MAKES FRAMED CHARACTER GRAPHIC BOX
50 ' AND PUTS WORDING IN BOX
60 CLS
70 PRINT@(8,26),STRING$(28,191)   ]
80 FOR R=9 TO 11                  ]
90    PRINT@(R,26),CHR$(191)      ] <------ Print outer ring
100   PRINT@(R,53),CHR$(191)      ]
110 NEXT R                        ]
120 PRINT@(12,26),STRING$(28,191) ]
130 FOR R=9 TO 11                   ]
140   PRINT@(R,27),STRING$(26,132); ] <--- Print inner shading
150 NEXT R                          ]
160 PRINT@(10,34),"STUDENT NAME"; <---- Print student name
170 PRINT@(18,1),"" <------------------ Move print point off
180 END                                 graphic so okay at end of
                                        program run won't ruin it
```

Example:

```
10 ' C14E13
15 ' FOR TRS-80 MODEL III
20 ' STUDENT NAME, CHAPTER 14, EXAMPLE 13
30 ' MAKES FRAMED CHARACTER GRAPHIC BOX
40 ' AND PUTS WORDING IN BOX
50 CLS
60 FOR ROW=274 TO 530 STEP 64 <-------- One line at a time:
70    PRINT@ROW,; <-------------------- Locate the printing point
80    FOR CHAR=1 TO 28 <--------------- Loop across the line length
90       READ CODE <------------------- Read code from DATA line
100      PRINT CHR$(CODE); <----------- Print code's character
110   NEXT CHAR
120 NEXT ROW
```

```
130 PRINT@410,"STUDENT NAME" ←———— Print student name
140 PRINT@800, ←———— Move print point off graphic
150 END
200 DATA 191,191,191,191,191,191,191,191,191,191,191,191,191,191
210 DATA 191,191,191,191,191,191,191,191,191,191,191,191,191,191
220 DATA 191,132,132,132,132,132,132,132,132,132,132,132,132,132
230 DATA 132,132,132,132,132,132,132,132,132,132,132,132,132,191
240 DATA 191,132,132,132,132,132,132,132,132,132,132,132,132,132
250 DATA 132,132,132,132,132,132,132,132,132,132,132,132,132,191
260 DATA 191,132,132,132,132,132,132,132,132,132,132,132,132,132
270 DATA 132,132,132,132,132,132,132,132,132,132,132,132,132,191
280 DATA 191,191,191,191,191,191,191,191,191,191,191,191,191,191
290 DATA 191,191,191,191,191,191,191,191,191,191,191,191,191,191
```

Example:

```
10 ' C14E13
15 ' FOR TRS-80 MODEL 4
20 ' STUDENT NAME, CHAPTER 14, EXAMPLE 13
30 ' MAKES FRAMED CHARACTER GRAPHIC BOX
40 ' AND PUTS WORDING IN BOX
50 CLS
60 FOR R=8 TO 12 ←———— One line at a time:
70    PRINT@(R,26),; ←———— Locate the printing point
80    FOR CHAR=1 TO 28 ←———— Loop across the line length
90       READ CODE ←———— Read code from DATA line
100      PRINT CHR$(CODE); ←———— Print code's character
110   NEXT CHAR
120   PRINT
130 NEXT R
140 PRINT@(10,34),"STUDENT NAME"; ←———— Print student name
150 PRINT@(18,1),"" ←———— Move print point off graphic
160 END
200 DATA 191,191,191,191,191,191,191,191,191,191,191,191,191,191
210 DATA 191,191,191,191,191,191,191,191,191,191,191,191,191,191
220 DATA 191,132,132,132,132,132,132,132,132,132,132,132,132,132
230 DATA 132,132,132,132,132,132,132,132,132,132,132,132,132,191
240 DATA 191,132,132,132,132,132,132,132,132,132,132,132,132,132
250 DATA 132,132,132,132,132,132,132,132,132,132,132,132,132,191
260 DATA 191,132,132,132,132,132,132,132,132,132,132,132,132,132
270 DATA 132,132,132,132,132,132,132,132,132,132,132,132,132,191
280 DATA 191,191,191,191,191,191,191,191,191,191,191,191,191,191
290 DATA 191,191,191,191,191,191,191,191,191,191,191,191,191,191
```

VOCABULARY WORDS

The following terms were introduced in this chapter:

character graphics	pixel	pixel graphics
graphics		

KEYWORDS

The following keywords were introduced for IBM:

COLOR	PSET	RND
LINE	RANDOMIZE	SCREEN
LOCATE	TIMER	WIDTH

The following keyword was introduced for TRS-80 Models III and 4:

PRINT@

PROGRAMS TO WRITE

For each of the programs, prepare the necessary documentation before writing the BASIC code. If you are using a TRS-80 Model III or 4 or an IBM PC with no pixel graphics capability, you can complete only Programs 1 through 5.

Program 1

Using character graphics, write a program to draw a rectangle in the top left corner of the screen and print your name inside the rectangle.

Program 2

Using character graphics, write a program that prints a reasonable facsimile of a checkerboard.

Program 3

Assume that you are planning to write an accounting program that you call "Accounting Master." Write the program lines to print an "opening screen" for the program. The screen, which is to be displayed immediately upon execution of the program, should contain the name of the program and your name as the writer of the program. Make the screen attractive by the use of boxes around the lines of data. At the bottom of the screen there should be the message: "Hit any key to continue." When the user strikes a key, the screen should clear and program execution should end.

Program 4

Write a program that uses character graphics to print a team mascot. (If you're not the world's greatest artist, that's okay!)

Program 5

Using character graphics, write a program that prints two patterned vertical columns rising from a baseline. If your computer has color capability, include the capability to allow the user to specify the colors to be used each time the program is executed.

Program 6

Write a program that will display one colored pixel in each of the four corners of the screen.

Program 7

Write a program that uses pixel graphics to print a single row of dots horizontally across the screen and a single row vertically on the screen to form a large plus sign.

Program 8

Modify your solution to Program 7 so that the plus sign is "fat" rather than consisting of two lines of single dots. If your computer has color capability, allow the user to specify different colors each time the program is executed.

Program 9

Write a program that uses pixel graphics to draw a box of any desired size on the screen. The program should get keyboard input for the beginning and ending points for the box as well as for the colors.

Program 10

Write a program that runs continuously until interrupted. It should draw lines on the screen, with each line beginning at the end of the previous line and going to a randomly generated position. The background color should be written into the program, but the color of each individual line segment should be randomly generated.

PROJECT 6

In Chapter 14, you learned how to make graphics using either characters or pixels. For this project, you have the opportunity to apply that graphic knowledge, along with things you learned in previous chapters, to produce a useful graphing program.

The program you write should produce a bar graph done with automatic scaling, which means that the program should use the full available length for the bar representing the largest quantity, with other bars being proportionately shorter. The graph should have a centered main title and should have the capability of graphing anywhere from 1 to 6 quantities. Each of the quantities should be labeled with a name. All data, including the main title and the labeling for the bars, should be input by the user from the keyboard when the program is executed.

To test your program, make a graph of monthly sales for July 19--, with the following data: Susan Smith, $39,832; Fred Martin, $24,389; William McMicken, $37,321; Ami Lawrence, $27,398; Brad Wyley, $14,398; and Lea Brown, $43,233. Run the program again, omitting the last two persons.

GLOSSARY

Alphanumeric data—Data that consists of any combination of letters, numbers, and symbols. The same as character data. (pg. 187)

Array—A variable that can store more than one piece of data at a time; a table. (pg. 186)

Ascending sequence—Arranging data in order from smallest to largest. (pg. 212)

BASIC—A high-level language. BASIC is an acronym for Beginner's All-purpose Symbolic Instruction Code. (pg. 4)

Buffer—A special area of computer memory used for the writing and reading of data files. (pg. 303)

Bug—A program error. (pg. 29)

Case structure—A control structure under which one of several possible actions is taken based on conditions. (pg. 74)

Catenation—Connecting data items together. Also known as concatenation. (pg. 168)

Character graphics—Graphics made with a computer's built-in characters. (pg. 340)

Column heading—A heading over a column of data. (pg. 159)

Command—A word telling the computer to take immediate action. (pg. 13)

Compare variable—A variable that is used to determine when the control variable has changed. (pg. 245)

Compiler—A program that translates a high-level programming language into machine language. (pg. 3)

Computer—An information processing machine that can accept data, make comparisons, and perform calculations. (pg. 2)

Conditional count—A count of the data items or operations meeting a predetermined requirement, as opposed to a count of all items. (pg. 242)

Conditional total—A sum of data items meeting a predetermined requirement, as opposed to a sum of all data items. (pg. 242)

Constant—An actual number used for processing by the computer. (pg. 8)

Control break—A change in program action caused by a change in a control field. (pg. 245)

Control module—A program part that controls the operation of other parts of the program. Also called the main module. (pg. 47)

Control structure—One of several methods used to control the order of execution of program steps. (pg. 68)

Control variable—A field (variable) whose change in value causes a subtotal to be printed. (pg. 245)

Controlled loop—A loop that executes the number of times determined in the program. (pg. 91)

Count—The number of data items that have been processed or the number of operations that have been performed. (pg. 242)

CRT—Cathode ray tube—the television-like display screen of a computer. (pg. 6)

Cursor—A dash, an underscore, or a block that marks the printing position on the CRT. (pg. 14)

Data terminator—A dummy data item, the existence of which can be detected by an IF . . . THEN statement to determine that the end of data has been reached. (pg. 115)

Data validation—Examining data by methods designed to help insure data correctness. (pg. 135)

Debugging—Finding and correcting the errors in a program. (pg. 29)

Decision structure—A control sequence under which an action is taken if a specified condition is true. (pg. 69)

Default drive—The drive used when a drive identification is not specified by the operator or program. (pg. 17)

Descending sequence—Arranging data in order from largest to smallest. (pg. 212)

Detail line—A report line containing an output line for each item of data processed. (pg. 159)

Detail printing—Printing a line on a report for each data item processed. (pg. 248)

Dimensioning—Creating a table in the computer's memory. (pg. 187)

Disk drive—A storage device that records data on a magnetic disk. (pg. 3)

Do . . . Until loop—A loop that repeats until a condition in the program comes true. (pg. 92)

Do . . . While loop—A loop that repeats while a condition in the program remains true. (pg. 92)

Double precision variables—Variables that can contain a maximum of fifteen digits. (pg. 329)

Editing—Improving the appearance of output by spacing, underlines, dollar signs, decimal points, and trailing zeros. (pg. 160)

Elements—Data items stored in a table. (pg. 185)

Enhanced decision structure—A decision structure that takes one action under a true condition and a different action under a false condition. (pg. 73)

Error messages—A message printed by the computer stating the existence of an error such as incorrect syntax, misspelled keywords, etc. (pg. 15)

Expression—A formula stating the operation to be performed on data. (pg. 11)

Field—Each individual data item in a record. (pg. 278)

Fielding—Dividing a file buffer into named variables for purposes of writing and reading of a random data file. (pg. 311)

File—A group of data stored on disk or tape. (pg. 277)

Floating dollar sign—A dollar sign that moves to the right as far as necessary to be printed immediately before the amount. (pg. 172)

Floppy diskette—An oxide-coated plastic disk upon which data may be recorded by a disk drive. (pg. 17)

Graphics—Pictorial representations. (pg. 338)

Group printing—Printing lines on a report only for subtotals and totals. No detail lines are printed. (pg. 248)

Hard copy—Computer output printed on paper. (pg. 16)

Hierarchy chart—A diagram showing the relationship of the main module and the submodules of a program. (pg. 46)

High-level languages—Computer languages using English-like instructions that are translated into machine language by the computer. (pg. 3)

Inner loop—The second loop in a nested pair of loops. (pg. 98)

Input—Raw facts, numbers, and characters entered into the computer and stored in its memory. (pg. 3)

Interactive program—A program that calls for the user to enter data as it executes. (pg. 25)

Interpreter—A program that translates a program written in a high-level language into machine language. (pg. 3)

Keywords—English words that have a special meaning to the translator program of the computer. (pg. 4)

Leaders—A string of periods connecting data items on a report. (pg. 167)

Literal—A message enclosed in quotation marks for printing by the computer. (pg. 7)

Logic errors—Errors involving use of incorrect logic to solve a problem. (pg. 28)

Logical operators—Keywords that allow the computer to determine if data items have AND, OR, or NOT relationships to each other. (pg. 71)

Loop—A series of statements that are repeated a number of times. (pg. 91)

Machine language—Computer language containing coded instructions having special meanings to the computer's electronic circuitry. (pg. 3)

Main module—A segment of the program that controls the operation of other parts of the program. (pg. 47)

Matrix—A variable that can store more than one piece of data at a time; a table. (pg. 186)

Menu—A list of options available to the user of a program. (pg. 74)

Minor totals—Subtotals that are printed before all data items are processed. (pg. 243)

Module—A part or segment of a computer program. (pg. 46)

Module documentation sheet—A form describing in detail the operation of a part or module of a program. (pg. 49)

Nested loop—A loop totally contained within another loop. (pg. 98)

Null—A "nothing" character. A character variable that has not been assigned a value will contain a null. (pg. 188)

One-dimensional table—A table with multiple rows but only one column. (pg. 186)

Operators—Symbols written in a computer program to perform arithmetic, such as +, −, /, and *. (pg. 11)

Outer loop—The first loop in a nested pair of loops. (pg. 98)

Output—Processed information that can be displayed on a screen, printed, or stored for future use. (pg. 3)

Page heading—A heading that appears at the top of each page. (pg. 159)

Pixels—Picture elements. (pg. 343)

Pixel graphics—Graphics made by manipulating pixels. (pg. 343)

Program—Step-by-step instructions to be followed by a computer. (pg. 3)

Program design—The English language steps to be followed in solving a problem. (pg. 28)

Program documentation sheet—A form used for writing the identification and description of a program as part of the program's documentation. (pg. 24)

Programmer—A person who writes computer programs. (pg. 3)

Prompts—Instructions to the user of an interactive program. Prompts are usually printed on the CRT when input is required by the program. (pg. 32)

Random data file—A file that can be written and read in random order. (pg. 300)

Record—A group of one or more related data fields. (pg. 278)

Record number—The number of the record in a random file into which data are to be placed. (pg. 304)

Relational operators—Operators that allow the computer to compare one value with another. (pg. 70)

Report heading—A heading appearing at the beginning of a report; it includes the title of the report and may also include a company name, an identification number, or other data. (pg. 159)

Row heading—A heading that appears at the beginning of a report row. (pg. 159)

Rulings—Lines made from hyphens, underlines, or other characters. Used to improve the appearance and readability of reports. (pg. 160)

Searching—The process of looking up a desired value in a table. (pg. 186)

Sequential—Recording items one after another. (pg. 280)

Single precision variables—Variables that can contain a maximum of seven digits. (pg. 328)

Sorting—Arranging data in alphabetic or numeric order. (pg. 212)

Spacing chart—A form used for planning the location of data on an output report. (pg. 25)

Statement—A step in a computer program. (pg. 4)

Storage device—Electronic device that can store data by use of magnetic tape or disk. (pg. 3)

String—One or more characters (as opposed to numbers). (pg. 31)

Structured programming—Breaking a program into segments or modules for programming purposes. (pg. 45)

Stubbing in—Coding submodules in skeleton form so that testing of the main module may be done. (pg. 56)

Submodule—A small program part under the control of a main module. (pg. 47)

Subscript—In a table, the number of the row or element to which reference is being made. (pg. 185)

Subtotals—Totals that are printed at intermediate points during computer processing. (pg. 243)

Summarizing—The process of producing a summary. (pg. 240)

Summary—A method of presenting information that makes the "big picture" easier to see. (pg. 240)

Syntax errors—Errors in the usage of a computer language. (pg. 29)

Table—A variable that can store more than one piece of data at a time. (pg. 184)

Top-down design—A planning method whereby you start with the "big picture" and work down to the details. (pg. 46)

Total—The sum of two or more numbers. (pg. 241)

Truncated—Cut off. A data item that is too long for the space allowed may be truncated. (pg. 174)

Two-dimensional table—A table with multiple rows and multiple columns. (pg. 186)

Unconditional count—A count of all data items processed or all operations performed. (pg. 242)

Unconditional total—A sum of all data items processed. (pg. 242)

Variable—The label or name used for the location storing particular data in the computer's memory. (pg. 31)

White space—Blank space between the rows and columns of a report. Used to improve the appearance and readability of the report. (pg. 160)

APPENDIX A

QUICK REFERENCE GUIDE TO COMMONLY USED KEYWORDS

Note: Keywords that vary on different computers and are unique to a particular computer are indicated in the computer column. Their usage can be checked on the referenced page. Computers will be indicated as (I)BM and compatibles and (T)RS-80 Model III. It is assumed that all statements in the example column are preceded by line numbers. Each keyword is followed by a brief definition. Refer to the reference manual of your computer for keywords not included in this chart.

KEYWORD	EXAMPLE	PAGE	COMPUTER
APPEND	OPEN "PEOPLE" FOR APPEND AS #1 Allows data to be added to existing file.	285	I
ASC	PRINT ASC(B$) Returns ASCII code of first character in string.	144	I, T
CHR$	PRINT CHR$(34) Returns a one-character string defined by code.	144	I, T
CLEAR	CLEAR 1500 On TRS-80 Model 3 reserves memory for storage of character data.	00	I, T
CLOSE	CLOSE #1 Closes data files.	288	I, T
CLS	CLS Clears the screen.	31	I, T

CVS	F=CVS(R$) Converts to single precision after GET.	316	I, T
DATA	DATA 45,67,34 Holds data for access by READ statement.	116	I, T
DIM	DIM P(25),A$(25) Allocates storage for a table.	188	I, T
ELSE	IF A>25 THEN 240 ELSE GOSUB 300 Alternates action for conditional statement.	78	I, T
END	END Terminates program.	12	I, T
EOF	IF EOF(1) THEN 900 Determines if end of file has been reached.	287	I, T
FIELD	FIELD#3,15 AS NM$,10 AS TE$ Organizes a random file buffer into fields.	311	I, T
FOR	FOR X=1 TO 10 Opens a FOR . . . NEXT loop and sets limits.	93	I, T
GET	GET #1,RECNO Gets record from random file and places it in file buffer.	315	I, T
GOSUB	GOSUB 2000 Branches to a subroutine.	55	I, T
GOTO	GOTO 50 Branches unconditionally to a specified line number.	86	I, T
IF . . . THEN	IF A>B THEN RATE=R Makes decision regarding program flow based on result of expression.	70	I, T
INKEY$	C$=INKEY$ Reads a character from the keyboard.	142	I, T
INPUT	INPUT "WHAT IS YOUR NAME?";N$ Allows input from keyboard during program execution.	32	I, T

INPUT#	INPUT#1,R$,F,E Reads items from sequential disk file and assigns them to program variables.	287	I, T
INPUT$	C$=INPUT$(3) Reads a given number of characters from keyboard into a variable.	143	I
INSTR	P=INSTR(N$,",") Searches for first occurrence of string and returns the position at which it is found.	140	I
LEFT$	PRINT LEFT$(A$,2) Returns requested number of left-most characters in a string.	139	I, T
LEN	PRINT LEN(X$) Returns the number of characters in a string.	146	I, T
LET	LET B=25 Assigns value of expression to variable.	34	I, T
LINE INPUT	LINE INPUT R$ Allows input from keyboard, including blanks, commas, and colons.	145	I, T
LSET	LSET ST$="OHIO" Left-justifies data into a random access file buffer.	312	I, T
MID$	PRINT MID$(B$,9,7) Returns the mid-portion of a character string, starting with the character specified by the first number and continuing for the number of characters specified by the second number.	149	I, T
MKD$	LSET AV$=MKD$(AMT) Makes double-precision number ready for random file disk write.	329	I, T
MKI$	LSET AV$=MKI$(300) Makes integer number ready for random file disk write.	330	I, T

MKS$	LSET AV$=MKS$(AMT) Makes single-precision number ready for random file disk write.	312	I, T
NEXT	NEXT Y Closes a FOR . . . NEXT loop.	93	I, T
ON...GOSUB	ON CHOICE GOSUB 1000,2000 Goes to a subroutine based on the value contained in the variable.	78	I, T
OPEN	OPEN "PEOPLE" FOR INPUT AS #1 Opens data file on disk.	284	I
PRINT	PRINT "THE ANSWER IS";A Displays data on the screen.	6	I, T
PRINT USING	PRINT USING "###.##";A+B Prints strings or numbers using a specified format.	170	I, T
PRINT#	PRINT#1,X Writes data sequentially to a file.	286	I, T
PUT	PUT#1,RECNO Writes a record from a random buffer to a random file.	312	I, T
READ	READ A$,B,J Reads values from a DATA statement into variables.	116	I, T
REM	REM ** SORT ROUTINE ** Allows explanatory remarks to be placed in program.	5	I, T
RESTORE	RESTORE Allows DATA statements to be reread.	123	I, T
RETURN	RETURN Ends a subroutine and returns to statement following GOSUB.	55	I, T
RIGHT$	PRINT RIGHT$(A$,7) Returns the right-most specified characters of a string.	149	I, T
RND	X=RND(1) Returns a random number.	358	I, T

SPACE$	F$ = SPACE$(5) Returns a string consisting of a specified number of spaces.	166	I
SPC	PRINT "RIGHT";SPC(10);"HERE" Prints indicated number of spaces.	36	I
STEP	FOR J = 1 TO 20 STEP 2 Specifies increment in FOR . . . NEXT loop.	95	I, T
STR$	PRINT STR$(A + B) Returns a string representation of value specified.	148	I, T
STRING$	PRINT STRING$(30,"–") Returns a specified number of character symbols.	166	I, T
SWAP	SWAP A,B Exchanges the value of two variables.	224	I
TAB	PRINT TAB(10)"SALES REPORT" Tabs to specified position.	36	I, T
VAL	PRINT VAL(C$) Returns the numeric value of the string.	147	I, T
WEND	WEND Terminates loop beginning with WHILE statement.	99	I
WHILE	WHILE A = 25 Begins execution of a series of statements in a loop as long as given condition is true.	99	I

APPENDIX B

DEBUGGING

Many program errors are fairly easy to find and correct. If a program stops running and the computer prints an error message, the message is a guide to locating the problem. There are situations, however, in which errors are not easily identified even though an error message is printed. There are also situations in which the program runs without error but produces incorrect results. This appendix presents two methods that are helpful in locating hard-to-find errors.

EXAMINING THE CONTENTS OF VARIABLES

The contents of variables may be examined to see if they contain values the programmer believes they should contain. If they don't, a search can be made to determine where the incorrect values were assigned.

Extra PRINT statements may be temporarily inserted into a program to display the selected variables as the program executes. A STOP statement may be placed in the program at the point at which you want to see the values. When the computer stops, print commands may be entered to see the variables. For example:

PRINT N$ *or* PRINT C

The contents of variables may also be examined at the time a program stops execution and the computer prints an error message. Be sure to enter the print commands before changing any program line, however. Changing a line may set the variables back to nulls or zeros. Since the IBM and TRS-80 go into edit mode automatically when an error is found, the edit mode must be exited with no changes made in the program. When the IBM stops with the error line displayed, press CTRL and Break to get out of edit mode. When the TRS-80 stops with the number of the error line displayed, strike the letter Q (for quit edit) and press the ENTER key to take the computer out of edit mode. If you just press ENTER with either machine, the contents of all variables will be destroyed. Once you have left edit mode, enter the print commands to display the variables you want to see.

TRACING THE EXECUTION OF PROGRAM STEPS

The IBM and TRS-80 can display the line numbers being executed when the program is run. This technique, known as trace mode, is especially useful when the program runs but produces incorrect results. By examining the line numbers, you can determine whether the program is executing the lines you think it should. If it isn't, the necessary statements may be changed to make it work correctly.

When the trace mode is turned on, the number of each program line is printed on the screen as the statement on that line is executed. The program will still function as usual. The screen display, however, will be cluttered or broken up by the printed line numbers.

TRACING WITH THE IBM AND TRS-80

The trace mode on the IBM and TRS-80 is turned on with the keyword **TRON** (trace on). The keyword may be used as a command or included as a statement in a program. The keyword **TROFF** (trace off) turns off the trace mode. This keyword may also be used either as a command or program statement.

Trace mode with the IBM and TRS-80 works properly with all programs, including those using the printer and data files on diskette.

APPENDIX C

ASCII CODE

Inside the computer, each character is stored as a numeric code. The code is known as the American Standard Code for Information Interchange, or ASCII. There are 128 characters represented by the standard code, using code numbers of 0 to 127. IBM and TRS-80 computers, however, have added codes 128–255 and use these extra codes for additional characters, including graphics.

Codes 0 to 31 are known as control characters. Most of them do not have separate keys on the keyboard and do not appear on the screen when printed. If your computer has a control key (CTRL), the control codes can be produced by holding down that key while striking a regular character key. The characters represented by the codes may be printed by using the CHR$ function, such as PRINT CHR$(7). Codes used for the same purpose by most computers are described. On the IBM and TRS-80, using the proper procedure can cause the control codes to make graphics when printed (see Chapter 14). These graphic characters are shown. Since the effects of control codes vary widely from one computer to another, check the reference manual for your computer.

ASCII CONTROL CHARACTERS

CODE	NAME	CONTROL KEY	DESCRIPTION
0		@	
1	☺	A	
2	☻	B	
3	♥	C	

CODE	NAME	CONTROL KEY	DESCRIPTION
4	♦	D	
5	♣	E	
6	♠	F	
7	BEL	G	Bell. On computers that can "beep," printing ASCII code 7 will produce the sound. For example, a BASIC statement of PRINT CHR$(7) may be used.
8	◘	H	Backspace. In addition to being produced by striking the H key while holding down the CTRL key, code 8 is produced by the backspace key.
9	HT	I	Horizontal tab. On computers with a TAB function, printing of this code moves the cursor to the next tab stop. Produced also by the TAB key, if present.
10	LF	J	Line feed. When printed, causes the cursor to move to the next line on the screen. It does not cause the cursor to return to the left side of the screen.
11		K	
12	FF	L	Form feed. With many printers, printing of this code causes the paper to move to the top of the next page.
13	CR	M	Carriage return. Printing of the carriage return code causes the cursor to move to the left side of the screen.

CODE	NAME	CONTROL KEY	DESCRIPTION
14	♫	N	
15	☼	O	
16	►	P	
17	◄	Q	
18	↕	R	
19	‼	S	
20	¶	T	
21	§	U	
22	▬	V	
23	↨	W	
24	↑	X	
25	↓	Y	
26	→	Z	
27	←	Varies	Escape. On computers with an escape key (ESC), this code is produced when that key is struck. The response of the computer to this key depends on the software being used.
28			
29			
30			
31			

ASCII CHARACTER CODES

The character codes are used for characters that appear on the screen when printed. Each code is produced by a key on the keyboard. Printing the CHR$ function of one of the codes is the same as printing the character inside quotation marks. For example, PRINT "A" and PRINT CHR$(65) will both print the letter A on the screen. The codes for the letters and numerals are the same on all computers using the ASCII code. However, there is some variation from one machine to another on the codes for some of the symbols. For this reason, you should check the reference manual for your machine if using the codes for symbols. Here are the codes:

CODE	CHARACTER	CODE	CHARACTER
32	Space	44	,
33	!	45	- (hyphen)
34	"	46	.
35	#	47	/
36	$	48	0
37	%	49	1
38	&	50	2
39	'	51	3
40	(	52	4
41	)	53	5
42	*	54	6
43	+	55	7

CODE	CHARACTER
56	8
57	9
58	:
59	;
60	<
61	=
62	>
63	?
64	@
65	A
66	B
67	C
68	D
69	E
70	F
71	G
72	H
73	I
74	J
75	K
76	L
77	M
78	N
79	O
80	P
81	Q
82	R
83	S
84	T
85	U
86	V
87	W
88	X
89	Y
90	Z
91	[
92	\
93	]
94	^
95	_(underscore)

CODE	CHARACTER	CODE	CHARACTER
96	‘	112	p
97	a	113	q
98	b	114	r
99	c	115	s
100	d	116	t
101	e	117	u
102	f	118	v
103	g	119	w
104	h	120	x
105	i	121	y
106	j	122	z
107	k	123	{
108	l	124		
109	m	125	}
110	n	126	~
111	o	127	Delete

Codes 128–255 are extended codes. The IBM character can be displayed by using the ASC function (e.g., PRINT ASC(192)) or POKEing the number into a memory location representing a screen position. For displaying some of the TRS-80 characters, refer to the reference manual for special procedures.

CODE	CHARACTER IBM	CHARACTER TRS-80
128	Ç	(BLANK)
129	ü	
130	é	
131	â	
132	ä	
133	à	
134	å	
135	ç	
136	ê	
137	ë	
138	è	
139	ï	
140	î	
141	ì	
142	Ä	
143	Å	
144	É	
145	æ	
146	Æ	
147	ô	
148	ö	
149	ò	
150	û	
151	ù	
152	ÿ	
153	Ö	
154	Ü	
155	¢	
156	£	
157	¥	
158	₧	
159	ƒ	
160	á	
161	í	
162	ó	
163	ú	
164	ñ	
165	Ñ	
166	ª	
167	º	

CODE	CHARACTER IBM	CHARACTER TRS-80
168	¿	🬦
169	⌐	🬧
170	¬	▐
171	½	🬨
172	¼	🬩
173	¡	🬪
174	«	🬫
175	»	🬬
176	░	🬭
177	▒	🬮
178	▓	🬯
179	│	🬰
180	┤	🬱
181	╡	🬲
182	╢	🬳
183	╖	🬴
184	╕	🬵
185	╣	🬶
186	║	🬷
187	╗	🬸
188	╝	🬹
189	╜	🬺
190	╛	🬻
191	┐	█
192	└	♠
193	┴	♥
194	┬	♦
195	├	♣
196	─	☺
197	┼	☹
198	╞	≤
199	╟	≥
200	╚	α
201	╔	β
202	╩	γ
203	╦	δ
204	╠	ε
205	═	ζ
206	╬	η
207	╧	θ

CODE	CHARACTER IBM	CHARACTER TRS-80
208	╨	ι
209	╤	κ
210	╥	λ
211	╙	μ
212	╘	ν
213	╒	ξ
214	╓	ο
215	╫	π
216	╪	ρ
217	┘	σ
218	┌	τ
219	█	υ
220	▄	φ
221	▌	χ
222	▐	ψ
223	▀	ω
224	α	Ω
225	β	√
226	Γ	÷
227	π	Σ

CODE	CHARACTER IBM	CHARACTER TRS-80
228	Σ	≈
229	σ	Δ
230	µ	∫
231	τ	≠
232	Φ	[illegible]
233	Θ	[illegible]
234	Ω	[illegible]
235	δ	∞
236	∞	✓
237	Ø	§
238	∈	[illegible]
239	∩	©
240	≡	✕
241	±	¶
242	≥	¢
243	≤	®
244	⌠	[illegible]
245	⌡	[illegible]
246	÷	⇒
247	≈	℞

CODE	CHARACTER IBM	CHARACTER TRS-80
248	°	%
249	•	♂
250	·	♀
251	√	⊏
252	ⁿ	?
253	²	웃
254	■	♣
255	(BLANK 'FF')	Å

APPENDIX D

FLOWCHARTING

OBJECTIVES

1. Define flowcharting.
2. Explain the uses of various symbols in flowcharting.
3. Explain how to use flowcharting to document the control structures commonly used in programming.
4. List the advantages and disadvantages of using flowcharting.

WHAT IS FLOWCHARTING?

Some program designers find it convenient to use flowcharting to plan and document their programs. Flowcharting is a method of using pictorial representations to show the design of a program. For an example of flowcharting, let us convert the following program design to a flowcharting representation. The steps of the program design are the steps to calculate and display the amount of sales tax on an item.

1. Assign the price of the item and the tax rate to variables.
2. Display the price.
3. Display the rate.
4. Calculate and display the sales tax.
5. End of problem.

To show the design of a program in flowchart form, each step of the program is placed inside a symbol that indicates what kind of action is taking place at each step. Arrows known as flow lines are used to connect the different steps. The steps generally go from top to bottom and left to right, although there may be exceptions.

At the simplest level, a rectangle can be used for all sequential steps. Since all steps of the program design we are currently working with are sequential, the rectangular symbol is all that will be required. Study Figure D-1 to see how the steps can be shown. Note that each step has simply been placed inside a rectangle.

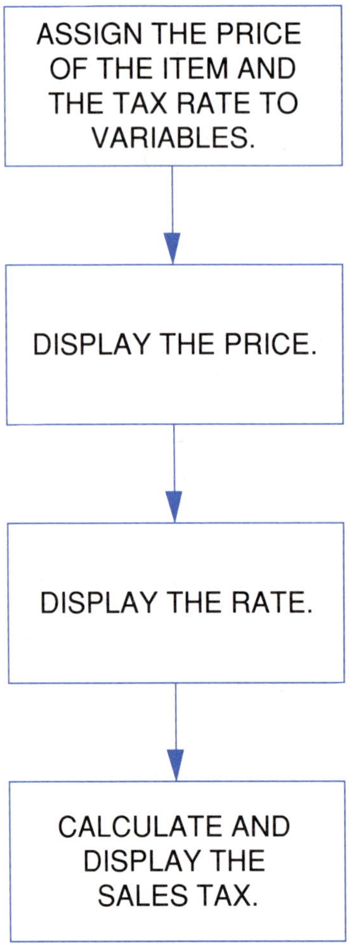

Figure D-1 Flowchart of a Sequential Program

SYMBOLS USED IN FLOWCHARTING

There are many symbols that can be used in flowcharting. However, the logic of just about any program can be shown by using only a few symbols. Using a small number of symbols helps make the production of flowcharts much easier. Study Table D-1, which shows the commonly used symbols and describes their use.

Use of the Rectangle for Steps in Processing

In the previous section, you became familiar with the rectangle that can be used to indicate all sequential steps in a program. When desired, the rectangle may be used to show input and output as well as computations. This is true in spite of the fact that a separate symbol has been designated for input and output operations.

Symbol	Use
Rectangle 	Used to show a sequential step—some action is to be taken.
Parallelogram 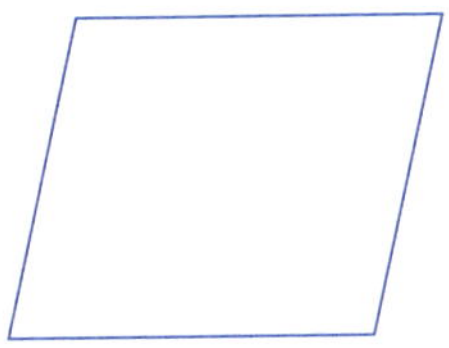	Used to show actions that accept input or produce output.
Diamond 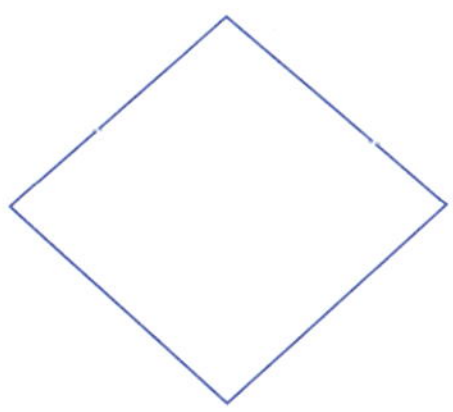	Used to show a decision point. Program control goes one way or another based on whether a logical condition is true.
Oval 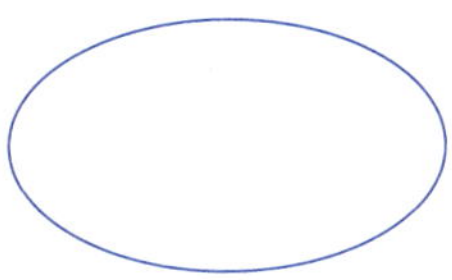	Used to indicate the beginning and end of a flowchart.
Circle 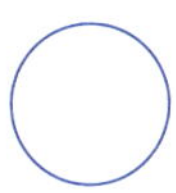	Used as a connector between different parts of the flowchart.

Table D-1 Commonly Used Flowcharting Symbols

Use of the Oval for Beginning and Ending the Flowchart

The oval may be used to indicate both the beginning and ending points of a flowchart. Examine Figure D-2 to see how the symbol has been added to the flowchart from Figure D-1.

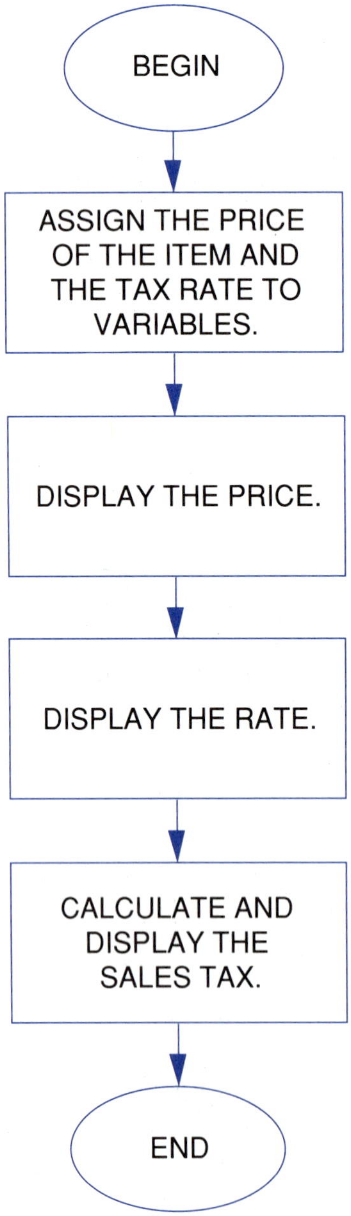

Figure D-2 Flowchart of a Sequential Program

Use of the Parallelogram for Input and Output

Now, examine how the flowchart from Figure D-2 can be changed to include the symbol used for output. This time, the steps that produce output will be in parallelograms (see the result in Figure D-3). Note that the original "calculate and display the sales tax" step from Figure D-2 must be divided into two steps this time, since it performs a computation as well as produces output.

Use of the Diamond for Decisions

The diamond symbol is used whenever a decision must be made based on some logical condition. As the introduction to this symbol, we will use a different example. This program calculates and prints the gross pay for several employees. The data is contained in DATA lines. The steps of the program design are as follows:

1. Print the headings at the top of the report.
2. Read the employee's name, the hours worked, and the rate of pay.
3. Check to see if the terminator was read. If it was, go to the end statement.
4. Calculate the gross pay by multiplying the hours worked by the rate of pay.
5. Print the employee name, the hours worked, the rate of pay, and the gross pay.
6. Go back to step 3 and read the next record.
7. End.

Study Figure D-4 to see how the steps have been represented in a flowchart. Note that the diamond is used to represent step 3 of the program design. At this point, control either continues or is transferred to the END statement, depending on whether the terminator was read. The two possible answers to the question, yes and no, are written at points of the diamond to indicate the direction to be taken depending on the answer. The arrows then point the way from the answer. One thing that we have done to make the flow better follow the top-to-bottom guideline, is to place the END statement at the bottom of the flowchart. It could have been placed at the right of the decision symbol, although such a location would not be preferred.

Use of the Connector

The connector symbol, the circle, is used to connect different parts of a flowchart. This becomes necessary whenever the chart

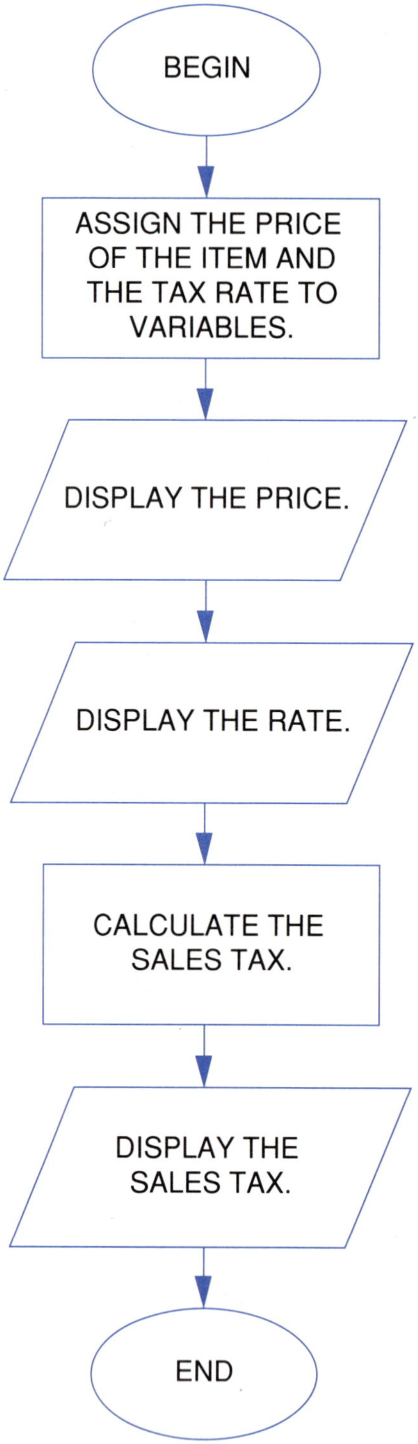

Figure D-3 Flowchart Showing Use of the Output Symbol

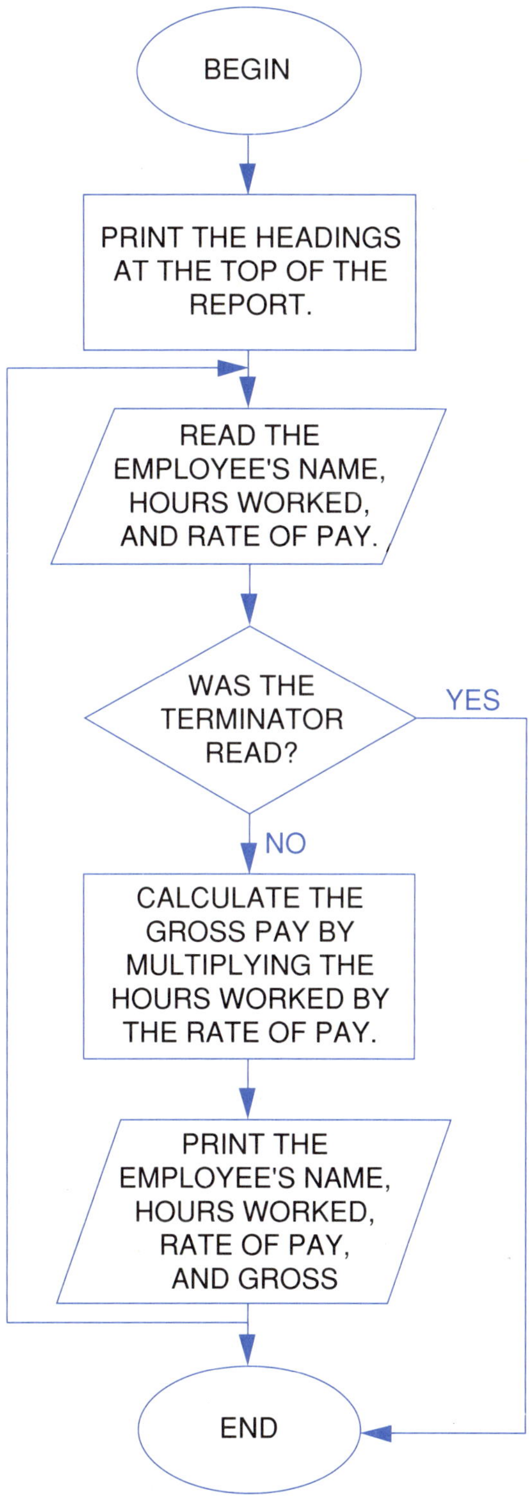

Figure D-4 Illustration of the Operation of a Decision Statement

is too large for one page, or when it is impractical to draw a flow line in the required path. Connectors are labeled to show the connection; the label may be either alphabetic or numeric. Suppose we have a payroll program that calculates both hourly pay and commissions. The methods for doing these obviously vary and can become rather complex. Therefore, the flowchart for computing hourly pay might consume one page, while the flowchart for computing commissions might consume another page. A connection could be made to either page based on the pay type. Figure D-5 shows the departure for the connections between the flowchart sections. This shows that if the pay type is hourly, control should go the connector labeled as A, which will be on another page. If the pay type is commission, control will go to the connector labeled B, which will also be on another page. Note that the beginning of the flowchart is not shown.

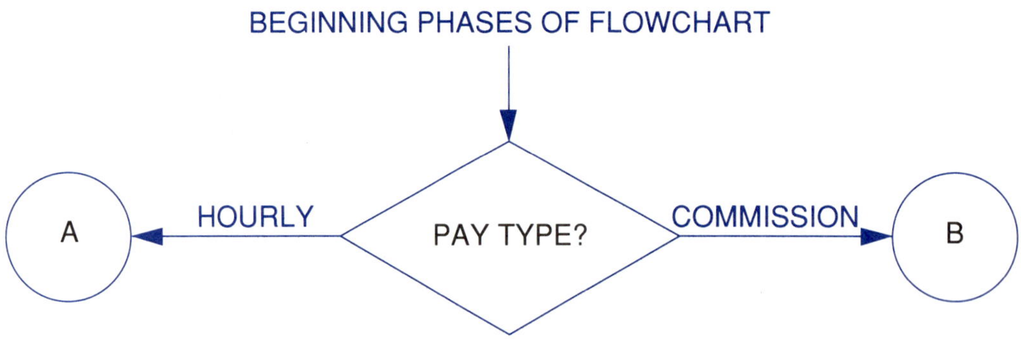

Figure D-5 Use of "Departure" Connectors

On the additional pages, each flowchart will begin with a circle containing the appropriate alphabet letter—either A or B. Figure D-6 shows how those flowcharts will look.

USING FLOWCHARTS TO DOCUMENT PROGRAM DESIGN

There are four main design structures with which all programs may be written. Known as control structures, they are: (1) sequential steps, (2) alternate actions (IF . . . THEN . . . ELSE), (3) case (also known as selection), and (4) iteration. When drawing flowcharts, only these structures should be used. On the flowchart, each structure should be complete in itself, with one way to get in the structure and one way out of the structure. In other words,

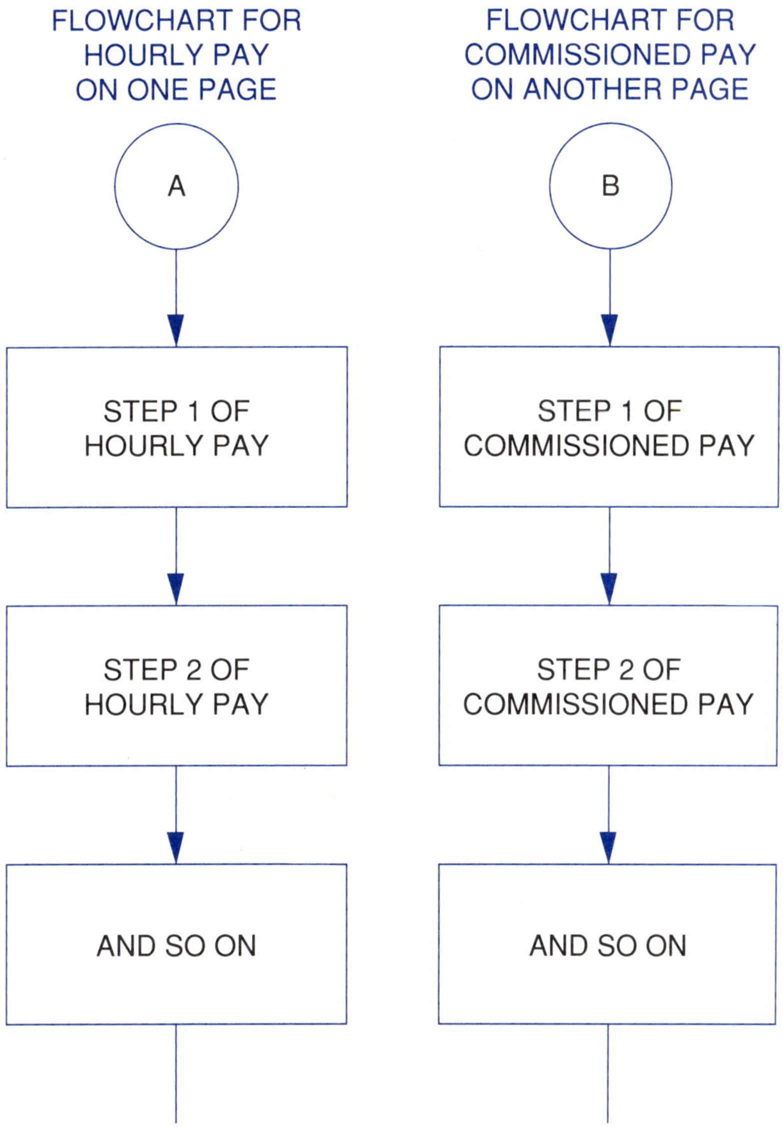

Figure D-6 Flowcharts Beginning With "Continuation" Connectors

on a flowchart you should be able to identify everything as one of these four structures. If you encircled each structure, there should be only one flow line going into the box and one flow line coming from the box. This will help ensure that the principles of structured programming are followed. The following sections illustrate how to chart each of the control structures.

Sequential Steps Structure

Sequential steps are shown in a flowchart as one symbol after another. The steps may indicate the beginning of a program, a computation or other action to take, an input step, an output step, or the end of a program. Figure D-7 indicates the general form of sequential steps in a flowchart.

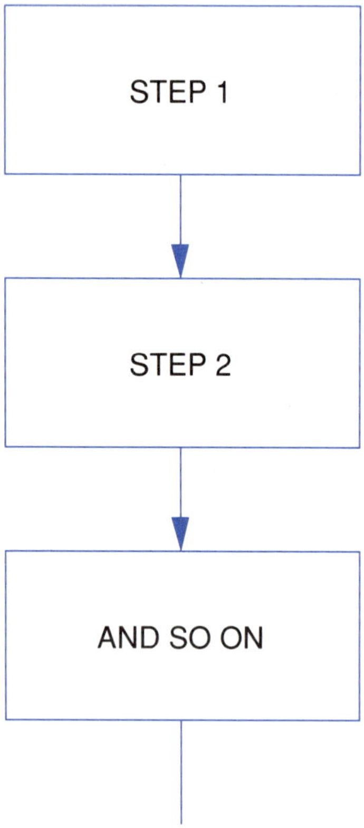

Figure D-7 Sequential Control Structure

Alternate Actions Structure

Alternative actions are most frequently implemented in BASIC with IF . . . THEN statements. When alternate actions are to be taken based on a logical comparison, it is very easy to produce flowcharts that are difficult to follow. However, by using the pattern suggested here, flowcharts will be easier to construct and follow.

The most frequently occurring difficulty in flowcharting alternate actions is that of where to place the two different actions. That can be solved by, in effect, making two distinct flowcharts,

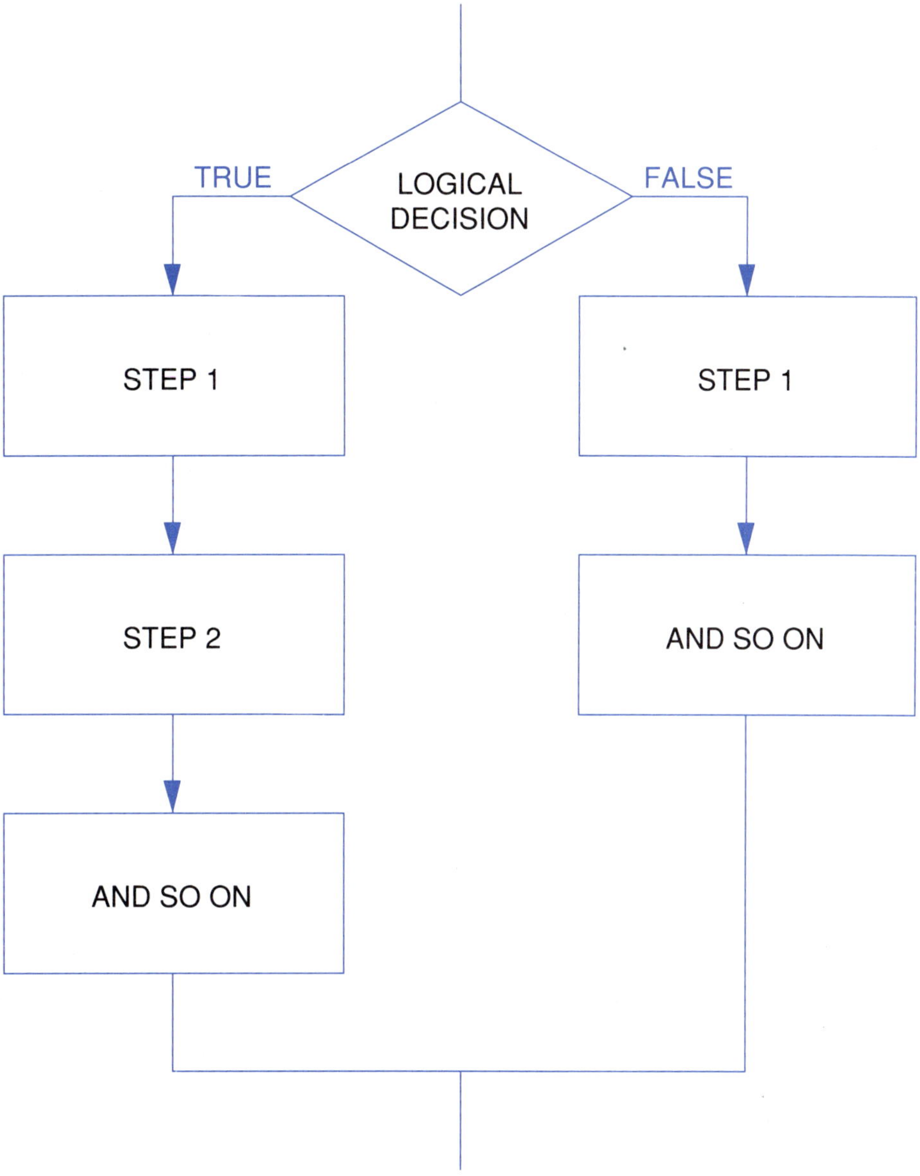

Figure D-8 General Form for Alternate Action Structure

one for each action. Then a decision is made as to which to follow, with the flow lines coming back together at the end of the actions. This maintains the idea of one way into and one way out of each control structure. Study Figure D-8 for an example of alternate actions to be taken. Note that the choices need not contain the same number of steps.

Sometimes, an action is to be taken if a logical condition is true, while no action of any kind is to be taken if the condition is false. When flowcharting such a structure, both possible outcomes are still shown. Figure D-9 shows how it is done.

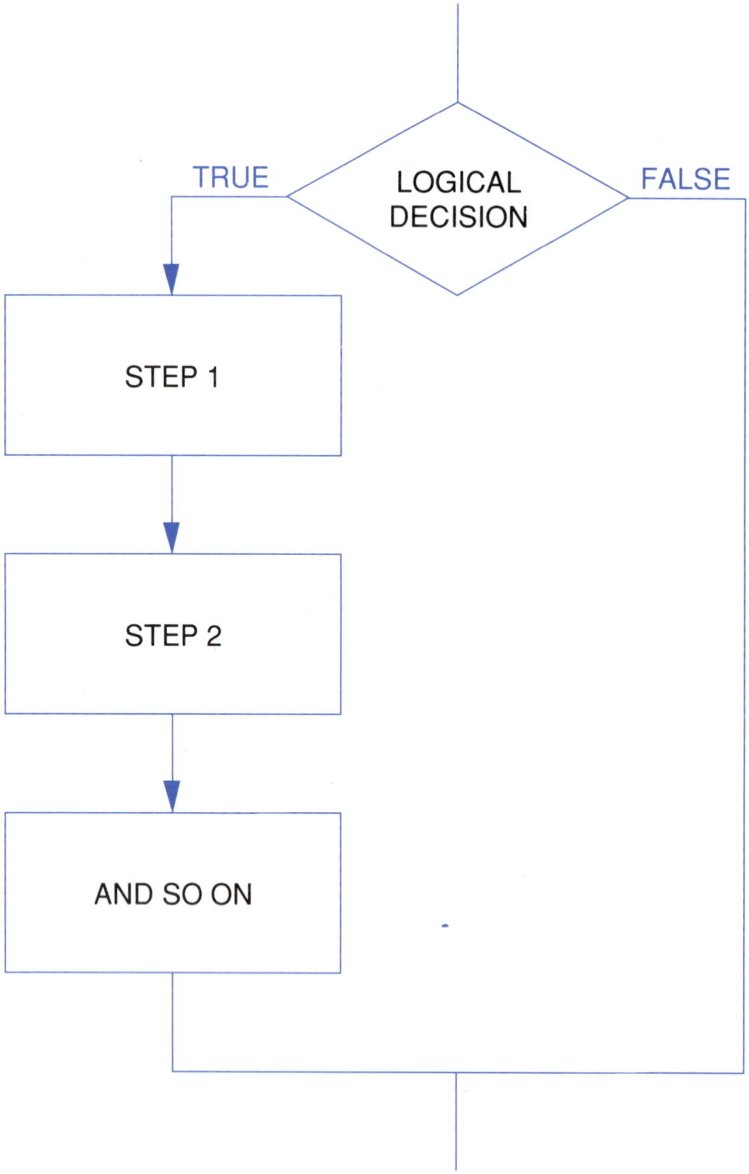

Figure D-9 General Form for Action/No Action Structure

Case Structure

The case structure, also known as selection, is used to cause a program to perform one action from a selection of possibilities. One of the most frequent applications is in the use of menus, where the user chooses which of several actions the program should take. Other applications might involve selecting from among multiple types of pay methods to process or taking different actions depending on how long an account receivable is past due.

While the case structure may be drawn in several ways in a flowchart, one of the better ones involves the use of connectors. Each connector indicates a separate flowchart documenting the steps to be performed in that case. Study Figure D-10 for an example of the case structure for a menu. The beginning and end of the case structure are easy to see. Note that only one of the cases is true when the program is executed. Therefore, only one of the flowcharts referenced by the connectors will come into play. In case the selected choice is invalid, no action will be taken. While most versions of BASIC do not have a real case structure statement, the ON . . . GOSUB statement can handle most cases.

Iteration Structure

Iterations, commonly known as loops, may be of two types as far as structure is concerned. Both types repeat until some terminating condition becomes true. The difference is that one type tests for the terminating condition before taking action, while the other tests for the terminating condition after taking action. In making flowchart segments for these two kinds of loops, we still follow the guideline of one way in and one way out. Examine the following two figures to learn how to make these structures. Figure D-11 shows the "test first" loop, while Figure D-12 shows the "test last" loop.

ADVANTAGES AND DISADVANTAGES OF FLOWCHARTING

Whether to use flowcharting has been a topic of much discussion. There are some factors in favor of flowcharting. Flowcharting may make the design of a program easier for someone other than the designer to understand. Also, it may point out some logic problems before coding of a program begins.

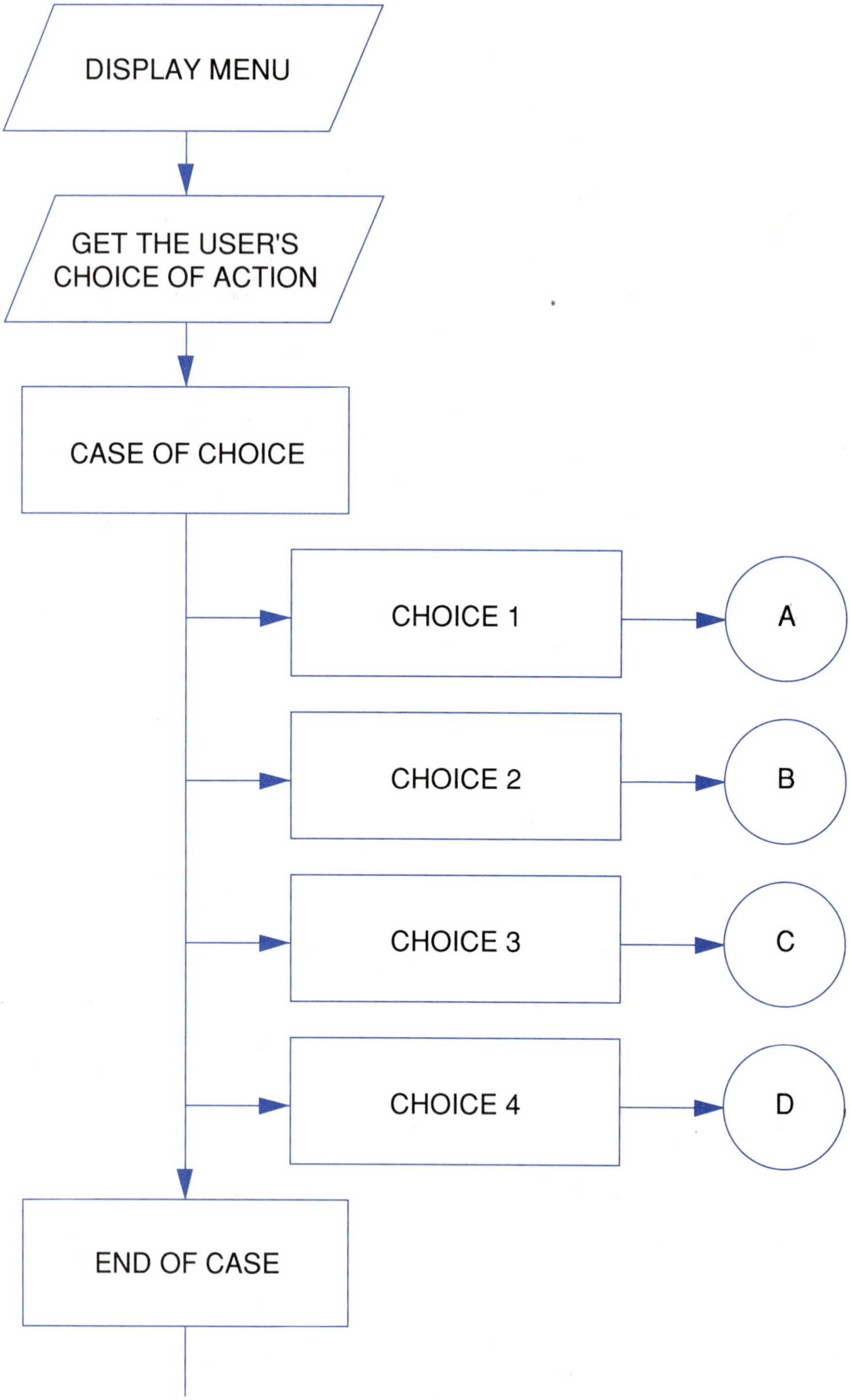

Figure D-10 Flowchart of Case Structure

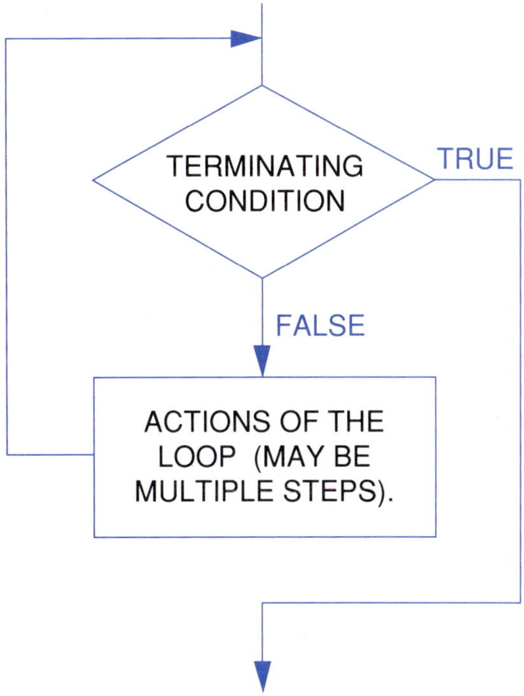

Figure D-11 "Test First" Loop

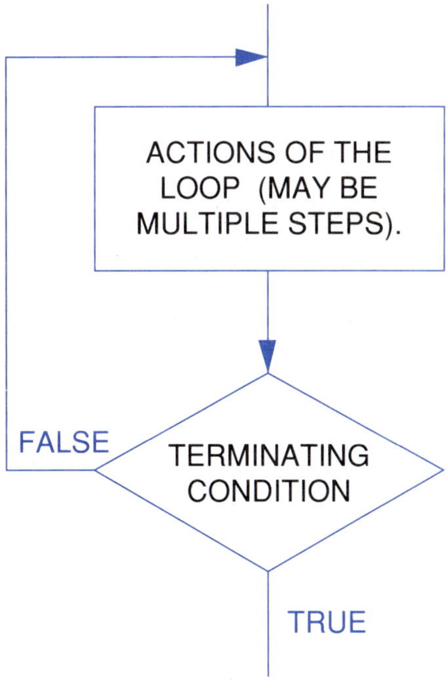

Figure D-12 "Test Last" Loop

On the negative side of flowcharting, there are also some factors. First, the preparation of flowcharts is very tedious and time consuming. Most programmers will not make flowcharts unless directed to do so by their superiors. At that, they may be made only after a program is completed, contributing nothing to the planning process. The biggest disadvantage, however, has to do with program maintenance. Remember that one of the most important purposes of program documentation is to enable someone else to make corrections or modifications in the program. Remember also that the programmers spend much of their time making program modifications. Assuming that a flowchart has been made originally, it is next to impossible to keep it up to date as changes are made in a program. Therefore, it becomes useless. It is much better to make the code of the program as self-documenting as possible. When the code is self-documenting, there is no doubt that the program and documentation match. In other words, the ideal is for a person to be able to determine how a program works by reading the program itself.

INDEX

D

K

N

O

P

U

V

W

Z